L. ANNAEUS CORNUTUS
GREEK THEOLOGY, FRAGMENTS,
AND TESTIMONIA

WRITINGS FROM THE GRECO-ROMAN WORLD

General Editor
John T. Fitzgerald

Editorial Board
Christopher A. Baron
Andrew Cain
Margaret M. Mitchell
Teresa Morgan
Ilaria L. E. Ramelli
Clare K. Rothschild
David T. Runia
Karin Schlapbach
James C. VanderKam
L. Michael White

Number 42
Volume Editor
Glenn Most

L. ANNAEUS CORNUTUS:
GREEK THEOLOGY, FRAGMENTS, AND TESTIMONIA

Translated with an Introduction and Notes by
George Boys-Stones

SBL PRESS

Atlanta

Copyright © 2018 by SBL Press

All rights reserved. No part of this work may be reproduced or transmitted in any form or by any means, electronic or mechanical, including photocopying and recording, or by means of any information storage or retrieval system, except as may be expressly permitted by the 1976 Copyright Act or in writing from the publisher. Requests for permission should be addressed in writing to the Rights and Permissions Office, SBL Press, 825 Houston Mill Road, Atlanta, GA 30329 USA.

Library of Congress Cataloging-in-Publication Data

Names: Cornutus, Lucius Annaeus, active 1st century, author. | Boys-Stones, G. R., editor.
Title: L. Annaeus Cornutus : Greek theology, fragments, and testimonia / by George Boys-Stones.
Other titles: Greek theology, fragments, and testimonia
Description: Atlanta : SBL Press, 2018. | Series: Writings from the Greco-Roman world ; number 42 | Includes bibliographical references and index.
Identifiers: LCCN 2018014639 (print) | LCCN 2018017637 (ebook) | ISBN 9780884142942 (ebk.) | ISBN 9781628372106 (pbk. : alk. paper) | ISBN 9780884142935 (hbk. : alk. paper)
Subjects: LCSH: Greece—Religion—Early works to 1800. | Virgil—Criticism and interpretation—Early works to 1800. | Lucan, 39–65—Criticism and interpretation—Early works to 1800. | Persius—Criticism and interpretation—Early works to 1800. | Cornutus, Lucius Annaeus, active 1st century.
Classification: LCC PA6375.C8 (ebook) | LCC PA6375.C8 B69 2018 (print) | DDC 878/.01—dc23
LC record available at https://lccn.loc.gov/2018014639

Printed on acid-free paper.

CONTENTS

Acknowledgments vii
Sigla and Abbreviations ix

1. Introduction: Cornutus the Philosopher 1
   1.1. Preface   1
   1.2. The Life of Cornutus   2
   1.3. Stoicism in the First Century CE   7
      1.3.1. Stoicism as an International Movement   7
      1.3.2. Stoicism as a Textual Community   9
      1.3.3. The Intellectual Program of Post-Hellenistic Stoicism   12
   1.4. Cornutus's Philosophical Views   13
      1.4.1. Dialectic   14
      1.4.2. Physics   29
      1.4.3. Ethics   32
   1.5. Summary: Cornutus's Profile as a Philosopher   35
   1.6. Works by Cornutus and Their Titles   36
      1.6.1. Transmitted Works   36
      1.6.2. Other Titles Attested   36
      1.6.3. Dubious   37
      1.6.4. Spurious   37
      1.6.5. Speculative Modern Attributions   37
   1.7. Notes on Texts and Referencing   38
      1.7.1. The *Greek Theology*   38
      1.7.2. *On Pronunciation or Orthography*   40
      1.7.3. Fragments   40
      1.7.4. Persius   40

2. The *Greek Theology* 41
   2.1. Preface   41
   2.2. Text and Translation   51

3. *On Pronunciation or Orthography* 139
    3.1. Preface   139
    3.2. Text and Translation   141

4. Fragments and Testimonia 157
    4.1. Preface   157
    4.2. Texts and Translations   157
        4.2.1. Life   157
        4.2.2. Exegesis of Greek Theology   163
        4.2.3. On Aristotle's *Categories*   167
        4.2.4. Physics and Metaphysics   176
        4.2.5. Rhetoric   178
        4.2.6. Fame as a Critic   182
        4.2.7. On Virgil   182
        4.2.8. On Lucan   194
        4.2.9. Miscellaneous   195

5. Cornutus and Persius 197
    5.1. *Life of Persius*   198
    5.2. Persius, *Sat.* 5   202

6. Index of Sources for the Fragments 217

7. Concordances 223

Bibliography 229

General Index 239

Acknowledgments

The translation of Cornutus's *Greek Theology* in this volume has benefited from the input of Simon MacPherson and Steven Kennedy, and I am very grateful to José Torres for sharing his work on the new (2018) Teubner edition. A number of colleagues have offered invaluable specialist advice: Johannes Haubold on Tzetzes; Monica Hellström, Amy Russell, and Mark Woolmer on Roman and Phoenician nomenclature; and Stephen Menn on the *Categories* material. Timothy Greenwood supplied the Armenian text and English translation of F10. James Zetzel generously shared forthcoming work on Roman philology. Improvements of every sort were made throughout in light of comments and advice from the volume editor, Glenn Most. Finally, my thanks to Nicole Tilford and Bob Buller at SBL Press for their care in editing and preparing the text and introducing many improvement in doing so.

Sigla and Abbreviations

Sigla

[ ]	in Greek and Latin texts, encloses material that is in our manuscripts but ought to be deleted (and is not translated)
< >	encloses Greek and Latin text that is a conjectural supplement to our manuscripts
<…>	indicates a lacuna
†	indicates an undiagnosed problem with the text
F	a text ("fragment") in chapter 4 of the present work
T	a title of a work ascribed to Cornutus; see the introduction, §1.6

Abbreviations

acc.	accusative
Ad Aen.	Servius, *Commentary on the Aeneid*
Ad Ecl.	Servius, *Commentary on the Eclogues*
ad fin.	*ad finem*, at or near the end
Ad Georg.	Servius, *Commentary on the Georgics*
ad loc.	*ad locum*, at the relevant place
Ad Lyc.	Tzetzes, *Commentary on Lycophron*
Adv. math.	Sextus Empiricus, *Adversus mathematicos*
AE	*L'Année Épigraphique*
Aen.	Virgil, *Aeneid*
AGP	*Archiv für Geschichte des Philosophie*
Agr.	*On Agriculture*
Alc.	Euripides, *Alcestis*
All.	Heraclitus, *Homeric Problems*
All. Il.	Tzetzes, *Allegories of the Iliad*

All. Od.	Tzetzes, *Allegories of the Odyssey*
ANRW	Temporini, Hildegard, and Wolfgang Haase, eds. *Aufstieg und Niedergang der römischen Welt: Geschichte und Kultur Roms im Spiegel der neueren Forschung*. Part 2, *Principat*. Berlin: de Gruyter, 1972–.
Ars gramm.	Marius Victorinus, *Ars grammatica*
BAGB	*Bulletin de l'Association G. Budé*
BCG	Biblioteca clásica Gredos
Bel. civ.	Lucan, *Civil War*
Bibl.	Photius, *Bibliotheca*
BICSSup	Bulletin of the Institute of Classical Studies Supplement Series
BJS	Brown Judaic Studies
BKA	Bibliothek der klassischen Altertumswissenschaft
BSGRT	Bibliotheca Scriptorum Graecorum et Romanorum Teubneriana
BZ	*Byzantinische Zeitschrift*
CAG	Commentaria in Aristotelem Graeca
Cas.	Plautus, *Casina*
Cat.	Aristotle, *Categories*
CCS	Cambridge Classical Studies
CCTC	Cambridge Classical Texts and Commentaries
Chron.	Eusebius, *Chronicle*
CID	*Corpus des inscriptions de Delphes*. Paris: de Boccard, 1977–.
cod.	codex
CP	*Classical Philology*
CPF	*Corpus dei papiri filosofici greci e latini: Testi e lessico nei papiri di cultura greca e latina*. Vol. 1.1*. Florence: Olschki.
CQ	*Classical Quarterly*
CSEL	Corpus Scriptorum Ecclesiasticorum Latinorum
[Dan.]	scholia first published in P. Daniel's 1600 edition of Servius
Def. med.	Pseudo-Galen, *Definitiones medicae*
Def. orac.	Plutarch, *Abandoned Oracles*
del.	delete(s) text transmitted in the manuscripts; often indicated by placing square brackets around the relevant text

Diatr.	Epictetus, *Diatribes*
DK	Diels, Hermann, and Walther Kranz. *Die Fragmente der Vorsokratiker*. 6th ed. 3 vols. RKLW 10. Zurich: Weidmann, 1954.
EAA	Etudes d'Antiquités africaines
Ecl.	Virgil, *Eclogues*; Stobaeus, *Eclogae*
EK	Edelstein, Ludwig, and Ian Gray Kidd, eds. *The Fragments*. Vol. 1 of *Posidonius*. 2nd ed. Cambridge: Cambridge University Press, 1989.
Ench.	Epictetus, *Encheiridion*
Enn.	Plotinus, *Enneads*
Ep.	Seneca, *Moral Epistles*
Epist.	Jerome, *Letters*
EPRO	Études préliminaires aux religions orientales dans l'empire romain
Exp. Buc.	Junius Philargyrius, *Commentary on the Bucolica*
Exp. Cat.	Porphyry, *On the Categories*
Exp. serm. antiq.	Fulgentius, *Expositio sermonum antiquorum*
FD	Homolle, Théophile, et al., eds. *Fouilles de Delphe*. Paris: de Boccard, 1906–.
frag.	fragment
FRH	Cornell, Tim J., ed. *The Fragments of the Roman Historians*. 3 vols. Oxford: Oxford University Press, 2013.
gen.	genitive
Georg.	Virgil, *Georgics*
Gloss.	Pseudo-Placidus, *Glossary*
Graec. affect. cur.	Theodoretus, *Graecarum affectionum curatio*
Gramm.	Suetonius, *Lives of the Grammarians*
GRBS	*Greek, Roman, and Byzantine Studies*
HCS	Hellenistic Culture and Society
Hist. eccl.	Eusebius, *History of the Church*
Hist. Rom.	Dio Cassius, *Roman History*
IJCT	*International Journal of the Classical Tradition*
Il.	Homer, *Iliad*
ILAfr	Cagnat, René, and Alfred Merlin with Louis Chatelain. *Inscriptions latines d'Afrique (Tripolitaine, Tunisie, Maroc)*. Paris: Leroux, 1923.
Inst.	Quintilian, *Institutes of Oratory*
Int.	Aristotle, *On Interpretation*

IRT	Reynolds, Joyce Maire, and John Bryan Ward-Perkins. *The Inscriptions of Roman Tripolitania*. Rome: British School at Rome, 1952.
JCPSup	Jahrbücher für classische Philologie Supplementsband
Leg.	Plato, *Laws*
LSJ	Liddell, Henry George, Robert Scott, Henry Stuart Jones. *A Greek-English Lexicon*. 9th ed. with revised supplement. Oxford: Clarendon, 1996.
Metaph.	Aristotle, *Metaphysics*
Mid.	Demosthenes, *Against Midias*
Mnemosyne	*Mnemosyne: A Journal of Classical Studies*
Mor.	Plutarch, *On Moral Virtue*
Nat. d.	Cicero, *On the Nature of the Gods*
Noct. att.	Aulus Gellius, *Attic Nights*
nom.	nominative
NT	*Novum Testamentum*
OCM	Oxford Classical Monographs
OCT	Oxford Classical Texts/Scriptorum classicorum bibliotheca Oxoniensis
Od.	Homer, *Odyssey*
OLD	Glare, P. G. W., ed. *Oxford Latin Dictionary*. Corrected ed. Oxford: Clarendon, 1982.
om.	omit(s)
Onom.	Hesychius, *Onomatologi*
Op.	Hesiod, *Works and Days*
Or.	Maximus, *Oration*
PCG	Kassel, Rudolf, and Colin Austin, eds. *Poetae comici Graeci*. Berlin: de Gruyter, 1983–.
PhA	Philosophia antiqua
Phaed.	Plato, *Phaedo*
Phaedr.	Plato, *Phaedrus*
Phil. min.	Michael Psellus, *Philosophica Minora*
PhilSup	Philologus Supplement
PhTS	Philosophical Texts and Studies
PIR[2]	*Prosopographia Imperii Romani, saec. I. II. III.* 8 vols. 2nd ed. Berlin: de Gruyter, 1933–2015.
P.Oxy.	Oxyrhynchus papyrus
Pseud.	Plautus, *Pseudolus*
Quaest. conv.	Plutarch, *Quaestiones Convivales*

Quaest. rom.	Plutarch, *Aetia romana et graeca*
q.v.	*quod vide*, which see
RA	Roma Aeterna
Rer. nat.	Lucretius, *De rerum natura*
REG	*Revue des études grecques*
Resp.	Plato, *Republic*
RFIC	*Rivista di filologia e di istruzione classica*
RIP	*Revue internationale de philosophie*
RKLW	Rowohlts Klassiker der Literatur und der Wissenschaft
RM	*Rheinisches Museum*
RW	Paulys *Real-Encyclopädie der classischen Altertumswissenschaft*. New edition by Georg Wissowa and Wilhelm Kroll. 50 vols. Stuttgart: Metzler & Druckenmüller, 1894–1980.
SAPERE	Scripta antiquitatis posterioris ad ethicam religionemque pertinentia
Sat.	Macrobius, *Saturnalia*
Sat.	Persius, *Satires*
SBLTT	Society of Biblical Literature Texts and Translations
SC	Sources chrétiennes
sc.	*scilicet*, understand
Schem. dian.	[Julius Rufinianus], *De schematis dianoeas*
Scut.	[Hesiod,] *Shield*
SPhiloA	Studia Philonica Annual
SRPF	Ribbeck, Otto, ed. *Scaenicae Romanorum poesis fragmenta*. 2nd ed. 2 vols. Leipzig: Teubner, 1871–1873.
Sull.	Plutarch, *Sulla*
s.v.	*sub verbo*, under the heading
SVF	Arnim, Hans Friedrich August von, ed. *Stoicorum veterum fragmenta*. 4 vols. Stuttgart: Teubner, 1903–1924.
TF	Texte zur Forschung
Theaet.	Plato, *Theaetetus*
Theog.	Hesiod, *Theogony*
Tim.	Plato, *Timaeus*
TK	Texte und Kommentare

TrGF	Snell, Bruno, Richard Kannicht, and Stefan Radt, eds. *Tragicorum Graecorum fragmenta*. 5 vols. Göttingen: Vandenhoeck & Ruprecht, 1971–2004.
Tro.	Euripides, Trojan Women
Util. cred.	Augustine, *The Usefulness of Believing*
Viol.	Eudocia, *Violarium*
Vit. phil.	Diogenes Laertius, *Lives of Eminent Philosophers*
Vit. Plot.	Porphyry, *Life of Plotinus*
Vit. Prob.	*Vita Probiana*
Vit. soph.	Philostratus, *Lives of the Sophists*
Vit. Verg.	Donatus, *Life of Virgil*
WGRW	Writings from the Greco-Roman World

1
Introduction: Cornutus the Philosopher

1.1. Preface

This is the first complete collection of the surviving evidence for the life of Cornutus and his "many philosophical and rhetorical works" (F2, F3; cf. *Life of Persius* 20).[1] This is probably to be explained, in part at least, by the uneven assessment of the several parts of his legacy. In particular, the fragments of Cornutus's specifically philosophical output have not seemed much worth studying. The surviving *Greek Theology* has always found readers and has made Cornutus a prominent figure in discussions of ancient allegorical exegesis; historians of ancient literary scholarship have been keenly aware of him as one of the very earliest commentators on Virgil (and collections *have* been made of his grammatical fragments). But the philosophical views for which many of the remaining fragments give evidence have suggested a thinker who, outside these two fields, is derivative at best and scholastic at worst. It has not helped that deflationary accounts of the wider philosophical culture of the early Roman Empire have set low expectations all around and diverted the attention of commentators towards authors whose surviving works we can, whatever we think of their content, at least admire for their literary qualities.

But there has been a reevaluation of Roman philosophy in recent decades and a new appreciation of its integrity and originality. What is more, substantial new ground has been broken in recognizing and understanding topics and questions distinctive of the period—notably, for example, the

---

1. The first, that is, to be formally published. It is also, and just as remarkably, the first time that the *Greek Theology* has been published in English translation. On both scores, however, it is preceded by Hays (1983), an unpublished thesis in wide circulation. For texts and other modern-language translations of the *Greek Theology*, see the bibliography; for fragments, see the concordances.

discussion of Aristotle's *Categories*, to which Cornutus made an early contribution. (As he is one of the earliest commentators on Virgil of whom we know, so he is on the *Categories*.) This sets the scene for a reassessment of Cornutus's philosophical achievements—and, with that, a fuller account of his intellectual profile in the round. The introductory remarks that follow are intended in this spirit. I do not pretend that they give in themselves a definitive or even, it might be felt, a balanced description of Cornutus's intellectual interests and entanglements. What I hope, however, is that they will help to make such a description possible in the future by supplementing existing accounts of his linguistic work with a study of his philosophical profile—or, better, a study of what he looks like if we think of him, with many in antiquity, *as a philosopher*. I hope that students of ancient philosophy will find that the results enlarge our understanding not just of Cornutus but to some degree of his period as well, and that those who do not wish to take his philosophy as their principal route into Cornutus will recognize at least that it is a perspective that needs to be taken seriously.

1.2. The Life of Cornutus

Lucius Annaeus Cornutus was born, probably during the second decade of the first century CE, in the Phoenician city of Leptis Magna in what was by then the Roman province of Africa (F2, F3, F4).[2] The rough parameters for his dates are given by these facts: that he was older than the poet Persius, who was born in 34 CE (*Life of Persius* 1–2); that he probably completed his *Orthography*, which notes the absence of the digamma from the Latin alphabet, before the Emperor Claudius introduced that letter in the (short-lived) reforms of 48 CE (see *Orthography* 2, with n. 6); that he had achieved sufficient prominence by the mid-60s to have attracted Nero's displeasure (F2, F3, F7, F8, F10); and, just possibly, that he lived to see something of the *Punica*, the epic poem on which Silius Italicus began work in the 80s (see F57 with note).

We know nothing about the family or social circumstances into which Cornutus was born. In first-person remarks, he is capable of identifying as a Roman, although in all likelihood he was not a Roman citizen by birth.[3]

---

2. The ruins of the city—now a World Heritage Site—lie in the district of Khoms, modern Libya.

3. On his identifying as a Roman, see *Orthography* 2; by contrast, Cornutus can appear to distance himself from the Greeks in the *Greek Theology* (Most 1989, 2030,

That does not mean that he lacked social privilege, however (at this period, possession of Roman citizenship was still a rarity in the wider empire, even in the most privileged circles).[4] Nor is this implied by the probability that he acquired Roman citizenship later on under the patronage of some member of the Annaeus family, whose name, as was customary, he subsequently adopted.[5] It is often assumed that Cornutus must have been a freedman of the family—and thus that he was born a slave.[6] But it is far more likely that

---

n. 123; Torres 2011, esp. 49—although he does make first-person identifications with Greek speakers in that work as well). Even the claim that he was not a Roman citizen by birth is something of which we cannot be quite certain. We tend to assume that Cornutus became a citizen through an acquaintance with the Annaeus family that was forged in Rome, but nothing in our evidence rules out that it was his father or grandfather who first acquired citizenship and the name Annaeus.

4. Before Caracalla extended citizenship to all freeborn members of the empire in an edict of 212, Roman citizens could be made only by birth, on emancipation from slavery to a Roman master, as a reward for (substantial) military service, or by direct grant from the emperor, normally achieved through patronage.

5. We cannot know who this was; the only member of that family we can be sure Cornutus knew was Lucan, who was certainly too junior to be a plausible candidate for the role of sponsor. But it is at least an attractive possibility that Cornutus was acquainted with Lucan's uncle, the philosopher Seneca (another Stoic). In fact, it is unthinkable that Cornutus was not at least aware of Seneca. But there seems to be little at stake in the question. Scholars have struggled to find clear traces of either philosopher in the other's works; see, e.g., Nock 1931, 1004 (Cornutus a polemical target for Seneca?); Cizek 1972, 254; cf. 350; and Rocca-Serra 1982, 65 (Seneca an influence on Cornutus?). Setaioli (2003–2004, 351) and Torre (2003) note that what thematic and methodological similarities there are may be due to common sources.

6. As, e.g., Hadot 2005, 414, n. 10—where the connection with Epictetus suggests one reason why the theory has been so readily and uncritically accepted: the adoption of Epictetus in our historiography as a typical "Roman philosopher" (see below with n. 20). Another reason concerns the manner in which the theory was introduced. As far as I can tell, the suggestion that Cornutus had servile origins was first made by Bouhier (1729, 1137); it was rejected by Martini (1825, 25, n. 1) but made again, apparently independently, by Marx (1894, 2227), who went on to specify *who* Cornutus might have been freed by (Seneca the Elder). He thereby sparked a debate about the identity of Cornutus's owner that has had the effect of distracting attention from the hypothetical character of the claim that he had one at all. (The other main contender in this secondary debate is Lucan's father, Mela; see, e.g., Nock 1931, 996. Others, e.g., Cizek [1972, 253], suggest his brother, the younger Seneca.) Geymonat (1984, 877) adds fictive support to the picture by claiming that Cornutus lived in the house of the Annaei (although *Life of Persius* 24 rather implies that he had his own). Some discussions use the supposed fact of Cornutus's servile status as the springboard for substantive claims

he was a friend of an Annaeus who sponsored him for citizenship—much as his younger Greek contemporary Plutarch acquired Roman citizenship under the patronage of Mestrius Florus (ending his days, then, as Mestrius Plutarchus).[7] There are certainly much stronger reasons to doubt that Cornutus might ever have been a slave than there are reasons to support the hypothesis that he was. One wonders, for a start, whether he would have been known in antiquity as Cornutus the Leptite (F2, F3)—let alone chosen by ancient encyclopedists to exemplify the use of the toponym (F4)—if he had not been a freeborn citizen of Leptis. Then there is the matter of his own name—Cornutus. This is clearly a Roman rather than a Phoenician name; indeed, it is the name of at least one prominent Roman family.[8] But we know that the philosopher was not either a member or a freedman of this family—or else, of course, he would not have become an Annaeus (*pace* Martini 1825, 24). (Nor is there any Cornutus branch of the Annaeus family from which he might have acquired both names at once.) On the other hand, it is quite unthinkable that a slave or ex-slave would have been allowed to appropriate the name of a Roman family, especially a well-known family, without being adopted in some way by them. So the only reasonable hypothesis is that Cornutus is a *Romanization* of the philosopher's own Phoenician birth name.[9] We can even make a plausible guess at how it came about: the Latin word *cornutus* means "horned," and it may not be a coincidence that horns (specifically rams' horns) were

---

about social inversion involved in his activities: e.g., Bellandi 2003, 189; Pià Comella 2011, esp. 6, 12, 13, 14, cf. 15 for Cornutus's "condition modeste"). Morford (2002, 192–93) is a rare voice of skepticism.

7. This is how he is recorded in inscriptions: *FD* 3.4.472 = *CID* 4.150.

8. See PIR^2, s.v. We know of one distinguished *Cornutus* active in North Africa the later first/early second century CE (perhaps as a legate of the consul): PIR^2 C.1058 = *ILAfr* 591 (from Aunoberis, modern Kern el-Kebch, a little inland from Carthage) mentions a *clarissimus vir* of that name. If the subject of F6 is not the philosopher, then it might possibly belong to a Roman contemporary of that name in Leptis itself. There seems to have been a well-known historian called Cornutus as well; see F2 with note.

9. It was quite common for people travelling between linguistic communities in the ancient world to adopt local monikers—which might be quite unrelated to their original name but very often translate it, either literally or through some form of association. We have an example of both moves in the case of the third-century Platonist philosopher Malkos, from the African city of Tyre. He was sometimes referred to by a straightforward Greek translation of his birth name, Basileus, "king," but he himself adopted a more allusive moniker, based on the Greek word for (royal) purple; see, in his own words, Porphyry, *Vit. Plot.* 17.

the principal attribute of the principal deity of the African Phoenicians, namely, Baal Hammon—also known as Baal Qarnaim, "Two-Horned Baal." In fact, Baal is a very common component in names from the region.[10] So Cornutus quite likely represents a Latin substitution for a birth name that placed Cornutus under the protection of Baal (a substitution made all the smoother for the assonance between *Cornu*tus and *Qarna*ium). But, again, such a name would certainly not have been given to a slave.[11]

If we can approximate certainty about anything in Cornutus's life, then, it is that he was a freeborn citizen of Leptis. Given the cultural and economic prosperity of the city, there is no reason to doubt that an education equal to his talents was available there, but how long it was before he went to Rome, we do not know. All we know is that he was in Rome by 50 CE, the year in which the sixteen-year-old Persius first encountered him (*Life of Persius* 12).

Cornutus taught in Rome—but there are different ways of construing what this might mean, with implications for our understanding both of his biography and of his output. At one extreme, his activities have been supposed to extend, whether through choice or economic necessity, to the tutoring of relatively young children.[12] In favor of this view is the occasional reference to Cornutus as *grammaticus* (which could mean an elementary teacher, not just a student of language) (F41). His publications include at least two contributions to a genre mostly associated with the classroom, the *Orthography* and the commentaries on Virgil.[13] The *Greek Theology*, meanwhile, is addressed to a *pais*, that is, a young child—perhaps a pupil, actual or ideal.

On the other hand, the content of the *Greek Theology*, Cornutus's Virgil commentary, and the *Orthography* seems variously sophisticated, critical,

---

10. A philosophical example is the third-century Carthaginian philosopher Hasdru-*bal*, who found fame in Athens as Clitomachus (Diogenes Laertius, *Vit. phil.* 4.67).

11. There is another possibility, too, albeit one that tends to the same general conclusion. If F6 is the philosopher, then Cornutus dedicated a shrine to Poseidon in Leptis. But Cornutus himself tells us that horns—bull's horns, this time—have an iconographical association with dependents of Poseidon: *Greek Theology* 42.16–17. So his choice of Roman name might be meant to signal a particular attachment to Poseidon—or Yam(m), his Phoenician equivalent.

12. See esp. Most 1989, esp. 2029–31; also, e.g., Pià Comella 2011, 15; 2014, ch. 3, esp. pp. 213, 250, 254.

13. For the educational context of works on orthography, see my introductory remarks to the translation below; for commentaries, see Zetzel 1981, 27.

and controversial in ways that *at the very least* engage mature scholarly interest as well and may actually rule them out as suitable classroom material.[14] The only two people we know as beneficiaries of Cornutus's teaching are Lucan and Persius (F10; *Life of Persius* 18–19)—who were not only exceptionally talented individuals but probably both came to Cornutus after they had done with their formal education, in their late teens, as Persius certainly did. It may also be relevant that the *Life* describes Persius's relationship with Cornutus as one of friendship, rather than pedagogy, from the outset (13). If F41 calls Cornutus *grammaticus*, it is in a very particular context (see note ad loc.): he is normally characterized as a philosopher (F2, F3, F4, F5, F10, F17), specifically a Stoic (Persius, *Sat.* 5.86; *Life of Persius* 20; F1)—even by those who have the full range of his works in view (F2, F3).[15] His situation as described in the *Life of Persius* suggests a philosopher more than a schoolteacher: the *Life* sets him in a circle of philosophically inclined friends meeting at his house, a circle that includes men of his own age, Claudius Agathinus and Petronius Aristocrates, as well as Lucan and Persius (*Life of Persius* 24–28). The case of Plutarch is available as a parallel in this matter, too—down to the demographic mix of this circle. (Plutarch's own sons, and those of his friends, took part in discussions as equals, not pupils.)[16]

If there is room for debate about the kind of life Cornutus led in Rome, the complete lack of evidence for its particularities ensures unanimous ignorance for the rest. We do not know whether he married or whether he had children, for example.[17] I noted above that he probably

---

14. See §1.4.1.2 below for the Virgil commentary and introductory remarks to the translations of the other two works in what follows.

15. In other words, the evidence seems to me to encourage the view that Cornutus's wide-ranging intellectual interests were united in a certain understanding of philosophy and not that he had an unconnected diversity of interests (*pace*, e.g., Most 1989, 2026; Pià Comella 2011, 14).

16. *Pace*, e.g., Clarke (1971, 93), who suggests that Stoics in general were less given to sociability (albeit "Persius recalls pleasant evenings spent with Cornutus"). In encouraging the comparison with Plutarch, I am deliberately offering an alternative to the comparison that is more commonly made with Epictetus (e.g., Pià Comella 2011, 13)—cf. n. 6 above and n. 20 below.

17. One manuscript of the *Greek Theology* (Laurentianus 60.19) asserts that it is dedicated to a son called George (see note to the text ad loc.). But this is impossible, since *Georgios* is (1) a Greek name that is (2) unattested this early and that (3) could not have been used as a Roman *praenomen* anyway. (Most [1989, 2033] argues that it

took Roman citizenship while in Rome, and we know that he was sent into exile by Nero (F7) in 65 or 67 CE (F10), but we do not know why, we do not know where, and we do not know if he returned to Rome after Nero's death in 68.[18]

1.3. Stoicism in the First Century CE

1.3.1. Stoicism as an International Movement

Before turning to see how far one can go in developing the picture of Cornutus as a philosopher, it is worth pausing to consider the context for his philosophical activity. As I noted above, the first century CE has usually been considered a relatively barren period for philosophy—one in which its practice survived only in an etiolated and scholastic form as part of the rich cultural life of the capital. The work of the philosophical schools in Athens had suffered catastrophic disruption during the Mithradatic Wars in the previous century, and the effective closure of these schools (so the thinking goes) left the philosophical movements they had nurtured, Stoicism included, adrift. Without centers for their activity and without hierarchical structures, they survived not as live research communities but more as historical ideals: at best, the support for practical systems of ethics, at worst, material for intellectual display.[19]

This picture can appeal to the survival of some truly great works of Roman philosophical literature dating from the first century BCE through to the later second century CE: works by Lucretius, Cicero, Seneca, and the

---

was added by a scribe who was disconcerted by the unusual absence of the name of the addressee in what he argues is a school text.) Stroux finds evidence for a son named Titus in F63 (q.v. with note)—which is within the bounds of historical possibility, even if the argument is speculative.

18. Fuentes González (1994, 464) reports an argument from Rocca-Serra (1988) that the true date was 63, when Lucan was forbidden from publishing. F2 and F3 say that Cornutus was executed rather than exiled—but that might be traced back to a mistransmission of the phrase "all but executed" in F7 and F9. The story reported in F7 and F8 sounds like it might have been invented after the fact, and it would be incautious to take it as historical—or even (as Fuentes González [1994, 464] suggests) that it is evidence that Cornutus had a reputation for *parrhēsia*, i.e., saying just what he thought.

19. Perhaps the fullest recent account of philosophy in Cornutus's time that follows this sort of narrative is Trapp (2007).

emperor Marcus Aurelius.[20] But at the same time, it is becoming increasingly clear that one has to ignore a lot of other evidence in order to claim either that Rome inherited a monopoly on philosophical activity at this period or that the circumstances of the time put dampers on innovative and boundary-pushing work across the full range of philosophical subjects. In fact (to address the first of these points), the extension and consolidation of the empire seems to have made it easier than ever before for communities of common interest to subsist over a large geographical area.[21] One need only think about how quickly Christianity was able to *become* an international community to understand the extent of the infrastructures that must already have been in existence. Thanks to the heroic logistical work of Richard Goulet, it is becoming possible to think more clearly and precisely about how widely dispersed philosophers were at this period.[22] The evidence that we have is, it should be admitted at the outset, very imperfect. For example, we rather infrequently know either where philosophers studied or where they were based. But we do quite often know where they come from: all around the Mediterranean, with the largest concentration in the east, especially around the coastline of modern-day Turkey (the Roman provinces of Asia, Lycia-Pamphylia, and Cilicia). If it is reasonable to infer that a large number of philosophers *coming from* a particular area testifies to an exceptional number of philosophers teaching there in the first place, then Cornutus is more typical among Stoics of whom we know for coming from the wider Mediterranean than he is for working at Rome.[23]

---

20. Epictetus is typically added to the list of Roman Stoics, *honoris causa*. This itself is an interesting phenomenon; there is an uncomfortable awareness that Epictetus ought not to be included in our evidence for *Roman* Stoicism: he was not a Roman by birth, did not work in Latin, and spent the later part of his career in exile in Greece (Long 2003, 207). He is no more Roman than Plutarch is. Yet his popular style of philosophy answers so well to what our histories would like Roman philosophy to be that he is rarely omitted from accounts of it (e.g., Morford 2002, ch. 8), even in authors who are aware of the need for special pleading (e.g., Thorsteinsson 2010, 20–21).

21. See Hadot (2005, 414) on the existence of schools outside the major cities (using Epictetus as an example).

22. The completion of the monumental *Dictionnaire des Philosophes Anciennes* (Goulet 1994– 2018) allows a new generation of proper statistical work. Goulet (2013) and (1994–2018) vol. 7, 1175–271 ("Epimetrum") begin this work and provide the starting point for my observations in what follows.

23. So, for example, P. Ignatius Celer (first century, from Beirut) learned his Sto-

There is more we can say about this as well. If the east is a geographical center of gravity for members of movements bequeathed by Hellenistic Athens, the newer schools of the period—including the increasingly dominant forces of Platonism, Pythagoreanism, and Aristotelianism—are overwhelmingly based there.[24] Indeed, while there is substantial evidence for the presence of Stoics and Epicureans in Rome during the first century and even through the second, there is vanishingly little evidence for the activity of any representatives of these movements in the capital.[25] It is important to bear this in mind as evidence that Rome—whatever its cultural attractions—was simply not the natural locus for frontline philosophical debate. But this means that if we want to make an assessment of Cornutus's philosophical heft, the proper context for doing so is the Mediterranean as a whole, not his immediate neighbors in Rome.

1.3.2. Stoicism as a Textual Community

There is a concern that will naturally arise at this point: it is one thing to say that philosophical movements, include Stoicism, had a *presence* all around the Mediterranean, but it is quite another thing to say that a philosopher on one side of the Mediterranean had any consciousness of philosophers on the other side of the Mediterranean—or any means of meaningful philosophical interaction. Stoicism, for example, might have been *international*, but was it in any sense *a community*?

There is, I think, significant work that remains to be done on this question, but if we do not yet have agreed models for the way in which members of dispersed intellectual movements found ways of cohering and commu-

---

icism in Tarsus; Chaeremon (first century) worked in Alexandria as well as Rome; in exile, Epictetus (late first/early second century) set up school in Nicopolis, on the West coast of the Greek mainland; Galen was taught, either in Smyrna or Pergamum, by the Stoic physician Aeficianus (see below p. 13).

24. The case could be made that Aristotelianism is as much a Hellenistic school as Stoicism or Epicureanism; certainly, it is more closely linked to the Hellenistic Peripatos than Platonism is to the Hellenistic Academy. But one way or another, Aristotelianism found a second wind in the later first century BCE after relative quietude during the Hellenistic centuries, and it seems reasonable to link its success then to the new opportunities of the age.

25. A fact recognized even at Rome: in 176, Marcus Aurelius established—in Athens (!)—chairs in Platonism and Aristotelianism, alongside chairs in Epicureanism and Stoicism: Dio Cassius, *Hist. rom.* 71.31.3–32.1; Philostratus, *Vit. soph.* 2.2.

nicating during this period, it would be wrong to suppose that they did not do so. Indeed, there is some evidence that movements such as Stoicism had begun to adopt strategies very similar to those that modern scholarship is starting to trace in the newer movements such as Platonism. These newer movements lacked institutional structures, acknowledged leaders, and geographical centers from their very inception, yet their members found coherence and common purpose in a way that enabled them to develop into powerful philosophical forces. The way in which they did this seems to have been to constitute themselves as what have been described as *textual communities*—that is, as groups whose adversative identity is linked to a shared commitment to the authority of a textual corpus (see esp. Niehoff 2007 and Baltzly 2014). Platonists, most obviously, are united by their shared orientation to the dialogues of Plato. The study of these dialogues can unite Platonists on opposite sides of the Mediterranean, not just spiritually, but in the very concrete sense that it gives a common point of reference to their individual deliverances (publications, letters, conversations): a rallying point for common concerns and the evolution of a common language. The texts give a substructure to support an intellectual *network* of ideas and activity, through which every member is linked to every other—through intermediaries, if not directly. The newly revived Aristotelianism of the period can be seen in a similar light; it seems, indeed, to have received its impetus from new prominence achieved by the so-called esoteric texts of Aristotle, perhaps through the publication of a new edition of them by Andronicus in the later first century BCE.[26]

It is true that this model works better to give plausible grounds to the idea of a diasporic community of Platonists or Aristotelians than of Epicureans or (especially) Stoics; there are no tightly defined and easily shared corpora of texts that can stand proxy for the schools in their cases. Nevertheless, it seems to me no coincidence that Stoics at this time constantly reference their work to the first three heads of the school—Zeno, Cleanthes, and Chrysippus. The ancient biography of Persius mentions his collection of Chrysippus—indeed, they are the only books that it mentions; the reason may be that this is the way to indicate his philosophical affiliation, that is, as a Stoic (see *Life of Persius* 38–39 with note). Cornutus must have been delighted to inherit them for the same reason (*Life of Persius*

---

26. This is the traditional view, based on Plutarch, *Sull.* 26.1–2 (see Porphyry, *Vit. Plot.* 24 for Andronicus's work as an editor); see Barnes 1997b for a skeptical evaluation of it.

38–39). His overt deference to earlier authorities at the end of the *Greek Theology* (at 76,6–8, he says that he only wanted to summarize what they had to say) should, I suggest, be seen in this light; it is far from a confession that he is thoughtlessly *retailing* older material—any more than Platonists are merely retailing Plato when they write commentaries on his works.[27] If we can assume that ancient readers would have seen in the earlier philosophers a reference to, imprimis, the older Stoics (but see also p. 47 n. 9 below), then this amounts to a statement of his philosophical identity and the tradition within which he wants the *Greek Theology* to be read; it is the way in which he can establish common purpose with other contemporary members of the Stoic community.[28]

There is something else that can be said here as well. The process of forming one network, or textual community, does not take place in isolation from the formation of others, and identity can be constructed through *opposition* to those others as well. So, just as one can make a constructive claim to philosophical identity by aligning oneself with the classics of a particular movement, one can also make the claim *adversatively*, that is, by the *polemical* treatment of works underpinning the identity of rival movements. So, if the Stoic canon is just too unwieldy for fine-grained allusion, a Stoic can nevertheless go some way towards marking affiliation by *polemical* engagement with well-known Aristotelian and Platonic texts.[29] This is exactly what Cornutus does when he sets out to mobilize Stoicism against the logical system of the renascent Aristotelians (or so at least I shall argue in §1.4.1.1 below). His approach is not to write commentary on logical works by Chrysippus that might be completely inaccessible to others; he rather does it by criticizing a

---

27. Most (1989, 2015–16) points out that in only one place is a source named (Cleanthes, at 64.16)—and that is to note disagreement.

28. It is worth noting that the word he uses for passing on what his predecessors had said, παραδοῦναι (76.8), is precisely the word that Cornutus uses to talk about the way in which the privileged wisdom of the earliest generations of humankind has reached us. Indeed, it is only ever used by Cornutus to refer to the material that is *worth preserving*, that preserves the truth—the material that lies underneath the later corruptions and accretion. So the word implies much more than passing on; it is a matter of *salvaging* and *selecting*—active and constructive intellectual engagement with his own intellectual past.

29. Few people would have had access to the hundreds of works written by Chrysippus (see *Life of Persius* 35–40 with note to the translation below), let alone know them by heart.

work by Aristotle that is accessible to everyone—the *Categories*. I have argued before—although the case is admittedly less transparent—that he takes similar pains to define his position in physics by allusively critical engagement with the most widely known work of ancient physics, Plato's *Timaeus* (see Boys-Stones 2009).

1.3.3. The Intellectual Program of Post-Hellenistic Stoicism

I have noted above that the standard picture of Stoicism (and of other movements) in the post-Hellenistic era downplays the extent to which original work in the more theoretical branches of philosophy was pursued; the focus was, we are told, on practical ethics instead. But this view is closely bound up with the idea that the Roman Stoics are our best, or only, window on the activity of the movement. As soon as one stands back to consider the pan-Mediterranean context, the plausibility of this picture comes under intolerable strain.

In fact, it takes some manipulation of the evidence to be able to make the claim that ethics, let alone practical ethics, is *even* the main preoccupation of Roman Stoics. One can point to the *Moral Epistles* of Seneca, or Marcus Aurelius's work *To Himself* (the so-called *Meditations*)—although the former at least builds in physical and logical theory and high-level, polemical engagement with Platonist metaphysics. On the other hand, we know that interest in logic had never been greater, and we actually possess a number of major scientific works by Roman-era Stoics. For example, there is the *Astronomica* of Manilius, published early in the first century CE, and there is the corpus of zoological works by Claudius Aelianus from the turn of the third century. (Aelian, as he is generally known in English, also wrote on theology.) Alongside Seneca's *Moral Epistles*, we have to reckon with his own major work of physics, the *Natural Questions*.

But when one leaves Rome, the picture is even more striking. There is, of course, the ethical work of Epictetus, but even that is richly informed by physics and logic—in fact he tells us that there was much more interest in logic in his day than there had been in the Hellenistic period (*Diatr.* 3.6.1).[30] His amanuensis, Arrian, wrote his own work on

---

30. His point is to ask why, for all this, the *advances* had been greater in the past—but that only guarantees that he is not exaggerating the extent of the interest. See further Barnes 1997a.

1. Introduction: Cornutus the Philosopher   13

meteorology. We know that work only through quotations,[31] but we still have Cleomedes's *On the Heavens* (translated into English for the first time in Bowen and Todd 2004) and Geminus's *Introduction to [Astronomical] Phenomena* (of uncertain date, but earlier than Alexander of Aphrodisias, who cites him; translated into English for the first time in Evans and Berggren [2006]). Cornutus's friends and contemporaries, the medical scientists Agathinus and Aristocrates, were at least interested in Stoicism (*Life of Persius* 24–28, with note) and might well have counted themselves as Stoics; in any case, we know of one (other) Stoic physician in the period: Aeficianus, one of Galen's teachers (Galen, *On His Own Books*, 19:58,3–4 [Kühn 1821–1833]). Chaeremon of Alexandria—someone who might conceivably have met Cornutus in Rome and in F11 is coupled with him for their shared interest in allegorical interpretation—was cited in later antiquity for his views on metaphysics.[32] At least one Stoic prior to Cornutus engaged with the technicalities of Aristotle's *Categories*, namely, Athenodorus, who was probably writing at the end of the first century BCE (see F19, F20, F21, F22, and F24; Hijmans 1975).[33]

1.4. Cornutus's Philosophical Views

The purpose of the foregoing sections has been to argue that we ought to come to Cornutus with high expectations. He is not a freedman made good in the last refuge of a dying school; he is a cosmopolitan intellectual, more than likely of high social standing, aligned with a vibrant and well-connected international community of like-minded scholars. Against this background, we can start to ask what case can be made for his own views. For the remainder of the introduction, then, I turn to discuss what philosophical positions and motivating concerns it might be possible to

---

31. Arrian's work is generously excerpted in Stobaeus, *Ecl.* 1.28–31 (Wachsmuth and Hense 1884–1912, 1:229,10–231,8; 235,9–238,12; 246,1–247,13); see also Photius, *Bibl.*, cod. 250, 460b17–20.

32. For Chaeremon in general, see van der Horst 1987. We are told that he taught the emperor Nero (van der Horst 1984, Test. 3 = Suda α.1128), which is what raises the possibility that he overlapped in Rome with Cornutus. (Martini [1825, 34] speculates that he might have himself have taught Cornutus—a hypothesis that relies, of course, on the idea that Cornutus received his education in Stoicism in Rome.)

33. He will presumably be one of the philosophers named Athenodorus in F1. Barnes (2005) speculates that L. Sergius Plautus, writing at a similar time, may also have been interested in the work.

reconstruct for Cornutus from the surviving evidence. I do this under the standard, threefold division of Hellenistic philosophical systems that Cornutus himself accepted: dialectic, ethics, and physics.[34]

1.4.1. Dialectic

On the standard Hellenistic view, dialectic typically divides into the study of knowledge (i.e., epistemology), on the one hand, and logic and rhetoric, on the other, as, according to need and context, the modes of its communication.[35] We have little that can be attributed to Cornutus under the heading of epistemology narrowly conceived—although in line with earlier Stoic thought, he seems to think that innate concepts form the bedrock of our rationality, and since he refers in particular to the knowledge of "the will of the gods" allowed us by these concepts, the claim might be taken as an assertion of epistemological optimism against relativism or skepticism (*Greek Theology*, 22,2–3, with note ad loc.). But there is a great deal to be said about how he thinks knowledge is to be codified and beliefs communicated. Indeed, one way of approaching the question of how to balance our view of Cornutus as a grammarian with our view of him as a philosopher would be to ask whether his philosophy subserves, or complements, a primary concern with literary or rhetorical topics—or whether, conversely (and this is the case that I am putting in the present account of him), one rather thinks that his rich interests in literature and rhetoric, and even mythology, are conceived by him within a framework of philosophical dialectic. After all, we know that Cornutus did some important first-order work in the field of logic (quite apart from a conventional remark in *Greek Theology*, ch. 16 that the wise man will understand sophisms); at least, I shall argue below that the standing debate between Aristotelian and Stoic systems of logic provides the best context for understanding his pioneering engagement with the interpretation of Aristotle's *Categories*. If this is right, it becomes at best uneconomical to think that he saw his work in rhetoric as part of a separate intellectual discipline: grammar *rather than* philosophy.[36] On the contrary, his study of poetics and the mechanisms by

---

34. See *Greek Theology*, 15,4–5 with note ad loc.

35. For philosophical interest in rhetoric at this period in particular, see Long 2003, 191–92.

36. It is relevant to note that a work dedicated to rhetoric gives us some of our evidence for Cornutus's thinking about the *Categories*, too: F20.

which ancient wisdom has been transmitted through wider cultural traditions naturally fall within the field of what one might think of as applied dialectic: where formal logic traces the scope of legitimate inference in theoretical terms, these subjects address the ways in which human beliefs are codified and preserved within living cultural practice.[37]

1.4.1.1. Logic: Cornutus on Aristotle's *Categories*

One of the liveliest emerging sites for philosophical debate in the time of Cornutus was Aristotle's *Categories*—a text in which earlier generations had shown very little interest but one that suddenly achieved prominence in the mid-first century BCE, perhaps thanks to its promotion in the editorial work of Andronicus.[38] The work was discussed not only by Aristotelians but also by their enemies, and it attracted an unparalleled level of comment and even formal commentary from Pythagoreans and Platonists as well as Stoics. Of the Stoics, two were remembered in the later tradition by name: Athenodorus (see above with n. 33) and Cornutus. If one takes the view that Cornutus is more grammarian than philosopher (so, e.g., Martini 1825, 48; Fuentes González 1994, 468), his interest in the *Categories* can certainly be explained in other terms—as having to do with his broader interests in language, for example. Indeed, as we shall shortly see, Cornutus was criticized already in antiquity for treating the work precisely as if it were a work of linguistics. But the *Categories* is not an obvious text for the grammarian (much more relevant in their different ways would be Aristotle's *On Interpretation* or *Rhetoric*). If Cornutus had a grammarian's interest in the work, he was the only person in antiquity who did—and it is far from clear what lessons he derived from it. It is, conversely, relevant that his thoughts on the work enjoyed an exclusively philosophical reception; we know about Cornutus's treatment of the *Categories* (even that he read it "as if it were a work of linguistics"—an accusation I shall return to below) only because later philosophers found his criticisms of Aristotle enough of a threat to their own interests that they required explicit refutation.

---

37. And note the emphasis Cornutus places on the social context and utility of rhetorical study when he touches on it in the *Greek Theology*; see 17,6–10; 25,2–8.

38. See n. 26 above. For the importance of the *Categories* at this period, see in general Moraux 1984, 592–601; Griffin 2015, esp. ch. 5.

Leaving Cornutus himself to one side for a moment, we can in any case be sure that the principal debate over the *Categories*, the debate that brought it to prominence in the first century BCE and kept it there for the rest of antiquity, concerned philosophical and not grammatical issues. The *Categories* famously gets its name from a tenfold list of *predicates* (κατηγορήματα) whose discussion forms its bulk (1b25–27, quoted in F20 [86,15–19]):

> Every word which can be spoken on its own signifies either substance, or quantity, or quality, or relation, or where, or when, or disposition, or possession, or action, or affection.[39]

This list gives ten classes into which meaningful words can be sorted. But how did Aristotle arrive at just this list? And what exactly is the purpose of the classification?

Platonist commentators of Cornutus's era (who include the Lucius and Nicostratus mentioned in F23) thought that the purpose of the *Categories* was to categorize reality (τῶν ὄντων, as Aristotle says; *Cat.* 1a20), and read this way, they found it a handy reference point for a criticism of what they saw as the defective ontology of the Peripatetics, notably their failure to acknowledge the existence (indeed, the primary existence) of Plato's forms.[40] Peripatetics, on their side, put more emphasis on the linguistic content of the work—but not to argue that it ought to be considered a grammatical treatise; rather, they saw it as a work concerned with *meaning*: to be precise, with what Aristotle elsewhere calls the "significant vocalization" (φωνὴ σημαντική; *Int.* 16a19; see Diogenes Laertius, *Vit. phil.* 7.56 for the Stoics' adoption of the phrase).

The Peripatetic view seems to have been that the *Categories* was doing a job of work for scientific inquiry. After all, Aristotle's system of formal logic trades exclusively in simple predications: in any syllogism, each premise, and the conclusion, takes the form "A is true of [all, some, not all, or no] B"—where A stands for a predicate. So by classifying different types of predicate (the different options for A), the *Categories* offers a vocabulary to describe the component parts of a syllogism. This is in fact what another later commentator on the *Categories* says (in the course of a passage quoted more fully below): "The elements of significant vocaliza-

---

39. Unless otherwise indicated, all translations in this volume are my own.
40. Evidence and discussion in Boys-Stones 2018, ch. 15.

tion which, thought of as parts of a simple categorical premise, provide the terms out of which one is properly constituted—these are among the categories" (cf. Morison 2005). But this is far from making the *Categories* about language *rather than* ontology—grammar rather than philosophy. The simple reason for this is that the predications allowed by the *Categories* had better be *true to the world* if they are going to be used in the process of acquiring knowledge about the world. (No ancient system of logic has as its end the exploration of purely formal relationships: its ultimate concern is always with the assessment of claims to knowledge about the world based on inference.) The account that Aristotelians soon came to agree on is formulated carefully to acknowledge this fact, without tipping over into the initial Platonist view that the *Categories* is only or principally about ontology. According to Aristotelians, then, the *Categories* is a work that classifies meaningful words according to the divisions of reality. This view was accepted by later Platonists, who became its best-known and most powerful advocates. As Porphyry put it in the third century CE, the *Categories* concerns meaningful words *insofar as they signify things*.[41] Another way Porphyry expresses this is to say that it is about words in their "primary imposition" (see F19): the contrast is with their "secondary imposition," which refers to the strictly *derivative* use of words to refer to words themselves, as when someone says, "'Dog' is a noun."

An understanding of Porphyry's perspective on the *Categories* is essential background to the study of Cornutus (and Athenodorus as well) because Porphyry is the immediate or ultimate source for almost everything we know about the earlier Stoic treatment of the text—including what comes to us through Simplicius.[42] But Porphyry and Simplicius are not impartial in their reports of the Stoics. Whatever, exactly, the Stoics believed, we know that it was both different from the view shared with the Aristotelian tradition by Porphyry and Simplicius and, what is worse to them, that it was critical of Aristotle's text.

---

41. Porphyry himself tells us that this way of viewing the work was already firmly in place in the Peripatetic tradition of the later first century BCE, with Andronicus's successor Boethus (*Exp. Cat.* 59,17–25).

42. We have one commentary by Porphyry that survives; another, longer commentary, known as the *Ad Gedalium* (from its dedication to Gedalius), is now lost but seems to have been a major source for the surviving sixth-century commentary by Simplicius, which is our own immediate source for much of the earlier debate.

It is nowhere more important to bear the polemical context of our evidence in mind than in the case of the programmatic F19. Porphyry here offers us a seductive and speciously exhaustive alternative: one might, he says, read the *Categories* as concerned with the *primary* imposition of words, that is, words considered as signifiers of things in the world; or one might read it as concerned with the *secondary* imposition of words—words *as* words. Porphyry, as we know, takes the *Categories* the former way; given that the Stoics do not take it this way, he encourages us to think, they must suppose that the *Categories* is concerned *only* with words—something that is confirmed (says Porphyry) if you consider the fact that they criticize Aristotle for neglecting details of linguistic analysis such as the distinction between the literal and the metaphorical.

This is the proof text for the prevailing view that Cornutus and Athenodorus were pedantic interlocutors in a debate they did not understand, nit-picking at the *Categories* for failing to do what they would have wished from a Greek grammar. But Porphyry is engaging in polemical simplification here. One could guess as much just from reading the *Categories* oneself: it would take a considerable feat of imagination to think that anyone could have intended the ten kinds, which are at the heart of the work and are the immediate the subject of Porphyry's discussion in F19, as grammatical categories, comparable to *yet excluding* verbs, nouns, prepositions, and so on (see F25 [359,7–9]). But we do not need to guess. We can know with absolute certainty that Cornutus and Athenodorus did not believe that the *Categories* was a narrowly linguistic text of this sort.[43] Simplicius makes this explicit when he tells us in F21 that one of their complaints was that the work dealt rather haphazardly with a whole range of subjects, *including* real-world issues of ethics, physics, and theology (i.e., metaphysics; see n. 39 ad loc.; cf. Duhot 1991, 223–24). We also know from Simplicius that Stoics entered a debate about whether mass and weight are to be considered under the category of quantity (F23), which is not a linguistic question. Cornutus actually denies a purely linguistic criterion for identifying relatives in F24.

---

43. Porphyry would no doubt be surprised himself to see that the scholarship has largely taken his remark in F19 at face value—even when the contradiction with the evidence is unmissable and unmissed. Moraux (1984, 594), for example, recognizes Cornutus's development of a realist definition of the relative in F24, *despite* what he believes to be his "principled commitment" to interpreting the categories as a matter of *lexis* ("trotz seines prinzipiellen Bekenntnisses").

There is no countervailing evidence: Porphyry does not, for example, quote Athenodorus or Cornutus expressing the view that the *Categories* makes a poor introduction to the Greek language. Rather, he invites us to *infer* that they think of the *Categories* as a work of linguistics; specifically, he invites us to infer this from the fact that they object to the omission of certain classes of words. When we are clear about this, we can begin to discern, at least in outline, what Porphyry's accusation really amounts to. Porphyry is not objecting that the Stoics *actually believed* that the *Categories* was a narrowly linguistic work but that, in criticizing Aristotle for omitting certain classes of words from consideration, they treated it *as if* it were. To put this another way, what the Stoics count as omissions in the *Categories* would in Porphyry's eyes only be omissions from a work of linguistics. We shall see that this question of scope, what the *Categories* ought to have included, will get us to the heart of a much more fundamental and long-standing disagreement between the Stoics, on one side, and Porphyry with the Aristotelian tradition, on the other, over the resources needed for an adequate system of logic.

One text that is especially helpful for understanding Cornutus's concerns is Dexippus, *On the Categories* (Busse 1887, 11,1–12,31, the longer passage from which I had occasion to quote a line above). It does not mention Cornutus and is not included among the fragments in this edition, but, as Michael Griffin has argued, Dexippus's resistance to attempts to expand the scope of the *Categories* dovetails with Porphyry's explicit account of Cornutus and Athenodorus (note, for example, the exclusion of figurative language here) and helps us to flesh out what they must have thought.[44] In fact it is useful enough as such to be well worth quoting in full:

> [Seleucus:] But how are we going to work out whether the expressions in question fall under the categories or not? Give me some criterion by which we can exclude what does not fall under the division of categories.
>
> [Dexippus:] Well, I say that the class of *the significant* as a whole must be prior, since it underlies this kind of division and is to be ranged among its starting points; without this kind of vocalization, you could never predicate anything as one thing said of another. So no one would rightly place the following sort of thing among the categories: an element

---

44. Griffin 2015, 153–65, also comparing Simplicius, *On the Categories* (Kalbfleisch 1907, 14,33–15,5) (also 15.30–34).

that is meaningless in itself, such as *blityri*, or is significant only insofar as it refers back to another [linguistic] element, as in the case of so-called referents when they identify something only insofar as they refer back to an indefinite element [11,10] (e.g., the word "he" when it refers back to "someone"),[45] or something that signifies [only] in combination with something else, such as articles and conjunctions.

Again, he intends each category to form a proper class conforming to some reality and following the divisions among things—since a significant word has, first and foremost, to do with the primary employment of language, that by which we try to reveal things to each other. For example, the word "human" conforms to substance, "whiteness" to quality, and so on with the rest. So words which are so formed that they are not part of the primary significance of some utterance, but acquire their character from their components (e.g., "from Dio," "from home," "finest," "rightest," [11,20] "wisest," "most poetic") or from the interweaving of thoughts with each other (as in a hypothetical [syllogism] expressing consequence, such as "if it is day," or one by exhaustive alternative, such as "either it is day")[46]—no such words belong among the categories. For all these uses of language stand at a remove from the primary coordination of the categories with things.

Again, mental activity that cannot be put into words, as in the case of groaning and moaning, and inarticulate noises, as in the case of tutting, and nonrepresentational vocalizations, as in the case of humming, and nouns that do not pick anything out—none of these are categories at all: they do not in any sense possess the property of what it is to be a category.

[11,30] Again, the highest differentiations among the genera—or, if one wants to say this, among the most generic words—are mutually exclusive. So there cannot be, above them, anything real that exists in its own right or is used as a predicate. Indeed, by this account, if you are on the right track for the categories, you should not even claim that *being* is common to them all (otherwise, [12,1] there will not be ten of

---

45. The point seems to that a pronoun (e.g., "he") signifies its antecedent, but it *only* signifies something in the world as well if the antecedent picks out a determinate individual (if the antecedent is, e.g., "Socrates," naming the man Socrates). When its antecedent is indefinite (e.g., "someone"), the pronoun inherits its failure to pick out, and so to signify, anything in particular. (Dexippus would presumably say that an indefinite antecedent does not signify *anything all*, which is why the pronoun, which at least signifies the antecedent, is his example at this point.)

46. The examples are abbreviated from arguments that have the form: (1) If it is day, then it is light; it is day; therefore it is light. (2) Either it is day or it is night; it is day; therefore it is not night.

them after all, but they will be reduced to a single genus). Nor should you invent a category of "movement" shared by acting and being affected (they would not then be two genera, but the one they have in common, movement). Look for what is simple and incomposite in the genera of beings, or in the most generic words that have significations, or both; it is this that defines the distinguishing character of the categories. So neither composites of words, such as "Dio walks," nor compound words, such as <...>,[47] nor abbreviated or elliptical expressions, nor made-up words, nor modifications, nor epithets, nor anything else that properly belongs to poetry or rhetoric [12,10] have anything at all to do with the categories. This sort of thing is recognized by a different, posterior study: linguistics. A category tracks the primary significations of words and the principal substantial commonalities among things, which are to be found in the highest genera—not common meanings that are seen to be accidental and secondary.

Figures of speech and the endless possibilities for connotation are useless for knowledge, but generic significant words, our grasp of the primary genera, give us something definite within this infinity and produce clear understanding, both of language and at the same time of reality. So you should use these as your starting points, which are rightly the objects of special attention by those who are interested [12,20] in language and reality. And tropes or metaphors, like "rein in" or "the farthest foot of Ida" [Homer, *Il.* 2.824] are not to be ranged among the categories, nor modalities (being necessarily, possibly, or actually), nor quantifications (all, no, some, none). Nothing like this captures a concrete nature proper to anything. So one might reasonably dismiss them as inappropriate to the scope of the discussion we are now having about categories. I think, in fact, that what is above all relevant to the categories is what has regard to truth in language, that in which speaking truly or falsely is properly encompassed. So the elements of significant vocalization that, thought of as parts of a [12,30] simple categorical premise, provide the terms out of which one is properly constituted—these are among the categories.

The passage is useful not just for an insight into the kind of things that Cornutus and Athenodorus believed the *Categories* ought to have covered but did not; it is also useful for clarifying the rule for inclusion against which the Stoics were objecting. In particular, it emerges clearly from Dexippus that, behind the headline claim made by Porphyry for the Aristotelian/Neoplatonist tradition that the *Categories* is interested in the primary imposition

---

47. The text is corrupt here, but all that is required is an example of a compound word: forethought (fore+thought) would be one English example.

of words, there is a *further* set of restrictions about the sort of words that are going to count. This tradition is only interested, in fact, in expressions whose primary imposition *immediately* signifies something in the world. It is not interested, for example, in *derivative* formulations, such as propositions—even though one might think of these, too, as having a primary and secondary imposition ("The cat runs" versus "'The cat runs' is a proposition"). Similarly, it is not interested in conjunctions, which only acquire meaning in the context of the verbal expressions they join. This is why it is not interested in derivative uses of words, for example, metaphorical usage (although, again, a metaphor might refer to something in the world).

In short, it turns out that the Aristotelian tradition is interested not broadly in language insofar as it names things but much more specifically in words that (1) on their own and (2) in their primary meaning signify something in the world. This is a legitimate way of understanding the text itself, which claims to deal with "things said *without any combination*" (1b25).[48] But it is also precisely what we should expect if the purpose of the work is closely tied to the formation of the predications specifically intended for syllogisms.

It is here that the opening obviously exists for objection from the Stoics. The Stoics could simply point out that there is no philosophical merit, and potentially some harm, to be had from operating with a logical system restricted to such a narrow set of meaningful ways of talking about the world. It might not even be possible consistently to maintain the restriction.

Consider F25. At first glance this fragment might seem to be good evidence for the view that Cornutus was reading the *Categories* in purely linguistic terms. On one natural reading, Cornutus in this fragment is pointing out problems *if* (i.e., since) Aristotle intended to distinguish categories "by the way that words are characterized." In this case, Cornutus's worries are purely formal; they would concern the fact that Aristotle does not in fact always place similar linguistic expressions together. But a more serious and interesting criticism is available if we suppose that Cornutus is raising a problem with the principles restricting the linguistic expressions encompassed within the *Categories*. Start from the fact that Aristotle thought that to be a place (e.g., Durham) or a time (e.g., a year) is to be a

---

48. Boethus also tried to secure their exclusion by arguing that "combinations of words" do not fall under "things said"; see Simplicius, *On the Categories* (Kalbfleisch 1907, 41,16–18), where "it is day" is his example. (Cf. 64,23–26, where conjunctions are not "said" either.)

1. Introduction: Cornutus the Philosopher

quantity of some sort, so that place and time both belong to "quantity" as a category. But being *at* some place (the answer to the question "where?": e.g., "at Durham") or *at* some time (the answer to "when?": e.g., "last year") are, according to Aristotle, distinct ways of being—each of which constitutes a category of its own (the categories, namely, of "where" and "when"). But what, exactly, makes them distinct? This is an awkward case for the Aristotelians because many of the ways we have for saying "at a place/time" precisely involve *derivative* expressions—expressions derivative, in fact, from the names for places. The Lyceum is a place (and so falls under the category of "quantity"), but "*in* the Lyceum" is one of Aristotle's examples for "where" (ἐν Λυκείῳ; *Cat.* 2a1).[49] So it turns out that the rule against *combined* expressions is not strictly adhered to—and Cornutus can reasonably ask: if "*in* the Lyceum" is allowed a category of its own, why not something like "*with* Dion"?

Simplicius's answer—in the pattern set by Porphyry—is to accuse Cornutus of making a superficial linguistic point at the expense of meaning: since Dion does not name a place but a person, he says, locating yourself by reference to Dion is at best an indirect way of saying where you are. But Cornutus has his eye on meaning as well; he is not claiming, as Simplicius implies, that all uses of a particular grammatical case or a particular preposition ought to fall under the same category. In fact his example, εἰς Δίωνα, "to Dion," may be carefully chosen to prove the point. In Greek, as in English, this could be a dedication rather than a direction, but in this case, Cornutus could not be trying to show, for example, that all uses of εἰς with the accusative belong in the same category. What Cornutus is shrewdly pointing out is that, here, Aristotle does not, and perhaps cannot, keep strictly to the rule that excludes derivative expressions from the categories. But if the restriction does not apply in this case, then why should it in others? It is precisely with an eye on the world as well as language that Cornutus criticizes Aristotle for trying so hard to exclude some forms of expression that succeed in talking about the world—here, by showing that the attempt has led him to inconsistency.

The point is no mere cavil, and it should be starting to become clear why. We have seen that the restriction the Aristotelians place on themselves

---

49. The awkwardness is implicitly acknowledged in some ancient accounts of the categories, which "correct" Aristotle by substituting "time" and "place" for "when" and "where" in the list of categories. (Many modern accounts and translations make this amendment as well—and often without acknowledging the change.)

in enumerating the categories has to do with the purpose of the work in supplying a classification of terms to be used in their logic. But the Stoics do not adopt Aristotle's logical system, and their own is much more capacious in the propositions that it can deal with—precisely, in fact, because its component parts are propositions (ἀξιώματα) rather than terms. In fact, the Stoics use the very word *predication* in a tellingly different way. Where, for Aristotle, a predication brings one term into some relationship with another, for the Stoics it is a matter of completing a thought about some subject—typically expressed by a verb in the appropriate conjugation (e.g., "walks" attached to a name, "Dion"). The logical figures of Stoicism express relationships between predications, that is, propositions like this. But this means that the figures can be populated by *any* meaningful statement at all. So were a Stoic to set about writing a book exploring meaningful expressions relevant to logic, they would need to cover all of the verbal elements from which a proposition can be formed. By this standard, of course it is the case that the *Categories* falls short.[50]

In other words, Cornutus's worries about the scope of the *Categories* cohere perfectly with the kind of criticism that a Stoic logician would have about Aristotelian logic. In fact, to trace the deficit in the *Categories* would be an elegant way of highlighting the significant restrictions (as a Stoic would see them) in what Aristotelian syllogistic can process—and so, in turn, in the knowledge, properly speaking, that his system is able to support (given, that is, that the most robust form of knowledge, scientific knowledge, is identified by Aristotle with the conclusion of a certain kind of syllogism, the demonstrative syllogism). If Cornutus was not a shrewd logician, one can at the very least see why he looked like one to Porphyry.

1.4.1.2. Rhetoric: The Social Context for Wisdom Traditions

If I am right, Cornutus was interested in logic and interested in it as the theoretical framework for the organization of knowledge. But he was also interested in the ways in which knowledge was communicated and transmitted.[51] On the face of it, there might seem to be little in common

---

50. For the related, but narrower, case made by the Stoics that their logical system has priority over Aristotelian syllogistic because any deduction made in the terms of the latter can be reformulated as valid arguments in the former, see also Mueller 1969.

51. In this context it might be worth noting a hint at Cornutus's view about meaning. In 21.2–3 he claims that speech conducts "thoughts into the souls of those

between what we know of his *Orthography*, his commentary on Virgil, the grammatically inflected work on rhetoric, and the allegorical fireworks of his *Greek Theology*. In fact, however, they share precisely this core concern: the relationship between information to be communicated and the way our linguistic practices—orthographical, rhetorical, and poetic—actually operate. These practices can obscure meaning or distort it; they can do so deliberately, as in the case of an unscrupulous rhetorician; or carelessly, as in the case of poetic invention, which pursues pleasure rather than truth; or altogether unwittingly, as when changes in orthography unhitch a word from its etymological sense. The fragments of Cornutus's more narrowly rhetorical and poetical works (including his works on Virgil) might be too meager for this to be obvious, but the theme is of paramount importance to the *Greek Theology*.[52]

The *Greek Theology* was at one time typically treated as an exercise in uncovering the allegorical meaning of the canonical Greek poets—the philosophical thought that they *really* intended to communicate under the cloak of stories that were not always, at their literal level, quite so edifying. But it became generally recognized that Cornutus—and the older Stoics before him—in fact had rather little regard for the so-called wisdom of the poets.[53] Their interest in the poets turned out to be purely instrumental: they preserved, albeit they at the same time tended to distort, the learning of earlier human beings, going back to the very first generations of the human race. What the Stoics were actually interested in was the recovery of their outlook on the world, on the understanding that these first human beings had a perspective on the world that was uncomplicated by the sort of errors and misunderstandings introduced in later generations by their less virtuous progeny. If we could only recover this perspective, it might serve as an effective test for the success of contemporary philosophical theory. With this in mind, it became common to say that the Stoics were not interested in *allegory* at all, in fact; they were much more interested in *etymology*—insights into the true or original meanings of words that have

---

nearby"; if it is not reading too much into this to say that words are indexed directly to mental concepts, which would be their *meanings*, rather than to items in the world, then he holds an *indirect reference* theory of meaning.

52. But for the Virgil commentary read in light of the *Greek Theology*, see Setaioli 2003–2004, 356–64.

53. The turning point was Steinmetz (1986); see also Long 1992. Setaioli (2003–2004, 343–46) gives a useful survey.

reached us through various channels of cultural transmission as testimony to the thought of our primitive ancestors. So, for example, the word *Zeus* is used by the poets to refer to the most powerful agent in a dynasty of powerful gods, but this is not what the word *originally* meant; it originally referred to life, and presumably (if we are to explain the poets' error of understanding) to the life associated with the whole cosmos in particular (see *Greek Theology*, ch. 2).

This is not quite the full story, however. For one thing, it is not just single words that entered the poetical tradition from the ancients, but whole propositions involving them—and these (given the poets' misunderstanding of the words) manifest as what one might think of as de facto allegories. To take a simple example: the story that Rhea gave birth to Hera is a de facto allegory of the philosophical insight that *air* (the original meaning of Hera) derives from the *flow* (Rhea) of precosmic matter (*Greek Theology*, ch. 3). This may never have been intended as an allegory, either by the ancients (who were speaking plainly in their own terms) or by the poets (who simply missed the true meaning), but it is functionally similar to an allegory as far as we are concerned, and it takes the same exegetical tools to unpack it.

But Cornutus goes further than this as well; he seems to think that the earliest human beings were not merely prelapsarian in their outlook but philosophically reflective and that they also constructed allegories quite deliberately—perhaps as means of preserving or promulgating their wisdom (see *Greek Theology*, 76,2–5).[54] Traces of these allegories, too, are to be found in the poetical tradition. So Cornutus does have an interest in allegory after all—in fact we can say that he is on the lookout for as many as two distinct types of allegory (see Boys-Stones 2003b; Pià Comella 2014, 203–12). The one thing that does not interest him is any deliberate attempt at allegory that later poets might have made—just because he is not interested in their own thought at all.[55]

---

54. To this extent, Cornutus seems to have aligned himself with the view of Posidonius (early first century BCE), who argued the point against earlier Stoics. See Sextus Empiricus, *Adv. math.* 9.28 = Posidonius F305 (Theiler 1982), with Most 1989, 2021; and discussion in Seneca, *Ep.* 90, with Boys-Stones 2001, 8–26.

55. *Pace* Setaioli (2003–2004), who claims that there is allegorical interpretation of poets as well as their primitive sources; his examples are better explained either as the preservation of allegories (whether of the real or de facto kind) inherited from the ancients. Also to be taken into account in assessing the evidence is the ancient prac-

1. Introduction: Cornutus the Philosopher   27

One ought not to carry away the impression from all this that Cornutus has no time for poets, let alone that he holds them in disdain. If he uses them as *sources* for something else in the *Greek Theology*—sources whose imperfections to the task at hand he properly acknowledges—this does not mean that he cannot also enjoy them as ends in their own right. This is where reflection on, and comparison with, Cornutus's views of the Roman poetical tradition can help. Cornutus evidently devoted considerable energy to the study of Virgil. As many commentators have noticed, much of what is reported from Cornutus is critical, at least in the sense that he had improvements to suggest. He also notes Virgil's poetical "habit of invention" (*de nihilo fabulam fingit*; F50); indeed, this is a crucial moment of continuity between Cornutus's work as a researcher of ancient wisdom and as a commentator on Virgil (see Setaioli 2003–2004, 359).[56] Yet we should certainly not want to infer that Cornutus actively *disliked* the poetry of Virgil or wished to discourage its study (see Timpanaro 1986, 71–72).[57] It seems rather more likely that, to the contrary, Cornutus

---

tice of correcting or improving poets to make them more edifying (the Greek word is *epanorthōsis*). At its crudest, this might involve rewording lines (as at, e.g., *SVF* 3.167), but it might equally involve the imposition of a figurative meaning on them. We do not have a surviving example from the Stoics involving poetry (although there is a precedent of sorts in Plato, *Phaedr.* 229d), but (*pace* Most 1989, 2026) it is probably what Chrysippus intended with the cosmological lesson he associated with a painting depicting Zeus and Hera engaged in a sex act (*SVF* 2.1071–1074).

56. Most (1989, 2031) suggests that the paucity of ethical—and logical—terms implies that the *Greek Theology* is an introductory work of physics and that Cornutus believed that physics ought to be taught before ethics and logic. For an alternative view, see Boys-Stones 2007.

57. This is not to say that Cornutus might not have had reasons independent of his philosophical views to dislike some things in Virgil, but it is worth noting that the only fragments in this collection that explicitly use the language of *blame* or *censure* are the two that do not mention Cornutus by name (F51 and F54): F50, on the basis of which these are associated with Cornutus, is by contrast quite neutral in tone. The occasional suggestion that Cornutus was a savage critic of Virgil might have more to do with the hyperreverential attitude of our sources. It is instructive, for example, to see how Servius can respond to a comment on one of Virgil's characters as if it were a criticism of Virgil himself (F52 with note ad loc.) or how Aulus Gellius in F53 is able to gloss what seems to have been a very minor reservation (to judge by the quotation) as a major attack. The harshest comment we can be sure Cornutus made is the claim that Virgil did something "jarring" (*indecore*; F47; on this occasion, Servius in his own comment on the same passage uses the slightly weaker *incongrue*, "inconsistent").

enjoyed and admired Virgil as a poet—even while finding him wanting as a philosopher.[58] Perhaps the two-headed message of his commentary on Virgil was precisely that we ought to engage with him as, already, a figure of considerable cultural importance to Rome—even while reminding us that the distinctive evolution of a single cultural tradition tends *away* from the truths of philosophy that are the common heritage of all humankind.

Cornutus's project with the *Greek Theology* can be understood in just the same light. The work contains nothing like a call to *reject* the authors of accretion around its primitive truth—nothing comparable to the expulsion of Homer from Plato's *Republic*. Of course, one way to read that might be to say that Cornutus is more of a realist than the Socrates of Plato's *Republic* and that it is only, as it were, through gritted teeth that he exhorts the young addressee of the work to conventional religious observance (76,8–16). But another way to say that is, with Cornutus's work in hand, one is liberated to enjoy the traditions of one's own culture for what they are. When Cornutus peels back the layers of confusion, poetical fiction, history, and so on to show us the kernel of primitive truth within them, he is *also* showing us the storytelling, the poetry, the history of our own ancestors. Virgil, too, is not to be expelled from Rome because he does what poets do. On the contrary, he is to be studied and cherished and appreciated—but that means appreciating him *as* a poet and understanding what that entails.

If I am right, then Cornutus's technical interest in how language operates—especially perhaps on topics such as ambiguity (F34, F35), but in general the potential gap between author and audience that is the preoccupation of rhetoric—in this sense is intimately bound up with his work on poetry and his work on the theological tradition. It is not subordinate to it, as if it is all about getting past the medium to uncover the message; it is about appreciating the medium *even while hearing* the message.

---

58. So what might seem like a correction of Virgil in F44 (and conceivably, in its original context, F41) might actually have been meant as emendation (see note ad loc.). It could also be relevant context for such criticism as there is of Virgil's moral judgment in F47, F53, and F41 that Virgil's philosophical sympathies lay with the Epicurean school (see *Vit. Prob.* 10–11).

1.4.2. Physics

Cornutus's *Greek Theology*, the principal source for our knowledge of his physics, is sometimes represented as a work introducing Stoic physics. In fact, it rather assumes a good knowledge of Stoic physics even in the way that it sets its material out; the *disiecta membra* of the physical system on which Cornutus relies are scattered through the work and never systematically introduced. What is more, the system is described through a constellation of synonyms and homonyms whose effect on someone new to the system could only be one of confusion and misdirection. An example of synonymy: the primal, precosmic state of substance (οὐσία) might be described as *flow* (ῥύσις; 3,19; 5,10; 8,1; 31,4), *fire* (πῦρ; 4,6; 28,9, 11), or *moisture* (τὸ ὑγρόν; 28,8). But fire and moisture are both homonyms, too, since the same words are used for the elemental states of matter produced out of this substance, fire and water.[59] (Cornutus also recognizes a third type of fire: the combustible mixture of aether and air that he identifies with Hephaestus at 33,12–18.) Air (ἀήρ) is likewise used of at least two quite distinct states of substance: a *precosmic* state (28,12) and the elemental form more familiar to us.[60] Despite the terminological complexity, however, the underlying physics (set out in chs. 3–5 and with a bit more detail in ch. 17 [28,7–15]) is both conventional and straightforward. The following paragraphs are intended to pull together everything of doctrinal relevance to physics from the *Greek Theology*. (Parallels with other Stoic sources will be found in notes to the translation.)

According to Cornutus, then: (1) substance (οὐσία), before the processes which lead to cosmic order (διακόσμησις), exists in a radically fluid state; (2) its first transformation is to become a form of precosmic air (the process is called quenching at 28,12); (3) this precosmic air then becomes elemental water (i.e., water as the substance familiar to us within the cosmic order that results); (4a) part of elemental water in turn solidifies further to give elemental earth as a sort of precipitate, which settles at the center of the cosmos—giving us what we call *"the* earth"; (4b) meanwhile, another part of elemental water evaporates, as we might say, or

---

59. (Elemental) fire, πῦρ: 3,20; 33,12; cf. αἰθήρ: 4,6; 29,15; 33,13. Water, ὕδωρ: 4,10; 28,13; τὸ ὑγρόν: 27,9; 28,7–8; 29,14.

60. Air, ἀήρ—(1) a denser form, as mist: 3,20; 4,18; 29,14; 74,6; (2) a thinner form: 3,16; 4,6. The fourth and final elemental form of substance, earth, γῆ (e.g., 3,17; 8,2), does not suffer from homonyms.

"breathe[s] out," as Cornutus puts it—that is, it becomes more rarefied to give us elemental air and fire, which form earth's surrounding atmosphere and the heavens.[61]

It is worth remarking that, in this model, elemental air and fire do not derive directly from *pre*cosmic air, as one might have expected—let alone from precosmic fire. Rather, they are produced as exhalations from the characteristically terrestrial elements, water and earth (see 29,10–11; 49,14–16; 53,3–5). This is interesting as a matter of physics, but it may have a certain axiological significance as well because it establishes the priority as well as the literal centrality of the earth to the cosmic system, something that Cornutus seems keen to emphasize; see especially comments in chapters 6 (7,11–16), 17 (29,10–11, 16–18), and 28 (52,4–14; 53,5–18). It is hard to resist the sense of contrast here with Aristotelian and Platonist physics, both of which conceive of the earth and its environs as something that is both cosmologically and axiologically the *lowest* and most dependent thing in the cosmos—its solidity a regrettable drag on its receptiveness to divine order rather than an anchor and foundation for it.[62] This supports a view of ethical and philosophical activity intended to orient us away from the physical world, to identify ourselves as much as we can with the higher divinities that govern it. For Platonists, this includes the recognition of our true selves as immortal souls that are sent down to earth to fulfill the work of providence but that do not properly belong there at all (see Boys-Stones 2018, ch. 10). But for the Stoics, who deny the reality of the incorporeal in general, the ideal of fleeing the world is absurd: as humans, we are embedded parts of the physical cosmos, and our end is to find fulfillment as such. It is at least worth considering, then, that Cornutus's emphasis on the cen-

---

61. Cornutus evidently follows the scheme set out more clearly in a single sentence of Diogenes Laertius, *Vit. phil.* 7.142 (see also 7.135–136): "The cosmos comes about when, from fire (πῦρ, sc. precosmic fire), substance turns through air (ἀήρ, sc. precosmic air) into moisture (ὑγρότης, sc. water); then the denser constituent of that produces earth (γῆ), while the rarefied constituent is thinned out further; this, when it has become even more rarefied, gives rise to fire (πῦρ)."

62. The idea that what is higher is better is not a way of thinking alien to Stoicism; see, e.g., Cicero, *Nat. d.* 2.17 for its application to cosmology. But the Stoics might claim, with some plausibility, that Platonists and Aristotelians talk as if they would prefer it if the earth had not been a necessary part of the cosmos at all. (In Aristotelianism at this period, the sublunary realm does not even enjoy divine providence, which "stops at the moon"; see Boys-Stones 2016, 322–26.)

1. Introduction: Cornutus the Philosopher

trality of the earth is meant as a subtle challenge to the Platonist world view—its anthropology and ethics as much as its cosmology.

However that might be, the basic physics here is certainly Chrysippean (see, e.g., Hahm 1977, ch. 3; Salles 2015); and almost everything else we can discern of Cornutus's physics follows what we know of Chrysippean orthodoxy, too. The cosmos is unique (49,13–14); it exhibits variety (6,10–11; 30,1–2), especially in the heavens (49,18–15,1); it is evidently well ordered (2,4–6): this is because it was created by reason (8,13–14), which is an essential property, in fact the very *nature* of substance (4,6–7; see 4,18–5,2 for nature as a name for substance itself).[63] The cosmos in its current state manifestly exhibits the rationality that created it (37,3–5) and that now animates and governs it as its soul (3,3–15; 32,1–2), a soul whose seat is in the heavens (3,13–15; 35,12–15; 38,7–9; 49,7–8). Nothing whatsoever eludes this rationality (11,18–12,1), which arranges everything for the best (for example, it ensures that the wicked are always punished: 9,20–10,2; 10,20–11,18). This is not always obvious, but present ills are sometimes the price that has to be paid for greater benefits in the future (cf. 12,8–10 on prayers that go unanswered); even warfare has beneficial effects (it can help to promote virtue: 40,9–13). Since everything falls under the providential government of this intelligence, it is properly thought of as ineluctable fate (ch. 13). There is nothing outside the cosmos that could impede or destroy it (see 49,4–5), but its own internal dynamic, and especially the fact that the fires of the heavens continue to be nourished by evaporation of moisture in the cosmos, without there being any mechanism for replenishing it, means that the lifespan of the created order is not indefinite; it will be ultimately destroyed as substance reverts to its original homogeneous state (28,10–12; 51,21–52,1; 66,4–6)—before the process begins all over again.[64] Within the cosmos, there are two kinds of rational being: created gods and humans (the latter originally born from the earth: 32,3–5; 39,15); animals lack rationality (20,20–21).[65] Souls, human and divine, are fiery (3,14–15); this fact might imply that, when

---

63. The point that the cosmos is unique might have had some currency for Cornutus, since there seem to have been Platonists at this time who entertained the possibility that there were five *cosmoi* (something allowed by Plato, *Tim.* 55d); see Plutarch, *Def. orac.* 426c–e; 428c–e.

64. See 28,12 with note ad loc.

65. This is a point on which Stoics disagreed with at least some Platonists, namely, those who allowed the transmigration of the human soul into animal bodies. See esp.

Cornutus says that souls inhabit the (mundane) air on death (74,5–8), what he really means is that their substance is turned to colder air, so that there is no personal survival. This would be the standard Stoic view (e.g., *SVF* 1.146), and it might gain some support from F27, where Cornutus suggests that the death of an animal follows the extinction of the soul.[66]

Finally, it may be worth noting that the *Greek Theology* shows an interest in explaining a number of natural phenomena, rather in the spirit of Seneca's *Natural Questions*: the genesis of rainstorms ("from the mountains"; 5,16–17); the formation of seas and mountains (29,16–30,1), earthquakes (41,3–5), and pestilence (65,11–13); the link between animal gestation and the periods of the moon (73,15–18).

1.4.3. Ethics

For Cornutus's ethics, we are once again almost entirely reliant on what can be inferred from the *Greek Theology*—where, however, ethics is less in evidence, and what is there is less technical. There are a number of ways in which one could account for this without suggesting that Cornutus is actually uninterested in ethics—or even that he is uninterested in ethics for the purposes of the work in hand. It might, for example, be due to the nature of the material that he is working with. On my account, the *mythological turn*, the period at which the original philosophy began to be passed on as half-remembered tradition, and ultimately as picaresque amusement, was by definition a period of downturn for philosophy: poetry appeals to a desire for amusement, not philosophy. But while such moral decadence entails the loss of a firm grasp on ethical principles, there may well have been a period when people still had access to the scientific insights of their immediate forefathers. For this reason, we might expect that there is a bias built into the process towards the preservation of good physics over the preservation of systematic ethics.

Or again, the imbalance could be due to a choice on Cornutus's part—not to *prefer* physics over ethics, but more subtly to insinuate ethical principles in the background of his apparent focus on details of physics. As I

Plutarch's works *Whether Land or Sea Creatures Are More Clever* and *Gryllus, or: On the Use of Reason by the Nonrational Animals*.

66. In this case, Cornutus does not follow those, such as Cleanthes and Chrysippus, who think that the soul can remain for some time out of the body (*SVF* 2.774, 809–11).

noted above, we should not too quickly infer from the wealth of details drawn from physics that the work is intended to *teach* physics; it might, on the contrary, be intended to activate and encourage the reader to build on a knowledge of physics that it presupposes. The very absence of the technical vocabulary of philosophical ethics might be explained by a desire to maximize the accessibility of its ethical message (see Boys-Stones 2007). For it is true, in any case, that the stated aim of the work, or at least what Cornutus hopes will be its effect, is broadly ethical: that is, to counter the dangers of *superstition* latent in traditional religious forms (76,12–13). (By this, Cornutus presumably has in mind, for example, the danger of believing that the gods may intend ill towards humans and might need to be feared and propitiated.)[67] Along the way, Cornutus does in fact highlight a number of central ideas in Stoic ethics, for example, in his insistent and repeated emphasis on the centrality of reason. Virtue and happiness, he says, involve structure, internal harmony, and consistency (17,12–13; 25,9–11), and these, along with strength and protection, come from reason (20,23; 21,5–8; 36,11–13).

According to the account I gave above in §1.4.1.2, Cornutus's view of early humans, and the presence of philosophy among them, converges with that of the later Stoic Posidonius (see again n. 54). It is possible that Posidonius himself thought that there had better be philosophy among early humans to counteract the nonrational inclinations that he—unusually for a Stoic—ascribed to the human soul alongside reason. However that might be, there is no evidence that Cornutus shared Posidonius's psychological model. One could find a trace of it in Cornutus's claim that our conceptions, the basis of our rationality, were evoked to control human aggression (39,15–20)—as if our anger can be engaged independently of our beliefs.[68] But it is not clear that this is how the passage needs to be read. Cornutus might here be saying only, in effect, that the seeds of reason are what separate us from the animals; the thought is not so much that they actually had to be stirred up at some point, but that *were they not active*, we would be driven by the aggressive and self-serving instincts

---

67. This concern about superstition is given its classic expression in the philosophical tradition by Plato, whose response to it is to drive the poets out of the ideal state altogether. Its dangers were also explored by Cornutus's younger contemporary Plutarch, in the work *On Superstition*.

68. This would frame 32,16–21, the observation that pain can be hard to negotiate.

of animals.⁶⁹ The pattern of education that Cornutus recommends is consistent with the intellectualist view characteristic of earlier Stoics: the emphasis is on the education of reason (see chs. 14, 16) rather than on the training of the body (one should not put all one's trust in the strength of the body, he says at 26,2–6) or even of manners (what one might think of as properly moral education in the Aristotelian sense).⁷⁰

Cornutus tells us that the virtues are inseparable (15,13–15)—a view shared with other schools, but having special explanation in Stoicism in the numerical identity of all the virtues with wisdom. Since philosophical reflection informs our ability to achieve virtue, there is no choice to be made between the contemplative and practical lives (15,5–8).⁷¹ Indeed, Cornutus insists on the social dimension of virtue, the social virtues having divine mandate (e.g., 9,20–10,2; cf. 6,6, which, by referencing the idea of the cosmos as city, also reminds us of the naturalistic basis for virtue in general and social virtue in particular), and when he says that the divine is the model for virtuous action (15,18), presumably it is because god is the ideal cosmic agency, as well as the ideal of rationality.⁷²

---

69. On this reading, Cornutus's exegesis itself remains allegorical to some extent (see Boys-Stones 2009, 151–52).

70. Cornutus makes one comment relevant under this heading, on the emasculating effect of the *aulos* (38,18–20), but this need not imply that it has its effect (which is described in terms of strength, not emotion) on a putative nonrational part of the soul, and it may actually stand in tension with Posidonius's view that music has an important role to play in training, specifically in soothing, the nonrational parts (EK F168).

71. The possibility that there might be (and which way one ought to choose if there is) is a topic in ancient ethics that goes back at least to Aristotle. The way Cornutus's point is put at Diogenes Laertius, *Vit. phil.* 7.130 (= *SVF* 3.687) is that there is a *third* life, the rational, which we ought to choose, as preparing us for both contemplation and action. Platonists contemporary with Cornutus also claimed that the practical and contemplative lives were compatible—but with the proviso that we should keep our engagement with practical concerns, for example, involvement in politics, to the minimum necessary from time to time (see Boys-Stones 2018, ch. 17, §17.2.2).

72. Again, one might make a connection here with the thought of contemporary Platonists, who define virtue as "coming to be like god." Since the highest god of Platonism is not involved with the cosmos, this definition feeds into Platonist discussions of the relative merits of the contemplative and practical lives (see again the previous note).

1.5. Summary: Cornutus's Profile as a Philosopher

This, then, is the case for Cornutus, as a philosopher who deserves our interest both for his own originality and for the light he might be able to shed on the conditions of philosophy in the first century CE. I have argued, to begin with, that his intellectual horizons reach far beyond Rome: he had native fluency in Greek and Latin and may well have retained strong ties to African Leptis (see F6 with note), and he is closely engaged with contemporary movements around the Mediterranean. Among his broad intellectual interests, he proves to be especially well versed in physics and in dialectic (including, but not limited to, formal logic). His core philosophical commitment is to Stoicism, and specifically the Stoicism of Chrysippus and Cleanthes (esp. Persius, *Sat.* 5.63–64), but he can disagree with both, for example, in his outlying views on the nature of death and in his apparent agreement with Posidonius on the philosophical activity of the first generations of human beings. Even to the extent that Cornutus is faithful to the earlier Stoics, his faith is grounded in independent judgment of the issues. When, for example, he defends Chrysippean logic against Aristotelians, he does so through an original and independent critique of a work that had only recently come to wider philosophical notice, the *Categories*. (It is relevant to note here, as further evidence that he is thinking the issues through for himself, that Cornutus occasionally disagrees with Athenodorus, the only Stoic before him who was remembered for work in the same field.) I have argued elsewhere that it might be possible to trace polemical engagement with the *Timaeus* in Cornutus's *Greek Theology* (Boys-Stones 2009); if that is right, then it involves a similarly original and thoroughly contemporary confrontation of Platonism in defense of Chrysippean physics (and note testimony to his explicit engagement with the Platonist theory of forms in F28 and F29).

Cornutus, in short, seems to me no antiquarian or dilettante. On the contrary, he offers evidence of real philosophical vitality in the early empire—to the extent, indeed, that, if further study of the material in this volume vindicates that view, Cornutus may also prove to be a lens through which we are ultimately forced to reassess our entire historiographical model for the first and second centuries CE.

1.6. Works by Cornutus and Their Titles

1.6.1. Transmitted Works

T1. *Survey of the Greek Theological Tradition* (one book, Greek). This is the formal title normally reconstructed for the work, but see the textual note ad loc. Outside the manuscript tradition for the work itself, it is referred to as *On Greek Theology* (F18) or simply *Greek Theology* (F17)—which is how it is referred to in discussions in this volume.

T2. *On Pronunciation or Orthography* (probably one book, Latin). Extracts. Referred to in this volume as *Orthography*. I take the full title to be a single one, since Cornutus himself makes it clear early on in the work that he is dealing with how Latin is to be written hand in hand with how it is to be spoken (see *Orthography* 1), but it could be that the work was known by alternative titles: *On Pronunciation* or *On Orthography*.

1.6.2. Other Titles Attested

T3. *On Haveables* (two books, Greek): F28. Probably a work of metaphysics (see note ad loc.).

T4. *Against Athenodorus and Aristotle* (more than one book, Greek): F22. In fact it is unclear from this reference whether there was a single multivolume work or two separate books: one *Response to Athenodorus* (the title given in F20), one *Against Aristotle*. In either case, Simplicius makes it clear that they dealt with Aristotle's *Categories*.

T5. *Rhetorical Handbook* (Greek): F20 testifies that this work, too, contained material on Aristotle's *Categories*—although this was presumably not its principal purpose.

T6. *On Figures of Thought* (at least two books, Latin): F53. Another rhetorical work, of which F31 might also be a fragment.

T7. *On Virgil (To Italicus)* (Latin): F57. Opinions differ over whether this is the same work as the *Commentary on Virgil* (T8 below).[73] If it is, then the work was at least ten books long (see F57 with note).

T8. *Commentary on Virgil* (Latin): F58; see F53. See above on T7.

---

73. Leo's arguments that the two works are distinct (1904, 259; cf. Reppe 1906, 28–29) are accepted by Timpanaro (1986, 71). On the other side, see Ribbeck 1866, 12–14; and in more recent times, Duret 1986, 3320.

1.6.3. Dubious

T9. (Tragedies). The transmitted text of the *Life of Persius* 19–20 calls Cornutus a "tragedian" (*tragicus*), a reading embraced even by commentators who do not think he authored the surviving *Octavia* (see §1.6.5 below): for example, Kragelund (2016, 103, 145). There is no corroborating evidence, however, and the text might be in need of emendation (see note ad loc.).

T10. *Satires* (Latin): F64. But this title is ascribed to one *Marcus* Cornutus, and a more credible source gives the philosopher's *praenomen* as Lucius (F58). Although Cornutus felt able to edit the work of Persius (for whom he seems to have acted as a sort of literary executor [*Life of Persius* 43–49; 56–59]), there is no independent evidence that he wrote poetry of his own.

T11. *Record of His Father's Camps* (Latin): F63. But the title itself is a matter of debate; it is not clear whether F63 ascribes the work in question to Cornutus (it does not in the translation offered here), and it is debated whether the philosopher Cornutus is meant in any case (see notes ad loc.).

1.6.4. Spurious

T12. *On Gods and Comets.* Following the texts of Cornutus's *Theology* in one of our manuscripts (Codex Laurentianus 58), there appears the line: Φουρνούτου περὶ θεῶν καὶ κομήτων. But this is an evident conflation of Cornutus's name as author of the forgoing work with the title of what follows, which is a section "on comets" from John Lydus's work *De ostentis* (= chs. 10–15b [Wachsmuth 1897, 23,12–40,21]).

T13. *Commentary on Persius.* Scholia falsely transmitted under Cornutus's name (Clausen and Zetzel 2004).

T14. *Commentary on Juvenal.* Another work falsely transmitted under Cornutus's name (Höhler 1867, 379–442).

T15. *Disticha Cornuti.* A glossary that actually dates from the middle ages (Liebl 1888).

1.6.5. Speculative Modern Attributions

In addition to the foregoing, a number of purely speculative attributions have been made. Ciaffi (1937) and others subsequently (e.g., albeit cautiously, Sullivan 1985, 72–33) make him the author of the anonymous tragedy *Octavia* (but see Most 1989, 2044–46; Kragelund 2016, 145); Herrmann (1980) makes him the author of the *Rhetoric to Herennius* (which from time to time has also been credited to Cicero) (the argument has not seemed compelling). In order to explain F27, Finamore and Dillon (2002, 178) speculate redundantly that Cornutus might have written a work *On Death* (see Duret 1986, 3322).

1.7. Note on Texts and Referencing

The editions used for the texts printed in this volume, and the conventions for referencing them, are explained in what follows. As a matter of principle, divergences from the source edition have been kept to a minimum; each case of divergence is explained and accounted for in its place; textual issues are not otherwise discussed.

1.7.1. The *Greek Theology*

The text that follows is based on that of Lang (1881).[74] The Greek text includes page and line references to Lang's edition; both text and translation include the standard chapter divisions found in the manuscripts (although they are not due to Cornutus himself; see Schmidt 1912, 32–33; and Most 1989, 2025): references in this volume are always to the former unless "ch[apter]" is specified. Paragraph breaks, and section headings in the translation are my own (as explained in the preface, §2.1 below).

I have benefited enormously from the opportunity to consult, ahead of publication, José Torres's new, improved Teubner edition (Torres 2018)[75] but have not adopted his readings in preference to Lang unless they seemed grammatically uncontroversial or to yield superior sense. These and all other divergences from Lang are noted, with two classes of

---

74. Previous important editions include Osann (1844); and, with Latin translation, Gale (1688) ("Phurnuti de natura deorum commentarius" at 137–236) and Welare (1549). Translations into modern languages include, into German: Berdozzo (2009) and Busch and Zangenberg (2010); into Italian: Ramelli (2003) (reprinted in two further Bompiani volumes: Ramelli 2007, 2008); into Polish: Wojciechowski (2016); into Spanish: Torres (2009a). There is an unpublished English translation in Hays (1983) and an unpublished French translation in Rocca-Serra (1988).

75. The need to replace Lang (1881) was noted by Nock (1931, 998) and articulated in Rocca-Sara (1963); Krafft (1975) helped prepare the way with a new and more comprehensive survey of the manuscript tradition.

1. Introduction: Cornutus the Philosopher

exception. On the one hand, Lang's bracketed deletions (and similarly his supplements) have as a rule been accepted without note where they are motivated by linguistic considerations; however, on the other hand, they have been ignored without note (except in the few cases where they are adopted by Torres) where they indicate suspected glosses or expansions of the text. (Lang's grounds for suspicion are sometimes stronger, sometimes weaker, but always, in the end, subjective.) Differences in the text of Torres with respect to that of Lang that are not adopted and noted in the text that follows are these (references, as usual, are to Lang page and line numbers):

4.12 εἴτ᾽ οὖν, 4.14 [φύσει ἰδίων], 4.14 εἴθ᾽ ὅσον, 5.1 αὐτῇ, 5.2 ἢ τάχα ὅτι, 5.16 καταράσσουσι, 6.9 ἐπιτιθέασιν, 7.9 λάθρᾳ, 8.14 ἡ ἐπὶ τῶν 8.16–17 θάτερον μόνον ἄμικτον, 13.14 ἑαυτήν, 15.8 τέσσαρες, 15.12 τοῦ ἐνδομενείας, 15.15 αὐτῶν, 16.9 αὐτῶν, 17.15 παραδίδοται, 18.11 εὑρήματα, 19.11 καὶ χαρίζεσθαι, 20.5 δ᾽ εὐεργετεῖν, 20.9 εὐείδειαν, 20.23 ἡμῖν, 22.6 διὰ τόδε, 23.13 τῷ τὸ ἑδραῖόν τε καί, 25.14 ἐνιδρύσαντο, 26.15 δύο, 28.2 πείθεσθαι, 30.6 Ἀφορίην καὶ Σόφην, 31.13 Ἡσιόδου τελειοτέρα, 34.2 αὐτῆς, 34.5 τούτῳ, 34.6 πυρίνων, 34.12 μυθεύονται, 35.5 τι καί, 35.21 καθ᾽ ὅλου, 36.1 δ᾽ ὄνομα, 36.12 δυσχερεστάτους, 39.9 μάλιστα. καί, 41.22 γινόμενα 42.5 θαλάσσης, 42.7 ποιεῖ. ἀποτελουμένων δέ, 42.8 ῥῆξιν εὐλόγως, 43.5–6 "καὶ δ᾽αὐτὸς, 43.9 πλεονάζοντος ἐν αὐτῇ, 43.19 θαλάσσης, 44.12 θάλασσαν, 44.13 τοὺς Κύκλωπας, 44.14 Ἀλωάδας, 44.15 γενέσθαι (for εἶναι), 44.16 θάλασσά, 44.23 θαλάσσῃ, 48.18 παρισταμένους, 51.8 διακάθαρσιν, 51.21 ἐπεὶ (for ἢ ἐπεὶ), 51.21 ἄμα ἀλδαίνει, 52.13 δαιτεῖσθαι, 52.18–53.1 τὴν … ὕλην, 53.7 ἱδρύεσθαι, 53.9 χεῖσθαι, 53.22–3 οἰκουμένης Τριπτόλεμος, 55.17 εἶναι υἱὸς ἔδοξεν, 57.7 ὁ Ζεὺς λέγεται, 57.8 ἡμῖν (for καθ᾽ ἡμᾶς), 58.1 παρὰ τὸ τὴν διάνοιαν ἐπομβρεῖν καὶ καταβρέχειν ἐσχηκὼς τὴν προσηγορίαν ἀπὸ τῆς ὕσεως (added after ἡδέως ἤ), 58.2 λύσειον, 58.16 δὲ ἡ, 59.20 τούτου, 60.6 ὑποκρυπτομένου, 61.6 παραφερόμενον, 61.16–19 (καθαιρετικὸς … θρίαμβον placed after ἀφιέναι at 62.2), 62.15 σύρρευσις, 63.9–10 προσηγορίας Ἀλκμήνης, 63.10 υἱὸς ὤν, 64.5 ὡς γάρ, 64.8–9 πιθανώτερον, 65.13 αὐτοῖς θανάτους, 66.16 εὐειδέστεροι, 69.6 συνεχέστερον καθ᾽, 70.18 κατὰ τῶν, 71.11 δικτύννης, 71.19 καὶ τούς, 73.9 αὐταῖς, 74.5 τὰς ψυχὰς τῶν τελευτώντων, 74.23 προήχθη, 75.13 μεμυθεῦσθαι ἐν Ἅιδου εἶναι, 76.15 ἐπιβάλλουσι

1.7.2. On Pronunciation or Orthography

Extracts of the *Orthography* come from a sixth-century work *On Orthography* by Cassiodorus (Keil 1880, 147,23–154,11). References in square brackets in the text are to page and line number in Keil (1880); the other numbers, common to text and translation, count out paragraphs in Keil (1880), which he takes to be discrete extracts from Cornutus's work (although nothing explicit marks the breaks, and para. 19 seems to me to follow directly on para. 18, for example).

1.7.3. Fragments

Details of the editions of texts used for the fragments are given in full in the index of sources. References are either standard or to page and line numbers in the specified edition.

1.7.4. Persius

Texts for the *Life of Persius* and Persius, *Sat.* 5 are from Clausen (1959).

2
The *Greek Theology*

2.1. Preface

2.1.1. Structure

2.1.1.1. Introduction

Glenn W. Most may be right to say that the survival of the *Greek Theology* has done Cornutus's reputation more harm than good. For one thing, it appears to be highly derivative; Cornutus himself seems to tell us that it is a cursory distillation of earlier work (76,6–8). For another, it lacks a clear sense of structure. In the introduction, I offered a reason not to think that Cornutus's deference to his philosophical ancestors should be taken too quickly as a confession of mindless dependence, suggesting that it was rather a move, conventional for the period, by which he meant to establish the Stoic credentials of the work. By way of a preface to the work itself, I would like to address the question of structure. I do this in two stages. First of all, and most importantly, I show that there are more structural markers *within* the text than is sometimes appreciated and that Cornutus is actually quite clear in directing us towards a broad sense of the work's shape. Once that is established, I shall make a more speculative suggestion—that this shape in its turn tracks the most famous of all cosmological texts, the *Timaeus*. If the structure of the *Greek Theology* is not self-evident, that may be because Cornutus did not mean it to be self-standing, but he precisely (once again) invites his readers to see it in dialogue with a longer tradition of thought.

2.1.1.2. Structural Markers in the *Greek Theology*

Most (1989, 2023) himself discerns a broad trajectory of the *Greek Theology* from the top of the physical system to the bottom (from Ouranos to Hades, as he puts it, although in fact Hades is the air above the earth, and Cornutus goes lower than that), but this is a broad trajectory, and within it (still according to Most), transitions are merely *associative*. But there are signs that Cornutus has a more deliberate sense of composition. There are many explicit back references, for example, suggesting a conscious choice of what to treat when, and at least two forward references that show that a higher principle than mere association is at least sometimes at work.[1] Cornutus also marks out moments of division and transition within the text, which carve the work into a number of clearly demarcated sections. The most obvious of these ways is his use of words such as "first," "next" (or "after this…"), and "finally"—words that not only signal transition but also make it clear that Cornutus has a particular order in mind for his material.[2] Another important marker is Cornutus's periodic address to an unnamed boy (variously παιδίον/παῖς/τέκνον), the imagined reader of the *Greek Theology*.[3] It is reasonable to assume that these addresses occur at significant moments within the text. Again, Cornutus occasionally marks the end of a stretch of discussion with a summative epilogue of some sort, wrapping the discussion up while at the same time implicitly signaling the start of a new train of thought. Finally, there are a few cases of sudden thematic transition—jarringly *non*associative leaps that, considered in isolation, might precisely indicate a *lack* of structure but that in practice complement the more formal and explicit compositional markers to produce something like the effect of beginning a new paragraph.

---

1. Specific and explicit back references at: 7,3; 7,22–8,1; 8,4; 18,14; 30,7; 31,8–9; 41,19–20; 73,6–7, 12–14; 74,6 (and cf. 38,9 and 60,18–19, which make little sense unless one remembers what was said earlier). Forward references: 4,15–16; 17,15–16.

2. *Pace*, e.g., Torres (2016, 196), who sees here "evidence of an order previously established in the source from which he [Cornutus] is drawing."

3. Since he is not given a name, or any identifying feature, it would probably not be appropriate to think of him as its dedicatee. He is more like an ideal reader, representing, that is, the intended demographic of the *Greek Theology*—although, as I have noted, it does not exhaust the potential interest of the work to think that it is aimed only at children, and one might suspect an element of conceit in this (see above, introduction, §1.2).

I collect these markers below and show how they can be used to build a sense of structure for the *Greek Theology*. I have added my own descriptive titles for the sections that seem to emerge.[4]

A. First Survey of the Physical System
A.1. Cosmos: Origins and Structure   chs. 1–8
- begins with invocation of the boy (ὦ παιδίον; 1,1)

A.2. Cosmos: Order and Justice/A.3. Education and Ethics   chs. 9–16
- begins with "next" (μετὰ δὲ ταῦτα; 9,1)

B. Wisdom and Its Transmission
B.1. Theological Traditions   ch. 17.1–3
- begins with a sudden transition to higher-level methodological reflection (26,7)
- ends with an epilogue, containing methodological advice (27,19–28,2)

B.2. Hesiod   ch. 17.4
- begins anew: πάλιν τοίνυν (28,2–3)
- addresses the boy (ὦ παῖ, at 28,11)[5]
- ends with another epilogue, rounding off the discussion of Hesiod (31,12–17)

B.3. Science and Philosophy   chs. 18–21
- begins with an introduction phrased as the answering (δέ) clause to the (μέν) clause containing the epilogue to the previous section (νῦν δέ; 31,17–18)

---

4. There is substantial, and reassuring, overlap with chapter groupings suggested (on independent grounds) by others. Lang's use of capitalization also suggests new beginnings that match my A.1, A.2, B, C.1, C.2, C.3. Nock (1931, 998) marks my A.1, A.2, B.1, B.3, C.1, C.3. Ramelli's modification of this scheme (2003, 103–4; accepted by Berdozzo [2009, 26–28]) also marks C.4, but shifts Nock's division at ch. 32 back to ch. 30 (in the middle of my C.2).

5. Slightly delayed from the very beginning of this putative section (so that Torres [2010, 97] adduces this as evidence that the address does not always have structural significance), but it comes just at the point where we arrive at the payoff in Stoic physics for the references to Hesiod with which it begins.

C. Second Survey of the Physical System

C.1. Water (and the Principles of Fertility) (Poseidon)   chs. 22–27
- begins with "next" (μετὰ δὲ ταῦτα; 41,18)
- immediately addresses the boy (ὦ παῖ; 41,19)

C.2. Earth (and Principles of Stability) (Demeter/Hestia)   chs. 28–30
- begins with "next" (ἑξῆς; 52,4)
- immediately addresses the boy (ὦ παῖ; 52,4–5)

C.3. Fire (Apollo/Artemis)   chs. 32–34
- begins with "next" (ἐχομένως τοίνυν; 65,1)
- immediately addresses the boy (ὦ τέκνον; 65,1)

C.4. Air (Hades)   ch. 35.1–2
- begins with "finally" (τελευταῖον; 74,5)

D. Epilogue   ch. 35.3
- begins with a sudden transition to generalization (75,17)
- addresses the boy (ὦ παῖ; 76,2)

2.1.1.3. The *Greek Theology* and Plato's *Timaeus*

On my analysis, then, Cornutus marks ten divisions within the *Greek Theology*, which seem to fall into three major sections, supplemented by a brief epilogue: (A) a section that thematically addresses (1) the physical structure of the cosmos as (2) the context for an exploration of ethics;[6] (B) a section which has less obvious thematic unity but seems to focus on Hesiod as a kind of case study in exegetical methodology, moving on to human ingenuity and activity in general (the idea being, perhaps, to see how both the emergence and the exegesis of the mythological tradition are, for good or for bad, characteristically human endeavors); and (C) a section that returns to an account of the cosmos—but this time a sort of bottom-up account (compared with the top-down and more ethically

---

6. I make a further division here at ch. 14, where there seems to me a significant thematic shift from (A.2) the structures that embed justice in the fabric of the cosmos at large to (A.3) the means by which the individual acquires virtue. This, however, is not flagged by explicit markers.

inflected cosmology of section A), which is very clearly articulated around the four elements from which it is constructed: water, earth, fire, air.[7]

That section C involves a return to material covered in section A is something of which Cornutus is conscious—indeed, something that he self-consciously intends. This is clear from the explicit back references to A from the very outset of C (e.g., προείρηται at 41,19). But why would he *knowingly* and *deliberately* return to earlier themes in this way? (The less one thinks he has a structure in mind the odder this is; one might suppose that he would simply have grouped related material together to start with.) It is tempting to think that at least part of the reason must lie with one very distinguished and very well-known precedent for just such a move; for Plato does something strikingly similar in the *Timaeus*:

ὧδε οὖν πάλιν ἀναχωρητέον, καὶ λαβοῦσιν αὐτῶν τούτων προσήκουσαν ἑτέραν ἀρχὴν αὖθις αὖ, καθάπερ περὶ τῶν τότε νῦν οὕτω περὶ τούτων πάλιν ἀρκτέον ἀπ' ἀρχῆς.
So we need to go back again, take up a new starting point suitable for these things, and begin again from the beginning, just as we did before about for the matters that concerned us then. (*Tim.* 48b)

This comes after what the reader might be forgiven for thinking was a reasonably full and coherent account of the cosmos at 27d–40d. But this earlier account focused on what we might call a god's-eye view of the universe, tracing its origin and nature from the higher causes on which it depends. What we did not get then—but what we return to now—is a complementary story about the *elements* from which the cosmos is made:

τὴν δὴ πρὸ τῆς οὐρανοῦ γενέσεως πυρὸς ὕδατός τε καὶ ἀέρος καὶ γῆς φύσιν θεατέον αὐτὴν καὶ τὰ πρὸ τούτου πάθη.

---

7. It is worth emphasizing that the four elements around which the discussion here is articulated operate as far more than just the starting points for these sections: they govern them thematically. This might not be immediately obvious in all cases, but, for example, the theme of sexual desire, fertility, and generation in chs. 24–27 are governed by the common idea that water is the vehicle for generative principles (see already 3,10–11); again, the focus on peace (and the activities of peacetime, embodied by Dionysus in ch. 30) and the robust nature of the cosmos (in ch. 31) are clearly related to the idea of *earth* as the most solid and immobile of the elements.

We should look at the nature of the fire, water, air, and earth that came about prior to the heavens, and at their qualities. (*Tim.* 48b)

Just as in Cornutus, in fact, the second cosmology of the *Timaeus* is to be distinguished by having an examination of the four elements at its heart.

Working from this broad observation, the basic structure I have identified in the *Greek Theology* can readily be made to answer to the broad structure of the *whole* cosmological section of the *Timaeus*. This begins (call it A′) with the top-down account of the cosmos from 27d, with a focus on its divine causes and global structures. It turns to a digression of sorts (B′) from 40d—a digression that resonates with section B in the *Greek Theology* all the more because among the things that Plato talks about here is the transmission of belief through mythology:

> Περὶ δὲ τῶν ἄλλων δαιμόνων εἰπεῖν καὶ γνῶναι τὴν γένεσιν μεῖζον ἢ καθ᾽ ἡμᾶς, πειστέον δὲ τοῖς εἰρηκόσιν ἔμπροσθεν, ἐκγόνοις μὲν θεῶν οὖσιν, ὡς ἔφασαν.
> It is beyond us to talk or know about the other divinities; we have to believe what predecessors said, since they were, they said, children of the gods. (*Tim.* 40d)

Timaeus alludes specifically to Hesiod, and indeed, specifically, to a part of the divine genealogy that is also explored in section B of the *Greek Theology*:

> Γῆς τε καὶ Οὐρανοῦ παῖδες Ὠκεανός τε καὶ Τηθὺς ἐγενέσθην, τούτων δὲ Φόρκυς Κρόνος τε καὶ Ῥέα καὶ ὅσοι μετὰ τούτων, ἐκ δὲ Κρόνου καὶ Ῥέας Ζεὺς Ἥρα τε καὶ πάντες ὅσους ἴσμεν ἀδελφοὺς λεγομένους αὐτῶν, ἔτι τε τούτων ἄλλους ἐκγόνους.
> Okeanos and Tethys were the children of Earth and Heaven; they gave birth to Phocys, Kronos, and Rhea and others besides; Kronos and Rhea gave birth to Zeus, Hera, and all the others we know of who are said to be their siblings; and they in turn had further offspring. (*Tim.* 40e–41a; compare *Greek Theology*, ch. 17)

Timaeus's weary tone and ironic deference in talking about these mythological genealogies (furnished, as he says with neither necessary nor convincing proofs: ἄνευ τε εἰκότων καὶ ἀναγκαίων ἀποδείξεων; 40e) might suggest to us the problems explicitly identified, but then also addressed, by Cornutus.

So, finally, at 47e we come to (C′)—the second beginning, the bottom-up account of the cosmos (motivated in the case of the *Timaeus* by the need to bring *necessity* and the so-called receptacle into Timaeus account).

Of course, if these observations have merit, one might still wonder what to make of them. Perhaps one ought to reflect that it is not surprising if Cornutus was influenced in writing the *Greek Theology* by what was, no doubt, a profound acquaintance with the *Timaeus*.[8] But it remains a question whether there is more to be discovered than this. Did Cornutus intend his readers to make the connection as well? If so, to what end? Could it even be that we are meant to see the *Greek Theology* as part of a conversation with Plato?[9]

2.1.2. Cornutus and the Tradition of Allegorical Reading

The use of allegorical and etymological exegesis in reading mythological and poetical traditions has a very long history in Greece, and no doubt a longer prehistory. A method that allowed generations of later readers to discover hidden treasuries of wisdom in Homer can already be found in use by Homer himself (Most 1993). One of the earliest exponents of this mode of reading recognized by the Greeks themselves was Theagenes of Rhegium in the sixth century BCE (see DK 8, frag. 2), and it was well enough established by the fourth century that when Plato expelled Homer from his ideal city, it was explicitly *despite* the possibility that allegorical readings could turn his picaresque narratives of the gods into serious and edifying philosophy (*Resp.* 378d).

As this will suggest, allegorical and etymological exegesis was often applied to uncovering or decoding the intentions and beliefs of the poets themselves—sometimes for apologetic purposes, sometimes with other aims more or less clear to us. But the same techniques early on became applied to material that had been more or less accidentally preserved in

---

8. Quite apart from the fact that the *Timaeus* was far and away the most famous and important philosophical text on cosmology in antiquity, it had always been an important starting point for the Stoics' own thinking on the subject; see Sedley (2002). In the early first century BCE, Posidonius was not just drawing on the *Timaeus* but writing about it (EK F85 = Sextus Empiricus, *Adv. math.* 7.93).

9. I give my own answer to this in Boys-Stones 2009, where I argue for an anti-Platonist agenda on Cornutus's part. One might, conversely, think that Plato is one of the "older philosophers" of 76,6–7 and that Cornutus hopes to benefit from his authority—rather as the spokesman for Stoic physics at Cicero, *Nat. d.* 2.32 ("Let us listen to Plato," he says, "a kind of god among philosophers").

the poets as what I called in the introduction de facto allegory (see above, introduction §1.4.1.2). The idea is that pearls of ancient wisdom were misconceived and transmitted by subsequent poets as idle fantasies and stories. They were never intended as allegories, but to treat them as if they were is to find your way back to the thinking of our *pre*historical ancestors. Aristotle, *Metaph.* Λ.12 gives a famous example of this practice; Plato's *Cratylus*, at least in recent interpretations such as that of Sedley (2003), is a wholesale attempt to apply this approach to the Greek language itself. There is general agreement now that this is exactly the sort of consideration that originally motivated Stoic interest in allegory and etymology: the excavation of primitive wisdom (above, introduction, §1.4.1.2).

The Stoics, needless to say, had their own agenda in pursuing this study, but their techniques, and even their individual readings and reconstructions, were shared by thinkers with quite diverse agendas. It is possible in fact to find precedents or parallels to individual points that Cornutus makes across a wide range of literature. Indeed, it is probably safe to assume—without reducing Cornutus to the status of a mere epitomizer—that most of his claims will have had parallels and precedents somewhere. It is for this very reason that the translation of the *Greek Theology* that follows is not heavily annotated with cross-references of this sort—except, that is, where identifying a parallel helps to explain the point that Cornutus himself wishes to make. Readers hoping for such a resource are already very well served by the notes in Ramelli (2003), but for most purposes, there is no substitute for seeking out the original texts from which the parallels tend to be drawn. The important sources are not many, and it is invaluable to see the very different contexts and uses to which the same results of allegorical exegesis could be put.[10] (Whatever it is, the *Greek Theology* is not part of a homogenous culture of allegorical reading.) The most important of these sources—both because they survive entire and because they are directly relevant to understanding Cornutus's own intellectual orientation and background—are, first and foremost, Plato's *Cratylus* (which we must assume Cornutus knew); next, the *Homeric Problems* by Heraclitus Homericus (so called to distinguish him from the Presocratic; *this* one was probably a rough contemporary of Cornutus and likely a Stoic as well); and, finally, the account of Stoic theology in Cicero, *Nat. d.*

---

10. Except for the *Cratylus*, the texts mentioned in what follows, and more, can be found translated into Italian in Ramelli 2007.

2.[11] Going further beyond Cornutus's own intellectual tradition, and back to the fourth century, the most relevant texts are the *Incredibilia* (*Unbelievable Tales*) by Palaephatus (the author mentioned alongside Cornutus in F13 and F16), which contains important cognate material, and the Derveni papyrus, which is an instructive and important document for the subject (albeit with little direct overlap with Cornutus).[12] The most important fragmentary sources are collected in *SVF*, which contains a great deal of relevant material from the older Stoics, and *FrGHist* 244, including fragments from *On the Gods* by the second-century Apollodorus of Athens—at one time considered an especially important source for Cornutus.

The classic work in the secondary literature on ancient allegorical interpretation in general is Pépin (1958); the stage for more recent discussion is set by two books in particular: Dawson (1992) and Struck (2004). See also papers in Boys-Stones (2003a). For Stoicism, which necessarily includes Cornutus in particular, see Steinmetz (1986), Most (1989), and Long (1992); also Lévy (2004) and Gourinat (2005 and 2008).

---

11. Heraclitus in Russell and Konstan 2005; see also in this series Fitzgerald and White 1983.

12. For Palaephatus, see Stern 1996; for Derveni, Betegh 2004.

2.2. Text and Translation

Κορνούτου

Ἐπιδρομὴ τῶν κατὰ τὴν ἑλληνικὴν θεολογίαν παραδεδομένων[1]

A.1.

(1) [1,1] Ὁ οὐρανός, ὦ παιδίον, περιέχει κύκλῳ τὴν γῆν καὶ τὴν θάλατταν καὶ τὰ ἐπὶ γῆς καὶ τὰ ἐν θαλάττῃ πάντα καὶ διὰ τοῦτο ταύτης ἔτυχε τῆς προσηγορίας, οὖρος ὢν ἄνω πάντων καὶ ὁρίζων τὴν φύσιν· [2,1] ἔνιοι δέ φασιν ἀπὸ τοῦ ὠρεῖν ἢ ὠρεύειν τὰ ὄντα, ὅ ἐστι φυλάττειν, οὐρανὸν κεκλῆσθαι, ἀφ' οὗ καὶ ὁ θυρωρὸς ὠνομάσθη καὶ τὸ πολυωρεῖν· ἄλλοι δὲ αὐτὸν ἀπὸ τοῦ ὁρᾶσθαι ἄνω

---

1. Ἐπιδρομὴ τῶν κατὰ τὴν ἑλληνικὴν θεωρίαν παραδεδομένων most manuscripts (*Survey of the Greek Theoretical Tradition*); θεολογίαν is a suggestion, apparently in Cardinal Bessarion's hand, found in one of the manuscripts (Venetus gr. 924). Most (1989, 2034, n. 163) notes that this title echoes the self-characterization of the work at 75,18–76,8 (but that could tell either for or against its originality). Laurentianus plut. 60 cod. 19 has Πρὸς τὸν υἱὸν Γεώργιον περὶ θεῶν (*To His Son George: On the Gods*); Bodleianus Barroccianus 125 and Vindobonensis 253 have Θεωρία περὶ τῆς τῶν θεῶν φυσέως (*Study of the Nature of the Gods*).

Cornutus

Survey of the Greek Theological Tradition[2]

A. First Survey of the Physical System

A.1. Cosmos: Origins and Structure

(1) 'Heaven' [*ouranos*], my child, encircles earth and sea and everything on the earth and in the sea, and this is how it acquired its name—being the *upper limit* [*ouros*] of all things[3] and the *limit* [*hor(izōn)*] of nature. But some say that it is so called from the fact that it *cares for* [*ōr(ein)*] or *takes care of* things [*ōr(euein)*], that is, guards them. (This is where the word for 'doorkeeper' [*thur-ōros*] comes from; also, 'to treat with care' [*polu-ōrein*].) Others find its etymology in the words for *looking upwards*

---

2. In the translation, words for which etymologies are offered are put in single quotes (' '); words in *italics* translate the etymologies themselves. Double quotation marks (" ") are used for mere quotation or mention. In transcriptions, I place curved brackets around elements of the words given by Cornutus (for example, prefixes and morphological features) that suggest a greater distance than there actually is between the term under analysis and the proposed etymology. "Cf." indicates that Cornutus's text has a cognate form of the relevant word; "sc." indicates that he uses a synonym of what he actually has in mind. Divine epithets are sometimes translated and sometimes not; it depends on how familiar the epithet is in its original form and to what extent it has plain meaning in Greek. The pronouns *he* and *she* are used to refer to the persons of the deities, but *it* is used when the subject of some claim is clearly intended to be the feature of the cosmos they represent. (Where it is not clear, the default is *he* and *she*.) (The fact that all nouns in Greek are gendered and that they are usually aligned with the corresponding gender of deity—see 15,10–11!—means that this is not a distinction Cornutus generally had to make.)

3. This seems to make best sense in the immediate context, although it relies on taking *ouros* as the Ionic dialect form of Attic *horos* (limit). In Attic Greek, *ouros* means "guardian"—also a possible translation, especially in light of what follows.

ἐτυμολογοῦσι. καλεῖται δὲ σὺν [2,5] πᾶσιν οἷς περιέχει κόσμος ἀπὸ τοῦ κάλλιστα διακεκοσμῆσθαι. τινὲς δὲ τῶν ποιητῶν Ἄκμονος ἔφασαν αὐτὸν υἱὸν εἶναι, τὸ ἄκμητον τῆς περιφορᾶς αὐτοῦ αἰνιττόμενοι, ἢ προλαβόντες ὅτι ἄφθαρτός ἐστι τοῦτο παριστᾶσι διὰ τῆς ἐτυμολογίας· κεκμηκέναι γὰρ λέγομεν [2,10] τοὺς τετελευτηκότας. ἡ δὲ οὐσία αὐτοῦ πυρώδης ἐστίν, ὡς δῆλον ἐκ τοῦ ἡλίου καὶ ἐκ τῶν ἄλλων ἄστρων. ὅθεν καὶ αἰθὴρ ἐκλήθη τὸ ἐξωτάτω μέρος τοῦ κόσμου ἀπὸ τοῦ αἴθεσθαι· τινὲς δέ φασιν ἀπὸ τοῦ ἀεὶ θεῖν οὕτως αὐτὸν ὠνομάσθαι, ὅ ἐστι ῥοίζῳ φέρεσθαι. καὶ [2,15] τὰ ἄστρα γὰρ οἱονεὶ ἄστατά ἐστιν ὡς οὐδέποτε ἱστάμενα, ἀλλ' ἀεὶ κινούμενα. εὔλογον δὲ καὶ τοὺς θεοὺς ἀπὸ τῆς θεύσεως ἐσχηκέναι τὴν προσηγορίαν· πρῶτον γὰρ οἱ ἀρχαῖοι θεοὺς ὑπελάμβανον εἶναι οὓς ἑώρων ἀδιαλείπτως φερομένους, αἰτίους αὐτοὺς νομίσαντες [2,20] εἶναι τῶν τοῦ ἀέρος μεταβολῶν καὶ τῆς σωτηρίας τῶν [3,1] ὅλων. τάχα δ' ἂν εἶεν θεοὶ θετῆρες καὶ ποιηταὶ τῶν γινομένων.

(2) Ὥσπερ δὲ ἡμεῖς ὑπὸ ψυχῆς διοικούμεθα, οὕτω καὶ ὁ κόσμος ψυχὴν ἔχει τὴν συνέχουσαν αὐτόν, καὶ [3,5] αὕτη καλεῖται Ζεύς, πρώτως καὶ διὰ παντὸς ζῶσα καὶ αἰτία οὖσα τοῖς ζῶσι τοῦ ζῆν· διὰ τοῦτο δὲ καὶ βασιλεύειν ὁ Ζεὺς λέγεται τῶν ὅλων, ὡς ἂν καὶ ἐν ἡμῖν ἡ ψυχὴ καὶ ἡ φύσις ἡμῶν βασιλεύειν ῥηθείη. Δία δὲ αὐτὸν καλοῦμεν ὅτι δι' αὐτὸν γίνεται καὶ σώζεται πάντα. [3,10] παρὰ δέ τισι καὶ Δεὺς λέγεται, τάχα ἀπὸ τοῦ δεύειν τὴν γῆν ἢ μεταδιδόναι τοῖς ζῶσι ζωτικῆς ἱκμάδος· καὶ ἡ γενικὴ πτῶσις ἀπ' αὐτῆς ἐστι Δεός, παρακειμένη πως τῇ Διός. οἰκεῖν δὲ ἐν τῷ οὐρανῷ λέγεται, ἐπεὶ ἐκεῖ ἐστι τὸ κυριώτατον

[*hor(asthai) anō*]. Considered with everything it embraces, it is called 'cosmos,' from the fact that everything is *arranged* [(*diake*)*kosm*(*ēsthai*)] in the best possible way. Some of the poets said that he was the son of 'Akmon,' hinting at the *unwearied* [*a-kmēton*] nature of its circuit—or else they established this on the basis of the etymology because they assumed that heaven is indestructible;[4] for we call the dead *worn out* [(*ke*)*kmē*(*kenai*)]. Its substance is fiery, as is clear from the sun and the other stars. This is why the outermost part of the cosmos is called 'aether': because it *blazes* [*aith*(*esthai*)]—although some say that it is named this way because it *always runs* [*aei th*(*ein*)], that is, is carried along at a rush. And the 'stars' [*astra*] are, as it were, *unstable* [*a-stata*], since they are never fixed in place but always in motion. It is reasonable to think that the 'gods' [*theoi*] acquired their name from *hurrying* [*theu*(*sis*)]; for, in the first place, the ancients conceived their notion of god from those things they saw unceasingly borne along, reckoning that they were responsible for changes in the air and for sustaining the universe. But perhaps the 'gods' are those who *establish* [*the*(*tēres*)] and make those things that come into being.

(2) Just as we are governed by a soul, so the cosmos has a soul that holds it together, and this is called 'Zeus'—who *lives* [*zōsa*] preeminently and in everything and is the cause of *life* [*zēn*] in those things that live. Because of this, Zeus is said to reign over the universe—just as our soul and nature might be said to reign over us.[5] And we call him 'Dia' because *through* [*dia*] him everything comes to be and is sustained. Among some people he is called 'Deus' as well, perhaps because he *bedews* [*deu*(*ein*)] the earth or gives a share of life-giving moisture to the living. (Its genitive is 'Deos,' which is quite close to *Dios*.)[6] He is said to live in heaven, since that

---

4. But assumed wrongly; see 5,7–8 below.
5. See *SVF* 1.532; 2.1076.
6. *Deos* is plausibly the genitive of *Deus*, if we take *Deus* to be the Aeolian (specifically, Boeotian) dialect form of *Zeus* and not (*pace* Torres 2009a) the Latin word for "god" (genitive *dei*). (*Orthography* 2 proves Cornutus's awareness of Aeolian.) *Dios* could be the adjective meaning "heavenly," but it is better understood here as the regular genitive form of "Zeus" in Attic Greek. The point of this parenthesis is to confirm the connection between (Attic) "Zeus" and (Boeotian) "Deus."

μέρος τῆς τοῦ κόσμου ψυχῆς· καὶ γὰρ αἱ [3,15] ἡμέτεραι ψυχαὶ πῦρ εἰσιν.

(3) Γυνὴ δὲ καὶ ἀδελφὴ αὐτοῦ παραδέδοται ἡ Ἥρα, ἥτις ἐστὶν ὁ ἀήρ. συνῆπται γὰρ εὐθὺς αὐτῷ καὶ κεκόλληται αἰρομένη ἀπὸ τῆς γῆς ἐκείνου αὐτῇ ἐπιβεβηκότος· καὶ γεγόνασιν ἐκ τῆς εἰς τὰ αὐτὰ ῥύσεως, ῥυεῖσα γὰρ εἰς λεπτότητα ἡ οὐσία τό τε [3,20] πῦρ καὶ τὸν ἀέρα ὑφίστησιν. ἐφ' ᾧ καὶ Ῥέαν τὴν [4,1] μητέρα αὐτῶν ἐμύθευσαν εἶναι, πατέρα δὲ τὸν Κρόνον ἤτοι διὰ τὸ ἐν τεταγμένοις χρόνου μέτροις γενέσθαι ταῦτα ἢ διὰ τὸ κατὰ σύγκρισιν καὶ βρασμὸν τῆς ὕλης τὴν εἰς τὰ στοιχεῖα διάκρισιν ἀποτελεῖσθαι ἤ, [4,5] ὅπερ πιθανώτατον, διὰ τὸ τηνικαῦτα ὑφίστασθαι τὸν αἰθέρα καὶ τὸν ἀέρα, ἡνίκ' ἂν ἐκ πυρὸς κινῆται ἡ φύσις ἐπὶ τὸ κραίνειν καὶ ἀποτελεῖν τὰ ὄντα. (4) διὰ δὲ ταύτην τὴν αἰτίαν καὶ τὸν Ποσειδῶνα ἔφασαν οἱ ἀρχαῖοι Κρόνου καὶ Ῥέας υἱὸν εἶναι· καὶ γὰρ τὸ [4,10] ὕδωρ ἐκ τῆς εἰρημένης μεταβολῆς γίνεται. Ποσειδῶν δέ ἐστιν ἡ ἀπεργαστικὴ τοῦ ἐν τῇ γῇ καὶ περὶ τὴν γῆν ὑγροῦ δύναμις, εἴτουν ἀπὸ τῆς πόσεως οὕτω κληθεῖσα καὶ τοῦ διδόναι ταύτην, εἴτε λόγος καθ' ὃν ἰδίει ἡ φύσις φυσιιδίων ἐστίν, εἴθ' οἱονεὶ πεδοσείων [4,15] ὠνόμασται κατὰ τὴν παραδειχθησομένην αὐτοῦ ἰδιότητα. (5) ἀδελφὸς δὲ αὐτῶν καὶ ὁ Ἅιδης εἶναι λέγεται. οὗτος δέ ἐστιν ὁ παχυμερέστατος καὶ προσγειότατος ἀήρ· ὁμοῦ γὰρ αὐτοῖς γίνεται καὶ αὐτὸς ἀρξαμένης [5,1] ῥεῖν καὶ κραίνειν τὰ ὄντα κατὰ τοὺς ἐν αὐτῇ λόγους τῆς φύσεως. καλεῖται δὲ Ἅιδης ἢ ὅτι καθ' ἑαυτὸν ἀόρατός ἐστιν, ὅθεν καὶ διαιροῦντες Ἀΐδην αὐτὸν ὀνομάζουσιν, ἢ κατ' ἀντίφρασιν ὡσὰν ὁ ἀνδάνων [5,5] ἡμῖν· εἰς τοῦτον γὰρ χωρεῖν ἡμῖν κατὰ τὸν θάνατον αἱ ψυχαὶ

is where the most important part of the cosmic soul is[7]—and indeed, our souls are fire, too.[8]

(3) Tradition relates that his wife and sister is 'Hera,' that is, *air* [*aēr*], which is linked and bonded to him[9] directly: she *rising* [*air(omenē)*] from the earth, he having come down to her. And they were born as a result of a *flow* [*rhu(sis)*] in the same direction; for when substance *flowed* [*rhueisa*] toward fineness, it gave rise to both fire and air.[10] This is why mythology makes 'Rhea' their mother. It makes their father 'Kronos' either because these things came to be in ordered measures of *time* [*chronos*], or because the elements are *distinguished* [*(dia)kri(sis)*] by the *combination* [*(sun) kri(sis)*] and agitation of matter; or, as is most plausible, because aether and air come about whenever nature is roused to *make* [*krain(ein)*] out of fire the things that exist and bring them to completion. (4) For this reason, the ancients said that Poseidon is also the son of Kronos and Rhea; for water is a product of the aforementioned change as well. 'Poseidon' is the power which produces moisture in the earth and around the earth[11]—whether so called from *drink* [*posis*] and the fact that he provides the same; or whether he is the principle responsible for *nature sweating* [*phys(is) idi(ei)*], "Physi-idion";[12] or whether it is as if he were called *Earth Shaker* [*pedo-seiōn*], in line with what will be shown to be his characteristic activity.[13] (5) Hades is said to be their brother. He is the most dense form of air, closest to the earth, and is produced along with them when nature starts to flow and make the things that exist according to the principles within it. It is called 'Hades' either because it is in itself unseen [cf. *a-idein*] (so that he is also called 'Aïdes,' with a diaeresis) or, by antithesis, as if it is *the one who pleases* us [cf. *hadein*]—for it appears that this is where our souls go at

---

7. See *SVF* 2.644. Cornutus agrees with Chrysippus and Posidonius as reported here, against Cleanthes (the sun) and Archedemus (the earth: *SVF* 3, Archedemus, frag. 15; cf. *SVF* 2.642), who identified the "ruling part" of the cosmic soul with the earth. Later on, Cornutus seems to side more specifically with Chrysippus's view that the ruling part is, properly, the aether (see 35,13–15).

8. See *SVF* 1.134; 2.773, 775.

9. I.e., Zeus, as identified in the previous line as (intelligent, heavenly) fire.

10. See introduction, p. 29–30.

11. Note this more precise formulation, according to which Poseidon is not the sea itself but the power or principle in nature that is responsible for the sea (similarly 41,19–20 below). Cf., perhaps, *SVF* 2.1093, where Poseidon is (not the sea but) the "breath," *pneuma*, in the sea (similarly Cicero, *Nat. d.* 2.71 = *SVF* 2.1080).

12. Cf. Empedocles DK 31.A25: "The sea is … the earth's sweat."

13. See ch. 22 below.

δοκοῦσιν ἥκιστα ἀνδάνοντος ἡμῖν τοῦ θανάτου. καὶ Πλούτων δὲ ἐκλήθη διὰ τὸ πάντων φθαρτῶν ὄντων μηδὲν εἶναι ὃ μὴ τελευταῖον εἰς αὐτὸν κατατάττεται καὶ αὐτοῦ κτῆμα γίνεται.

(6) Τῆς [5,10] δὲ Ῥέας κατὰ τὴν παραδεδειγμένην ῥύσιν εἰδοποιουμένης εἰκότως ἤδη καὶ τὴν τῶν ὄμβρων αἰτίαν ἀνατιθέντες αὐτῇ, ὅτι ὡς ἐπὶ τὸ πολὺ μετὰ βροντῶν καὶ ἀστραπῶν συμβαίνει γίνεσθαι, καὶ ταύτην παρεισήγαγον τυμπάνοις καὶ κυμβάλοις καὶ κεραυλίαις καὶ [5,15] λαμπαδηφορίαις χαίρουσαν. ἐπεὶ δ' ἄνωθεν οἱ ὄμβροι καταράττουσι, πολλαχοῦ δὲ καὶ ἀπὸ τῶν ὀρῶν ἐπερχόμενοι φαίνονται, πρῶτον μὲν τὴν Ἴδην ἐπωνόμασαν αὐτῇ, μετέωρον ὄρος καὶ ὃ μακρόθεν ἔστιν ἰδεῖν, ὀρείαν αὐτὴν προσαγορεύοντες[14] καὶ τὰ γενναιότατα τῶν [6,1] ἐν τοῖς ὄρεσι γινομένων ζῴων, τοὺς λέοντας, ἡνιοχουμένους ὑπ' αὐτῆς παρεισήγαγον· τάχα δὲ καὶ ἐπεὶ οἱ χειμῶνες ἀγριωπόν τι ἔχουσι. πυργωτὸν δὲ περίκειται στέφανον ἤτοι διὰ τὸ καταρχὰς ἐπὶ τῶν ὀρῶν [6,5] τίθεσθαι τὰς πόλεις ὀχυρότητος ἕνεκεν ἢ ἐπεὶ ἀρχηγός ἐστι τῆς πρώτης καὶ ἀρχετύπου πόλεως, τοῦ κόσμου. κωδίαν δ' ἀνατιθέασιν αὐτῇ παριστάντες ὅτι αἰτία τῆς ζῳογονίας αὕτη ἐγένετο. κατὰ τοῦτο δὲ καὶ ἄλλους τινὰς τύπους περὶ τὸ στῆθος αὐτῆς περιτιθέασιν, ὡς [6,10] τῆς τῶν ὄντων ποικιλίας καὶ παντὸς χρήματος δι' αὐτῆς γεγονότος. ἔοικε δ' αὕτη καὶ ἡ παρὰ Σύροις Ἀταργάτις εἶναι, ἣν καὶ διὰ τοῦ περιστερᾶς καὶ ἰχθύος ἀπέχεσθαι τιμῶσι, σημαίνοντες ὅτι τὰ μάλιστα δηλοῦντα τὴν τῆς οὐσίας ῥεῦσιν[15] ἀὴρ καὶ ὕδωρ.

Φρυγία [6,15] δ' ἰδίως εἴρηται διὰ τὸ θρησκεύεσθαι παρὰ τοῖς Φρυξὶν ἐξόχως, παρ' οἷς καὶ ἡ τῶν γάλλων ἐπεπόλασε παρεδρία τάχα τι τοιοῦτον ἐμφαίνουσα, ὁποῖον καὶ παρὰ τοῖς Ἕλλησι περὶ τῆς τοῦ Οὐρανοῦ ἐκτομῆς μεμύθευται. [6,20] Πρῶτον μὲν γὰρ ὁ Κρόνος λέγεται καταπίνειν τὰ [7,1] ἐκ τῆς Ῥέας αὐτῷ γινόμενα τέκνα· εἴληπται μὲν οὖν οὕτω πάνυ εἰκότως, ἐπειδὴ ὅσα ἂν γίνηται κατὰ τὸν εἰρημένον τῆς κινήσεως λόγον πάλιν κατὰ τὸν αὐτὸν ἐν περιόδῳ ἀφανίζεται· καὶ ὁ χρόνος δὲ τοιοῦτόν τί [7,5] ἐστι· δαπανᾶται γὰρ ὑπ' αὐτοῦ τὰ γινόμενα ἐν αὐτῷ. εἶτα τὴν Ῥέαν φασὶν γεννωμένου αὐτῇ τοῦ Διὸς λίθον ἀντ' αὐτοῦ προσενεγκεῖν ἐσπαργανωμένον τῷ Κρόνῳ, τοῦτον εἰποῦσαν τετοκέναι· κἀκεῖνον μὲν καταποθῆναι ὑπ' αὐτοῦ, τὸν δὲ Δία λάθρα τραφέντα

---

14. προσηγόρευσαν Lang (1881), Torres (2018).

15. Wyttenbach (Osann 1844: see ad loc. and p. xii); αἵρεσιν Lang (1881), Torres (2018) (with manuscripts).

death, and death is least pleasing to us. It is called 'Pluto' as well because, all things being perishable,[16] there is nothing that does not in the end get allocated to him and become his property.[17]

(6) The characterization of 'Rhea' is appropriate to the *flow* [*rhu(sis)*] she represents. To her is ascribed the cause of rainstorms, and because it usually happens that storms are accompanied by thunder and lightning, it became a custom that Rhea rejoices in drums and cymbals, the playing of horns, and torchlit processions. And since rainstorms pour down from above, and often seem to come from the mountains, first of all, they gave her the name of 'Ida'—a skyscraping mountain, *visible* [*id(ein)*] from a long way off—addressing her as being 'of the mountains,' and they made it a custom that her chariot should be pulled by lions, which are the most noble of the animals that live in the mountains—although perhaps it is because storms have a rather wild aspect. And she wears a turreted crown, either because the first cities were built on mountains for reasons of fortification, or because Rhea founded the first and archetypal city, the cosmos. The poppyhead is dedicated to her, suggesting that she was the cause of animal generation. For this reason, too, certain other symbols are placed around her breast, to show that each thing, and the variety and colors of the things that exist, have come about thanks to her. The Syrian Atargatis seems to be the same as Rhea, and she is honored by abstention from the dove and from fish, signifying that air and water make the flow of substance especially manifest.

Rhea is known, distinctively, as Phrygian because her worship is especially cultivated among the Phrygians. Here, the service of Galli is not uncommon and perhaps represents something like the Greek myth about the castration of Ouranos. First of all, Kronos is said to swallow the children born to him from Rhea. This is understood in a way that is completely reasonable: whatever comes about according to the principle of motion mentioned earlier[18] disappears again in its turn according to the same thing—and time is indeed something like this; for everything born in it is consumed by it. Next, Rhea, they say, having given birth to Zeus, gave Kronos a swaddled stone instead of him, saying that this is what she had given birth to; he swallowed it, and Zeus, who was raised in secret, came to

---

16. For the ultimate destruction of the world order and everything in it, see below 28,10–12, with n. 92.

17. The implicit etymology, then, is with *ploutos*, "wealth."

18. I.e., time; see 4,1–3 above.

βασιλεῦσαι [7,10] τοῦ κόσμου. ἐνταῦθ' οὖν ἄλλως εἴληπται ἡ κατάποσις· συντέτακται γὰρ ὁ μῦθος περὶ τῆς τοῦ κόσμου γενέσεως, ἐν ᾧ τότε ἀνετράφη ἡ διοικοῦσα αὐτὸν φύσις καὶ ἐπεκράτησεν, ὅτε εἰς τὸ μεσαίτατον αὐτοῦ ὁ λίθος οὗτος, ὃν καλοῦμεν γῆν, οἱονεὶ καταποθεὶς ἐγκατεστηρίχθη. [7,15] οὐ γὰρ ἂν ἄλλως συνέστη τὰ ὄντα, εἰ μὴ ὡς ἐπὶ θεμελίου ταύτης ἡρείσθη, γινομένων καὶ τρεφομένων ἐντεῦθεν πάντων. (7) τελευταῖον δὲ ὁ μὲν Κρόνος ἱστορεῖται συνεχῶς κατιόντα ἐπὶ τῷ μίγνυσθαι τῇ Γῇ τὸν Οὐρανὸν ἐκτεμεῖν καὶ παῦσαι τῆς ὕβρεως, [7,20] ὁ δὲ Ζεὺς ἐκβαλὼν αὐτὸν τῆς βασιλείας καταταρταρῶσαι. διὰ γοῦν τούτων αἰνίττονται ὅτι ἡ τῆς τῶν ὅλων γενέσεως τάξις, ἣν ἔφαμεν ἀπὸ τοῦ κραίνειν [8,1] Κρόνον εἰρῆσθαι, τὴν γινομένην τέως πολλὴν ῥύσιν τοῦ περιέχοντος ἐπὶ τὴν γῆν ἔστειλε λεπτοτέρας ποιήσασα τὰς ἀναθυμιάσεις. ἡ δὲ τοῦ κόσμου φύσις ἐπισχύσασα, ἣν δὴ Δία ἐλέγομεν καλεῖσθαι, τὸ λίαν [8,5] φερόμενον τῆς μεταβολῆς ἐπέσχε καὶ ἐπέδησε μακροτέραν διεξαγωγὴν δοὺς αὐτῷ τῷ κόσμῳ. πάνυ δ' εἰκότως καὶ ἀγκυλομήτην καλοῦσι τὸν Κρόνον, ἀγκύλων ὄντων καὶ δυσπαρακολουθήτων μήτι ἃ ἐτέλεσε[19] τοσούτους ἀριθμοὺς ἐξελίττων.

(8) [8,10] Κατ' ἄλλον δὲ λόγον τὸν Ὠκεανὸν ἔφασαν ἀρχέγονον εἶναι πάντων—οὐ γὰρ μία μυθολογία περὶ τοῦτον ἐγένετο τὸν τόπον—τούτου δ' εἶναι γυναῖκα τὴν[20] Τηθύν. ἔστι δ' Ὠκεανὸς μὲν ὁ ὠκέως νεόμενος λόγος καὶ ἐφεξῆς μεταβάλλων, Τηθὺς δὲ ἡ τῶν ποιοτήτων [8,15] ἐπιμονή. ἐκ γὰρ τῆς τούτων συγκράσεως ἢ μίξεως ὑφίσταται τὰ ὄντα· οὐδὲν δ' ἂν ἦν, εἰ θάτερον ἄμικτον ἐπεκράτει.

---

19. Torres (2018); ἃ μητιάσεται Lang (1881).
20. Torres (2018); om. Lang (1881).

reign over the cosmos. Here the swallowing is not understood literally; the myth has been composed about the origin of the cosmos, whose governing nature was raised and brought to power when this stone which we call the earth had been, as it were, 'swallowed' and fixed firmly at the very center of it. Nothing that exists could have come about if it were not supported on this foundation, and all things are born and raised from it. (7) And finally, it is said that Kronos castrated Ouranos, who was continually descending for intercourse with Earth, and put an end to the outrage. But Zeus expelled him from his throne and threw him down to Tartarus. By all this, then, they hint that the plan for the universe to come into being—which we said was called 'Kronos' from *make* [*krain(ein)*]²¹— sent the great flow of what until then had been surrounding the earth down toward it, making the exhalations finer.²² Cosmic nature (which we said was called Dia)²³ was strong and restrained the excessive impetus in this change, giving a longer course of life to the cosmos itself. And it is entirely appropriate that they also call Kronos Intricate in Counsel, since the things he skillfully accomplishes when he unfolds such a great number of items²⁴ are intricate and hard to follow.

(8) In a different account, Okeanos was said to be the progenitor of all things—for there was more than one story about this topic—and his wife was said to be Tethys. 'Okeanos' is reason, as it *moves swiftly* [*ōkeōs ne(omenos)*] and makes changes in due sequence; 'Tethys' is the stability of qualities.²⁵ What exists comes about from the combination or mixing of these two; there would be nothing if either prevailed unmixed.²⁶

---

21. See 4,7 above—which means that the "plan" here, or perhaps better, the "order of things" (*taxis*), must be a way of referring to nature.

22. This seems to be an elaboration of the thoughts, in ch. 3, that (1) "substance flowed toward fineness" (3,19) and (2) the production of air involves earth "rising" (the "exhalations") to meet the descending fire (3,17–18).

23. See 3,8–9 above.

24. The sense of *arithmoi* (lit. "numbers") here is probably that of individual cosmological principles, as, e.g., in SVF 2.744.

25. We are probably meant to be put in mind of *tithēmi*, "to place."

26. It might seem tempting to read this "different account" either as some form of dualism (but most dualistic systems, for example, that of certain forms of Platonism, presuppose that the *rational* principle is the one associated with stability) or as a reference to the active and passive principles of Stoicism (but the Stoics do not think that matter defines the qualities available to the activity of reason; see, e.g., SVF 2.1168). So more likely, what underlies this myth is simply a cursory summary of creation, according to which the divine mind plans the cosmos as a fluid sequence of qualitative change.

A.2.

(9) [9,1] Μετὰ δὲ ταῦτα ἄλλως ὁ Ζεὺς πατὴρ λέγεται θεῶν καὶ ἀνθρώπων εἶναι διὰ τὸ τὴν τοῦ κόσμου φύσιν αἰτίαν γεγονέναι τῆς τούτων ὑποστάσεως, ὡς οἱ πατέρες γεννῶσι τὰ τέκνα. νεφεληγερέτην δ' αὐτὸν καὶ [9,5] ἐρίγδουπον καλοῦσι καὶ τὸν κεραυνὸν αὐτῷ καὶ τὴν αἰγίδα ἀνατιθέασι τῷ ἄνω ὑπὲρ ἡμᾶς τὰ νέφη καὶ τὰς βροντὰς συνίστασθαι καὶ τοὺς κεραυνοὺς ἐκεῖθεν καὶ τὰς καταιγίδας ἐνσκήπτειν, ἄλλως ἤδη[27] τῷ τὸν οὐρανὸν λελογχότι θεῷ παντὸς τοῦ ὑπὲρ τὴν γῆν τόπου [9,10] ἀπονεμομένου. καὶ διὰ μὲν τὰς αἰγίδας, αἳ δὴ ἀπὸ τοῦ ἀΐσσειν τὸ ὄνομα ἔσχον, αἰγίοχος ἐκλήθη, δι' ἄλλας δὲ ὁμοειδεῖς καὶ εὐεπιγνώστους αἰτίας ὑέτιος καὶ ἐπικάρπιος καὶ καταιβάτης καὶ ἀστραπαῖος καὶ ἄλλως πολλαχῶς κατὰ διαφόρους ἐπινοίας. καὶ σωτῆρα καὶ ἕρκειον [9,15] καὶ πολιέα καὶ πατρῷον καὶ ὁμόγνιον καὶ ξένιον καὶ κτήσιον καὶ βουλαῖον καὶ τροπαιοῦχον καὶ ἐλευθέριον αὐτὸν προσαγορεύουσιν, ἀπεριλήπτων ὅσων ὀνομασιῶν αὐτοῦ τοιούτων οὐσῶν, ἐπειδὴ διατέτακεν εἰς πᾶσαν δύναμιν καὶ σχέσιν καὶ πάντων αἴτιος καὶ [9,20] ἐπόπτης ἐστίν. οὕτω δ' ἐρρήθη καὶ τῆς Δίκης πατὴρ εἶναι—ὁ γὰρ παραγαγὼν εἰς τὰ πράγματα τὴν κοινωνίαν [10,1] τῶν ἀνθρώπων καὶ παραγγείλας αὐτοῖς μὴ ἀδικεῖν ἀλλήλους οὗτός ἐστι—καὶ τῶν Χαρίτων—ἐντεῦθέν τε γάρ εἰσιν αἱ τοῦ χαρίζεσθαι καὶ εὐεργετεῖν ἀρχαί—καὶ τῶν Ὡρῶν, τῶν κατὰ τὰς τοῦ περιέχοντος [10,5] μεταβολὰς σωτηρίους τῶν ἐπὶ γῆς γινομένων καὶ τῶν ἄλλων ὠνομασμένων ἀπὸ τῆς φυλακῆς. παρεισάγουσι δ' αὐτὸν τελείου ἀνδρὸς ἡλικίαν ἔχοντα, ἐπεὶ οὔτε τὸ παρηκμακὸς οὔτε τὸ ἐλλιπὲς ἐμφαίνει, κατηρτυκότι δὲ οἰκεῖον, διὰ τοῦτο καὶ τελείων αὐτῷ [10,10] θυομένων. τὸ δὲ σκῆπτρον τῆς δυναστείας αὐτοῦ σύμβολόν ἐστι, βασιλικὸν φόρημα ὑπάρχον, ἢ τοῦ ἀπτώτως αὐτὸν ἔχειν καὶ ἀσφαλῶς ὡς τοὺς ἐπὶ βάκτροις ἐρηρεισμένους· τὸ δὲ κράτος,[28] ὃ ἐν τῇ δεξιᾷ χειρὶ κατέχει, σαφεστέρας ἢ κατ' ἐπεξήγησιν ὀνομασίας ἐστί. [10,15] πολλαχοῦ δὲ καὶ Νίκην κρατῶν πλάττεται· περίεστι γὰρ πάντων καὶ ἡττᾶν αὐτὸν οὐδὲν δύναται. ἱερὸς δ' ὄρνις αὐτοῦ ἀετὸς λέγεται εἶναι διὰ τὸ ὀξύτατον τοῦτο τῶν πτηνῶν εἶναι. στέφεται δ' ἐλαίᾳ διὰ τὸ ἀειθαλὲς καὶ λιπαρὸν καὶ πολύχρηστον ἢ διὰ τὴν

---

27. Torres (2018); κατασκήπτειν, [ἄλλως] Lang (1881).
28. Torres (2018) (with manuscripts); βέλος Lang (1881) ("weapon," sc. thunderbolt).

A.2. Cosmos: Order and Justice

(9) Next: Zeus is called "father of gods and men" because cosmic nature caused these things to exist, as fathers give being to their children. They call him Cloud Gatherer and Thundering and give him the thunderbolt and aegis as attributes because he is responsible for the clouds and thunder above us and hurls down storms and thunderbolts from there. In any case, the whole space above the earth is allocated to the god to whose lot heaven fell. And he was called Aegis Bearer because of 'hurricanes' [*aigides*], which are so called from the word for *rushing* [*aiss(ein)*], and for other, similar reasons which are easy to understand, he was called Bringer of Rain, Guardian of Fruits, God of the Thunderbolt, God of the Lightning Flash—and various other things, too, according to the different views people had of him. They also call him Savior, and Bulwark, and Guardian of the City, and God of Our Forefathers, God of Our Race, God of Hospitality, Protector of Property, Counselor, God of the Trophy, and Deliverer: these names are endless, since he extends to every power and state and is the cause and overseer of everything. Likewise, he was also said to be the father of Justice because it was he who brought community to the affairs of men and ordered them not to wrong each other; and of the Graces because this is the source of gracious and beneficent action; and of the 'Seasons' [*hōrai*], which are named from guarding,[29] the thought being that changes in what surrounds the earth preserve what grows on it, among other things. By tradition, he has the age of a mature man, since he shows neither deficiency nor excess, but what is appropriate to someone fully grown. For this reason, too, mature animals are sacrificed to him. The scepter is a symbol of his power, being something carried by kings; or of his sure and steady bearing, like those supported by staffs. And the power[30] which he holds in his right hand has a name too clear to need explanation; in fact, he is often depicted dominating even Victory, for he is superior to everything, and nothing can defeat him. The eagle is said to be his sacred bird because this is the swiftest of birds. He is crowned with olive because olive is evergreen, lustrous, and useful for many things, or

---

29. We are meant to think of the verb "take care of," *ōreu(esthai)*; see 57,7–8 below.
30. Sc. *Nikē*, "Victory."

ἐμφέρειαν [10,20] τῆς πρὸς τὸν οὐρανὸν γλαυκότητος. λέγεται δ' ὑπό τινων καὶ ἀλάστωρ καὶ παλαμναῖος τῷ τοὺς ἀλάστορας καὶ παλαμναίους κολάζειν, τῶν μὲν ὠνομασμένων [11,1] ἀπὸ τοῦ τοιαῦτα ἁμαρτάνειν, ἐφ' οἷς ἔστιν ἀλαστῆσαι καὶ στενάξαι, τῶν δὲ ἀπὸ τοῦ ταῖς παλάμαις μιάσματα ἀνέκθυτα ἀποτελεῖν.

(10) Κατὰ τοῦτον τὸν λόγον καὶ αἱ λεγόμεναι Ἐρινύες γεγόνασιν, [11,5] ἐρευνήτριαι τῶν ἁμαρτανόντων οὖσαι, Μέγαιρα καὶ Τισιφόνη καὶ Ἀληκτώ, ὡσπερεὶ μεγαίροντος τοῖς τοιούτοις τοῦ θεοῦ καὶ τιννυμένου τοὺς γινομένους ὑπ' αὐτῶν φόνους καὶ ἀλήκτως καὶ ἀπαύστως τοῦτο ποιοῦντος. Σεμναὶ δ' ὄντως αὗται αἱ θεαὶ καὶ Εὐμενίδες [11,10] εἰσί· κατὰ γὰρ τὴν εἰς τοὺς ἀνθρώπους εὐμένειαν τῆς φύσεως διατέτακται καὶ τὸ τὴν πονηρίαν κολάζεσθαι. φρικώδεις δὲ τὰς ὄψεις ἔχουσι, πυρὶ καὶ μάστιγι τοὺς ἀσεβεῖς διώκουσαι καὶ ὀφιοπλόκαμοι λεγόμεναι, τῷ τοιαύτην τοῖς κακοῖς φαντασίαν ποιεῖν, [11,15] ἃς ἂν ἀποτίνωσι ποινὰς ἀντὶ τῶν πλημμελημάτων. ἐν Ἅιδου δὲ οἰκεῖν λέγονται διὰ τὸ ἐν ἀσαφεῖ κεῖσθαι τὰς τούτων αἰκίας καὶ ἀπροόρατον ἐφίστασθαι τὴν τίσιν τοῖς ἀξίοις. (11) ἀκολούθως δὲ τούτοις λέγεται καὶ ὅτι [11,20] "πάντ' ἐφορᾷ Διὸς ὀφθαλμὸς καὶ πάντ' ἐπακούει." πῶς γὰρ οἷόν τέ ἐστι τὴν διὰ πάντων διήκουσαν δύναμιν [12,1] λανθάνειν τι τῶν ἐν τῷ κόσμῳ γινομένων;

Προσαγορεύουσι δὲ καὶ μείλιχον τὸν Δία, εὐμείλικτον ὄντα τοῖς ἐξ ἀδικίας μετατιθεμένοις, οὐ δέοντος ἀδιαλλάκτως ἔχειν πρὸς αὐτούς· διὰ τοῦτο γὰρ καὶ ἱκεσίου [12,5] Διός εἰσι βωμοὶ (12) καὶ τὰς Λιτὰς ὁ ποιητὴς ἔφη τοῦ Διὸς εἶναι θυγατέρας, χωλὰς μὲν οὔσας διὰ τὸ πίπτειν τοὺς γονυπετοῦντας, ῥυσὰς δὲ ἐπὶ παραστάσει τῆς ἀσθενείας τῶν ἱκετευόντων, παραβλῶπας δὲ τῷ παριδόντας τινάς τινα ὕστερον ἀνάγκην ἴσχειν [12,10] λιτανείας.

because of the similarity of its gray color to heaven.[31] He is called by some 'Avenger' [*alastōr*] and 'Blood Avenger' [*palamnaios*] because he punishes 'those who deserve vengeance' [*alastores*] and are 'guilty of blood' [*palamnaioi*][32]—the former being named from the fact that they commit crimes in the face of which one might feel *hatred* [*alast(ēnai)*] and grief, the latter from the fact that they acquire inexpiable pollution from crimes of *violence* [*palamiai*].

(10) The so-called 'Erinnyes' came about in the same way, as *investigators* [*ereun(ētriai)*] of crimes: 'Megaira' and 'Tisiphone' and 'Alekto'—as if god *holds a grudge* [*megairōn*] against such men and *punishes* [cf. *tisis*] *the murders* [*phonoi*] done by them and does this *unremittingly* [*alēktōs*] and unceasingly. These goddesses truly are holy and kindly;[33] for nature's benevolence toward men has also provided for the punishment of wickedness. Their gaze is terrifying; they pursue the impious with fire and goads, and they are called "snake haired" because this is the impression made on the minds of the wicked by the penalties they pay for their crimes. They are said to live in Hades because the sufferings that come to these men lie in hiding, and punishment comes to those who deserve it out of the blue. (11) Consistent with this is the line: "The eye of Zeus sees all, and he hears all."[34] For how can anything that happens in the cosmos elude the power that pervades everything?[35]

And they call Zeus Gentle, since he is easily appeased by those who repent of their injustice—he does not want to be irreconcilable toward them. For this reason there are altars dedicated to Zeus, God of Suppliants. (12) And the Poet said that the Prayers are daughters of Zeus.[36] They are lame because those who supplicate fall down; they are wrinkled because of the suppliants' display of weakness; they squint because they overlook some prayers, intent on whatever future necessity.[37]

---

31. *Glaucos* is a notoriously hard color term to translate, but it generally refers to a pale hue, usually gray or green (although one might not want to call heaven green); see 36,15–20 below for the gray eyes of Athena and 38,20–21 for the gray olive dedicated to her on this account.
32. Cf. *SVF* 2.1176.
33. "Eumenides" = the "kindly ones."
34. Hesiod, *Op.* 267.
35. Cf. *SVF* 2.937 (269,10–12).
36. See Homer, *Il.* 9.502.
37. See, perhaps, *SVF* 2.1169, 1181.

(13) Ὁ Ζεὺς δέ ἐστι καὶ ἡ Μοῖρα διὰ τὸ μὴ ὁρωμένη διανέμησις εἶναι τῶν ἐπιβαλλόντων ἑκάστῳ, ἐντεῦθεν ἤδη τῶν ἄλλων μερίδων μοιρῶν ὠνομασμένων. Αἶσα δέ ἐστιν ἡ ἄιστος καὶ ἄγνωστος αἰτία [12,15] τῶν γινομένων—ἐμφαίνεται δὲ νῦν ἡ τῶν κατὰ μέρος ἀδηλότης—ἤ, ὡς οἱ πρεσβύτεροι, ἡ ἀεὶ οὖσα. Εἱμαρμένη δέ ἐστι καθ' ἣν μέμαρπται καὶ συνείληπται πάντα ἐν τάξει καὶ στοίχῳ μὴ ἔχοντι πέρας τὰ γινόμενα σύλληψιν ἢ ει συλλαβὴ περιέχει καθάπερ [13,1] καὶ ἐν τῷ εἱρμῷ. Ἀνάγκη δέ ἐστιν ἣν ἄξαι καὶ ἧς περιγενέσθαι οὐκ ἔστιν ἢ ἐφ' ἣν πᾶν ὃ ἂν γένηται τὴν ἀναγωγὴν λαμβάνει. κατ' ἄλλον δὲ τρόπον τρεῖς Μοῖραι παρεισάγονται κατὰ τὸ τρισσὸν τῶν χρόνων· καὶ [13,5] Κλωθὼ μὲν ὠνόμασται μία αὐτῶν ἀπὸ τοῦ κλώσει ἐρίων[38] ἐοικέναι τὰ γινόμενα ἄλλων ἄλλοις ἐπιπιπτόντων, καθὸ καὶ νήθουσαν αὐτὴν πρεσβυτάτην διατυποῦσι, Λάχεσις δ' ἄλλη ἀπὸ τοῦ τῇ κατὰ τοὺς κλήρους λήξει τὰ ἀποδιδόμενα ἑκάστῳ προσεοικέναι, Ἄτροπος δὲ ἡ [13,10] τρίτη διὰ τὸ ἀτρέπτως ἔχειν τὰ κατ' αὐτὴν διατεταγμένα· ἡ δ' αὐτὴ δύναμις οἰκείως ἂν δόξαι τῶν τριῶν προσηγοριῶν τυγχάνειν. αὕτη δέ ἐστι καὶ Ἀδράστεια, ἤτοι παρὰ τὸ ἀνέκφευκτος καὶ ἀναπόδραστος εἶναι ὠνομασμένη ἢ παρὰ τὸ ἀεὶ δρᾶν τὰ καθ' αὑτήν, ὡσὰν ἀειδράστεια [13,15] οὖσα, ἢ τοῦ στερητικοῦ μορίου πλῆθος νῦν ἀποδηλοῦντος ὡς ἐν τῇ "ἀξύλῳ ὕλῃ"· πολυδράστεια γάρ ἐστι. Νέμεσις δὲ ἀπὸ τῆς νεμήσεως προσηγόρευται—διαιρεῖ γὰρ τὸ ἐπιβάλλον ἑκάστῳ—Τύχη δὲ ἀπὸ τοῦ τεύχειν ἡμῖν τὰς περιστάσεις καὶ τῶν συμπιπτόντων [13,20] τοῖς ἀνθρώποις δημιουργὸς εἶναι, Ὄπις δὲ ἀπὸ τοῦ λανθάνουσα καὶ ὥσπερ παρακολουθοῦσα ὄπισθεν καὶ [14,1] παρατηροῦσα τὰ πραττόμενα ὑφ' ἡμῶν κολάζειν τὰ κολάσεως ἄξια.

---

38. Lang (1881); Torres (2018) follows the manuscripts to read ἔργων ("of deeds").

(13) And Zeus is 'Lot' [*Moira*] because the distribution of the things that are assigned to each person is *not seen* [*mē hor(ōmenē)*]—which is why other portions are called "lots."[39] 'Destiny' [*aisa*] is the *unperceived* [*a-is(tos)*] and unknown cause of things that come about—in which case it indicates the obscurity of things considered piecemeal.[40] Or, according to earlier people,[41] it is *what always exists* [*aei ousa*]. What is 'fated' [*heimarmenē*] is that by which all the things that come about have been *seized* [*(me)mar(ptai)*] and put together in an order and series that has no limit—the syllable *hei-* contains the idea of "putting together," as in 'series' [*heirmos*]. 'Necessity' [*anankē*] is what it is impossible [sc. *an-*] to *break* [*axai*] and overcome; or it is the point to which everything that comes about *develops* [*anagōgē*]. In another approach, the tradition gives us three Lots, corresponding to the three aspects of time. One of them is named 'Klotho' from the fact that events are like the *spinning* [cf. *klōthein*] of fleeces: one thing comes on top of another (and this is also why they represent the spinner as the oldest).[42] Another is called 'Lachesis' from the fact that what is assigned to each person is like the *apportionment* [cf. *lach(ein)*] of what is allotted. The third is called 'Atropos' because the things arranged by her are *unchangeable* [*atrep(tōs)*]. It might appropriately seem that the three names all have the same force, which is 'Adrasteia,' named either because of being ineluctable and *inescapable* [*a(n)(apo)draston*] or from the fact that the things for which she is responsible are *always active* [*aei dran*], as if it were "Aiei-drasteia," or else the privative particle [i.e., initial *a-*] is indicative of magnitude in this case, as in the phrase "unharvested wood";[43] for it *does* a great deal [*(polu)drasteia*]. It is called 'Nemesis' from *distribution* [*nemēsis*]—for it divides out what happens to each person, 'Fortune' [*Tuchē*] from the fact that it *builds* [*teuchein*] our surroundings and is the craftsman of those things which befall men, and 'Opis' because it escapes notice and, as it were, follows *behind* [*opis(then)*] and keeps an eye on our actions, so as to punish those that are worthy of punishment.

---

39. See *SVF* 2.913.

40. Cf. *SVF* 2.966, 967.

41. The word for "earlier," *presbuteroi*, is used of Cornutus's philosophical predecessors at 76,6–7, and they might be in his mind here.

42. See Hesiod, [*Scut.*] 258.

43. Literally, a wood that has not been turned into useable timber—the idea perhaps being that for this very reason it is *richer* in (potential) timber (there is more to harvest just because it is "unharvested").

A.3.

(14) Λέγεται δ' ἐκ Μνημοσύνης γεννῆσαι τὰς Μούσας ὁ Ζεύς, ἐπειδὴ καὶ τῶν κατὰ παιδείαν μαθημάτων [14,5] αὐτὸς εἰσηγητὴς ἐγένετο, ἃ διὰ μελέτης καὶ κατοχῆς ἀναλαμβάνεσθαι πέφυκε ὡς ἀναγκαιότατα πρὸς τὸ εὖ ζῆν ὄντα. καλοῦνται δὲ Μοῦσαι ἀπὸ τῆς μώσεως, τουτέστι ζητήσεως, καθὸ εἴρηται "ὦ πονηρέ, μὴ τὰ μαλακὰ μῶσο, μὴ τὰ σκλήρ᾽ ἔχῃς." [14,10] ἐννέα δ' εἰσὶ διὰ τὸ τετραγώνους, ὥς φησί τις, καὶ περιττοὺς τοὺς προσήχοντας[44] αὐταῖς ἀποτελεῖν· τοιοῦτος γάρ ἐστιν ὁ τῶν ἐννέα ἀριθμός, συνιστάμενος κατὰ τὸ ἐφ᾽ ἑαυτὸν γεννᾶσθαι[45] τὸν πρῶτον ἀπὸ τῆς μονάδος τελειότητός τινος μετέχειν δοκοῦντα ἀριθμόν. [15,1] λέγονται δὲ παρά τισι καὶ δύο μόναι εἶναι, παρ᾽ οἷς δὲ τρεῖς, παρ᾽ οἷς δὲ τέτταρες, παρ᾽ οἷς δὲ ἑπτά· τρεῖς μὲν διὰ τὴν προειρημένην τῆς τριάδος τελειότητα ἢ καὶ διὰ τὸ τρία γένη σκεμμάτων εἶναι, δι᾽ ὧν [15,5] ὁ κατὰ φιλοσοφίαν λόγος συμπληροῦται· δύο δὲ ἀπὸ τοῦ θεωρεῖν τε καὶ πράττειν τὰ δέοντα ἐπιβάλλειν ἡμῖν καὶ ἐν δυσὶ τούτοις συνίστασθαι τὸ πεπαιδεῦσθαι· τέτταρες δὲ καὶ ἑπτὰ τάχα διὰ τὸ τὰ παλαιὰ τῶν μουσικῶν ὄργανα τοσούτους φθόγγους ἐσχηκέναι. [15,10] θήλειαι δὲ παρήχθησαν τῷ καὶ τὰς ἀρετὰς καὶ τὴν παιδείαν θηλυκὰ ὀνόματα ἐκ τύχης ἔχειν πρὸς σύμβολον τοῦ ἐξ ἐνδομενείας καὶ ἑδραιότητος τὴν πολυμάθειαν περιγίνεσθαι. σύνεισι δὲ καὶ συγχορεύουσιν ἀλλήλαις πρὸς παράστασιν τοῦ τὰς ἀρετὰς ἀχωρίστους [15,15] αὐτῶν καὶ ἀδιαζεύκτους εἶναι. περὶ δὲ τοὺς τῶν θεῶν ὕμνους καὶ τὴν θεραπείαν κατασχολοῦνται μάλιστα, ἐπειδὴ στοιχεῖον παιδείας ἐστὶ τὸ ἀφορᾶν πρὸς τὸ θεῖον καὶ τοῦθ᾽ ὑπόδειγμα τοῦ βίου ποιησαμένους ἀνὰ στόμα ἔχειν δεῖ. ἄλλως δὲ Κλειὼ μὲν μία [15,20] τῶν Μουσῶν ἐστιν ἀπὸ τοῦ κλέους τυγχάνειν

---

44. Torres (2018); προσέχοντας Lang (1881).

45. Osann (1844); Lang (1881) and Torres (2018) follow the manuscripts to read γενέσθαι, but this passage needs to be construed in such a way as to ascribe perfection to the number three, not nine, because it must be the object of the back reference at 15,3–4.

A.3. Education and Ethics

(14) Zeus is said to have been father of the Muses by Mnemosyne ["Memory"], since he was the author of those curricular subjects which are acquired through hard work and retention; they are the things most necessary for a good life. They are called 'Muses' [*Mousai*] from *seeking* [*mōsis*], that is, searching—in the sense of the line: "O wretch! Don't *seek* [*mōso*] the soft, don't hold the hard!"[46] They are nine because, as someone says, they render those who belong to them square [or: virtuous] and odd [or: learned]—that being what the number nine is like:[47] it is constituted when that number which seems to be the first, after one, to partake of some perfection [i.e., the number three] generates it from itself.[48] But some say that there are only two, some three, some four, others seven. Three because of the perfection of the triad, which has been mentioned, or because there are three kinds of investigation which make up a philosophical account of the world.[49] Two because it falls to us both to contemplate and to do what must be done,[50] and these two topics constitute education. Four and seven perhaps because the musical instruments of antiquity had that many strings. They were presented as women because the words for the virtues and for education happen to be feminine and symbolize the fact that learning comes from staying at home and from stability. They associate and dance with each other to show that the virtues are inseparable from each other and cannot be unyoked.[51] They spend time in particular in singing hymns and serving the gods, since it is a fundamental part of education to direct one's gaze away to the divine, and those who take it as their model for life ought to talk about it. In any case, 'Kleio' is

---

46. Epicharmus, *PCG* 1.236.

47. The number nine is the first odd square (or, if you prefer, the square of the first odd number); see, e.g., Plutarch, *Quaest. rom.* 288D; Theon, *On the Usefulness of Mathematics*, 106,3 (Hiller 1878). (Some manuscripts of Cornutus illustrate this with a block of nine alphas, three by three, drawn in the margin.) But the words for square and odd here can also be used of people, with the (positive) moral senses indicated—hence the point of the comparison with the Muses.

48. In other words: 3 x 3.

49. See Diogenes Laertius, *Vit. phil.* 7.39 = *SVF* 1.45, 2.37. The parts are: logic, physics, ethics.

50. Cornutus's answer to the question of whether we ought to live the contemplative or practical life. See the introduction, §1.4.3, with n. 71. Cf. 15,17–19 below, where we both contemplate and imitate the divine.

51. See *SVF* 1.200; 3.280.

τοὺς [16,1] πεπαιδευμένους καὶ αὐτούς τε καὶ ἑτέρους κλεΐζειν, Εὐτέρπη δὲ ἀπὸ τοῦ τὰς ὁμιλίας αὐτῶν ἐπιτερπεῖς καὶ ἀγωγοὺς εἶναι, Θάλεια δὲ ἤτοι διὰ τὸ θάλλειν αὐτῶν τὸν βίον ἢ διὰ τὸ ἔχειν αὐτοὺς καὶ τὴν συμποτικὴν [16,5] ἀρετὴν ἐπιδεξίως καὶ εὐμούσως ἐν ταῖς θαλείαις ἀναστρεφομένους, Μελπομένη δὲ ἀπὸ τῆς μολπῆς γλυκείας τινὸς φωνῆς μετὰ μέλους οὔσης—μέλπονται γὰρ ὑπὸ πάντων οἱ ἀγαθοὶ καὶ μέλπουσι καὶ αὐτοὶ τοὺς θεοὺς καὶ τοὺς πρὸ αὑτῶν γεγονότας—[16,10] Τερψιχόρη δὲ διὰ τὸ τέρπεσθαι καὶ χαίρειν αὐτοὺς τὸ πλεῖστον μέρος τοῦ βίου ἢ διὰ τὸ καὶ ἀπὸ τοῦ ὁρᾶσθαι παρέχειν τέρψιν τοῖς προσπελάζουσιν αὐτοῖς, ἑνὸς στοιχείου πλεονάζοντος ἐν τῷ ὀνόματι, τάχα δὲ ἐπεὶ καὶ χόρους ἵστασαν οἱ παλαιοὶ τοῖς θεοῖς, συντιθέντων [16,15] αὐτοῖς τὰς ᾠδὰς τῶν σοφωτάτων· ἡ δὲ Ἐρατὼ πότερον ἀπὸ τοῦ ἔρωτος λαβοῦσα τὴν ὀνομασίαν τὴν περὶ πᾶν εἶδος φιλοσοφίας ἐπιστροφὴν παρίστησιν ἢ τῆς περὶ τὸ ἔρεσθαι καὶ ἀποκρίνεσθαι δυνάμεως ἐπίσκοπός ἐστιν, ὡς δὴ διαλεκτικῶν ὄντων τῶν σπουδαίων· [16,20] Πολύμνια δέ ἐστιν ἡ πολυύμνητος ἀρετὴ ἢ μᾶλλον [17,1] ἴσως ἡ πολλοὺς ὑμνοῦσα καὶ ὅσα περὶ τῶν προγενεστέρων ὑμνεῖται παρειληφυῖα καὶ τῆς ἔκ τε ποιημάτων καὶ τῶν ἄλλων συγγραμμάτων ἱστορίας ἐπιμελουμένη. Οὐρανία δέ ἐστιν ἡ περὶ τὰ οὐράνια καὶ τὴν τῶν ὅλων [17,5] φύσιν ἐπιστήμη—τὸν γὰρ ὅλον κόσμον οὐρανὸν ἐκάλουν οἱ παλαιοί—Καλλιόπη δὲ ἡ καλλίφωνος καὶ καλλιεπὴς ῥητορική, δι' ἧς καὶ πολιτεύονται καὶ δήμοις προσφωνοῦσιν, ἄγοντες αὐτοὺς πειθοῖ καὶ οὐ βίᾳ ἐφ' ὅτι ἂν προαιρῶνται, δι' ἣν αἰτίαν ταύτην μάλιστά φησι [17,10] "βασιλεῦσιν ἅμ' αἰδοίοισιν ὀπηδεῖν." ἀποδίδοται[52] δὲ αὐταῖς ποικίλα ὄργανα, ἐμφαίνοντος ἑκάστου ὅτι ἥρμοσται καὶ σύμφωνος αὐτὸς ἑαυτῷ καὶ ὁμολογούμενος ὁ τῶν ἀγαθῶν βίος ἐστί. συγχορεύει δ' αὐταῖς ὁ Ἀπόλλων διὰ

---

52. Torres (2018), ἀποδίδονται Lang (1881).

one of the Muses because the educated obtain *renown* [*kleos*], and they themselves, along with others, *celebrate* them [*klei(zein)*].⁵³ 'Euterpe' is so called from the fact that associating with them is *pleasant* [*(epi)terpes*] and attractive, and 'Thaleia' because their life always *flourishes* [*thall(ein)*]—or because they also have the virtue of conviviality and conduct themselves with wit and decorum at *feasts* [*thaleiai*]. 'Melpomene' derives from the sweet *song* [*molpē*] which results when a voice has a tune—for the good are *sung* about [*melp(ontai)*] by everyone, and they themselves sing of the gods and of earlier men. 'Terpsichore' is so called because they *enjoy themselves* [*terp(esthai)*] and *rejoice* [*chair(ein)*] for most of their lives or because the very *sight* [*hor(asthai)*] of them gives *pleasure* [*terpsis*] to those who approach them. (In this case, one letter [i.e., -*c(h)*-] is redundant,⁵⁴ but perhaps it is there because the ancients instituted *dances* [*choroi*] for the gods, the wisest among them composing songs for them.) 'Erato' either takes her name from *love* [*erōtos*], because she cares about every kind of philosophy, or else she oversees the ability to *ask questions* [*er(esthai)*] and give answers, since the virtuous are skilled in dialectic. 'Polymnia' is virtue, whose *praises are much sung* [*polu-humnētos*], or rather, perhaps, she *sings the praises of many* [*pollous humnousa*], both having heard those things concerning our ancestors that are praised in song and pursuing her own research [into them] from poems and other writings. 'Ourania' is knowledge about the *heavenly* bodies [*ourania*] and the nature of the universe—for the ancients called the whole cosmos *heaven* [*ouranos*].⁵⁵ 'Kalliope' is rhetoric, which is beautiful of voice and *beautiful of word* [*kalliepēs*]; by this, men govern cities and address the people, leading them by persuasion, not force, to whatever they choose. This, in particular, is why Hesiod says that she "serves those who are kings and venerable."⁵⁶ Tradition assigns various instruments to them, each showing that the life of the good is well structured, harmonious with itself, and consistent.⁵⁷ Apollo dances with

---

53. I.e., the educated themselves celebrate educated people (cf. the good who sing about other good people in what follows).

54. I.e., the etymlogy is *terpsi-hor-*, with no semantic contribution made by -*c(h)*-.

55. Cf., perhaps, Plato, *Tim*. 28b: ὁ δὴ πᾶς οὐρανὸς ἢ κόσμος ἢ καὶ ἄλλο ὅτι ποτὲ ὀνομαζόμενος ("The whole heaven—or cosmos or whatever else it is called").

56. Hesiod, *Theog.* 79–80.

57. See *SVF* 3.674 (169,2–3) (structure); *SVF* 3.262 ad fin. and 293 (harmony). "Consistency" (*homologoumenos*; cf. *homologia* at 25,9–11) probably refers to the Stoic definition of virtue as consistency of one's (internal) disposition (Diogenes Laertius, *Vit. phil.* 7.89 = *SVF* 3.197) or of one's rationality (*SVF* 1.202), so that it is

τὴν κοινωνίαν τῆς μουσικῆς· [17,15] παραδέδοται γὰρ καὶ οὗτος κιθαριστὴς δι᾽ ἣν εἴσῃ μετ᾽ ὀλίγον αἰτίαν. ἐν δὲ τοῖς ὄρεσί φασι χορεύειν, ἐπειδὴ χρείαν ἔχουσι τοῦ μονάζειν καὶ συνεχῶς εἰς τὴν ἐρημίαν ἀναχωρεῖν οἱ φιλομαθοῦντες, "ἧς χωρὶς οὐδὲν σεμνὸν ἐξευρίσκεται" [17,20] κατὰ τὸν κωμικόν. τούτου δ᾽ ἕνεκεν καὶ ἐπὶ ἐννέα νύκτας λέγεται συγγενόμενος τῇ Μνημοσύνῃ ὁ Ζεὺς γεννῆσαι [18,1] αὐτάς· καὶ γὰρ τῆς ἐν νυκτὶ ζητήσεως δεῖ πρὸς τὰ κατὰ παιδείαν· εὐφρόνην γοῦν οὐ δι᾽ ἄλλο τι οἱ ποιηταὶ τὴν νύκτα ἐκάλεσαν, καὶ ὁ Ἐπίχαρμος αὐτίκα "αἴ τί κα, φησί, ζατῇς σοφόν, τᾶς νυκτος ἐνθυμητέον,"[58] [18,5] καὶ "πάντα τὰ σπουδαῖα νυκτὸς μᾶλλον ἐξευρίσκεται." τινὲς δ᾽ Οὐρανοῦ καὶ Γῆς ἔφασαν αὐτὰς φῦναι ὡς ἀρχαιότατον ἡγεῖσθαι τὸν περὶ τούτων λόγον δέοντος. στεφανοῦνται δὲ φοίνικι, ὡς μέν τινες νομίζουσιν, [18,10] διὰ τὴν ὁμωνυμίαν, ἀπὸ τοῦ Φοινίκων δοκεῖν εὕρημα εἶναι τὰ γράμματα, ὡς δ᾽ εὐλογώτερόν ἐστ᾽ ἔχειν, διὰ τὸ τρυφερὸν καὶ εὐερνὲς καὶ ἀείζωον καὶ δυσανάβατον καὶ γλυκύκαρπον τοῦ φυτοῦ.

(15) Ἐπιβάλλοντος δ᾽ ἡμῖν, ὡς εἴρηται, καὶ εὐεργετικοῖς [8,15] εἶναι, παραδεδώκασιν οἱ πλεῖστοι Διὸς θυγατέρας [19,1] τὰς Χάριτας οἱ μὲν ἐξ Εὐρυδόμης αὐτῷ γεγονυίας τῷ μάλιστα ἐξ εὐρέων καὶ διαβεβηκότων δόμων τὰς δωρεὰς φιλεῖν δίδοσθαι, οἱ δ᾽ ἐξ Εὐρυνόμης, καὶ τούτου παριστάντος ὅτι χαριστικώτεροί πώς εἰσιν ἢ [19,5] ὀφείλουσιν εἶναι οἱ μεγάλους κλήρους νεμόμενοι, τινὲς δ᾽ ἐξ Εὐρυμεδούσης, εἰς ταὐτὸ συντείνοντος καὶ τούτου τοῦ ἐτύμου, κυριεύουσι γὰρ τῶν ἰδίων οἱ ἄνθρωποι· τὴν δ᾽ Ἥραν ἄλλοι διδόασιν αὐταῖς μητέρα, ἵν᾽ εὐγενέσταται τῶν θεῶν ὦσιν, ὡς περὶ τῶν πράξεών εἰσι. πρὸς [19,10] ἄλλην δὲ ἔμφασιν γυμναὶ παρεισάγονται, ὡς καὶ τῶν μηδὲν κτῆμα ἐχόντων ὑπουργεῖν τινα ὠφελίμως χαρίζεσθαι πολλὰ δυναμένων καὶ οὐ περιουσιάζεσθαι πάντως, ἵνα τις εὐεργετικὸς ᾖ, δέοντος, ὡς εἴρηται καὶ τὸ

---

58. Torres (2018); αἴτε τι, φησί, ζατεῖ σοφόν τις, νυκτὸς ἐνθυμητέον Lang (1881).

them because of his affiliation with the arts. Tradition has it that he plays the kithara, for a reason you will learn in a little while.[59] They say that they dance in the mountains because those who love learning need to be alone and are always going into the wilderness, "without which nothing holy is discovered" as the comic poet has it.[60] Because of this, Zeus is said to have fathered them during nine nights of intercourse with Mnemosyne: nighttime research is necessary for the business of education. This, anyway, is why the poets called night "kindly"; and Epicharmus, then, says: "If there is wisdom you seek, consider it at night" and "All serious answers are best found at night."[61] Some say that they were born from Heaven and Earth, since one must think that the account of them is the most ancient. They are crowned with palm because, some think, of its homonym: writing is thought to have been an invention of the Phoenicians.[62] But it is more reasonable to hold that it is because the palm is a delicate plant, vigorous, perennial, difficult to climb, but sweet of fruit.

(15) Since, as has been said, we are capable of beneficial activity, too, the greater part of the tradition has it that that the Graces are the daughters of Zeus.[63] Some were born to him by 'Eurydome' because a love of giving gifts is especially characteristic of *wide* [*eureis*] and expansive *homes* [*domoi*]; some from 'Eurynome,' which establishes that those who are *apportioned* [*nemo*(*menoi*)] more as their lot are, or ought to be, more generous; and some from 'Eurymedousa,' for just the reason suggested by its etymology;[64] for men are masters of their own possessions. Others say that Hera was their mother, so that they might be the most noble of the gods by birth, as they are by their deeds. They are presented naked to make another point, which is that even those who have no possessions are able to provide help with some things, to do many useful favors, and that one does not have to be really wealthy in order to be a benefactor—as it is said:

---

effectively a gloss on the notions associated with it here, that is, of structure and of harmony *with oneself* (αὐτὸς ἑαυτῷ; 17,12) (see Torres 2016, 192). But it might be that we should see a slightly more allusive reference to the standard Stoic definition of the ethical end as "living consistently," i.e., *with nature* (e.g., *SVF* 3.16; see Rocca-Serra 1963, 349).

59. See 67,17–68,3 below.
60. *PCG* 8.143 (unidentified source).
61. *PCG* 1.259.1 and 1.259.2, respectively.
62. The word for "palm," *phoenix*, is the same as the word for "Phoenician."
63. See 10,2 above.
64. I.e., *eurus* ("wide") + *medeōn* ("guardian"/"ruler").

"ξενίων δέ τε θυμὸς ἄριστος"· [19,15] τινὲς δὲ οἴονται διὰ τῆς γυμνητείας αὐτῶν παρίστασθαι τὸ εὐλύτως καὶ ἀνεμποδίστως δεῖν ἔχειν πρὸς τὸ χαρίζεσθαι. λέγονται δ' ὑφ' ὧν μὲν δύο εἶναι, ὑφ' ὧν δὲ τρεῖς· δύο μέν, ἐπειδὴ τοὺς μὲν προκατάρχειν δεῖ χάριτος, τοὺς δὲ ἀμείβεσθαι· τρεῖς δέ, ἐπειδὴ [19,20] καλῶς ἔχει τὸν τετευχότα ἀμοιβῆς ἑστάναι πάλιν χαριστικῶς, ἵνα ἀκαταπαύστως τοῦτο γίνηται, τοιοῦτόν τι καὶ τῆς χορείας αὐτῶν ἐμφαινούσης. ἕτεροι δ' ἔφασαν [20,1] μίαν μὲν εἶναι Χάριν τὴν περὶ τὸν ὑπουργοῦντά τι ὠφελίμως, ἑτέραν δὲ τὴν περὶ τὸν δεχόμενον τὴν ὑπουργίαν καὶ ἐπιτηροῦντα τὸν καιρὸν τῆς ἀμοιβῆς, τρίτην δὲ τὴν περὶ τὸν ἀνθυπουργοῦντά τι καθ' αὑτὸν [20,5] ἐν καιρῷ. ἱλαρῶς δὲ εὐεργετεῖν δέοντος καὶ ἱλαροὺς ποιουσῶν τοὺς εὐεργετουμένους τῶν Χαρίτων, πρῶτον μὲν κοινῶς ἀπὸ τῆς χαρᾶς πᾶσαι Χάριτες ὠνομασμέναι εἰσί· καὶ εὔμορφοι δὲ λέγονται εἶναι καὶ εὐήδειαν καὶ πιθανότητα χαρίζεσθαι· εἶτα κατ' ἰδίαν [20,10] ἡ μὲν Ἀγλαΐα προσηγόρευται, ἡ δὲ Θάλεια, ἡ δὲ Εὐφροσύνη, διὰ τοῦτο ἐνίων καὶ Εὐάνθην φησάντων μητέρα αὐτῶν εἶναι, τινῶν δ' Αἴγλην. συνοικεῖν δ' Ὅμηρος ἔφη μίαν τῶν Χαρίτων τῷ Ἡφαίστῳ διὰ τὸ ἐπιχάριτα εἶναι τὰ τεχνικὰ ἔργα.

(16) [20,15] Ἡγεμόνα δὲ παραδιδόασιν αὐτῶν τὸν Ἑρμῆν, ἐμφαίνοντες ὅτι εὐλογίστως χαρίζεσθαι δεῖ καὶ μὴ εἰκῆ, ἀλλὰ τοῖς ἀξίοις· ὁ γὰρ ἀχαριστηθεὶς ὀκνηρότερος γίνεται πρὸς τὸ εὐεργετεῖν. τυγχάνει δὲ ὁ Ἑρμῆς ὁ λόγος ὤν, ὃν ἀπέστειλαν πρὸς ἡμᾶς ἐξ οὐρανοῦ οἱ [20,20] θεοί, μόνον τὸν ἄνθρωπον[65] τῶν ἐπὶ γῆς ζώων λογικὸν ποιήσαντες, ὃ παρὰ τἆλλα ἐξοχώτατον εἶχον αὐτοί. ὠνόμασται δὲ ἀπὸ τοῦ ἐρεῖν μήσασθαι, ὅπερ ἐστὶ λέγειν, ἢ ἀπὸ τοῦ ἔρυμα ἡμῶν εἶναι καὶ οἷον ὀχύρωμα. ἀλλ' [21,1] ἐνθένδε πρῶτον μὲν διάκτορος κέκληται ἤτοι ἀπὸ τοῦ διάτορος εἶναι καὶ τρανὸς ἢ ἀπὸ τοῦ διάγειν τὰ νοήματα ἡμῶν εἰς τὰς τῶν πλησίον ψυχάς· καθὸ καὶ τὰς γλώττας αὐτῷ καθιεροῦσιν. εἶτα ἐριούνιος ἐπονομάζεται [21,5] ἀπὸ τοῦ μεγαλωφελής τις εἶναι καὶ καθ' ὑπερβολὴν ὀνεῖν[66] τοὺς χρωμένους αὐτῷ καὶ σῶκος ὡσὰν σωτὴρ τῶν οἴκων ὑπάρχων ἤ, ὥς τινες, ἰσχυρός. καὶ τὸ ἀκάκητα δὲ αὐτὸν λέγεσθαι τοιούτου

---

65. Torres (2018); ἀνθρώπων Lang (1881).
66. Torres (2018); ἰσχύειν Lang (1881).

"In the gifts of a friend, it's the thought that counts."[67] And some think that their nakedness indicates that one must be at ease and unencumbered in order to do favors. They are said by some to be two in number, but by others to be three: two, counting those who first do the favor and those who repay it, but three because it is good when someone who has been repaid does another favor, so that there is no end to it. (Their dance illustrates something of the sort as well.) Others have said that there is one Grace to represent the man who does some useful service, another for the recipient of the service who looks out for the appropriate moment to repay it, and a third for the person who does his own service in return at the appropriate moment. Since one should do good deeds cheerfully, and since favors make their beneficiaries cheerful, first, the 'Graces' [*Charites*] were named in common from *joy* [*chara*] (and they are said to be beautiful and to favor people with charm and persuasiveness), but then, as individuals, they were called Aglaia ["Splendour"], Thaleia ["Plenty"], and Euphrosyne ["Cheer"]—some saying, because of this, that Euanthe ["Blooming"] is their mother, others Aigle ["Radiance"]. Homer says that one of the Graces lives with Hephaestus[68] because the technical arts give pleasure.

(16) The tradition gives Hermes as their leader, showing that one's favors must be reasonable—not given at random, but to those who are worthy of them, since someone who meets with a lack of gratitude becomes more reluctant to do good in the future. And 'Hermes' happens to be reason, the preeminent possession of the gods, which they sent to us from heaven, making man alone of the terrestrial animals rational.[69] He is named from *contriving to speak* [*er*(*ein*) *mēs*(*asthai*)], that is, to talk, or from being our *bulwark* [*eruma*] and stronghold, so to speak. In addition, he is called, first of all, 'Diaktoros,' either from being *piercing* [*diatoros*] and distinct, or from *conducting* [*diag*(*ein*)] our thoughts into the souls of those nearby—which is why they dedicate tongues to him. Secondly, he is called 'Eriounios,' from being a great help and profiting beyond measure those who use it [reason],[70] and 'stout' [*sōkos*], as being the *savior* [*sō*(*tēr*)] of homes—or, as some say, *strong* [*ischuros*]. Calling him 'guileless' [*akakēs*] signifies something similar; for reason is not [sc. *a*-] for doing *evil*

---

67. Source unidentifiable.
68. Homer, *Il.* 18.382–383.
69. See *SVF* 2.714, 725.
70. The etymology suggested combines the prefix is *eri*- ("exceedingly") with *ōnos* (price).

τινὸς σημεῖόν ἐστιν· οὐ γὰρ πρὸς τὸ κακοῦν καὶ βλάπτειν, [21,10] ἀλλὰ πρὸς τὸ σώζειν μᾶλλον γέγονεν ὁ λόγος, ὅθεν καὶ τὴν Ὑγίειαν αὐτῷ συνῴκισαν. ἀργειφόντης δέ ἐστιν οἷον ἀργεφάντης ἀπὸ τοῦ λευκῶς πάντα φαίνειν καὶ σαφηνίζειν—τὸ γὰρ λευκὸν ἀργὸν ἐκάλουν οἱ παλαιοί—ἢ ἀπὸ τῆς κατὰ τὴν φωνὴν ταχυτῆτος—καὶ [21,15] γὰρ τὸ ταχὺ ἀργὸν λέγεται—χρυσόρραπις δέ, ὅτι πολύτιμός ἐστι καὶ ὁ ἐξ αὐτοῦ ῥαπισμός, πολλοῦ γὰρ ἄξιαί εἰσιν εὔκαιροι νουθεσίαι καὶ ἐπιστροφὴ τῶν προσεχόντων αὐταῖς. παραδέδοται δὲ καὶ κῆρυξ θεῶν καὶ διαγγέλλειν αὐτὸν ἔφασαν τὰ παρ' ἐκείνων τοῖς ἀνθρώποις, [21,20] κῆρυξ μέν, ἐπειδὴ διὰ φωνῆς γεγωνοῦ παριστᾷ [22,1] τὰ κατὰ τὸν λόγον σημαινόμενα ταῖς ἀκοαῖς, ἄγγελος δέ, ἐπεὶ τὸ βούλημα τῶν θεῶν γινώσκομεν ἐκ τῶν ἐνδεδομένων ἡμῖν κατὰ τὸν λόγον ἐννοιῶν. πέδιλα δὲ φέρει πτερωτὰ καὶ δι' ἀέρος φέρεται συμφώνως τῷ [22,5] καθὼς εἴρηται τὰ ἔπη πτερόεντα· καὶ γὰρ τὴν Ἶριν ποδήνεμον διὰ τοῦτο καὶ ἀελλόποδα καλοῦσιν ἄγγελον, καὶ ἀπὸ τοῦ ὀνόματος παρεισάγοντες, ψυχοπομπὸν δὲ τὸν Ἑρμῆν ἐμύθευσαν εἶναι συμβάλλοντες, ὅπερ ἴδιον αὐτοῦ ἐστι, τὸ ψυχαγωγεῖν· διὰ τοῦτο γοῦν [22,10] καὶ ῥάβδον αὐτῷ ἐγχειρίζουσι, "τῇ τ' ἀνδρῶν ὄμματα θέλγει," τὰ τῆς διανοίας δηλονότι, "ὧν ἐθέλῃ, τοὺς δ' αὖτε καὶ ὑπνώοντας ἐγείρει"· καὶ παρορμᾶν γὰρ ῥᾳδίως τοὺς παρειμένους καὶ καταστέλλειν [22,15] τοὺς παρωρμημένους δυνατός ἐστιν. ἐντεῦθεν ἤδη καὶ τοὺς ὀνείρους ἐπιπέμπειν ἔδοξε καὶ μάντις εἶναι διὰ τοῦ τοιούτου τρόπου,[71] τρέπων ὡς βούλεται τὰς φαντασίας· "θεῶν δ' ἄγγελοι καὶ οἱ ὄνειροι." οἱ δ' ἀποπληροῦντες περὶ τὴν εἰρημένην ῥάβδον τὸ τοῦ κηρυκείου [22,20] σχῆμα δράκοντες σύμβολόν εἰσι τοῦ καὶ τοὺς θηριώδεις ὑπ' αὐτοῦ κηλεῖσθαι καὶ καταθέλγεσθαι, [23,1] λύοντος τὰς ἐν αὐτοῖς διαφορὰς καὶ συνδέοντος αὐτοὺς ἅμματι δυσλύτῳ· διὰ τοῦτο γὰρ καὶ εἰρηνοποιὸν δοκεῖ

---

71. διὰ τοῦ τρόπου del. Lang (1881), Torres (2018).

[*kak(oun)*] and harming but rather for sustaining—which is why they have Health live with him. And he is 'Argeiphontes,' as if the word were *argephantes*, because it *illuminates* [*phae(nien)*] everything brightly and *clarifies* [(*sa*)*phēn*(*izein*)] it—for the ancients used the word *argos* for 'bright,' or else because of the speed of sound, since *argos* means 'swift' as well. And he is Hermes 'of the Golden Wand' [*Chrusorrapis*] because even to be *struck* [*rapis*(*mos*)] by it [reason] is very valuable, since timely admonitions are worth a great deal, as is the repentance of those who take heed of them. The tradition makes him the herald of the gods, and he was said to announce their doings to men. He is a herald because a herald uses a loud voice to present rational meaning to an audience, and he is a messenger because we know the will of the gods from the concepts rationally instilled in us.[72] That he wears winged sandals and is carried through the air is consistent with the idea of 'winged words,' as they have been called.[73] (Iris is also for this reason called 'wind-footed' and 'whirlwind-footed' messenger—also on the basis of her name.)[74] And mythology represents Hermes as the Conductor of Souls, associating with him its proper task of guiding souls. Anyway, this is why they put in his hand a wand "with which he charms the eyes of those men he wishes" (obviously the eyes of the mind) "but again rouses others, even the sleeping."[75] For those who are slack, it [reason] is able to urge on, and those who have been stirred up it brings to order. This is why it was thought that he sends dreams as well and tells the future by this means, altering impressions as he wishes: "And dreams, too, are messengers of the gods."[76] And the snakes which twine around and complete the aforementioned wand, the wand which looks like a messenger's wand, are a symbol of the fact that the savage, too, are bewitched and charmed by it [reason]; it resolves their differences and binds them together with a knot which is hard to undo. For this reason the herald's wand seems to be

---

72. The point does not seem to be so much that we possess *innate* or *naturally acquired* concepts (e.g., *SVF* 2.83; or what are sometimes called *preconceptions*: *SVF* 3.69) because the immediate concern is with the operation of reason rather than its formation. Instead, it seems to refer more generally to the empiricist processes by which a rational being acquires concepts that accurately represent the world. (That would be a point worth making against Platonists, who actively deny the possibility that one can have such *concepts* without recollection of the forms; see Boys-Stones 2018, ch. 13.)

73. *Passim* in Homer.

74. "Iris" suggests *eirein*, to speak.

75. Homer, *Il*. 24.333–334 = *Od*. 5.47–48 = *Od*. 24.3–4.

76. Cf. Homer, *Il*. 2.26.

τὸ κηρύκειον εἶναι. φέρουσι δ' ἄλλως οἱ μετιόντες τὴν εἰρήνην καὶ θαλλοὺς μετὰ χεῖρας πρὸς ὑπόμνησιν τοῦ [23,5] γεωργεῖσθαι θέλειν τὴν χώραν καὶ φειδώ τινα εἶναι τῶν ἡμέρων καὶ καρποφόρων φυτῶν. ἐκ δὲ Μαίας ἔφασαν γεγεννῆσθαι Διὶ τὸν Ἑρμῆν ὑποδηλοῦντες πάλιν διὰ τούτου θεωρίας καὶ ζητήσεως γέννημα εἶναι τὸν λόγον· καὶ γὰρ αἱ μαιούμεναι τὰς γυναῖκας ἐντεῦθεν [23,10] εἴρηνται μαῖαι τῷ ὡσὰν ἐξ ἐρεύνης προάγειν εἰς φῶς τὰ βρέφη. πλάττεται δὲ ἄχειρ καὶ ἄπους καὶ τετράγωνος τῷ σχήματι ὁ Ἑρμῆς, τετράγωνος μὲν τῷ ἑδραῖόν τι καὶ ἀσφαλὲς ἔχειν ὥστε καὶ τὰς πτώσεις αὐτοῦ βάσεις εἶναι, ἄχειρ δὲ καὶ ἄπους, ἐπεὶ [23,15] οὔτε χειρῶν οὔτε ποδῶν δεῖται πρὸς τὸ ἀνύειν τὸ προκείμενον αὐτῷ. οἱ δ' ἀρχαῖοι τοὺς μὲν πρεσβυτέρους καὶ γενειῶντας Ἑρμᾶς ὀρθὰ ἐποίουν τὰ αἰδοῖα ἔχοντας, τοὺς δὲ νεωτέρους καὶ λείους παρειμένα, παριστάντες ὅτι ἐν τοῖς προβεβηκόσι ταῖς ἡλικίαις γόνιμος ὁ λόγος [23,20] καὶ τέλειός ἐστιν, ὃς δὴ καὶ τυχὸν τῷ ὄντι ἐστὶ τυγχάνων ὧν ἂν πρόθηται, ἐν δὲ τοῖς ἀώροις ἄγονος καὶ ἀτελής. ἵδρυται δὲ ἐν ταῖς ὁδοῖς καὶ ἐνόδιος λέγεται [24,1] καὶ ἡγεμόνιος ὡς αὐτῷ δέοντος πρὸς πᾶσαν πρᾶξιν ἡγεμόνι χρῆσθαι καὶ αὐτοῦ ὄντος τοῦ ἐν ταῖς βουλαῖς εἰς τὴν δέουσαν ἡμᾶς ὁδὸν ἀνάγοντος, τάχα δὲ καὶ ἐπεὶ ἐρημίας πρὸς τὴν ἐπισκευὴν αὐτοῦ καὶ [24,5] τὴν θεραπείαν δεῖ. διὰ δὲ τὸ κοινὸν αὐτὸν εἶναι καὶ τὸν αὐτὸν ἔν τε τοῖς ἀνθρώποις πᾶσι καὶ ἐν τοῖς θεοῖς, ὁπόταν τις εὕρῃ τι προάγων ἐν ὁδῷ, συνήθως ἐπιφθέγγεται[77] τὸ κοινὸν εἶναι τὸν Ἑρμῆν, ὃς δὴ συνίστωρ ἐστὶ τῆς εὑρέσεως ἐνόδιος ὤν, ἐμφαίνοντες ὅτι [24,10] κοινὸν ἀξιοῦσιν εἶναι καὶ τὸ εὑρημένον, ἐντεῦθεν καὶ τῶν εὑρημάτων ἑρμαίων λεγομένων. προσσωρεύουσι δὲ τοὺς λίθους τοῖς Ἑρμαῖς ἑκάστου τῶν παριόντων ἕνα τινὰ αὐτοῖς προστιθέντος ἤτοι ὡς χρήσιμόν τι τὸ παρ' αὐτὸν ἑκάστου καὶ κοινωνικὸν ποιοῦντος διὰ τοῦ [24,15] καθαίρειν τὴν ὁδὸν εἴτε μαρτυροποιουμένου τὸν Ἑρμῆν εἴτε ὡς ἐπισημαινομένου τὴν εἰς αὐτὸν τιμήν, εἰ μηδὲν ἄλλο ἔχει προσενεγκεῖν αὐτῷ, εἴτε ἐκδηλότερον τοῖς παριοῦσι τὸ ἀφίδρυμα ποιοῦντος εἴτε πρὸς [25,1] σύμβολον τοῦ ἐκ μικρῶν μερῶν συνεστάναι τὸν προφορικὸν λόγον. λέγεται δὲ καὶ ἀγοραῖος πρῶτος[78] εἰκότως· ἐπίσκοπος γὰρ τῶν ἀγορευόντων

---

77. Torres (2018); ἐπιφθέγγονται Lang (1881).
78. πρῶτος del. Lang (1881), Torres (2018).

a 'peacemaker.' (In any case, those who pursue peace also carry branches in their hands, as a reminder that the land wishes to be cultivated and to spare young and fruitful plants.) They said that Hermes was born to Zeus from 'Maia,' again suggesting through this that reason is the offspring of contemplation and inquiry; those who help women *deliver* [*maioumenai*] are thus called *midwives* [*maiai*] because, as in the case of inquiry, they bring something to light—the fetus.[79] Sculptures of Hermes lack hands and feet and are square in shape—square because there is something so steadfast and secure about it that however it falls, it serves as a basis.[80] He lacks hands and feet because it does not need hands or feet to complete the tasks before it. The ancients made the genitals of the older, bearded Herms erect, but those of the younger, smooth ones hang down: this shows that reason is fertile and ready in those advanced in age and might actually attain the goals it sets, but in the immature, it is infertile and imperfect. He is set up *on roads* [*en hodois*] and is called 'Wayside' [*enodios*] and 'Guiding,' as it is necessary to use it as *guide* in every action, and because it leads us in our planning down the path we need, and perhaps also because it needs solitude to be refreshed and cultivated. Because reason is shared, and the same in all men and in the gods, it is customary for someone who finds something as he goes along a road to say 'Hermes in common!' (Hermes of the Wayside being in fact witness to the find). This shows that people reckon the thing found to be common property—and so found objects are called *hermaia*. And people heap stones up in front of Herms, each passerby adding a stone, whether because this is a useful public service done by each individual (it clears the road), or because it invokes Hermes as a witness, or because it is a mark of honor to him (if one has nothing else to bring to him), or because it makes the statue more conspicuous to passersby, or because it acts as a symbol that uttered speech is made up of small elements. He is also, reasonably, the first to be called god 'of the Agora'; for

---

79. The thought has its root in Socrates's famous comparison of himself to a midwife, *maia* (Plato, *Theaet.* 149a).

80. The immediate point here concerns the geometrical stability of the cube, of course, but there are two further layers of meaning. (1) The word for "falls," *ptōseis*, can refer to the different ways in which cubic dice can fall, providing different but equally legitimate starting points for the players' next moves (see, e.g., Plato, *Rep.* 604c). (2) The link to reason comes in the fact that *ptōseis* can also be grammatical cases or (probably most to the point here) syllogistic moods. The point would be that arguments in different moods give formally diverse but equally secure bases for decision making. (For the general point, see Heraclitus, *All.* 72.6.)

ἐστίν· ἤδη δὲ ἀπὸ τῆς ἀγορᾶς διατείνει καὶ εἰς τοὺς ἀγοράζοντάς τι [25,5] ἢ πιπράσκοντας, ὡς πάντα μετὰ λόγου ποιεῖν δέοντος· ἐντεῦθεν καὶ τῶν ἐμποριῶν ἐπιστάτης ἔδοξεν εἶναι καὶ ἐμπολαῖος καὶ κερδῷος ἐπωνομάσθη, ὡσὰν μόνος τῶν ἀληθινῶν κερδῶν αἴτιος ὢν τοῖς ἀνθρώποις. τῆς δὲ λύρας εὑρετής ἐστιν οἷον τῆς συμφωνίας καὶ [25,10] ὁμολογίας καθ' ἣν οἱ ζῶντες εὐδαιμονοῦσιν, ἡρμοσμένην ἔχειν τὴν διάθεσιν ἐπιβάλλοντος. παραστῆσαι δὲ αὐτοῦ τὴν δύναμιν καὶ διὰ τῶν ἀπεμφαινόντων θέλοντες κλέπτην αὐτὸν παρέδωκαν καὶ Δολίου Ἑρμοῦ βωμὸν ἔνιοι ἱδρύσαντο· λανθάνει γὰρ ὑφαιρούμενος τὰ [25,15] προδεδογμένα τοῖς ἀνθρώποις καὶ κλέπτων ἔσθ' ὅτε τῇ πιθανότητι τὴν ἀλήθειαν, ὅθεν τινὰς καὶ ἐπικλόποις λόγοις χρῆσθαι λέγουσι· καὶ γὰρ τὸ σοφίζεσθαι τῶν εἰδότων λόγῳ χρῆσθαι ἴδιόν ἐστι. νόμιος δὲ λέγεται τῷ ἐπ' ἐπανορθώσει λόγος εἶναι, προστακτικὸς [25,20] ὢν τῶν ὡς ἐν κοινωνίᾳ ποιητέων καὶ ἀπαγορευτικὸς τῶν οὐ ποιητέων· διὰ γοῦν τὴν ὁμωνυμίαν μετήχθη καὶ ἐπὶ τὴν τῶν νομῶν ἐπιμέλειαν. σέβονται δ' αὐτὸν [26,1] καὶ ἐν ταῖς παλαίστραις μετὰ τοῦ Ἡρακλέους ὡς τῇ ἰσχύϊ μετὰ λογισμοῦ χρῆσθαι δέοντος· τῷ γὰρ μόνῃ πεποιθότι τῇ τοῦ σώματος δυνάμει, τοῦ δὲ λόγου, ὃς καὶ τέχνας ἐπήγαγεν εἰς τὸν βίον, ἀμελοῦντι πάνυ ἂν [26,5] τις οἰκείως ἐπείποι· "δαιμόνιε, φθίσει σε τὸ σὸν μένος."

B.1.

(17) Τοῦ δὲ πολλὰς καὶ ποικίλας περὶ θεῶν γεγονέναι παρὰ τοῖς παλαιοῖς Ἕλλησι μυθοποιΐας, ὡς ἄλλαι μὲν παρὰ Μάγοις γεγόνασιν, ἄλλαι δὲ παρὰ

he is overseer of *public speakers* [*agoreuontes*]. And from the 'agora,' he also extends to those who *trade* [*agorazontes*] and sell, as everything should be done in line with reason. From here he came to be thought of as the superintendent of the markets and was named god "of Business" and 'of Profit' [*kerdōios*], since it [reason] alone is the cause of true *profit* [*kerdos*] for men. He is the inventor of the lyre, as of the harmony and consistency by which those alive are happy, when it falls to them to have a well-adjusted disposition.[81] Some people wished to establish his power through incongruous images as well and made it part of the tradition that he was a thief, and there are those who build altars to Hermes the Deceitful because it stealthily erases the beliefs a man previously held,[82] and there are times when, by persuasion, it steals away the truth—in cases where it is said that someone is using "thieving words." And in fact the ability to use sophisms belongs to people who know how to use reason. He is called god 'of Law' [*nomios*] because the purpose of reason is rectification; it is prescriptive of those things that must, for the good of the community, be done and proscriptive of things not to be done.[83] (It is thanks to homonymy that he has been appropriated for the care of *pastures* [*nomoi*] as well.)[84] He is also honored in the wrestling grounds alongside Heracles because along with strength, one ought to employ reasoning; to someone trusting only in the power of the body, but neglecting reason (which also gave us the [technical] arts), one might very properly say, "Fool: your own strength destroys you!"[85]

B. Wisdom and Its Transmission

B.1. Theological Traditions

(17) That many and various myths about the gods arose among the ancient Greeks, as others among the Magi, others among the Phrygians, and again

---

81. See n. 57 above.
82. This might be a good or a bad thing, of course. Persius suggests that Cornutus himself taught by stealth (*Sat.* 5.37).
83. See, e.g., *SVF* 3.332.
84. The words for "law" (*nómos*) and "pasture" (*nomós*) are phonetically identical, although they differ in accent. So this is an example of a confusion in the tradition; Cornutus explains how Hermes comes to be associated with pasture, although this has nothing to do with *reason*.
85. Homer, *Il.* 6.407.

[26,10] Φρυξὶ καὶ ἤδη παρ' Αἰγυπτίοις τε καὶ Κελτοῖς καὶ Λίβυσι καὶ τοῖς ἄλλοις ἔθνεσι, μαρτύριον ἂν λάβοι τις καὶ τὸ παρ' Ὁμήρῳ λεγόμενον ὑπὸ τοῦ Διὸς πρὸς τὴν Ἥραν τοῦτον τὸν τρόπον· "ἢ οὐ μέμνῃ ὅτε τ' ἐκρέμω ὑψόθεν, ἐκ δὲ ποδοῖιν [26,15] ἄκμονας ἧκα δύω." ἔοικε γὰρ ὁ ποιητὴς μυθοῦ παλαιοῦ παραφέρειν τοῦτο ἀπόσπασμα, καθ' ὃν ὁ Ζεὺς ἐμυθεύετο κεκρεμακέναι τε ἐκ τοῦ αἰθέρος τὴν Ἥραν χρυσαῖς ἁλύσεσι τῷ χρυσοφανές τι ἔχειν τὰ ἄστρα καὶ ἐκ τῶν ποδῶν [26,20] αὐτῆς δύο ἄκμονας ἐξηρτηκέναι, τὴν γῆν δηλονότι καὶ [27,1] τὴν θάλατταν, ὑφ' ὧν τείνεται κάτω ὁ ἀὴρ μηδετέρωθεν ἀποσπασθῆναι δυνάμενος. ἑτέρου δὲ μύθου μέμνηται τοῦ κατὰ τὴν Θέτιν, ὡς ὑπ' αὐτῆς σεσωσμένου τοῦ Διός, [27,5] "ὁππότε μιν ξυνδῆσαι Ὀλύμπιοι ἤθελον ἄλλοι, Ἥρη τ' ἠδὲ Ποσειδάων καὶ Παλλὰς Ἀθήνη." φαίνεται δ' ὅτι κατ' ἰδίαν ἕκαστος τούτων τῶν θεῶν ἐπεβούλευε τῷ Διΐ συνεχῶς μέλλων ἐμποδίζειν ταύτην τὴν διακόσμησιν ὅπερ ἐγένετο, εἰ τὸ ὑγρὸν ἐπεκράτησε [27,10] καὶ ἐξυδατώθη πάντα ἢ τὸ πῦρ καὶ ἐξεπυρώθη ἢ ὁ ἀήρ. ἡ δὲ κατὰ τρόπον διαθεῖσα πάντα Θέτις τὸν ἑκατόγχειρα Βριάρεων ἀντέταξε τοῖς εἰρημένοις θεοῖς, καθ' ὃν ἴσως διανέμονται πανταχόσε αἱ ἐκ τῆς γῆς ἀναθυμιάσεις, ὡς διὰ πολλῶν χειρῶν τῆς εἰς πάντας [27,15] τοὺς ῥυθμοὺς[86] διαιρέσεως γινομένης· σκέψαι δ' εἰ παρὰ τὸ αἴρειν τὴν ὡσὰν βορὰν τῶν τοῦ κόσμου μερῶν ὠνόμασται Βριάρεως. Αἰγαίων μὲν γάρ ἐστιν ὁ ἀεὶ τεθηλὼς καὶ γαίων.[87] Δεῖ δὲ μὴ συγχεῖν τοὺς μύθους μηδ' ἐξ ἑτέρου τὰ [27,20] ὀνόματα ἐφ' ἕτερον μεταφέρειν μηδ' εἴ τι προσεπλάσθη ταῖς παραδεδομέναις κατ' αὐτοὺς γενεαλογίαις [28,1] ὑπὸ τῶν μὴ συνιέντων ἃ αἰνίττονται, κεχρημένων δ' αὐτοῖς ὡς καὶ τοῖς πλάσμασιν, ἀλόγως τίθεσθαι.

---

86. Reading with one manuscript; ἀριθμοὺς Lang (1881), Torres (2018).
87. Αἰγαίων to γαίων del. Lang (1881), Torres (2018).

among the Egyptians and Celts and Libyans and other races, one might take as witness the way Homer's Zeus speaks when he confronts Hera: "Or do you not remember when I hung you on high and fixed two anvils to your feet?"[88] For it seems that the poet hands down this fragment of an ancient myth, according to which Zeus is said to have hung Hera from the aether with golden chains (because the stars have a kind of golden appearance) and fixed from her feet two anvils (clearly the earth and the sea, by which the air was stretched down, unable to be torn away from either). Another myth, the one about Thetis, mentions that Zeus was saved by her "when the other Olympians wished to bind him—Hera and Poseidon and Pallas Athene."[89] It appears that each of these gods individually was always plotting against Zeus, intending to prevent the cosmic order that we have—something that would happen if the moist prevailed and everything became water, or if fire prevailed and everything were turned to fire, or if air prevailed.[90] But 'Thetis,' *disposing* [*(dia)theisa*] everything in due order, set 'Briareos' with his hundred hands against the gods that were mentioned—perhaps because the exhalations of the earth are distributed everywhere, as it is through many hands that *division* [*diairesis*] into all the various forms occur. Or consider whether he is named 'Briareos' from *raising up nourishment* [*boran airein*] (so to speak) for the parts of the cosmos. 'Aegean' is he who *always* [*aei*] flourishes and *rejoices* [*gaiōn*]—but one must not confuse the myths, nor transfer the names from one to another, nor set down unthinkingly something which has been made up and added to the genealogies handed down according to them by people who do not understand what they hint at but use them as they use fictions.[91]

---

88. Homer, *Il.* 15.18–19.

89. Homer, *Il.* 1.399–400.

90. The roots of this argument are to be found in Anaximander (DK 12.A16). Compare, perhaps, ch. 8 above, where similar language is used of movement and stability.

91. The syntax of this sentence as transmitted connects the injunction here to the etymology of "Aegean" in particular—a restriction that is presumably what motivated Lang (1881) to delete (i.e., bracket) the clause concerning "Aegean." But it might be relevant that "Aegean" was the name given by *humans* to the divinity known by the *gods* as "Briareos" (*Il.* 1.403–404); in this case, the double naming itself exemplifies the difference between merely human cultural accretion and the ancient (divine) core—just as these passages are also chosen to exemplify the process of fragmentation (they are literally, in Homer, fragments of their respective myths).

B.2.

Πάλιν τοίνυν πρῶτον μὲν ἐμύθευσαν τὸ Χάος γενέσθαι, καθάπερ ὁ Ἡσίοδος ἱστορεῖ, μετὰ δὲ αὐτὸ τὴν Γῆν καὶ [28,5] τὸν Τάρταρον καὶ τὸν Ἔρωτα, ἐκ δὲ τοῦ Χάους τὸ Ἔρεβος καὶ τὴν Νύκτα φῦναι, ἐκ δὲ τῆς Νυκτὸς τὸν Αἰθέρα καὶ τὴν Ἡμέραν. ἔστι δὲ Χάος μὲν τὸ πρὸ τῆς διακοσμήσεως γενόμενον ὑγρόν, ἀπὸ τῆς χύσεως οὕτως ὠνομασμένον, ἢ τὸ πῦρ, ὅ ἐστιν οἱονεὶ κάος· [28,10] καὶ αὐτὸ δὲ κέχυται διὰ τὴν λεπτομέρειαν. ἦν δέ ποτε, ὦ παῖ, πῦρ τὸ πᾶν καὶ γενήσεται πάλιν ἐν περιόδῳ. σβεσθέντος δὲ εἰς ἀέρα αὐτοῦ μεταβολὴ ἀθρόα γίνεται εἰς ὕδωρ, ὃ δὴ λαμβάνει τοῦ μὲν ὑφισταμένου μέρους τῆς οὐσίας κατὰ πύκνωσιν, τοῦ δὲ [28,15] λεπτυνομένου κατ' ἀραίωσιν. εἰκότως οὖν ἔφασαν μετὰ τὸ Χάος τήν τε Γῆν γενέσθαι καὶ τὰ ἠερόεντα Τάρταρα, ἃ δὴ μυχὸν Γῆς ὠνόμασεν ὁ προειρημένος ποιητὴς τῷ περιειληφέναι αὐτὴν καὶ κρύπτειν. ὁ δὲ Ἔρως σὺν αὐτοῖς ἐρρήθη γεγονέναι, ἡ ὁρμὴ ἡ ἐπὶ τὸ γέννᾶν· [29,1] ἅμα γάρ τι ἔκ τινος γίνεται καὶ παρεῖναι τῇ γενέσει νομιστέον ταύτην τὴν δύναμιν καλλίστην καὶ ἀξιοθέατον οὖσαν. τὸ δὲ Ἔρεβος ἐκ τοῦ Χάους ἐγένετο, ὁ ποιῶν ἐρέφεσθαι καὶ περιλαμβάνεσθαί τι ὑφ' [29,5] ἑτέρου λόγος, καθὸ καὶ τούτου τυχοῦσα ἡ Γῆ παραχρῆμα ὁμοιόσχημον αὐτῇ τὸν Οὐρανὸν ἐγέννησεν, "ἵνα μιν περὶ πάντα καλύπτοι, ὄφρ' εἴη μακάρεσσι θεοῖς ἕδος ἀσφαλὲς αἰεί," τοῖς ἐπ' αὐτῷ θέουσιν ἄστροις μακραίωσιν οὖσιν ἀσφαλὲς [29,10] οἰκητήριον. ἐγέννησε δὲ ἡ Γῆ τὸν Οὐρανὸν ἀπὸ τῶν ἀναθυμιάσεων, οὐρανοῦ νῦν κοινότερον λεγομένου παντὸς τοῦ περὶ αὐτὴν λεπτομεροῦς. τοῦ Χάους δὲ θυγάτηρ ἐστὶ καὶ ἡ Νύξ· ὁ γὰρ πρῶτος ἀρθεὶς ἀπὸ τοῦ ἀρχεγόνου ὑγροῦ ἀὴρ ζοφώδης καὶ σκοτεινὸς ἦν, εἶτα [29,15] λεπτυνόμενος εἰς αἰθέρα καὶ φῶς μετέβαλεν, εὐλόγως τούτων ἐκ τῆς νυκτὸς γεγονέναι ῥηθέντων. ἡ δὲ Γῆ τὰ ὄρη καὶ τὸ πέλαγος ἑξῆς λέγεται γεννῆσαι

B.2. Hesiod

Again, then, the myths say that Chaos was the first to be, as Hesiod relates; and after it, Earth and Tartarus and Eros; and from Chaos, Erebos and Night were born; and from Night, Aether and Day. 'Chaos' is the moisture that came about before cosmic order, so named from the word for *stream* [*chusis*] or fire, which is, as it were, a *burner* [*kaos*] and itself *streams* [*(ke)chu(tai)*] because of the fineness of its parts. Everything, my child, was once fire and will be again when the cycle comes round.[92] On being quenched to become air, an overwhelming change occurs to turn it into water, which it controls, compressing part of substance to make it settle and rarefying part to make it finer.[93] They say, reasonably enough, that Earth came to be after Chaos and misty Tartarus, which the aforementioned poet named the recess of Earth because it embraces and hides it.[94] Eros, the impulse to generation, was said to come into being with them; for one must suppose that, when one thing arises from another, this most beautiful and gorgeous power is present at the birth. And from Chaos was born 'Erebos,' which is reason making a thing to be *covered* [*ereph(esthai)*] and embraced by something else. This is why, when Earth met with it, she gave birth to Ouranos (a thing which is similar in appearance to it), "so that he might hide her all around, so that she might be the secure seat for the blessed gods"[95]—the secure home for the long-lived stars which rush along upon it. And Earth bore Ouranos from its exhalations—although the whole of the finer substance around it is now more commonly called Ouranos. Night is also the daughter of Chaos; for the first air which came up from the primeval moisture was dark and misty; then it was refined and changed to aether and light, which, reasonably enough, were said to be born from night. And Earth is said to have given birth in turn to the

---

92. See *SVF* 2.526 (= Diogenes Laertius, *Vit. phil.* 7.137), 626. As these parallel texts make clear, the standard view is that the cosmos is subsequently reborn (and is identical, or substantially identical, to the previous one). Cornutus does not say this in so many words, but it may be implied in the reference to "cycles"—here and below at 51,21.

93. See the introduction, pp. 29–30. Although the first part of the sentence says that the fire is quenched, we know that Zeus pervades the finished cosmos as a fiery soul (ch. 3, esp. 3,13–15), and this is what I take to be the subject of "it controls."

94. I.e., Hesiod; see *Theog.* 119 (Τάρταρά τ' ἠερόεντα μυχῷ χθονὸς εὐρυοδείης).

95. Hesiod, *Theog.* 127.

"ἄτερ φιλότητος ἐφιμέρου"· ἥ τε γὰρ θάλαττα ὑπέμεινεν ἐν τοῖς κοιλοῖς αὐτῆς μέρεσι κατὰ μεταβολὴν ὑποστᾶσα, [29,20] τά τε ὄρη περὶ τὸ ἀνώμαλον τῆς συνιζήσεως τὰς ἐξοχὰς [30,1] ἔλαβε.

Μετὰ δὲ ταῦτα ἡ τῶν λεγομένων Τιτάνων ἐστὶ γένεσις. οὗτοι δ᾽ ἂν εἶεν διαφοραὶ τῶν ὄντων. ὡς γὰρ Ἐμπεδοκλῆς φυσικῶς[96] ἐξαριθμεῖται "Φυσώ τε Φθιμένη τε καὶ Εὐναίη καὶ Ἔγερσις [30,5] Κινώ τ᾽ Ἀστέμφης τε πολυστέφανος τε Μεγιστώ" καὶ Φορυὴν καὶ Σιωπὴν τε καὶ Ὀμφαίην καὶ πολλὰς ἄλλας, τὴν εἰρημένην ποικιλίαν τῶν ὄντων αἰνιττόμενος, οὕτως ὑπὸ τῶν παλαιῶν Ἰαπετὸς μὲν ὠνομάσθη ὁ λόγος καθ᾽ ὃν φωνητικὰ ζῷα ἐγένετο καὶ [30,10] τὸ ὅλον ψόφος ἀπετελέσθη, ἰαφετός τις ὤν (ἰὰ γάρ ἐστιν ἡ φωνή)· Κοῖος δέ, καθ᾽ ὃν ποιά τινα τὰ ὄντα ἐστί (τῷ γὰρ κ πολλαχοῦ οἱ Ἴωνες ἀντὶ τοῦ π ἐχρῶντο) ἢ ὁ τοῦ κοεῖν αἴτιος, τουτέστι νοεῖν ἢ φρονεῖν· Κρῖος δέ, καθ᾽ ὃν τὰ μὲν ἄρχει καὶ δυναστεύει [30,15] τῶν πραγμάτων, τὰ δὲ ὑποτέτακται καὶ δυναστεύεται, ἐντεῦθεν τάχα καὶ τοῦ ἐν τοῖς ποιμνίοις κριοῦ προσαγορευομένου· Ὑπερίων δέ, καθ᾽ ὃν ὑπεράνω τινὰ ἑτέρων περιπορεύεται· Ὠκεανὸς δέ, καθ᾽ ὃν ἀνύεται ἐν τάχει, ὃς δὴ καὶ ἀκαλαρρείτης κέκληται τῷ ἡσύχιόν [30,20] τι καὶ σχολαῖον τὴν ῥύσιν αὐτοῦ ὡς τὴν τοῦ ἡλίου [31,1] κίνησιν ἐμφαίνειν καὶ βαθυδίνης τῷ βαθέως δινεῖσθαι· Τηθὺς δέ, καθ᾽ ἣν ἐπὶ μιᾶς καταστάσεως χρονίζει. Θεία δέ ἐστιν ἡ τῆς ὄψεως αἰτία, Ῥέα δὲ ἡ τῆς ῥύσεως, Φοίβη δὲ ἡ τοῦ καθαρά τινα καὶ λαμπρὰ [31,5] εἶναι, συνεκδέχεσθαι τούτοις καὶ τὰς τῶν ἐναντίων σχέσεων αἰτίας δέοντος· Μνημοσύνη δὲ ἡ τοῦ συναναφέρειν τὰ γεγονότα· Θέμις δὲ ἡ τοῦ συντίθεσθαί

---

96. Torres (2018); Φυσικοῖς Lang (1881) ("in the *Physics*").

mountains and the sea "without dear affection."[97] And the sea, being what the transformation had made it, remained in the hollow parts of the earth, and the mountains acquired peaks as it subsided irregularly.

After all this comes the birth of the so-called Titans. These would be the differences among the things that exist. They are, as Empedocles scientifically enumerates them: "Physo, Phthimene, Eunaie and Egersis, Kino, Astremphe, and many-crowned Megisto,"[98] and Phorye and Siope and Omphaie[99]—and many others, all hinting at the variety (as I said)[100] in the things that exist. In the same way, the process by which creatures with voices came to be, and sound in general was made, was called 'Iapetos' by the ancients: it is a sort of *archer* [*ia-phetos*], with the voice as an arrow [*ia*]. And 'Koios' is that by which the things that exist have *qualities* [*poia*] (the Ionians often use the sound *k* instead of *p*), or it is the cause of *perceiving* [*koein*], that is, of contemplating or thinking. 'Krios' is that because of which some things *rule* [*archei*] and hold sway, while others are commanded and ruled, perhaps also because the *ram* [*krios*] in the flock is so named. And by 'Hyperion' some things rise *above* [*huper(anō)*] others,[101] and by 'Okeanos' things are *accomplished* [*anu(etai)*] at speed.[102] (It is also called 'soft flowing' because its flow appears calm and leisurely, like the movement of the sun, and 'deep eddying' because it has deep eddies.) And by 'Tethys' things stay in the same state for some time.[103] And 'Theia' is the cause of vision,[104] 'Rhea' of *flux* [*rhu(sis)*], 'Phoebe' ["radiant"] of something's being pure and bright. (One has to understand that in all these are the causes for the opposite states as well.) Mnemosyne ["memory"] is the cause of recalling things that have

---

97. Hesiod, *Theog.* 132 (but the point of adding this is not obvious).

98. DK 31.B123. The names mean (or, rather, suggest): birth, decay, sleeping, waking, motion, unflinching, and (many-crowned) greatness. Note that the first six fall into pairs of opposites: this, as becomes clearer at 31,5–6, is why they are connected with "the differences among the things that exist."

99. These names suggest defilement, silence, and oracular deliverance. Phorye and Siope are both emendations of a confused manuscript tradition (Torres suggests *Aphorie*, "barrenness," and *Sophe*, "wisdom"), but they work to pick up from Megisto ("greatness") to complete two more pairs of opposites (see previous note): greatness/defilement, silence/prediction.

100. See 6,10 above.

101. The full etymology seems to be *hyper* ("above") with *iōn* ("going").

102. For "at speed," we are to understand *ōkeōs* (as at 8,13 above), giving *ōke(ōs) an(uetai)*.

103. See n. 25 above.

104. *Thea* is a word for the act of seeing or a view.

τι μεταξὺ ἡμῶν καὶ φυλάττεσθαι· Κρόνος δέ ἐστιν ὁ προειρημένος πάντων τῶν ἀποτελεσμάτων λόγος, δεινότατος [31,10] ὢν τῶν παίδων· ὁπλότατον δ' αὐτὸν γενέσθαι ἔφη διὰ τὸ καὶ μετὰ τὴν τῶν εἰρημένων γένεσιν ἐπιμένειν αὐτὸν ὡσὰν ἐν γενέσει ὄντα.

Ἀλλὰ τῆς μὲν Ἡσιόδου γενεαλογίας τελειοτέρα ποτ' ἂν ἐξήγησίς σοι γένοιτο, τὰ μέν τινα, ὡς οἶμαι, παρὰ τῶν ἀρχαιοτέρων [31,15] αὐτοῦ παρειληφότος, τὰ δὲ μυθικώτερον ἀφ' αὑτοῦ προσθέντος, ᾧ τρόπῳ καὶ πλεῖστα τῆς παλαιᾶς θεολογίας διεφθάρη· νῦν δὲ τὰ βεβοημένα παρὰ τοῖς πλείστοις ἐπισκεπτέον.

B.3.

(18) Παραδεδομένου τοίνυν ἄνωθεν ὅτι ὁ Προμηθεὺς [31,20] ἔπλασεν ἐκ τῆς γῆς τὸ τῶν ἀνθρώπων γένος, [32,1] ὑπονοητέον Προμηθέα εἰρῆσθαι τὴν προμήθειαν τῆς ἐν τοῖς ὅλοις ψυχῆς, ἣν ἐκάλεσαν οἱ νεώτεροι πρόνοιαν· κατὰ γὰρ ταύτην τά τε ἄλλα ἐγένετο καὶ ἐκ τῆς γῆς ἔφυσαν οἱ ἄνθρωποι, ἐπιτηδείως πρὸς τοῦτο ἐχούσης [32,5] καταρχὰς τῆς τοῦ κόσμου συστάσεως. λέγεται δὲ καὶ συνεῖναί ποτε τῷ Διΐ ὁ Προμηθεύς· πολλῆς γὰρ προμηθείας πᾶσα μὲν ἀρχὴ καὶ προστασία πλειόνων, μάλιστα δὲ ἡ τοῦ Διὸς δεῖται. καὶ κλέψαι δέ φασιν αὐτὸν τὸ πῦρ τοῖς ἀνθρώποις, ὡς τῆς ἡμετέρας ἤδη [32,10] συνέσεως καὶ προνοίας ἐπινοησάσης τὴν χρῆσιν τοῦ πυρός. κατενηνέχθαι δὲ αὐτὸ ἐμύθευσαν ἐκ τοῦ οὐρανοῦ διὰ τὸ πλεονάζειν ἐκεῖ ἢ ἐπεὶ οἱ κεραυνοὶ ἐκεῖθεν κατασκήπτουσι διὰ πληγῆς τἀνθάδε ἐξάπτοντες, τάχα τι τοιοῦτον καὶ διὰ τοῦ νάρθηκος αἰνιττόμενοι. [32,15] δεθεὶς δὲ ἐπὶ τούτῳ ὁ Προμηθεὺς ἐκολάσθη τοῦ ἥπατος αὐτῷ ὑπ' ἀετοῦ καταβιβρωσκομένου· ἡ γὰρ ἡμετέρα ἐντρέχεια, τὸ προειρημένον πλεονέκτημα σὺν τοῖς ἄλλοις ἔχουσα, πειρᾶταί τινος παρ' ἑαυτὴν δυσχρηστίας προσδεδεμένη ταῖς κατὰ τὸν βίον φροντίσιν ὀδυνηραῖς [32,20] οὔσαις καὶ ὥσπερ εἰς τὰ σπλάγχνα ὑπὸ τῆς λεπτομεριμνίας ἐκβιβρωσκομένη. ἀδελφὸν δ' ἔφασαν εἶναι νεώτερον τοῦ Προμηθέως τὸν Ἐπιμηθέα, εὐηθέστερόν πως ὄντα τὸν τρόπον διὰ τὸ προτερεῖν τῇ τάξει τὴν προόρασιν [33,1] τῆς ἐκ

happened, 'Themis' of *making an agreement* [(*sunti*)*the*(*sthai*)] about something between us and keeping to it. Kronos is the aforementioned reason behind all things brought to completion[105] and is the cleverest of the children. And he said that he was the youngest of them[106] because during their birth, he himself remained, as it were, in the process of being born.

There could be a more complete exegesis of the genealogy of Hesiod—who got some things, I think, from those more ancient than him but added other things for himself rather in the manner of a storyteller (and by this means, most of the ancient theology has been corrupted). Now, though, we should look at what is claimed by the majority.

B.3. Science and Philosophy

(18) It is a tradition passed down that Prometheus fashioned the race of men out of earth. It should be understood that 'Prometheus' is so called as the *forethought* [*prometheia*] exhibited by the soul of the universe. (More recent thinkers have called this "providence.")[107] For it was by forethought that everything else came into being, and men were born from the earth—the original constitution of the cosmos being suitably disposed for this.[108] And it is said that Prometheus used to be with Zeus, since all government and authority over many things—especially when it is that of Zeus—needs a great deal of forethought. They also say that he stole fire for men, since it was through our own understanding and providence that we worked out how to use fire. The myth says that Prometheus carried the fire out of heaven either because there is a superabundance of fire there or because thunderbolts crash down from there, setting fire to things that they strike down here. (Perhaps something of the sort is also hinted by the fennel stalk.) Prometheus was bound for this and punished by having his liver eaten by an eagle; for our skill set, which includes the accomplishment I have been talking about, among others, experiences some difficulty despite itself when it is bound up with the painful cares of life, having, as it were, its bowels gnawed at by petty concerns. 'Epimetheus' is said to be the somewhat simple-minded younger brother of Prometheus because foresight is worth more than education in things that have happened and *hindsight*

---

105. See 4,1–7 (reason, of course, is identical with nature in this context).
106. The subject of "he said" is Hesiod (talking about Kronos); see *Theog.* 137.
107. Cf. *SVF* 2.937, 1076, 1132; and ch. 20 below.
108. See *SVF* 2.323.

τῶν ἀποβαινόντων παιδείας καὶ ἐπιμηθείας· τῷ γὰρ ὄντι "ῥεχθὲν δέ τε νήπιος ἔγνω." διὰ τοῦτο γὰρ τῇ πρώτῃ γενομένῃ γυναικὶ συνοικῆσαι τοῦτον ἔφασαν· ἀφρονέστερον γάρ πως δὴ καὶ τὸ θῆλυ εἶναι [33,5] καὶ ἐπιμηθεῖσθαι μᾶλλον ἢ προμηθεῖσθαι πεφυκός.

Λέγεται δὲ ὑπό τινων καὶ τῶν τεχνῶν εὑρετὴς γενέσθαι ὁ Προμηθεὺς δι' οὐδὲν ἄλλο ἢ ὅτι συνέσεως καὶ προμηθείας δεῖ πρὸς τὴν εὕρεσιν αὐτῶν. (19) οἱ πλείους μέντοι τῇ Ἀθηνᾷ καὶ τῷ Ἡφαίστῳ αὐτὰς ἀνατιθέασι, [33,10] τῇ μὲν Ἀθηνᾷ, ἐπειδὴ φρόνησις καὶ ἀγχίνοια εἶναι δοκεῖ, τῷ δὲ Ἡφαίστῳ διὰ τὸ τὰς πλείστας τῶν τεχνῶν διὰ πυρὸς τὰ ἑαυτῶν ἔργα ἀποδιδόναι. ὁ μὲν γὰρ αἰθὴρ καὶ τὸ διαυγὲς καὶ καθαρὸν πῦρ Ζεύς ἐστι, τὸ δ' ἐν χρήσει καὶ ἀερομιγὲς Ἥφαιστος, ἀπὸ τοῦ [33,15] ἧφθαι ὠνομασμένος, ὅθεν καὶ ἐκ Διὸς καὶ Ἥρας ἔφασαν αὐτὸν γενέσθαι, τινὲς δὲ μόνης τῆς Ἥρας· αἱ γὰρ φλόγες παχυμερέστεραί πως οὖσαι ὡσὰν ἐκ μόνου τοῦ ἀέρος διακαιομένου τὴν ὑπόστασιν λαμβάνουσι. χωλὸς δὲ παραδέδοται τάχα μὲν διὰ τὸ παχεῖαν τὴν διὰ τῆς [33,20] ὕλης πορείαν ποιεῖσθαι τοῖς ἐπισκάζουσιν ὅμοιαν, τάχα δὲ ἀπὸ τοῦ μὴ δύνασθαι προβαίνειν δίχα ξυλώδους τινὸς ὡσὰν βάκτρου· τινὲς δέ, ἐπεὶ τὴν ἄνω [34,1] κίνησιν τῇ κάτω πρὸς τὴν τροφὴν[109] ἄνισον καὶ ἀνώμαλον ποιεῖται, βραδυτέρας ταύτης οὔσης, χωλαίνειν αὐτὸν ἔφασαν. ῥιφῆναι δ' ὑπὸ τοῦ Διὸς εἰς γῆν ἐξ οὐρανοῦ λέγεται διὰ τὸ τοὺς πρώτους ἴσως ἀρξαμένους χρῆσθαι [34,5] πυρὶ ἐκ κεραυνοβολίου καιομένῳ αὐτῷ περιτυχεῖν, μηδέπω ἐπινοίᾳ τῶν πυρίων ἐπιπεσεῖν δυναμένους. γυναῖκα δ' αὐτοῦ τὴν Ἀφροδίτην ἔφασαν εἶναι καθ' οἷον λόγον καὶ τῶν Χαρίτων μίαν· ὡς γὰρ χάριν φαμὲν ἔχειν τὰ τεχνικὰ ἔργα, οὕτω καὶ ἀφροδίτην τινὰ αὐτοῖς ἐπιτρέχειν [34,10] λέγομεν, εἰ μὴ πρὸς παράστασιν τοῦ πολὺ τὸ πυρῶδες εἶναι ἐν ταῖς πρὸς τὰς μίξεις ὁρμαῖς πέπλασται τοῦτο. δεδεκέναι δὲ μυθεύεται τὸν Ἄρην μοιχεύοντα τὴν γυναῖκα· καὶ γὰρ ὁ μῦθος παρὰ τῷ ποιητῇ ἐστι, παλαιότατος ὤν, ἐπειδὴ τῇ τοῦ πυρὸς δυνάμει [34,15] ὁ σίδηρος καὶ ὁ χαλκὸς δαμάζεται· τὸ δὲ τῆς μοιχείας πλάσμα παρίστησιν ὅτι οὐ πάνυ μὲν πέφυκε κατάλληλον τὸ μάχιμον καὶ βίαιον τῷ ἱλαρῷ καὶ μειλιχίῳ οὐδὲ κατὰ τὸν φυσικὸν αὐτῷ νόμον ἐπιπλέκεται, ἀντιποιούμενον δέ πως τῆς

---

109. Reading with some manuscripts; [πρὸς στροφὴν] Lang (1881); [πρὸς τὴν στροφὴν] Torres (2018).

[*epimētheia*]. For in truth "the fool, too, knows what has been done."[110] (This is why they say that Epimetheus lived with the first woman; for the female is somewhat less thoughtful by nature and inclined to hindsight rather than foresight.)

Prometheus is said by some to have invented the technical arts just because understanding and forethought were needed for their discovery. (19) Most people, however, ascribe them to Athena and Hephaestus: Athena because she seems to represent intelligence and cleverness and Hephaestus because most of the technical arts use fire to produce their works. Aether and bright, pure fire is Zeus;[111] 'Hephaestus' is the fire, mixed with air, which we use—named from *having been kindled* [*hēphthai*]. This is why some say that he was born from Zeus and Hera, but others from Hera alone; for these flames are somewhat denser, as if they exist only due to the air being burnt up. Traditionally, he is lame, perhaps because it makes slow progress through matter like those who limp, but perhaps it is from the fact that it cannot proceed without something wooden—as if it needs a staff. Others still explain his being lame by the inequality and unevenness of its movement—upwards, and downwards through what it consumes, the latter being slower. He is said to have been thrown to earth from heaven by Zeus, perhaps because the first people to use fire found it where it had been started by a thunderbolt—given that they could never have hit on the idea of fire sticks. They say that his wife is 'Aphrodite' for much the same reason as she is one of the Graces. For, just as we say that the works of technical art are pleasing, so we say that a certain *pleasure* [*aphroditē*] is diffused through them—unless this story was fabricated to show that the impulse toward sex is very fiery. There is a story that Hephaestus bound Ares while he was committing adultery with his wife (indeed, the myth comes through the Poet[112] and is extremely ancient), for iron and bronze are tamed by the power of fire. The fiction of the adultery shows that what is pugnacious and brutal does not at all go with what is cheerful and gentle, and it is not the law of nature that brings about their

---

110. Homer, *Il.* 17.32.

111. See n. 7 above for Chrysippus's identification of the ruling part of the cosmic soul with aether.

112. I.e., Homer: see *Od.* 8.266–366. The inference to its great antiquity cannot be from the very fact that the story is *in* Homer, but Cornutus might have it in mind that it is itself narrated by a bard (Demodocus) within the frame of the *Odyssey*, whose narrative it does nothing to advance—just as if this is an older, ready-made story transmitted forward by Homer.

μίξεως αὐτοῦ καλὸν καὶ γενναῖον [34,20] γέννημα, τὴν ἐξ ἀμφοῖν ἁρμονίαν, ἀποτελεῖ. λέγεται δὲ ὁ Ἥφαιστος μαιώσασθαι τὸν Δία, ὅτε ὤδινεν τὴν [35,1] Ἀθηνᾶν, καὶ διελὼν αὐτοῦ τὴν κεφαλὴν ἐκθορεῖν ἐκείνην ποιῆσαι· τὸ γὰρ πῦρ, ᾧ χρῶνται αἱ τέχναι, συνεργὸν πρὸς τὴν ἀπόδειξιν τῆς φυσικῆς τῶν ἀνθρώπων ἀγχινοίας γενόμενον ὥσπερ κεκρυμμένην αὐτὴν [35,5] εἰς φῶς προήγαγε· τοὺς δὲ ζητοῦντάς τι ὡς προσευρέσθαι κύειν αὐτὸ καὶ ὠδίνειν φαμέν.

(20) Ἡ δὲ Ἀθηνᾶ ἐστιν ἡ τοῦ Διὸς σύνεσις, ἡ αὐτὴ οὖσα τῇ ἐν αὐτῷ προνοίᾳ, καθὸ καὶ Προνοίας Ἀθηνᾶς ἱδρύονται ναοί. γενέσθαι δ' ἐκ τῆς τοῦ Διὸς κεφαλῆς λέγεται, [35,10] τάχα μὲν τῶν ἀρχαίων ὑπολαβόντων τὸ ἡγεμονικὸν τῆς ψυχῆς ἡμῶν ἐνταῦθ' εἶναι, καθάπερ καὶ ἕτεροι τῶν μετὰ ταῦτα ἐδόξασαν, τάχα δ' ἐπεὶ τοῦ μὲν ἀνθρώπου τὸ ἀνωτάτω μέρος τοῦ σώματος ἡ κεφαλή ἐστι, τοῦ δὲ κόσμου ὁ αἰθήρ, ὅπου τὸ ἡγεμονικὸν αὐτοῦ ἐστι [35,15] καὶ ἡ τῆς φρονήσεως οὐσία· "κορυφὴ δὲ θεῶν" κατὰ τὸν Εὐριπίδην "ὁ περὶ χθόν' ἔχων φαεννὸς αἰθήρ." Ἀμήτωρ δέ ἐστιν ἡ Ἀθηνᾶ διὰ τὸ ἀλλοίαν εἶναι τὴν τῆς ἀρετῆς γένεσιν καὶ οὐχ οἵα ἡ τῶν ἐκ συνδυασμοῦ γενομένων ἐστί. τὴν Μῆτιν οὖν καταπιὼν ὁ Ζεὺς [35,20] ἐγέννησεν αὐτήν, ἐπειδὴ μητιέτης καὶ συνετὸς ὢν οὐδαμόθεν ἄλλοθεν ἢ ἐκ τῆς καθ' αὑτὸν βουλῆς τὴν [36,1] ἀρχὴν τοῦ φρονεῖν ἔσχεν. τὸ δὲ ὄνομα τῆς Ἀθηνᾶς δυσετυμολόγητον διὰ ἀρχαιότητά ἐστι, τῶν μὲν ἀπὸ τοῦ ἀθρεῖν πάντα οἷον Ἀθρηνᾶν αὐτὴν εἰπόντων εἶναι, τῶν δὲ διὰ τὸ καίπερ θήλειαν οὖσαν ἥκιστα θηλύτητος [36,5] καὶ ἐκλύσεως μετέχειν τὴν Ἀθηνᾶν· ἄλλοι δὲ ἀπὸ τοῦ μὴ πεφυκέναι θένεσθαι καὶ ὑποτάττεσθαι τὴν ἀρετήν· τάχα δ' εἰ Ἀθηναία, ὡς οἱ παλαιοὶ τὴν Ἀθηνᾶν ἔλεγον, αἰθεροναία ἐστίν. ἡ δὲ παρθενία αὐτῆς τοῦ καθαροῦ καὶ ἀμιάντου σύμβολόν ἐστι· τοιοῦτον γάρ τι ἡ [36,10] ἀρετή.[113] καθωπλισμένη δὲ πλάττεται καὶ οὕτως ἱστοροῦσιν αὐτὴν

---

113. τοιοῦτον γάρ τι ἡ ἀρετή del. Lang (1881).

embrace. However, the former somehow manages it, and the offspring it produces from their intercourse is fine and noble—the harmony derived from both. It is said that Hephaestus stood midwife to Zeus, when he was giving birth to Athena, and that he cut open his head and made her leap out. For the fire which craftsmen use helps to demonstrate the natural ingenuity of men, as if leading it out into the light when it had been hidden before—and we say that those looking to discover something 'conceive' it and 'bring it to birth.'[114]

(20) Athena is the intelligence of Zeus, being the same thing as his *providence* [*pronoia*],[115] which is why temples are founded to 'Athena Pronoia.' She is said to have been born from the head of Zeus perhaps because the ancients got the idea that the ruling part of our souls is there—as others after them have thought[116]—but perhaps because the head is the highest part of the human body, as the aether, which is its ruling part and the substance of its wisdom, is the highest part of the cosmos.[117] As Euripides says: "The peak of the gods is the bright aether surrounding earth."[118] Athena is motherless because the genesis of virtue is different—it is not the kind possessed by those things that arise from a coupling.[119] Zeus, then, gave birth to her after swallowing 'Metis,' since, as a *counselor* [*mētietēs*] and an intelligent being, his thought has its roots nowhere else than in his own private deliberation. It is hard to give an etymology for the name of 'Athena' because of its antiquity. Some say that it comes from her *contemplating* [*athr(ein)*] everything, as if they said she was 'Athrene'; others that it is because, although 'Athena' is *female* [*thēleia*], she nevertheless participates least in [sc. *a-*] femininity and weakness; others again from the fact that virtue is not [sc. *a-*] the kind of thing to be *slain* [*then(esthai)*] and overcome. And perhaps, if it is 'Athenaia,' which is what the ancients called Athena, it means *aether dwelling* [*aithero-naia*]. Her virginity is a symbol of her being pure and unstained: that is what virtue is like. Athena

---

114. See n. 79 above.
115. See references in n. 107 above.
116. This is the view of Plato—and his later followers, but the Stoics (like Aristotle) thought the heart the seat of human rationality.
117. See n. 7 above.
118. *TrGF* 919, from an unknown play.
119. The switch to "virtue" here may be pointed. It is distinctive of Stoicism that virtue is identical with a certain state of reason; for Platonists (and others), virtue precisely involves the marriage of two things, namely the rational and nonrational parts of the soul: e.g., Maximus, *Or.* 27.7b–c; Plutarch, *Mor.* 443c–d.

γεγονέναι παριστάντες ὅτι αὐτάρκως πρὸς τὰς μεγίστας καὶ δυσφορωτάτους πράξεις παρασκευάζεται ἡ φρόνησις· μέγισται γὰρ δοκοῦσιν αἱ πολεμικαὶ εἶναι. διὰ ταύτην δὲ τὴν αἰτίαν καὶ τὸ ἔπανδρον καὶ γοργωπὸν [36,15] αὐτῇ ἀνατιθέασι πολὺ ἔχειν, τοιοῦτόν τι ἐμφαινούσης καὶ τῆς γλαυκότητος αὐτῆς· καὶ γὰρ τῶν θηρίων τὰ ἀλκιμώτατα, οἷον αἱ παρδάλεις καὶ οἱ λέοντες, γλαυκά εἰσι, δυσαντίβλεπτον στίλβοντα ἀπὸ τῶν ὀμμάτων· ἔνιοι δέ φασι τοιαύτην αὐτὴν παρεισάγεσθαι διὰ τὸ τὸν αἰθέρα [36,20] γλαυκὸν εἶναι. πάνυ δ' εἰκότως συμμετέχει τῷ Διῒ τῆς αἰγίδος, οὐχ ἑτέρα οὖσα τοῦ παρ' ὃ δοκεῖ [37,1] διαφέρειν ἁπάντων καὶ περιγίνεσθαι ὁ Ζεύς. προτομὴ δ' ἐν αὐτῇ Γοργόνος ἐστι κατὰ μέσον τῆς θεᾶς τὸ στῆθος ἔξω προβεβληκυῖα τὴν γλῶτταν ὡσὰν ἐκφανεστάτου ὄντος ἐν τῇ τῶν ὅλων οἰκονομίᾳ τοῦ λόγου. [37,5] οἱ δὲ δράκοντες καὶ ἡ γλαὺξ διὰ τὸ ἐμφερὲς τῶν ὀμμάτων ἀνατίθενται ταύτῃ γλαυκώπιδι οὔσῃ· σμερδαλέον γὰρ ὁ δράκων δέδορκε καὶ φυλακτικόν τι ἔχει καὶ ἄγρυπνον καὶ οὐκ εὐθήρατος εἶναι δοκεῖ· "οὐ χρὴ" δὲ "παννύχιον εὕδειν βουληφόρον ἄνδρα." λέγεται [37,10] δ' Ἀτρυτώνη μὲν ὡσανεὶ οὐ τρυομένη ὑπ' οὐδενὸς πόνου ἢ ὡς ἀτρύτου τοῦ αἰθέρος ὄντος, Τριτογένεια δέ, ὅτι ἡ τοῖς κακοῖς ἐγγεννῶσα τὸ τρεῖν καὶ τρέμειν αὕτη ἐστίν—ἦρται γὰρ πόλεμον πρὸς τὴν κακίαν—ἄλλοι δέ φασι διὰ τούτου παρίστασθαι τὰ [37,15] τρία γένη τῶν σκεμμάτων τῆς κατὰ φιλοσοφίαν θεωρίας, πανουργοτέραν διόρθωσιν ἢ κατὰ τὴν ἀρχαίαν ὁλοσχέρειαν ἔχοντος τούτου. λαοσσόον δὲ αὐτὴν ἐπονομάζουσι διὰ τὸ σεύειν ἐν ταῖς μάχαις τοὺς λαούς, ὡς ληῖτις ἐκλήθη ἀπὸ τῆς λείας,[120] ἢ μᾶλλον διὰ τὸ [37,20] σώτειραν αὐτὴν τῶν χρωμένων αὐτῇ λαῶν εἶναι· καὶ πόλεως γὰρ καὶ οἴκου καὶ τοῦ βίου παντὸς προστάτιν ποιητέον τὴν φρόνησιν· ἀφ' οὗ δὴ καὶ ἐρυσίπτολις καὶ [38,1] πολιὰς ὠνόμασται, καθάπερ ὁ Ζεὺς πολιεύς· ἐπίσκοποι γὰρ ἀμφότεροι τῶν πόλεων. Παλλὰς δὲ λέγεται διὰ τὴν μεμυθευμένην περὶ αὐτὴν νεότητα, ἀφ' οὗ καὶ οἱ πάλληκες καὶ παλλακαὶ προσαγορεύονται· σκιρτητικὸν [38,5] γὰρ καὶ παλλόμενον τὸ νέον. ἵδρυνται δὲ αὐτὴν ἐν ταῖς ἀκροπόλεσι μάλιστα, τὸ δυσκαταγώνιστον καὶ δυσπολιόρκητον ἐμφῆναι θέλοντες ἢ τὸ ἄνωθεν ἐφορᾶν τοὺς προσπεφευγότας αὐτῇ ἢ τὴν μετεωρότητα παριστάντες τοῦ καθ' ὃ μέρος

---

120. ὡς to λείας del. Lang (1881), Torres (2018).

2. The *Greek Theology* 95

is depicted armed, and the story is that she was born like that, which points out that wisdom is sufficiently well equipped for the greatest and most difficult deeds—for martial [deeds] strike us as the greatest. For this reason, her attributes also include masculinity and a steely gaze. The gray color [of her eyes] points to the same kind of thing; for the strongest wild animals, such as leopards and lions, are gray eyed, their flashing gaze hard to return. But some say that Athena was made like this because the aether is gray.[121] It is very appropriate that Athena shares the aegis of Zeus, since she is that very thing by which Zeus seems to surpass and excel everything. There is a Gorgon's head in the middle of the goddess's breast, its tongue sticking out—as if to show that reason is the most conspicuous thing in the design of the universe. Snakes, like the owl, are associated with her because their eyes, which are gray, have some similarity with hers; for the snake has a terrifying way of looking. Also, it is rather vigilant and sleepless and seems not to be easy prey, and "a counselor should not sleep all the night."[122] She is called 'Atryone,' as if not [sc. *a-*] *worn out* [*truomenē*] by any labor, or else because the aether is *unwearied* [*atrutos*], and 'Tritogeneia' because she it is who has *generated* [*(en)gennōsa*] *quaking* and *trembling* [*trein/tremein*] in evil people—for she declared war against vice. Others say that the name hints at the *three kinds* [*tria genē*] of subject matter in philosophical enquiry,[123] but that way of making sense of it is too contrived to represent the ancient outlook. She is called 'Laossoös' because she *rouses* [*seuein*] *the nations* [*laoi*] in battles (as she is called 'Dispenser of Booty' from *booty*) or, better, because she is the *salvation* [*sō(teira)*] of the *nations* [*laoi*] who use her—for intelligence should be made the guard of city and home and the whole of life. For this reason, she is also called Defender of the City and, like Zeus, Guardian of the City: both are overseers of cities. She is called 'Pallas' because of her youth in mythology, and for the same reason that 'lads' and 'lasses' [*pallēkes, pallakai*] are so named; for youth is skittish and *unstable* [*pall(omenon)*]. Temples are built for her especially in a city's acropolis, with the intention of showing that she is a tough opponent and hard to besiege, or that she looks down from above on those who flee to her, or to suggest the elevation of that by virtue of which Athena is a part

---

121. See n. 31 above.
122. Homer, *Il.* 2.24; 61.
123. See 15,3–5 above, with n. 49.

ἐστὶ τῆς φύσεως ἡ Ἀθηνᾶ. [38,10] ἀλαλκομενηΐδα δὲ αὐτὴν καλοῦσιν οἱ ποιηταὶ καὶ ἀγεληΐδα, τὸ μὲν ἀπὸ τοῦ ἀλαλκεῖν παράγοντες—ἱκανὴ γὰρ ἐπαμύνειν ἐστὶ καὶ προσβοηθεῖν, ἐξ οὗ καὶ Νίκη προσαγορεύεται—τὸ δ' ἤτοι ἀπὸ τοῦ ἄγειν αὐτὴν τοὺς λαοὺς ἢ ἀπὸ τοῦ ἀδάμαστον εἶναι ταῖς [38,15] ἀγελαίαις βουσὶν ὁμοίως, ἃς μάλιστα θύουσιν αὐτῇ. τοὺς δὲ αὐλοὺς εὑρεῖν μὲν λέγεται καθάπερ τἆλλα ἐν ταῖς τέχναις γλαφυρά, ἀφ' οὗ καὶ ἐπιστάτις τῆς ταλασιουργίας ἐστί, ῥῖψαι δὲ ὡς ἐκθηλύνοντος τὰς ψυχὰς τοῦ δι' αὐτῶν ἀποδιδομένου μέλους καὶ ἥκιστα [38,20] ἐπάνδρου καὶ πολεμικοῦ δοκοῦντος εἶναι. ἡ δ' ἐλαία δῶρον αὐτῇ διά τε τὸ ἀεὶ θάλλειν[124] καὶ διὰ τὸ γλαυκωπόν [39,1] τι ἔχειν· καὶ τὸ ἔλαιον δὲ οὐκ εὐνόθευτόν ἐστι δι' ἄλλου ὑγροῦ, ἀλλ' ἀκέραιον ἀεὶ μένει ὡς τῇ παρθενίᾳ κατάλληλον εἶναι δοκεῖ. ἄρεια δ' ἐκλήθη τῷ στρατηγικὴ εἶναι καὶ διοικητικὴ πολέμων καὶ ὑπερμαχητικὴ [39,5] τοῦ δικαίου· δεινότης γὰρ περὶ πάντα ἐστὶ καὶ συγκεφαλαίωμα πασῶν τῶν ἀρετῶν· καὶ ἱππίαν καὶ δάμνιππον καὶ δορυκέντορα[125] καὶ πολλαχῶς ἄλλως αὐτὴν προσαγορεύουσι, καὶ ἀνιστᾶσι τὰ τρόπαια ἐκ ξύλων ἐλαΐνων, μάλιστα δὲ καὶ τὴν Νίκην αὐτῇ πάρεδρον [39,10] διδόασιν, ἥτις ἐνὶ εἴκειν, τῷ περιγινομένῳ, ποιεῖ, πτερωτὴ παρεισαγομένη διὰ τὸ ὀξύρροπον καὶ εὐμετάβολον τῶν παρατάξεων. καὶ ἐν τῇ πρὸς τοὺς γίγαντας δὲ μάχῃ παραδίδοται ἠριστευκυῖα ἡ Ἀθηνᾶ καὶ γιγαντοφόντις ἐπονομάζεται κατὰ τοιοῦτον λόγον. [39,15] τοὺς γὰρ πρώτους ἐκ γῆς γενομένους ἀνθρώπους εὔλογον βιαίους καὶ θυμικοὺς κατ' ἀλλήλων γενέσθαι διὰ τὸ μηδέπω δύνασθαι διακρίνεσθαι μηδ' ἐρριπίσθαι τὸν ἐνόντα αὐτοῖς σπινθῆρα τῆς κοινωνίας. οἱ θεοὶ δὲ ὡσπερεὶ νύττοντες καὶ ὑπομιμνήσκοντες αὐτοὺς [39,20] τῶν ἐννοιῶν περιγεγόνασι· καὶ μάλιστα ἡ κατὰ τὸν λόγον ἐντρέχεια κατεπολέμησε καὶ ὑπέταξεν οὕτως ὡς [40,1] ἐξεληλακέναι καὶ ἀνῃρηκέναι αὐτοὺς ὡς τοιούτους[126]

---

124. Torres (2018); τὸ θάλλειν Lang (1881).

125. Torres (2018) (reading closer to the manuscripts); δαμάσιππον καὶ δορικέντορα Lang (1881).

126. Torres (2018); τοσούτους Lang (1881).

of nature.[127] The poets call her 'Alalkomeneida' and 'Ageleis'; they derive the former from *warding off* [*alalk(ein)*]—for she is capable of *protection* [(*ep*)*amun*(*ein*)] and help, which is why she is called Victory as well—and the latter from the fact that she *leads nations* [*agein laous*], or else from her being untameable, like *common cattle* [*agelaiai*], which especially are sacrificed to her. She is said to be the inventor of the aulos, as of the other subtleties of the technical arts, which is why she is patron of wool spinning. She threw the aulos away, since the tunes played on it emasculate the soul and seem to be the least manly and warlike.[128] The olive is her gift because it is evergreen and because it is somewhat gray. And olive oil is not easily adulterated with another liquid but always remains unmixed, so that it seems to have something in common with the virgin. She was called 'martial' because she is concerned with strategy and the organization of wars and the fight on behalf of justice. For she is cunning in all things and the summation of all virtues.[129] They call her Equestrian, too, and Horse Tamer and Spear Thrower and many other things. And they set up trophies made out of olive wood, and, especially, Victory is made to share her throne—Victory, who makes people yield to a single person (whoever prevails) and who is traditionally winged, because battle lines turn quickly and are easy changed. According to the tradition, Athena was the champion in the battle with the giants, and she was named Giant Slayer for this sort of reason.[130] For it is reasonable to think that the first men, who were born from the earth,[131] were violent and irascible with each other because they could not yet arrive at decisions or fan the spark of community that was in them. But the gods, as if spurring them on and reminding them of their concepts, prevailed.[132] The skill set that comes with reason, in particular, fought them down and put them in order so that it appears that they were changed and

---

127. This seems to look back to 35,9–15 above, where the governing intelligence represented by Athena is seated in the celestial aether.

128. Cf. Plato, *Rep.* 399a with d; and 59,24 below for the association of the *aulos* with Dionysus (who in turn is associated with peacetime activity and laxity). See the introduction, p. 34, with n. 70.

129. E.g., *SVF* 3.11.

130. As Vian (1952, 30) notes, Cornutus's pupil Lucan has Athena triumph against the Giants at *Bel. civ.* 9.655–658—and, it might be added, in virtue of the Gorgon that Cornutus mentions at 37,1–5 above.

131. See *SVF* 1.124; 2.739.

132. Cornutus's appropriation of the Platonist language of recollection here is striking; see discussion in Boys-Stones 2009, 149–52.

δοκεῖν· ἀλλοῖοι γὰρ αὐτοί τ' ἐκ μεταβολῆς ἐγένοντο καὶ οἱ γεγονότες ἐξ αὐτῶν συμπολισθέντες ὑπὸ τῆς Πολιάδος Ἀθηνᾶς.

(21) [40,5] Ἄλλοι δὲ περὶ τὰ πολεμικὰ ἀναστρέφονται θεοὶ μηκέθ' ὁμοίως τοῦ εὐσταθοῦς καὶ τοῦ κατὰ λόγον στοχαζόμενοι, ταραχωδέστεροι δέ πως, ὅ τε Ἄρης καὶ ἡ Ἐνυώ· καὶ τούτους δ' εἰσῆγεν εἰς τὰ πράγματα ὁ Ζεὺς ἐρεθίσας κατ' ἀλλήλων τὰ ζῷα καὶ οὐκ ἄχρηστον [40,10] οὐδὲ τοῖς ἀνθρώποις ἔσθ' ὅπου τὴν δι' ὅπλων διάκρισιν ἐμβαλών, ἵνα τε τὸ γενναῖον καὶ ἀνδρεῖον αὐτοί τε[133] ἐν ἑαυτοῖς καί γε ἐπ' ἀλλήλους τὸ οἰκεῖον τῆς εἰρήνης εὖ ἀσμενίζωσι. διὰ ταύτην μὲν οὖν τὴν[134] αἰτίαν Διὸς υἱὸς καὶ ὁ Ἄρης παραδέδοται οὐ κατ' ἄλλον λόγον[135] [40,15] ἢ καὶ ὀβριμοπάτρις ἡ Ἀθηνᾶ.

Περὶ δὲ τῆς Ἐνυοῦς οἱ μὲν ὡς μητρός, οἱ δ' ὡς θυγατρός, οἱ δ' ὡς τροφοῦ Ἄρεως διαφέρονται, διαφέροντος οὐδέν· Ἐνυὼ γάρ ἐστιν ἡ ἐνιεῖσα θυμὸν καὶ ἀλκὴν τοῖς μαχομένοις ἢ κατ' εὐφημισμὸν ἀπὸ τοῦ ἥκιστα ἐνηὴς καὶ ἐπιεικὴς εἶναι ὠνόμασται.[136]

Ὁ [40,20] δ' Ἄρης τὴν ὀνομασίαν ἔσχεν ἀπὸ τοῦ αἴρειν καὶ ἀναιρεῖν [41,1] ἢ ἀπὸ τῆς ἀρῆς, ἥ ἐστι βλάβη, ἢ πάλιν κατ' ἐναντίωσιν, ὡσανεὶ ἐκμειλισσομένων αὐτὸν τῶν προσαγορευσάντων· διαστατικὸς γὰρ καὶ λυμαντικὸς τῶν προσηρμοσμένων γίνεται οὖν ἀπὸ τοῦ ἄρσαι, ὅ ἐστιν [41,5] ἁρμόσαι, τοιούτου τάχα τινὸς ἐχομένης καὶ τῆς Ἁρμονίας, ἣν ἐμύθευσαν ἐξ αὐτοῦ γενέσθαι. εἰκότως δὲ καὶ μιαιφόνος λέγεται καὶ βροτολοιγός, καὶ ἀλαλάξιος καὶ βριήπυος, μεγίστης ἐν ταῖς παρατάξεσιν ὑπὸ τῶν μαχομένων ἀφιεμένης φωνῆς, ὅθεν καὶ ὄνους τινὲς [41,10] αὐτῷ σφαγιάζουσι διὰ τὸ ταραχῶδες καὶ γεγωνὸν τῆς ὀγκήσεως, οἱ πλεῖστοι δὲ κύνας διὰ τὸ θρασὺ καὶ ἐπιθετικὸν τοῦ ζῴου. τιμᾶσθαι δ' ὑπὸ Θρᾳκῶν μάλιστα καὶ Σκυθῶν καὶ τῶν τοιούτων ἐθνῶν λέγεται, παρ' οἷς ἡ τῶν πολεμικῶν ἄσκησις εὐδοκιμεῖ καὶ τὸ ἀνεπίστρεφὲς [41,15] τῆς δίκης. γῦπα δ' ἱερόν φασιν αὐτοῦ ὄρνιν εἶναι διὰ τὸ πλεονάζειν ὅπου πότ' ἂν πτώματα πολλὰ ἀρηΐφθορα ᾖ.

---

133. del. Lang (1881), Torres (2018).
134. Torres (2018); om. Lang (1881).
135. οὐ κατ' ἄλλον λόγον del. Lang (1881), Torres (2018).
136. ὠνόμασται is Lang's (1881) supplement (not adopted in Torres 2018).

destroyed and no longer seemed to be like that. For different men came out of this change, and those born from them lived together in cities under the protection of Athena Guardian of the City.

(21) Other gods concerned with military matters do not similarly aim at what is stable and reasonable but are somewhat more disruptive: Ares and Enyo. Zeus introduced these into things by stirring animals up against each other, and there are occasions when he decrees a settlement by arms which, even among men, is not without utility; it makes them welcome nobility and bravery in themselves, as well as behavior toward one another which is appropriate to peacetime.[137] (For this reason, then, tradition makes Ares the son of Zeus as well by exactly the same reasoning as that by which Athena is Daughter of a Mighty Sire.)

Accounts of Enyo differ; for some she is the mother of Ares, for some his daughter, for some his nurse. But it makes no difference: 'Enyo' is the one who *implants* [*enieisa*] in soldiers their spirit and strength, or else her name is a euphemism, because she is the least *kind* [*enēēs*] and seemly.

'Ares' got his name from *seizing* [*hair(ein)*] and *destroying* [*(an)air(ein)*]; or from *bane* [*arē*], that is, injury; or again by antithesis (as if to mollify him while addressing him), since he smashes and ruins things which are joined together—the name arises, then, from *join* [*arsai*], which is to fit together. ('Harmony' [*harmonia*] is perhaps one of these things—and mythology says that it was born from him.) He is appropriately called Murderous and the Bane of Men; also, God of the War-Cry and Loud-Shouting, since the loudest cry is made by those fighting in battle—and this is why some people sacrifice donkeys to Ares, their braying being so disruptive and loud. (Most, however, sacrifice dogs because they are daring and ready to attack.) Ares is said to be honored especially by the Thracians and Scythians and races like these, among whom the practice of warfare is highly esteemed, as is indifference for justice. The vulture is said to be the bird sacred to him because of their abundance wherever there are a lot of battle-slain corpses.

---

137. Cf., perhaps, *SVF* 3.206, which finds the silver lining for warfare in the opportunity it affords to display virtue.

C.1.

(22) Μετὰ δὲ ταῦτα περὶ τοῦ Ποσειδῶνος, ὦ παῖ, λεκτέον. προείρηται μὲν ὅτι ὁ αὐτός ἐστι τῇ [41,20] τεταγμένῃ κατὰ τὸ ὑγρὸν δυνάμει, νῦν δὲ παραμυθητέον τοῦτο. πρῶτον μὲν οὖν φυτάλιον αὐτὸν ἐπωνόμασαν, ἐπειδὴ τοῦ φύεσθαι τὰ ἐκ γῆς γενόμενα ἡ ἐν [42,1] αὐτῇ δηλονότι ἰκμὰς παραιτία ἐστίν· εἶτα ἐνοσίχθονα καὶ ἐνοσίγαιον καὶ σεισίχθονα καὶ τινάκτορα γαίας ὡς οὐ παρ' ἄλλην αἰτίαν τῶν σεισμῶν γινομένων ἢ παρὰ τὴν εἰς τὰς ἐν τῇ γῇ σήραγγας ἔμπτωσιν τῆς τε [42,5] θαλάττης καὶ τῶν ἄλλων ὑδάτων· στενοχωρούμενα γὰρ τὰ ἐν αὐτῇ πνεύματα καὶ ἔξοδον ζητοῦντα κλονεῖσθαι καὶ ῥήγνυσθαι αὐτὴν ποιεῖ, ἀποτελουμένων ἔσθ' ὅτε καὶ μυκημάτων κατὰ τὴν ῥῆξιν· εὐλόγως ὑπό τινων καὶ μυκητὰς εἴρηται τῆς θαλάττης τινα τοιοῦτον ἦχον [42,10] ἀποτελούσης, ἀφ' οὗ καὶ ἠχήεσσα καὶ ἀγάστονος καὶ πολύφλοισβος λέγεται· ἐντεῦθεν δὲ ἔδοξαν καὶ οἱ ταῦροι αὐτῷ προσήκειν, καὶ θύουσιν αὐτῷ ταύρους. παμμέλανας διὰ τὴν χροιὰν τοῦ πελάγους καὶ ἐπεὶ ἄλλως τὸ ὕδωρ μέλαν εἶναι λέγουσιν, εὐλόγως ἤδη [42,15] κυανοχαίτου αὐτοῦ εἰρημένου καὶ ἐν ἐσθῆτι εἰσαγομένου τοιαύτῃ· τούτου δ' ἕνεκεν καὶ τοὺς ποταμοὺς κερασφόρους καὶ ταυρωποὺς ἀναπλάττουσιν, ὡσὰν βίαιόν τι τῆς φορᾶς αὐτῶν καὶ μυκητικὸν ἐχούσης· καὶ γὰρ ὁ Σκάμανδρος παρὰ τῷ ποιητῇ [42,20] "ἤρυγεν ὡς ὅτε ταῦρος." κατ' ἄλλον δὲ τρόπον γαιήοχος λέγεται ὁ Ποσειδῶν καὶ θεμελιοῦχος ὑπό τινων καὶ θύουσιν αὐτῷ Ἀσφαλείῳ Ποσειδῶνι πολλαχοῦ ὡσὰν ἐπ' αὐτῷ κειμένου [43,1] τοῦ ἀσφαλῶς ἑστάναι τὰ οἰκήματα ἐπὶ τῆς γῆς καὶ αὐτοῦ δέοντος.[138] τρίαινα δ' αὐτοῦ φόρημά ἐστι πότερον ἐπεὶ χρῶνται αὐτῇ πρὸς τὴν τῶν ἰχθύων θήραν ἢ ὡς ἐπιτηδείου τούτου τοῦ ὀργάνου πρὸς τὴν κίνησιν [43,5] τῆς γῆς ὄντος, ὡς εἴρηται καὶ "αὐτὸς δ' ἐννοσίγαιος ἔχων χείρεσσι τρίαιναν ἡγεῖτ'· ἐκ δ' ἄρα πάντα θεμείλια χεῦε θύραζε." ἔχεταί τινος ἀποκεκρυμμένου ἐτύμου αὐτή τε καὶ ὁ Τρίτων καὶ Ἀμφιτρίτη, εἴτουν πλεονάζοντος τοῦ τ στοιχείου, [43,10] ἀπὸ δὲ τῆς ῥύσεως αὐτῶν οὕτως ὠνομασμένων, εἴτε καὶ παρ' ἄλλην αἰτίαν. ὁ δὲ Τρίτων δίμορφος ὢν τὸ μὲν ἔχει μέρος ἀνθρώπου, τὸ δὲ κήτους, ἐπειδὴ

---

138. καὶ αὐτοῦ δέοντος del. Lang (1881), Torres (2018).

C. Second Survey of the Physical System

C.1. Water (and the Principles of Fertility)

(22) After this, my child, we should speak of Poseidon. It has already been said that he is the same as the ordered power associated with the moist,[139] and now we need to justify this. First, then, they named him 'Nourishing' [*phutalios*], since, of things that come from the earth, it is clear that the moisture in it is a contributing cause of their *growth* [*phu(esthai)*]. And then he is called Earth Shaker and Land Shaker and Earth Quaker and Shaker of the Earth since earthquakes are caused precisely by the sea, and other waters, falling into the cavities of the earth: the air trapped inside seeks a way out and makes it surge and break up—sometimes producing a bellowing noise as it breaks. Some people understandably call him the 'Bellower' because the sea produces a noise like this, and this is why he is also called Roaring and Loud Groaning and Loud Roaring, and this is why bulls are thought to be associated with him and bulls are sacrificed to him—of pure black, because of the color of the sea (and in any case they say water is black).[140] (It also makes sense that he is called dark haired and is, by custom, made to wear dark clothes.) And because of this, rivers[141] are depicted with horns and the face of a bull: their current has something violent about it, so to speak, and bellows. So Skamander, according to the Poet, "bellowed like a bull."[142] A different approach leads some people to call Poseidon Earth Holder and Upholder of the Foundations. In many places they sacrifice to him as Poseidon the 'Steadfast,' since erecting buildings on land that are stable relies on him and needs him. He carries a trident, whether because this is something used to hunt fish or because it is a tool suited for moving the earth, so that it is also said that "he, the Earth Shaker, having in his hands a trident, led, and he poured out all the foundations."[143] ('Trident' contains some hidden etymology, along with 'Triton' and 'Amphitrite'—whether the letter t is irrelevant, and they are all named like this from the *flow* [*rhu(sis)*], or something else. Triton has a double form, part man, part

---

139. See 4,11–12 above, with n. 11.
140. "Black water" is, from Homer onward, a common poetical description of deep water (not only the sea). (That water really is black was famously argued by Anaxagoras (DK 59.A97). But there is no reason to think that this is what Cornutus has in mind.)
141. I.e., river *gods*.
142. Homer, *Il.* 20.403.
143. Homer, *Il.* 12.28–29.

καὶ τὸ εἰρημένον ὑγρὸν τὴν μὲν ὠφελητικὴν ἔχει δύναμιν, τὴν δὲ βλαπτικήν. καλεῖται δ' εὐρύστερνος [43,15] ὁ Ποσειδῶν διὰ τὸ πλάτος τοῦ πελάγους, ὡς εἴρηται καὶ "ἐπ' εὐρέα νῶτα θαλάσσης." λέγεται δὲ ἐκ τούτου καὶ εὐρυμέδων καὶ εὐρυβίας, ἵππιος δὲ τάχα ἀπὸ τοῦ ταχεῖαν τὴν διὰ θαλάττης [44,1] φορὰν εἶναι καθάπερ ἵπποις ἡμῶν ταῖς ναυσὶ χρωμένων, ἐντεῦθεν ἤδη καὶ ἐπίσκοπον αὐτὸν εἶναι τῶν ἵππων παραδεξαμένων τῶν μετὰ ταῦτα. λέγεται δὲ παρά τισι καὶ νυμφαγέτης καὶ κρηνοῦχος διὰ τὰς προειρημένας [44,5] αἰτίας· νύμφαι γάρ εἰσιν αἱ τῶν ποτίμων ὑδάτων πηγαί. ἀπὸ τοῦ ἀεὶ νέαι φαίνεσθαι ἢ ἀπὸ τοῦ φαίνειν οὕτως ὠνομασμέναι. τὰς δὲ γαμουμένας νύμφας καλοῦσιν ἀπὸ τοῦ νῦν πρώτως φαίνεσθαι κρυπτομένας τέως. τοῦ δ' αὐτοῦ λόγου ἔχεται [44,10] καὶ τὸ Ποσειδῶνος υἱὸν εἶναι τὸν Πήγασον, ἀπὸ τῶν πηγῶν ὠνομασμένον. διὰ δὲ τὴν θεωρουμένην βίαν περὶ τὴν θάλατταν καὶ πάντας τοὺς βιαίους καὶ μεγαλεπιβούλους γενομένους, ὡς τὸν Κύκλωπα καὶ τοὺς Λαιστρυγόνας καὶ τοὺς Ἀλωείδας, Ποσειδῶνος ἐμύθευσαν [44,15] ἐκγόνους εἶναι.

(23) Ὁ δὲ Νηρεὺς ἡ θάλαττά ἐστι, τοῦτον ὠνομασμένη τὸν τρόπον ἀπὸ τοῦ νεῖσθαι δι' αὐτῆς.[144] καλοῦσι δὲ τὸν Νηρέα καὶ ἅλιον γέροντα διὰ τὸ ὥσπερ πολιὰν ἐπανθεῖν τοῖς κύμασι τὸν ἀφρόν· καὶ γὰρ ἡ [44,20] Λευκοθέα τοιοῦτόν τι ἐμφαίνει, ἥτις λέγεται θυγάτηρ Νηρέως εἶναι, δηλονότι τὸ λευκὸν τοῦ ἀφροῦ.

(24) Πιθανὸν δὲ καὶ τὴν Ἀφροδίτην μὴ δι' ἄλλο τι παραδεδόσθαι γεγονυῖαν ἐν τῇ θαλάττῃ ἢ ἐπειδὴ πρὸς τὸ πάντα γενέσθαι κινήσεως δεῖ καὶ ὑγρασίας, [45,1] ἅπερ ἀμφότερα δαψιλῆ κατὰ τὴν θάλατταν ἐστιν. ἐστοχάσαντο δὲ τοῦ αὐτοῦ καὶ οἱ Διώνης αὐτὴν θυγατέρα εἰπόντες εἶναι· διερὸν γὰρ τὸ ὑγρόν ἐστιν. Ἀφροδίτη δέ ἐστιν ἡ συνάγουσα τὸ ἄρρεν καὶ τὸ θῆλυ δύναμις, [45,5] τάχα διὰ τὸ ἀφρώδη τὰ σπέρματα τῶν ζῴων εἶναι ταύτην ἐσχηκυῖα τὴν ὀνομασίαν ἢ, ὡς Εὐριπίδης ὑπονοεῖ, διὰ τὸ τοὺς ἡττωμένους αὐτῆς ἄφρονας εἶναι. καλλίστη δὲ παράγεται διὰ τὸ μάλιστα ἀρηρεκέναι τοῖς ἀνθρώποις τὴν κατὰ συμπλοκὴν ἡδονὴν ὡς πάντων [45,10] τῶν ἄλλων διαφέρουσαν, λέγεται δὲ καὶ φιλομειδὴς διὰ τοῦτο· οἰκεῖα γὰρ τὰ μειδιάματα καὶ ἡ ἱλαρότης τῶν τοιούτων συνόδων ἐστί. παρέδρους δὲ καὶ συμβώμους τὰς Χάριτας ἔχει καὶ τὴν Πειθὼ καὶ τὸν Ἑρμῆν διὰ τὸ πειθοῖ προσάγεσθαι καὶ λόγῳ καὶ χάρισι τοὺς ἐρωμένους [45,15] ἢ διὰ τὸ περὶ τὰς συνουσίας ἀγωγόν. Κυθέρεια δ' εἴρηται διὰ τὰς ἐκ τῶν μίξεων γινομένας κυήσεις ἢ διὰ τὸ κεύθεσθαι τὰ πολλὰ τὰς τῶν ἀφροδισίων ἐπιθυμίας.

---

144. Torres (2018); δι' αὐτῆς Lang (1881).

leviathan, since the aforementioned moisture has the power both to help and to harm.) Poseidon is called Wide Chested because of the breadth of the sea (as it is also said: "on the wide back of the sea").[145] This leads to his being called 'Wide Ruling' and 'Wide Powered.' He is 'God Of The Horse' perhaps because passage through the sea is swift, and it is as if we are on horses when we use ships. This led to the later tradition that he is the Guardian of Horses. He is called by some Leader of the Nymphs and Lord of the Springs for reasons already given: 'nymphs' [*numphai*] are the sources of fresh waters, thus named because they always *appear to be young* [*neai phain(esthai)*], or from the fact that they *shine as new* [*neai phain(ein)*]. (Brides are called 'nymphs' because they are *now appearing* [*nun phain(esthai)*] for the first time, after being hidden away.) The same line of reasoning is given for the fact that 'Pegasus' is the son of Poseidon: he is named from *springs* [*pēgai*]. Because of the observable force of the sea, mythology holds that all those who are violent, and who plot enormities, like the Cyclops, the Laistrygonians, and the Aloeidai, are offspring of Poseidon.

(23) 'Nereus' is a name given to the sea from one's *traveling* [*nei(sthai)*] through it. They also call Nereus 'Old Man of the Sea' because foam crowns the waves like gray hair. 'Leukothea,' who is said to be the daughter of Nereus, represents something of the sort as well: clearly the 'white' [*leukon*] of the foam.

(24) And it is plausible that Aphrodite is traditionally born in the sea just because movement and moisture are necessary for the generation of everything—and both are, in abundance, associated with the sea. Those who make Aphrodite the daughter of 'Dione' are getting at the same thing; for the moist is *wet* [*dieron*]. 'Aphrodite' is the power which brings male and female together. The name derives perhaps from the fact that the seed of animals is *foamy* [*aphrōdē*] or, as Euripides suggests, because those who are conquered by her are *fools* [*aphrones*].[146] She is supposed to be extremely beautiful because the pleasure of intercourse is especially pleasing to men and surpasses all others. And she is called 'Laughter Loving' because laughter and gaiety are appropriate to this kind of encounter. The Graces share her throne and altar, as do Persuasion and Hermes, because one seduces lovers through persuasion, speech, and favors, or because of the attraction of intercourse. She is called 'Kytheria' because of the *pregnancies* [*kuēseis*] that result from sex, or else because sexual desires are, for the most part, *hidden*

---

145. Hesiod, *Theog.* 781.
146. See Euripides, *Tro.* 989–990.

ἐκ τούτου δ' ἤδη καὶ ἱερὰ τῆς Ἀφροδίτης ἡ τῶν Κυθήρων νῆσος εἶναι δοκεῖ, τάχα δὲ καὶ ἡ [45,20] Κύπρος, συνᾴδουσά πως τῇ κρύψει κατὰ τοὔνομα. ἡ δὲ Πάφος ἴδιον αὐτῆς οἰκητήριόν ἐστι, Παφίας λεγομένης, τάχα κατ' ἔλλειψιν ἀπὸ τοῦ ἀπαφίσκειν, ὅ ἐστιν ἀπατᾶν· ἔχει γὰρ κατὰ μὲν τὸν Ἡσίοδον "μειδήματά τ' ἐξαπατάς τε," κατὰ δὲ τὸν Ὅμηρον [46,1] "πάρφασιν, ἥ τ' ἔκλεψε νόον πύκα περ φρονεόντων." ὁ δὲ Κεστὸς ἱμὰς ὡς οἷον κεκασμένος ἐστὶν ἢ διακεκεντημένος καὶ ποικίλος, δύναμιν ἔχων τοῦ συνδεῖν καὶ συσφίγγειν. καλεῖται δ' οὐρανία τε καὶ πάνδημος καὶ [46,5] ποντία διὰ τὸ καὶ ἐν οὐρανῷ καὶ ἐν γῇ καὶ ἐν θαλάττῃ τὴν δύναμιν αὐτῆς θεωρεῖσθαι. ἀκύρους δὲ καὶ οὐκ ἐμποινίμους τοὺς ἀφροδισίους ὅρκους ἔφασαν εἶναι, παρ' ὅσον κἂν ᾖ ῥᾳδία παρασχεθῆναι μεθ' ὅρκων ἐπάγεσθαι συμβέβηκε τοὺς πειρῶντας ἃς ἂν πειρῶσι. περιστερᾷ [46,10] δὲ τῶν ὀρνέων χαίρει μάλιστα τῷ καθάρειον εἶναι τὸ ζῷον καὶ φιλοφρονητικὸν διὰ τῶν ὡσανεὶ φιλημάτων, ἀνάπαλιν δ' ὗς διὰ τὴν ἀκαθαρσίαν ἀλλοτρία αὐτῆς εἶναι δοκεῖ. τῶν γε μὴν φυτῶν ἡ μὲν μυρσίνη διὰ τὴν εὐωδίαν Ἀφροδίτης εἶναι διείληπται, [46,15] ἡ δὲ φιλύρα διά τε τοὔνομα, ὅτι τῷ φιλεῖν παρακειμένως ἐξενήνεκται, καὶ ἐπεὶ πρὸς τὰς τῶν στεφάνων πλοκὰς εἰώθασιν αὐτῇ μάλιστα χρῆσθαι. τὴν δὲ πύξον φυλάττονται τῇ θεῷ προσφέρειν ἀφοσιούμενοι [47,1] πως ἐπ' αὐτῆς τὴν πυγήν.

(25) Οὐδὲν δὲ παράδοξον εἰ τοιαύτη οὔσῃ αὐτῇ συντιμᾶται καὶ συμπάρεστιν ὁ Ἔρως, τῶν πλείστων καὶ Ἀφροδίτης υἱὸν αὐτὸν παραδεδωκότων, ὃς δὴ παῖς μέν ἐστι διὰ τὸ ἀτελῆ τὴν [47,5] γνώμην καὶ εὐεξαπάτητον ἔχειν τοὺς ἐρῶντας, πτερωτὸς δέ, ὅτι κουφόνους ποιεῖ ἢ ὅτι ὡς ὄρνις ἀεὶ προσίπταται ταῖς διανοίαις ἀθρόως, τοξότης δ', ἐπεὶ πληγῇ τινι ὅμοιον ἀπὸ τῆς προσόψεως οἱ ἁλισκόμενοι αὐτῷ πάσχουσιν, οὔτε πλησιάσαντες οὔθ' ἁψάμενοι τῶν καλῶν, [47,10] ἀλλὰ μακρόθεν αὐτοὺς ἰδόντες· ἀποδίδοται δὲ καὶ λαμπὰς αὐτῷ, πυροῦν δοκοῦντι τὰς ψυχάς. Ἔρωτα δ' αὐτὸν εἰρῆσθαι πιθανὸν ἀπὸ τῆς ἐπιζητήσεως τῶν ἐρωμένων· τάττεται γὰρ ἐπὶ τοῦ ζητεῖν τὸ ἐρεῖν, ὡς εἴρηται τὸ [47,15] "Ἴφιτος αὖθ' ἵππους

[*keuth*(*esthai*)]. It is because of this that the island of 'Kythera' appears to be sacred to Aphrodite, and perhaps 'Cyprus,' too: the name sounds a bit like *hiding* [*krupsis*]. But her proper home is Paphos, and she is called the 'Paphian,' perhaps by ellipsis from *beguile* [*anaphisk*(*ein*)], which is to deceive. For according to Hesiod, she "smiles and deceives,"[147] and Homer talks about "allurement which steals even the mind of the thoughtful."[148] Her 'embroidered' girdle [*kestos*] is, as it were, something *adorned* [*kekas*(*menos*)] or elaborately pierced. It has the power of tying and binding together. She is called Heavenly and Demotic and Goddess of the Sea because her power is to be seen in the heaven and on earth and in the sea. They say that the vows of love are without authority and may be violated with impunity, and as long as she is readily invoked, the suitor can procure for himself any woman he can use oaths to persuade. Among birds, Aphrodite rejoices especially in the dove because it is a pure creature and, because of its "kisses," friendly. On the other hand, the pig seems to be alien to her because of its impurity. Among plants, the myrtle has been taken to be Aphrodite's because of its sweet smell, and the 'lime tree' [*philura*] because of its name, which turns out to be rather similar to *love* [*phil*(*ein*)], and since it tends to get heavy use for the wreaths of her crowns. And they reserve 'boxwood' [*puxos*] to offer the goddess in a kind of religious devotion to her *buttocks* [*pugē*].

(25) It is no paradox, given how Aphrodite is, that Eros should share her honor and be her companion—also her son, according to the majority tradition. He is a child because lovers are immature in their thinking and are easily deceived; he is winged because he makes people birdbrained or because he tends to fly suddenly into one's thoughts, bird-like; he is an archer because those captured by him experience something like a blow just from looking—not even approaching or touching someone beautiful, but seeing them from afar. He is given a torch, since he seems to set souls on fire. It is plausible that he is called 'Eros' from the search involved for those who are the objects of love; for *inquiry* [*erein*] is linked with searching, as in the line: "Iphitos inquiring after horses."[149] (It is from this, I think, that

---

147. Hesiod, *Theog.* 205.
148. Homer, *Il.* 14.217.
149. See Homer, *Od.* 21.22—although in fact Homer used the word translated "searching" here, *not* "inquiring." Berdozzo (2009, n. 327 ad loc.) suggests confusion with *Od.* 21.31, where "inquiring" does appear, but there is another possibility. The name "Iphitos" could suggest the word *ephiemai*, to desire; if so, then the point of quoting this is to give Homer's support to the *thematic* connection between desire and inquiry—and not merely (or perhaps not at all) to exemplify the use of the verb *erein*.

ἐρέων," ἐντεῦθεν, οἶμαι, καὶ τῆς ἐρεύνης ὠνομασμένης. καὶ πλείους δὲ Ἔρωτες παραδίδονται διὰ τὴν πολυτροπίαν τῶν ἐρώντων καὶ τὸ πολλοῖς τοιούτοις ὀπαδοῖς κεχορηγῆσθαι τὴν Ἀφροδίτην. καλεῖται δὲ καὶ Ἵμερος [47,20] εἴτουν παρὰ τὸ ἴεσθαι καὶ φέρεσθαι ἐπὶ τὴν ἀπόλαυσιν τῶν ὡραίων ὠνομασμένος εἴτε κατὰ μίμησιν τῆς περὶ τὴν διάνοιαν ἐκστάσεως ὡς μεμωρῶσθαι περὶ [48,1] ταύτην· Πόθος δ᾽ ἀπὸ τῆς τῶν φιλημάτων μιμήσεως, ὅθεν ἔσχε τὴν κλῆσιν καὶ ὁ πάππας, ἢ ἀπὸ τοῦ πολλὰ πυνθάνεσθαι περὶ τῶν ἐρωμένων τοὺς ἐρῶντας καὶ αὐτῶν ἐκείνων, πόθεν ἔρχονται καὶ ποῦ ἦσαν.

[48,5] Ἔνιοι δὲ καὶ τὸν ὅλον κόσμον νομίζουσιν Ἔρωτα εἶναι, καλόν τε καὶ ἐπαφρόδιτον καὶ νεαρὸν ὄντα καὶ πρεσβύτατον ἅμα πάντων καὶ πολλῷ κεχρημένον πυρὶ καὶ ταχεῖαν ὥσπερ ἀπὸ τοξείας ἢ διὰ πτερῶν τὴν κίνησιν ποιούμενον· (26) τοῦτον δ᾽ ἄλλως εἶναι καὶ τὸν [48,10] Ἄτλαντα, ἀταλαιπώρως ἀποδιδόντα τὰ κατὰ τοὺς ἐμπεριεχομένους ἐν αὐτῷ λόγους γινόμενα καὶ οὕτω καὶ τὸν οὐρανὸν βαστάζοντα, ἔχειν δὲ κίονας μακρὰς τὰς τῶν στοιχείων δυνάμεις, καθ᾽ ἃς τὰ μὲν ἀνωφερῆ ἐστι, τὰ δὲ κατωφερῆ· ὑπὸ τούτων γὰρ διακρατεῖσθαι [48,15] τὸν οὐρανὸν καὶ τὴν γῆν· ὀλοόφρονα[150] δ᾽ αὐτὸν εἰρῆσθαι διὰ τὸ περὶ τῶν ὅλων φροντίζειν καὶ προνοεῖσθαι τῆς πάντων αὐτοῦ τῶν μερῶν σωτηρίας. ἐκ δ᾽ αὐτοῦ τὰς Πλειάδας γεγονέναι παρισταμένου ὅτι πάντα τὰ ἄστρα πλείονα ὄντα ἐγέννησεν, Ἀστραίῳ τε καὶ Θαύμαντι [49,1] ὁ αὐτὸς ὤν· οὔτε γὰρ ἵσταται, τὸ σύνολον ἀνηρέμητος ὑπάρχων, εἰ καὶ ὅτι μάλιστα εὖ βεβηκέναι δοκεῖ καὶ ἀσάλευτος εἶναι, θαυμασμόν τε τοῖς ἐφεστῶσιν ἐπὶ τὴν διάταξιν αὐτοῦ πολὺν ἐμποιεῖ. (27) τοῦτον [49,5] εἶναι καὶ τὸν Πᾶνα, ἐπειδὴ τῷ παντὶ ὁ αὐτός ἐστι. καὶ τὰ μὲν κάτω λάσια καὶ τραγώδη διὰ τὴν τῆς γῆς δασύτητα ἔχειν, τὰ δ᾽ ἄνω ἀνθρωπόμορφα διὰ τὸ ἐν τῷ αἰθέρι τὸ ἡγεμονικὸν εἶναι τοῦ κόσμου, ὃ δὴ λογικόν ἐστι. λάγνον δὲ καὶ ὀχευτὴν αὐτὸν παρεισάγεσθαι [49,10] διὰ τὸ πλῆθος ὧνπερ εἴληφε σπερματικῶν λόγων καὶ τῶν κατὰ σύμμιξιν ἐξ αὐτῶν γινομένων. ἐν ταῖς ἐρήμοις δὲ διατρίβειν μάλιστα τῆς μονότητος αὐτοῦ διὰ τούτου παρισταμένης· εἷς γὰρ καὶ μονογενὴς ὁ κόσμος ἐστί. τὰς δὲ Νύμφας διώκειν, ἐπειδὴ χαίρει ταῖς ἐκ [49,15] τῆς γῆς ὑγραῖς ἀναθυμιάσεσιν, ὧν χωρὶς

---

150. See *SVF* 3.549; ὀλοόφρονα Lang (1881), Torres (2018).

'quest' [*ereunē*] *is* also named.) Traditionally, there is more than one Eros because there is a variety of lovers—and because Aphrodite is furnished with many of them as her attendants. Eros is called 'Desire' [*himeros*], named either from being *eager for* [*hi(esthai)*] and carried away toward the enjoyment to be had of those in their prime or to represent the distraction experienced by the mind, which becomes *silly* [*memōr(ōsthai)*] in the face of it. He is called 'Yearning' [*pothos*] from a representation of kisses (which is how we get the word 'pappa,' too);[151] or else from the fact that a lover *finds out* [cf. *puth(esthai)*] many thing about their beloved—and from their very questions: *whence* [*pothen*] they come and *where* [*pou*] they were.

Some think that Eros is also the whole cosmos: beautiful, desirable, young, and at the same time the oldest thing of all, rich in fire and the cause of swift motion, such as that produced by a bow or the use of wings. (26) In another sense, they say that it is 'Atlas,' *tirelessly* [*atalai(pōrōs)*] producing everything that comes to be according to the principles encompassed in it and thus holding up even the heavens. Its great pillars are the powers of the elements, which lead to some things being borne upwards and some downwards; heaven and earth are governed by them. Atlas is called 'Sagacious' [*holoophrōn*] because he is *concerned for the universe* [*holōn phront(izein)*] and provident in seeing to the welfare of all its parts. From him were born the 'Pleiades,' it being established that it [the cosmos] generated all the stars, of which there is a *superabundance* [*pleiona*]. He is identical with 'Astraios' and 'Thaumas' because it does not [sc. *a-*] *stand still* [(*hi*)*st*(*atai*)] (it is never everywhere at rest—although its progress is the best possible and calm), and it produces great *wonder* [*thaumas(mos)*] in those who contemplate its organization. (27) And it is 'Pan' as well, since it is identical with *everything* [*pan*]. He is hairy and goat-like in his lower parts because of the roughness of the earth; his upper parts have the form of a human because the ruling part of the cosmos, which is rational, is in the aether.[152] He is traditionally held to be lecherous and lewd because of the number both of the seminal principles it possesses and of the things that come about from their intermingling. He passes much of his time in the wilderness because it was established that he is solitary on the basis of the fact that the cosmos is single and unique.[153] He pursues Nymphs because

---

151. I.e., because *pothos*, like *pappa*, involves puckering the lips. There are other examples of this kind of gestural etymology in Chrysippus: e.g., *SVF* 2.895 (in *egō*, "I," the chin points to the self).

152. See n. 7 above.

153. See *SVF* 2.528, 530–531, 945.

οὐδ' οἷόν τ' ἐστὶν αὐτὸν συνεστάναι· τὸ δὲ σκιρτητικὸν αὐτοῦ καὶ παικτικὸν τὴν ἀεὶ κίνησιν τῶν ὅλων ἐμφαίνει. νεβρίδα δὲ ἢ παρδαλῆν αὐτὸν ἐνῆφθαι διὰ τὴν ποικιλίαν τῶν ἄστρων καὶ τῶν ἄλλων χρημάτων[154] ἃ θεωρεῖται [50,1] ἐν αὐτῷ. συρικτὴν δὲ εἶναι τάχα μὲν διὰ τὸ ὑπὸ παντοίων ἀνέμων διαπνεῖσθαι, τάχα δ' ἐπεὶ τὴν ἐμμέλειαν ἀγριοφανῆ καὶ αὐστηρὰν ἀλλ' οὐ πρὸς ἐπίδειξιν ἔχει. τῷ δὲ ἐν τοῖς ὄρεσιν αὐτὸν καὶ τοῖς [50,5] σπηλαίοις διαιτᾶσθαι καὶ τὸ τῆς πίτυος στέμμα ἐπηκολούθησεν, ὄρειόν τι καὶ μεγαλοπρεπὲς ἔχοντος τοῦ φυτοῦ, ἔτι δὲ τὸ Πανικὰς λέγεσθαι ταραχὰς τὰς αἰφνιδίους καὶ ἀλόγους· οὕτω γάρ πως καὶ αἱ ἀγέλαι καὶ τὰ αἰπόλια πτοεῖται ψόφου τινὸς ἐξ ὕλης ἢ [50,10] τῶν ὑπάντρων καὶ φαραγγωδῶν τόπων ἀκούσαντα. οἰκείως δὲ καὶ τῶν ἀγελαίων θρεμμάτων αὐτὸν ἐπίσκοπον ἐποιήσαντο, τάχα μὲν διὰ τοῦτο καὶ κεράστην αὐτὸν καὶ δίχηλον πλάττοντες, τάχα δὲ τὸ διττὸν τῶν ἐξεχόντων ἐν αὐτῷ ὤτων αἰνιττόμενοι. [50,15] Ἴσως δ' ἂν οὗτος καὶ ὁ Πρίαπος εἴη, καθ' ὃν πρόεισιν εἰς φῶς πάντα, τῶν ἀρχαίων δεισιδαιμόνως καὶ ἁδρῶς διὰ τούτων ἃ ἐφρόνουν περὶ τῆς τοῦ κόσμου φύσεως παριστάντων. ἐμφαίνει γοῦν τὸ μέγεθος τῶν αἰδοίων τὴν πλεονάζουσαν ἐν τῷ θεῷ σπερματικὴν [50,20] δύναμιν, ἡ δ' ἐν τοῖς κόλποις αὐτοῦ παγκαρπία τὴν δαψίλειαν τῶν ἐν ταῖς οἰκείαις ὥραις ἐντὸς τοῦ κόλπου φυομένων καὶ ἀναδεικνυμένων καρπῶν. παρεισάγεται δὲ καὶ αὐτὸς φύλαξ τῶν τε κήπων καὶ τῶν ἀμπέλων, [51,1] ἐπειδὴ κατὰ τὸν γεννῶντά ἐστι καὶ τὸ σώζειν ἃ γεννᾷ καὶ τοῦ Διὸς ἐντεῦθεν σωτῆρος εἶναι λεγομένου, καὶ τὸ μὲν πολυφόρον[155] καὶ καθαρὸν αἱ ἄμπελοι παριστᾶσι, μάλιστα δὲ τὸ ποικίλον καὶ ἐπιτερπὲς καὶ [51,5] ῥαδίαν τὴν γένεσιν ποιούμενον οἱ κῆποι, τοιαύτην ὡς ἐπίπαν αὐτοῦ καὶ τὴν ἐσθῆτα ἔχοντος. δρέπανον δὲ ἐν τῇ δεξιᾷ χειρὶ προτείνει πότερον ἐπεὶ τούτῳ χρῶνται πρὸς τὴν κάθαρσιν τῶν ἀμπέλων ἢ ἐπεὶ κατὰ τὸν τηροῦντά τί ἐστι καὶ καθωπλίσθαι πρὸς ἀσφάλειαν [51,10] αὐτοῦ ἢ ὡς τῆς αὐτῆς δυνάμεως μετὰ τὸ ἐνεγκεῖν τὰ ὄντα ἐκτεμνούσης αὐτὰ καὶ φθειρούσης.

Ἀγαθὸς δὲ Δαίμων ἤτοι πάλιν ὁ κόσμος ἐστὶ βρίθων καὶ αὐτὸς τοῖς καρποῖς ἢ ὁ προεστὼς αὐτοῦ λόγος, καθ' ὅσον δατεῖται καὶ διαμερίζει τὸ ἐπιβάλλον ἀγαθὸς διαιρέτης [51,15] ὑπάρχων. προστάτης δὲ καὶ σωτὴρ τῶν οἰκείων ἐστὶ τῷ σώζειν

---

154. my conjecture; χρωμάτων manuscripts. Without emendation, the reference would be, absurdly, to "stars and other colors."

155. Torres (2018); πολύφορον Lang (1881).

it rejoices in the moist exhalations of the earth, without which it could not be constituted.[156] His skittish and playful nature points to the ceaseless motion of the universe. He is clad in fawn skin or leopard skin because of the variety of the stars and of the other things which are observed in it.[157] He is said to play the panpipes, perhaps because it is swept by all sorts of winds or perhaps because they sound wild and austere, and they are not just for making a show. Because he spends time on mountains and in caves, the pine wreath was associated with him—the pine being an impressive tree associated with mountains. Also associated with him are the sudden and irrational disturbances called panic attacks; for this is how sheep and goats are frightened when they hear a sound from the wood or from underground caverns and in places where there are ravines. It was appropriate that they should have made him guardian of the young of the herds, and it is perhaps because of this that they depict him with horns and cloven hooves, and perhaps they were hinting at his double nature in his protruding ears. Perhaps it is 'Priapus' as well, by which all things *come into the light* [*proei(sin eis) phōs*]—the ancients thus suggesting in a superstitious and grandiose way what they thought about the nature of the cosmos. Anyway, the size of his genitals shows the abundant seminal power that is in god, while the collection of fruits held in the folds of his cloak indicates the wealth of fruits that grow in the bosom of the land and come forth in due season. Traditionally, he is guardian of orchards and vineyards, since it is the job of the parent to preserve what he has brought into being (Zeus, too, thence being said to be Preserver). Vineyards suggest bounty and purity, but fruits suggest more especially variety, pleasure, and making generation easy; he is mostly dressed that way as well. And he holds out a sickle in his right hand, either because this is used for pruning vines, or because he is guarding something and is armed to protect it, or because it is the same power that, after bringing things into being, cuts them off and destroys them.[158]

Again, the cosmos is 'Good Daemon,' he, too, being laden with fruits; or else he is the principle which rules it, considered insofar as it divides and *shares out* [*diamer(izei)*] what happens, thus being a good distributor. He is defender and preserver of household matters because it keeps its own

---

156. See *SVF* 2.572, 690.
157. See *SVF* 2.1009 (299,15–17).
158. Perhaps another reference to the destruction of the cosmos; see 28,10–12 with n. 92.

καλῶς τὸν ἴδιον οἶκον καὶ ὑπόδειγμα παρέχειν ἑαυτὸν καὶ τοῖς ἄλλοις. τὸ δὲ τῆς Ἀμαλθείας κέρας οἰκεῖον αὐτῷ φόρημά ἐστιν, ἐν ᾧ ἅμα πάντα ἀλδήσκει τὰ κατὰ τοὺς οἰκείους καιροὺς φυόμενα, [51,20] ἀλλ' οὐ περὶ ἕν τι αὐτῷ γινόμενα, περὶ πολλὰ δὲ ἀθρόως καὶ ποικίλα, ἢ ἐπεὶ ἐμπεριόδως ἀμαλδύνει [52,1] καὶ πάλιν κεραΐζει πάντα ἢ διὰ τὴν γινομένην ἐξ αὐτοῦ πρὸς τὸ πονεῖν προτροπὴν ὡς τῶν ἀγαθῶν τοῖς[159] μὴ μαλακιζομένοις προσγινομένων.

C.2.

(28) Ἑξῆς δὲ περὶ Δήμητρος καὶ Ἑστίας, ὦ [52,5] παῖ, λεκτέον· ἑκατέρα δ' ἔοικεν οὐχ ἑτέρα τῆς γῆς εἶναι. ταύτην μὲν γὰρ διὰ τὸ ἑστάναι διὰ παντὸς Ἑστίαν προσηγόρευσαν οἱ παλαιοὶ ἢ διὰ τὸ ταύτην ὑπὸ τῆς φύσεως ἐσωτάτω τεθεῖσθαι ἢ διὰ τὸ ἐπ' αὐτῆς ὡσανεὶ ἐπὶ θεμελίου τὸν ὅλον ἑστάναι κόσμον, διὰ δὲ τὸ μητρὸς [52,10] τρόπον φύειν τε καὶ τρέφειν πάντα Δήμητραν οἱονεὶ γῆν μητέρα οὖσαν ἢ Δηὼ μητέρα τῷ καὶ αὐτὴν καὶ τὰ ἐπ' αὐτῆς ἀφθόνως ἐφεῖσθαι τοῖς ἀνθρώποις δατεῖσθαι καὶ δαίνυσθαι ἢ ἐπ' αὐτῆς δήειν, ὅ ἐστιν εὑρίσκειν, ἃ μάλιστα[160] ἐπιζητοῦσι.

Παρεισάγεται τε ἡ [52,15] μὲν Ἑστία παρθένος διὰ τὸ τὴν ἀκινησίαν μηδενὸς εἶναι γεννητικήν—καὶ τούτου χάριν καὶ ὑπὸ παρθένων νεωκορεῖται—ἡ δὲ Δημήτηρ οὐκέτι, ἀλλὰ τὴν Κόρην τετοκυῖα οἷον τὴν Κόρον ἢ πρὸς τὸ τρέφεσθαι [53,1] μέχρι κόρου ὕλη. τὸ δ' ἀείζωον πῦρ ἀποδέδοται τῇ Ἑστίᾳ διὰ τὸ καὶ αὐτὸ δοκεῖν εἶναι ὄν, τάχα δ' ἐπεὶ τὰ πυρὰ τὰ[161] ἐν κόσμῳ πάντα ἐντεῦθεν τρέφεται καὶ διὰ ταύτην ὑφέστηκεν ἢ ἐπεὶ ζείδωρός ἐστι καὶ ζῴων [53,5] μήτηρ, οἷς αἴτιον τοῦ ζῆν τὸ πυρῶδές ἐστι. στρογγύλη δὲ πλάττεται καὶ κατὰ μέσους ἱδρύεται τοὺς οἴκους διὰ τὸ καὶ τὴν γῆν τοιαύτην εἶναι καὶ

---

159. Torres (2018); om. Lang (1881).
160. Torres (2018); om. Lang (1881).
161. Torres (2018); om. Lang (1881).

house in order and at the same time offers itself as an example to others. The 'horn [*keras*] of Amaltheia' is an attribute proper to him because of whom all things that are generated *in due season* [*kairoi*] *grow at the same time* [*hama aldē(skei)*]—not that he brings them into being for some single purpose; they crowd into being for many and various purposes. Or it [the 'horn of Amaltheia'] might indicate that the cosmos periodically *destroys* [*amaldunei*] and again *plunders* [*kera(izei)*] everything,[162] or it might be the exhortation to labor which comes from him, since good things come to those who are *not* [sc. *a*-] *made soft* [*malak(izomenoi)*].

C.2. Earth (and Principles of Stability)

(28) Next, my child, we must speak about Demeter and Hestia ["hearth"]: both seem to be none other than the earth. The ancients called this 'Hestia' because it is *stands firm* [*hest(anai)*] through everything, or because it was placed *innermost* [*esōtatō*] by nature, or because the whole cosmos *stands firm* [*hest(anai)*] on it as on a foundation. Since it gives birth to everything and nourishes it like a mother, the ancients called it 'Demeter,' as if it were *Earth Mother* [*gē-mētēr*], or else 'Mother Deo' because the earth and the things on it ungrudgingly produce what men can divide among themselves and *feast on* [*dai(nusthai)*] or because on it they *meet with* [*dē(ein)*], that is, find, what they most especially seek.

Hestia is traditionally a virgin because what is unmoving generates nothing. Because of this, she is also served by virgins.[163] (But Demeter is not also a virgin; she gave birth to 'Kore'—as it were, *Satiety* [*koros*]—she [Demeter] being the material for one's being nourished to satiety.) The eternal fire is associated with 'Hestia' because it, too, seems to be *what is* [cf. *esti*],[164] and perhaps because all the fires in the cosmos are nourished from the earth and subsist because of it or because the earth is life giving and the mother of living things, in which the fiery element is the cause of life. She[165] is formed circular and set in the middle of the home because

---

162. See once more 28,10–12 above, with n. 92.

163. Possibly a reference to the Vestal Virgins in Rome (see Most 1989, 2030 n. 123, with Cicero, *Nat. d.* 2.67).

164. As we have seen, fire is one characterization of precosmic "substance" (*ousia*, lit. "being" or "what is"): e.g., 28,10–11.

165. I.e., Hestia understood in concrete form as the hearth.

οὕτως ἱδρῦσθαι συμπεπιλημένην, ὅθεν κατὰ μίμησιν ἡ γῆ τε καὶ[166] χθὼν προσηγόρευται. τάχα δὲ ἡ χθὼν ἀπὸ τοῦ χείεσθαι [53,10] ἤτοι χωρεῖν πάντα οὕτως[167] ἐκλήθη, ὡς εἴρηται τὸ "οὐδὸς δ' ἀμφοτέρους ὅδε χείσεται." μυθεύεται δὲ πρώτη τε καὶ ἐσχάτη γενέσθαι τῷ εἰς ταύτην ἀναλύεσθαι τὰ ἀπ' αὐτῆς γινόμενα καὶ ἐξ αὐτῆς συνίστασθαι, καθὸ κἂν ταῖς θυσίαις οἱ Ἕλληνες [53,15] ἀπὸ πρώτης τε αὐτῆς ἤρχοντο καὶ εἰς ἐσχάτην αὐτὴν κατέπαυον. στέμματα δ' αὐτῇ λευκὰ περίκεινται τῷ στέφεσθαι καὶ καλύπτεσθαι πανταχόθεν αὐτὴν ὑπὸ τοῦ λευκοτάτου στοιχείου.

Ἡ μέντοι Δημήτηρ κατὰ τὸ ἀναδοτικὸν τῶν σπερμάτων εἰδοποιουμένη πάνυ οἰκείως [53,20] εἰσάγεται στάχυσιν ἐστεφανωμένη. τοῦτο γὰρ ἀναγκαιότατον ὂν κεχάρισται τοῖς ἀνθρώποις ἡ ἥμερος τροφή ἐστι. ταύτην δὲ μυθεύεται σπεῖραι διὰ τῆς οἰκουμένης ὁ Τριπτόλεμος ὁ Ἐλευσίνιος ἀναβιβασάσης αὐτὸν [54,1] ἐπὶ πτερωτῶν δρακόντων ὄχημα τῆς Δήμητρος. ἔοικε γὰρ πρῶτός τις τῶν παλαιῶν δρακεῖν καὶ συνιέναι θεοῦ τινος ἐπὶ μετεωροτέραν ἐπίνοιαν ἀναβιβάσαντος τὸν μεταχειρισμὸν τῆς κριθῆς, ὃν τρόπον τρίβεται καὶ [54,5] διακρίνεται διὰ τοῦ εἰς τὸν ἀέρα ἀναρριπτεῖσθαι ἀπὸ τῶν ἀχύρων· διὸ καὶ κριὸς ἐπιτηδείως ἔχει πρὸς τὴν σποράν.[168] ἐντεῦθεν δὲ τὴν ὀνομασίαν εἴληφεν, ὁ τρίψας τὰς οὐλάς· οὐλαὶ δὲ λέγονται αἱ κριθαί· Ἐλευσὶν δὲ ὁ τόπος, ὅπου πρώτως εὑρέθησαν. ἐκλήθη καὶ ἡ [54,10] Δημήτηρ Ἐλευσινία ἀπὸ τῆς αὐτόθι πρῶτον ἐλεύσεως γενομένης τοῖς ἀνθρώποις εἰς ἀνθρώπινον ὄντως βίον. ἁρπάσαι δ' ὁ Ἅιδης τὴν θυγατέρα τῆς Δήμητρος ἐμυθεύθη διὰ τὸν γινόμενον ἐπὶ χρόνον τινὰ τῶν σπερμάτων κατὰ γῆς ἀφανισμόν. προσεπλάσθη δ' ἡ κατήφεια [54,15] τῆς θεοῦ καὶ ἡ διὰ τοῦ κόσμου ζήτησις. τοιοῦτον γάρ τι καὶ παρ' Αἰγυπτίοις ὁ ζητούμενος καὶ ἀνευρισκόμενος ὑπὸ τῆς Ἴσιδος Ὄσιρις ἐμφαίνει καὶ παρὰ Φοίνιξιν ὁ ἀνὰ μέρος παρ' ἓξ μῆνας ὑπὲρ γῆν τε καὶ ὑπὸ γῆν γινόμενος Ἄδωνις, ἀπὸ τοῦ

---

166. ἡ γῆ [τε] καὶ Lang (1881); γῆ τε καὶ Torres (2018).
167. Torres (2018); om. Lang (1881).
168. διὸ to σποράν del. Lang (1881), Torres (2018).

the compression of earth gives it similar shape and setting.[169] This is why the earth is also, imitatively, called 'chthon'[170]—but perhaps it was called 'chthon' this way from the fact that it *contains* [*cheiesthai*] or has room for everything, as in the line: 'This road will contain us both.'[171] Mythology tells that she is first and last because the things that were born from the earth and sustained by it are dissolved into it, and this is also why the Greeks start and end their sacrifices with her. She is garlanded with white branches because it is crowned, and covered all over, by the whitest element.

Demeter, depicted according to her role in making seeds spring up, is quite appropriately shown crowned with ears of corn—for of all things whose cultivation benefits people, corn is the most essential. According to the myth, it was sown throughout the inhabited world by Triptolemos of Eleusis, mounted by Demeter in a chariot of winged 'serpents' [*drakontes*]. For it seems that there was among the ancients some first man who was mounted by god in a higher level of thought and *saw* [*drak(ein)*] and understood the use of 'barley' [*krithē*]—how it is ground and *separated* [*(dia)krin(etai)*] from its husk by being tossed in the air. (For the same reason, 'krios'[172] is also suited for sowing.) He took his name from the one who *grinds the oulai* [*tripsas tas oulas*] (barley seeds are called *oulai*). 'Eleusis' is the place where barley seeds were first *discovered* [*heurethēsan*], and Demeter is called 'Eleusinian' from the fact that human *progress* [*eleusis*] to a truly human life began there. There is a myth that Hades kidnapped the daughter of Demeter because of the disappearance of the seeds under the earth for a certain time. (The dejection of the goddess and her search throughout the cosmos are fictional additions.) Among the Egyptians, Osiris (who is sought and rediscovered by Isis) suggests the same sort of thing, and among the Phoenicians there is Adonis, who is alternately above the ground and below the ground for six-month periods—Demeter's pro-

---

169. "Compression" is one term used for the derivation of the denser elements from lighter ones (e.g., *SVF* 2.406; cf. Posidonius, frag. 336b (Theiler 1982) (from Arrian's *Physics*) at Stobaeus, *Anthology*, 1:246.6–9 (Wachsmuth and Hense 1884–1912). The denser elements are carried to the center of the universe (cf. "setting"), around which they cluster (hence explaining the circular shape of the earth): e.g., Cicero, *Nat. d.* 2.115 = *SVF* 2.549.

170. The thought here is not clear, but perhaps Cornutus is thinking that the mouth enacts compression when the word *chthon* is articulated (cf. the imitation in 48,1 above).

171. Homer, *Od.* 18.17.

172. A type of chickpea.

ἁδεῖν τοῖς [54,20] ἀνθρώποις οὕτως ὠνομασμένου τοῦ Δημητριακοῦ καρποῦ. τοῦτον δὲ πλήξας κάπρος ἀνελεῖν λέγεται διὰ τὸ τὰς ὗς δοκεῖν ληιβότειρας εἶναι ἢ τὸν τῆς ὕνεως [55,1] ὀδόντα αἰνιττομένων αὐτῶν, ὑφ' οὗ κατὰ γῆς κρύπτεται τὸ σπέρμα· διατετάχθαι δὲ ὧδε, παρά τε τῇ Ἀφροδίτῃ τὸν ἴσον χρόνον μένειν τὸν Ἄδωνιν καὶ παρὰ τῇ Περσεφόνῃ, δι' ἣν εἴπομεν αἰτίαν. ἐκάλεσαν δὲ [55,5] Περσεφόνην τὴν τῆς Δήμητρος θυγατέρα διὰ τὸ ἐπίπονον εἶναι καὶ πόνων οἰστικὴν τὴν ἐργασίαν ἢ τῷ ἐκ πόνων ὑπομονὴν φέρεσθαι. νηστεύουσι δ' εἰς τιμὴν τῆς Δήμητρος ἤτοι γεραίροντες αὐτὴν ἰδίῳ τρόπῳ τινὶ ἀπαρχῆς διὰ τοῦ πρὸς μίαν ἡμέραν ἀπέχεσθαι τῶν [55,10] δεδομένων αὐτοῖς ὑπ' αὐτῆς ἢ κατ' εὐλάβειαν ἐνδείας παρεισεληλυθότος τοῦ θεοῦ.[173] ἐπειδὴ δὲ ἔσπειρον, ἀφῄρουν ἀπὸ τῶν ἰδίων χρεῶν, καθὸ παρὰ τὸν τοῦ σπόρου καιρὸν τὴν ἑορτὴν αὐτῆς ἄγουσι. περὶ δὲ τὸ ἔαρ τῇ Χλόῃ Δήμητρι θύουσι μετὰ παιδιᾶς καὶ χαρᾶς, ἰδόντες [55,15] χλοάζοντα καὶ ἀφθονίας αὐτοῖς ἐλπίδα ὑποδεικνύντα. ἐντεῦθεν δὲ καὶ ὁ Πλοῦτος τῆς Δήμητρος υἱὸς ἔδοξεν εἶναι. καλῶς γὰρ εἴρηται τὸ [56,1] "σίτου καὶ κριθῆς, ὦ νήπιε, πλοῦτος ἄριστος." καὶ ἐναντίον πώς ἐστι τῷ λιμώττειν τὸ περιουσιάζεσθαι, εἰς ὃ καὶ ἀπιδὼν ὁ Ἡσίοδός φησιν· "Ἐργάζευ, Πέρση, δῖον γένος, ὄφρα σε λιμὸς [56,5] ἐχθαίρῃ, φιλέῃ δέ σ' ἐυπλόκαμος Δημήτηρ." θύουσι δ' ὗς ἐγκύμονας τῇ Δήμητρι πάνυ οἰκείως, τὸ πολύγονον καὶ εὐσύλληπτον καὶ τελεσφόρον παριστάντες. ἀνατιθέασι δ' αὐτῇ καὶ τὰς μήκωνας κατὰ λόγον· τό τε γὰρ στρογγύλον καὶ περιφερὲς αὐτῶν παρίστησι [56,10] τὸ σχῆμα τῆς γῆς σφαιροειδοῦς οὔσης, ἥ τε ἀνωμαλία τὰς κοιλότητας καὶ τὰς ἐξοχὰς τῶν ὀρῶν, τὰ δ' ἐντὸς τοῖς ἀντρώδεσι καὶ ὑπονόμοις ἔοικε, σπέρματά τε ἀνάριθμητα γεννῶσιν ὥσπερ ἡ γῆ. διὰ δὲ τὴν ἀφθονίαν τῶν σιτηρῶν ἐπαύσαντο οἱ ἄνθρωποι δυσπόριστον [56,15] καὶ ἀμφιδήριτον τὴν τροφὴν ἔχοντες, ὥστε καὶ συντιθέμενοί τινα πρὸς ἀλλήλους περὶ τῶν κατὰ τὰ ἠροτριωμένα μέτρων καὶ διανεμόμενοι τὰ γεννώμενα δικαίως ἀρχηγὸν ἔλεγον νόμων καὶ θεσμῶν τὴν Δήμητραν αὐτοῖς γεγονέναι· ἐντεῦθεν θεσμοθέτιν αὐτὴν προσηγόρευσαν [56,20] οἷον νομοθέτιν οὖσαν, οὐκ ὀρθῶς τινων θεσμὸν ὑπολαβόντων εἰρῆσθαι τὸν καρπὸν ἀπὸ τοῦ αὐτὸν ἀποτίθεσθαι καὶ θησαυρίζεσθαι. μυστήρια δ' ἄγειν ἤρξαντο αὐτῇ φιλοσοφοῦντες, ἅμα τῇ εὑρέσει τῶν πρὸς τὸν βίον χρησίμων

---

173. τοῦ † θεοῦ Lang (1881); προσεληλυθυίας τῆς θεοῦ Torres (2018) ("when the goddess has come forth").

duce being thus called 'Adonis' from the fact that people *enjoy* [*hadein*] it. It is said that a wild boar struck and killed him because pigs are known to devour the crops, or this all hints at the teeth of the ploughshare, by which seed gets covered in earth. He was assigned to be with Aphrodite and Persephone for equal periods of time, for the reason we said. They called the daughter of Demeter 'Persephone' because manual labor is hard work and *brings* [cf. *pherein*] hard work [*ponos*] or from the fact that *hard work brings* [(*ek*) *ponōn pheresthai*] endurance. Fasts are held in honor of Demeter, either as a special way of presenting her with the first fruits by abstaining for one day from those things given to people by her or through pious fear of want when the god withdraws within.[174] When they were sowing, they drew on their own stocks, which is why people hold her festival at the time of sowing. Around spring they sacrifice to Demeter 'Chloe' with games and good cheer, seeing *green* shoots [*chlo*(*azonta*)] which hint at the hope of plenty for them as well. Hence Wealth is thought to be the son of Demeter, and it is well said that "wealth in grain and barley is best, you fool!"[175] Being wealthy is in some way the opposite of starving; Hesiod notices this when he says, "Work, Perses, divine race, so that hunger may hate you but Demeter of the lovely hair will love you."[176] Pregnant sows are, quite appropriately, sacrificed to Demeter: it represents ease in fertility, conception, and birth. Poppies are dedicated to her for a reason: their round, spherical shape represents the shape of the earth, which is a globe, while the irregularity on their surface represents the hollows of the earth and the peaks of the mountains. Its interior is like caves and mines. They produce countless seeds, like the earth. Because of the plentifulness of corn, men no longer had any difficulty getting by, and their supply of food was no longer doubtful. This allowed them to agree with each other about the boundaries of cultivated land and to distribute its produce justly, and so they said that Demeter was the originator of their laws and *ordinances* [*thesmoi*]. Thus it is that they called her 'Thesmothetis,' as being a lawgiver—although some people wrongly think that her crops were called 'thesmos' because they are *laid aside* [(*apoti*)*thes*(*thai*)] and *stored up* [*thēsaur*(*izesthai*)]. It was with philosophical intent that they began to celebrate the 'mysteries' for her, rejoicing at the same time in the discovery of things beneficial for

---

174. If this is the right reading of the text, then "the god" (masculine) would be Adonis, representing the crops.

175. Traditional. A slightly different version is quoted in the scholia to Hesiod, *Theog.* 969, which mentions the birth of Wealth (Ploutos) to Demeter.

176. Hesiod, *Op.* 299–300.

καὶ τῇ πανηγύρει χαίροντες [57,1] ὡς μαρτυρίῳ χρώμενοι τοῦ πεπαῦσθαι μαχομένους αὐτοὺς ἀλλήλοις περὶ τῶν ἀναγκαίων μυσιᾶν τε, ὅ ἐστι κεκορῆσθαι· πιθανὸν γὰρ ἐντεῦθεν ὠνομάσθαι τὰ μυστήρια, ὅθεν καὶ μυσία παρά τισιν ἡ Δημήτηρ, [57,5] ἢ ἀπὸ τοῦ μώσεως δεῖσθαι τὰ δυσξύμβλητόν τι ἔχοντα. (29) διὰ δὲ ταύτην τὴν αἰτίαν καὶ ἐκ Θέμιδος λέγεται ὁ Ζεὺς γεννῆσαι τὰς Ὥρας, ὑφ' ὧν τὰ ἀγαθὰ πάντα καθ' ἡμᾶς ὡρεύεται καὶ φυλάττεται. καλεῖται δ' αὐτῶν ἡ μὲν Εὐνομία ἀπὸ τῆς τοῦ ἐπιβάλλοντος [57,10] διανεμήσεως, ἡ δὲ Δίκη ἀπὸ τοῦ δίχα χωρίζειν ἀπ' ἀλλήλων τοὺς διαφερομένους, ἡ δὲ Εἰρήνη ἀπὸ τοῦ διὰ λόγου καὶ οὐ δι' ὅπλων διακρίνεσθαι ποιεῖν· ἐκάλουν γὰρ τὸν λόγον εἰρήνην· ὁ δὲ πόλεμος ἀπὸ τοῦ πολλοὺς ὀλλύναι οὕτως ὠνόμασται ἢ ἀπὸ τοῦ παλάμαις [57,15] σπεύδειν περιγίνεσθαι τῶν ἐναντίων.

(30) Οἰκείως δ' ἔδοξεν Εἰρήνη κατά τι καὶ ὁ Διόνυσος εἶναι, τῶν ἡμέρων δένδρων ἐπίσκοπος ὢν καὶ δοτὴρ θεός, καὶ διὰ ταῦτα σπονδὰς ποιοῦνται·[177] δενδροκοποῦνται γὰρ αἱ χῶραι τοῖς πολέμοις· ἐν εἰρήνῃ [57,20] δὲ καὶ τὰ τῶν εὐωχιῶν θάλλει, οἷς ἀναγκαιότατος ὁ οἶνός ἐστι. τυγχάνει δὲ ὁ Διόνυσος ἤτοι διόνυξος [58,1] ὢν ἢ οἷον δίανυσος παρὰ τὸ διαίνειν ἡμᾶς ἡδέως ἢ ὡσανεὶ διάλυσος κεκλημένος, ἀφ' ἧς ἀρχῆς καὶ λύσιον αὐτὸν καὶ λυαῖον ἐπωνόμασαν λύοντα τὰς μερίμνας· τινὲς δέ φασιν ἀπὸ τοῦ τὸν Δία περὶ τὸ Νύσιον ὄρος [58,5] φῆναι πρῶτον τὴν ἄμπελον παρεληλυθέναι τοῦτο τὸ ὄνομα εἰς τὴν συνήθειαν. λέγεται δὲ διὰ πυρὸς λοχευθῆναι, τὸ θερμὸν αὐτοῦ καὶ πυρωτικὸν τῶν τε σωμάτων καὶ τῶν ψυχῶν παριστάντος τοῦ μύθου—ὄντως γὰρ οἶνός τι πυρὶ ἴσον μένος ἔχει κατὰ τοὺς [58,10] ποιητάς, ἐρραφθεὶς δ' εἰς τὸν μηρὸν τοῦ Διὸς ἐκεῖ τελεσφορηθῆναι διὰ τὸ πεπαίνεσθαι καὶ τελειοῦσθαι τὸν οἶνον <…>[178] ἐπεὶ πρώτη μὲν αὐτοῦ γέννησίς ἐστιν ἡ κατὰ [58,15] πέπανσιν τῆς ὀπώρας, ἥτις γίνεται τῶν[179]

---

177. καὶ to ποιοῦνται del. Lang (1881), Torres (2018).

178. Lang (1881) prints [διὰ τὸ πεπαίνεσθαι καὶ τελειοῦσθαι τὸν οἶνον † εἰ γὰρ μὴ πεφυκότα γενναῖον ἀποτιθέμενον, ἀτελῆ δ' ὡς πρὸς τὴν χρῆσιν συγκομισθέντα τάδε], as does Torres (2018) (with brackets but without obelisk); see note to translation.

179. Torres (2018); om. Lang (1881).

life, and in a festival which they used to bear witness to the fact that they had stopped fighting with each other over the necessities and were *replete* [*musia*], that is, satiated.[180] It is plausible that this is why the 'mysteries' [*mustēria*] are so named, and this is why some people know Demeter as a 'Mysian'—or else because matters which are to some extent difficult to understand need *investigation* [*musis*]. (29) For this same reason, Zeus is said to have generated the 'Seasons' [*hōrai*] from Themis: they *take care of* [*ōreu(etai)*] and guard all good things we have. One of them is called 'Eunomia,' from the [sc. *good, eu-*] *distribution* [*(dia)nemēsis*] of the things that fall to us; one is Justice [*Dikē*] because she gets those who are at variance *apart* [*dicha*] from one another; one is Peace [*eirēnē*], from judgments made through words not weapons; for they called the language of reason *peace* [*eirēnē*]. ('War' [*polemos*] is so named from the fact that *many are destroyed* [*pollous ollunai*] or from the hurry to *lay hands on* [*palamai*] each other that comes upon enemies.)

(30) It is appropriate that Dionysus was thought of as peace in some sense as well, since he is the overseer of cultivated trees and is a generous god—and this explains why "libations" are made;[181] for the countryside is deforested in wartime, but feasting, which requires wine above all else, thrives in peace. And 'Dionysus' is either 'Dionuxos' or, as it were, 'Dianusos'—named from the fact that we *weep* [*diainein*] with pleasure, or else it is as if it is 'Dialusos,' which is the origin of their calling him *Releaser*' [*lusios*] or *Deliverer* [*luaios*], releasing us from our cares. Some say that his name has entered common usage from the fact that *Zeus* [*Dia*] first made the vine appear on mount *Nysios*. He is said to have been born thanks to fire (a story which refers to the fact that his heat warms body and soul—for wine really does have the strength of fire, as the poets say), and he was stitched into the thigh of Zeus, where he came to full term (because wine needs to mellow and reach maturity) <...>[182] since its first birth is the ripening of the grapes in autumn, which happens when it is hottest, while its second

---

180. (*Ke*)*korē*(*sthai*)—see again 52,18 above on Kore.

181. The phrase "make libations" (of wine) is an idiom for making a peace treaty.

182. The text at this point is very corrupt. What Lang (1881) and Torres (2018) print might be translated: "unless it is naturally noble when it is laid down, and these things are not ready for use when they are gathered." Both recommend the excision of this, along with everything that falls within parentheses in the translation of this section—which has the merit of smoothing the way to the exegetical sentence that follows. But the problem might be the opposite of the one they diagnose: it could be that something we need has dropped out.

καυμάτων ἀκμαζόντων, δευτέρα δ' ἡ κατὰ τὴν πάτησιν, ἐκθλιβομένου [59,1] τοῖς ποσὶν αὐτοῦ, καὶ τοιοῦτόν τι ἐκ τοῦ μηροῦ συνεκδέχεσθαι δέοντος. βρόμιος δὲ καὶ Βάκχος καὶ Ἴακχος καὶ εὔιος καὶ βαβάκτης καὶ Ἰόβακχος καλεῖται διὰ τὸ πολλὰς τοιαύτας φωνὰς τοὺς πατοῦντας αὐτὸν [59,5] πρῶτον, εἶτα τοὺς ἕως μέθης μετὰ ταῦτα χρωμένους ἀφιέναι. τῆς δ' ἐν τοῖς πότοις παιδιᾶς, εἶτ' ἐκστάσεως σύμβολόν εἰσιν οἱ Σάτυροι τὴν ὀνομασίαν ἐσχηκότες ἀπὸ τοῦ σεσηρέναι καὶ οἱ Σκιρτοὶ ἀπὸ τοῦ σκαίρειν καὶ οἱ Σιληνοὶ ἀπὸ τοῦ σιλαίνειν καὶ οἱ Σευΐδαι [59,10] ἀπὸ τοῦ σεύειν, ὅ ἐστιν ὁρμᾶν. διὰ τούτων δ' ἴσως παρίσταται τὸ ὡσανεὶ μετ' ἐκλύσεως καὶ θηλύτητος παράφορον τῶν πινόντων. τούτου δὲ ἕνεκεν καὶ θηλύμορφος μὲν πλάττεται, κέρατα δὲ ἔχων, ὡσὰν τοὺς μὲν τόνους ἀποβαλλόντων τῶν μεθυσκομένων, βίᾳ δὲ χρωμένων [59,15] καὶ δυσκάθεκτόν τι καὶ ὁρμητικὸν ἐχόντων. καὶ τὸ μὲν τῆς ἐσθῆτος ἀνθηρὸν παρίστησι τὴν ποικιλίαν τῆς ὀπώρας, ἡ δ' ἐν τοῖς πλείστοις τῶν πλασμάτων γυμνότης τὸν παρὰ τοὺς πότους γινόμενον ἀπαμφιασμὸν τοῦ τρόπου, καθὸ δοκεῖ καὶ τὸ "οἶνος καὶ ἀλήθεια" [59,20] εἰρῆσθαι, τάχα διὰ τοῦτο καὶ μαντεῖα ἔσθ' ὅπου τοῦ Διονύσου ἔχοντος. τῷ δὲ θορυβώδει τῶν μεθυσκομένων οἰκεῖόν τι ἔδοξεν ἔχειν καὶ ὁ τῶν ῥόπτρων ψόφος καὶ τυμπάνων, ἃ παραλαμβάνουσιν εἰς τὰ ὄργια αὐτῶν.[183] χρῶνται δὲ πολλοὶ καὶ αὐλοῖς παρὰ τὴν συγκομιδὴν [60,1] τοῦ καρποῦ καὶ ἄλλοις τοιούτοις ὀργάνοις. ὁ δὲ θύρσος ἐμφαίνει τὸ μὴ ἀρκεῖσθαι τοῖς ἑαυτῶν ποσὶ τοὺς πολὺν οἶνον πίνοντας, τῶν δ' ὑποστηριούντων αὐτοὺς δεῖσθαι. τινὲς δὲ τῶν θύρσων καὶ ἐπιδορατίδας [60,5] κρυπτομένας ὑπὸ τοῖς φύλλοις ἔχουσιν ὡσὰν καὶ ὀδυνηφόρου τινὸς ἔσθ' ὅτε κρυπτομένου τῇ παρὰ τὴν πολυποσίαν ἱλαρότητι εἰς ὕβρεις ἐνίων καὶ παρακοπὰς ἐμπιπτόντων, ἀφ' οὗ δὴ μαινόλης τε ὁ Διόνυσος ἐκλήθη καὶ Μαινάδες αἱ περὶ αὐτὸν γυναῖκες. πλάττεται δὲ [60,10] καὶ νέος καὶ πρεσβύτης διὰ τὸ πάσῃ ἡλικίᾳ πρόσφορος εἶναι, τῶν μὲν νέων λαβρότερον αὐτῷ χρωμένων, τῶν δὲ πρεσβυτέρων ἥδιον. οἱ δὲ Σάτυροι παρεισάγονται ταῖς νύμφαις ἐπιμιγνύμενοι καὶ τὰς μὲν πείσαντες,[184] τὰς δὲ μετὰ παιδιᾶς βιαζόμενοι τῷ τὴν πρὸς [60,15] τὸ ὕδωρ κρᾶσιν τοῦ οἴνου συνῶφθαι χρησίμην οὖσαν. τὰς δὲ παρδάλεις ὑποζευγνύουσι τῷ Διονύσῳ καὶ παρακολουθούσας εἰσάγουσιν ἤτοι διὰ τὸ ποικίλον τῆς χροιᾶς, ὡς καὶ νεβρίδα

---

183. With some manuscripts; αὐτῶν Lang (1881), Torres (2018).

184. πειρῶντες Lang (1881) and Torres (2018) with the manuscripts, but "trying" seems inappropriate, when the stayrs *are already* ἐπιμιγνύμενοι.

2. The *Greek Theology* 119

is at the trampling of the grapes, when it is squeezed out by the feet—and something like this has to be understood from the reference to the thigh. He is called Bromios and Bacchos and Iacchos and Euios and Babaktes and Iobacchos because in the first place, people trampling the grapes let out many such cries, as, subsequently, people tend to do when they are drunk. The 'Satyrs' are a symbol of the playfulness and distraction of someone in their cups: their name comes from *grinning* [*sesērenai*]. There are also the 'Skirtoi,' from *dancing* [*skairein*]; and the 'Silenoi,' from *mocking* [*silainein*]; and the 'Seuidai,' from *hastening* [*seu(ein)*], that is, rushing. These perhaps suggest the way in which people who are drinking stagger about in a dissolute and effeminate way. This is also why he [Dionysus] is depicted as feminine in appearance—yet with horns: when drunk, people become lax,[185] but also violent, difficult to control and impulsive. His bright clothes suggest the colors of autumn, and the fact that he is naked in most statues suggests the stripping off of affectation, which happens among drinkers, and would seem to be what is meant by the line "wine and truth."[186] This might also be why there are places with an oracle of Dionysus. The noise of tambourines and drums, which are invitations to their rites, seem appropriate somehow to drunken rowdiness. Often the aulos is also played to accompany the harvest, along with other such instruments. The thyrsus represents the fact that people who drink too much wine cannot depend on their own feet but need something to prop themselves up. Some of the thyrsi have spearheads hidden within the leaves, as if to say that when the drinking is hard there is sometimes something painful hidden beneath the cheerfulness, which leads some to fall into violence and frenzy. This is why Dionysus was called Maddening [*mainolēs*], and the women around him 'Maenads.' He is depicted both as young and as old, because it [wine] is congenial at any age: more exciting for the young who use it, more pleasurable for the older. Tradition has it that the Satyrs had intercourse with the nymphs, as a result of seduction in some cases, by force in the course of sport in others. This came about because the mixing of wine with water was seen to be useful. Leopards were yoked to Dionysus's chariot and made to accompany him either because of their colorful skin (just as he him-

---

185. More literally, they "cast off their tone/tension" (*tonos*), a quality of strength and preparedness that can be applied to body or soul: e.g., (in Chrysippus's own words) *SVF* 3.473 (123,16–19). Its complete enervation spells death, as in F27.

186. The beginning of an otherwise lost poem of Alcaeus (Lobel-Page 1955, frag. 366).

αὐτός τε περιῆπται καὶ αἱ Βάκχαι, ἢ ὡς καὶ τὰ ἀγριώτατα ἤθη τῆς συμμέτρου [60,20] οἰνώσεως ἐξημερούσης. τὸν δὲ τράγον αὐτῷ θύουσι διὰ τὸ λυμαντικὸν δοκεῖν τῶν ἀμπέλων καὶ τῶν συκῶν εἶναι τοῦτο τὸ ζῷον, καθὸ καὶ ἐκδέροντες αὐτὸν εἰς τὸν ἀσκὸν ἐνάλλονται κατὰ τὰς Ἀττικὰς κώμας οἱ γεωργοὶ νεανίσκοι. τάχα δὲ ἂν χαίροι τοιούτῳ θύματι [60,25] ὁ Διόνυσος διὰ τὸ ὀχευτικὸν εἶναι τὸν τράγον, ἀφ' [61,1] οὗ καὶ ὁ ὄνος ἐν ταῖς πομπαῖς αὐτοῦ θαμίζει καὶ οἱ φαλλοὶ αὐτῷ ἀνατίθενται καὶ τὰ φαλλαγώγια ἄγεται· κινητικὸν γὰρ πρὸς συνουσίαν ὁ οἶνος, διὰ τοῦτ' ἐνίων κοινῇ θυόντων Διονύσῳ καὶ Ἀφροδίτῃ. ὁ δὲ νάρθηξ [61,5] διὰ τῆς σκολιότητος τῶν κώλων ἐμφαίνει τὸ τῇδε κἀκεῖσε περιφερόμενον τῶν μεθυόντων ἅμα δὲ καὶ ἐλαφροὺς καὶ εὐβαστάκτους αὐτοὺς εἶναι·[187] τινὲς δέ φασιν ὅτι καὶ τὸ ἄναρθρον[188] τῆς λαλιᾶς αὐτῶν ὡσανεὶ ἄρθρα ἔχον παρίστησιν. ὀρείφοιτοι δ' εἰσὶ καὶ φιλέρημοι [61,10] αἱ Βάκχαι διὰ τὸ μὴ ἐν ταῖς πόλεσιν, ἀλλ' ἐπὶ τῶν χωρίων γεννᾶσθαι τὸν οἶνον. διθύραμβος δ' ὁ Διόνυσος ἐκλήθη πότερον ὡς τὸ δίθυρον τοῦ στόματος ἀναφαίνων καὶ ἐκφερομυθεῖν τὰ ἀπόρρητα ποιῶν ἢ ὡς δι' αὐτὸν καὶ ἐπὶ τὰς θύρας ἀναβαινόντων τῶν [61,15] νέων ἢ ἐμβαινόντων εἰς αὐτάς, ὅ ἐστιν ἐμπιπτόντων καὶ διασαλευόντων τὰ κλεῖθρα. καθαιρετικὸς δὲ παντὸς οὑτινοσοῦν ὑπάρχων ἔδοξε καὶ πολεμιστὴς εἶναι καὶ πρῶτος καταδεδειχέναι τὸν ἐν ταῖς πολεμικαῖς νίκαις ἀγόμενον θρίαμβον. ὁ δὲ θρίαμβος ἀπὸ τοῦ [61,20] θροεῖν καὶ ἰαμβίζειν τὴν κλῆσιν ἔλαχεν, ὅθεν καὶ ἐν τοῖς κατὰ τῶν πολεμίων θριάμβοις οἱ πολλοὶ[189] ἀναπαίστοις σκώπτοντες χρῶνται. καὶ τὴν κίτταν δὲ ὡς λάλον [62,1] ὄρνεον καθιεροῦσιν αὐτῷ καὶ βασσαρέα καλοῦσιν ἀπὸ τοῦ βάζειν καὶ εἰραφιώτην ἀπὸ τοῦ ἔριν ἀφιέναι. τῷ κιττῷ δὲ στέφεται διὰ τὴν πρὸς τὴν ἄμπελον ἐμφέρειαν αὐτοῦ καὶ τὴν πρὸς τοὺς βότρυς ὁμοιότητα τῶν [62,5] κορύμβων· πέφυκε δὲ καὶ σφάλλειν τὰ δένδρα, ἀνέρπων δι' αὐτῶν καὶ περιπλεκόμενος βιαιότερον τοῖς πρέμνοις. τὰ δὲ θυμελικὰ ἀκροάματα τὸν Διόνυσον θεραπεύει διὰ τὴν πρὸς τὰς θαλίας οἰκειότητα αὐτῶν, οἷον ᾠδῆς καὶ κιθάρας· "τὰ γάρ τ' ἀναθήματα δαιτός." [62,10] μυθολογεῖται δ' ὅτι διασπασθεὶς ὑπὸ τῶν Τιτάνων συνετέθη πάλιν ὑπὸ

---

187. ἅμα to εἶναι del. Lang (1881), Torres (2018).
188. ἄναρθρον [μὲν] Lang (1881), Torres (2018).
189. Lang (1881), main text; πολλοὶ (without the article) Lang (1881), "Corrigenda et addenda," Torres (2018).

self and the Bacchai wear fawn skin)[190] or because of the taming effect a moderate amount of wine has on even the wildest dispositions. The goat is sacrificed to him because it is an animal known to destroy vines and figs—which is why young farmers in the Attic villages flay it and jump on the skin. And perhaps Dionysus enjoys this sort of sacrifice because the goat is lecherous—the same reason why the donkey also tends to feature in his processions, and phalli are dedicated to him, and phallic processions held. For wine moves a person to sex—which is why some people sacrifice to Dionysus and Aphrodite together.[191] The 'narthex,' a cane that has stems that twist around, suggests the way that drunk people stagger all over the place—and are likewise liable to be swayed and moved. Some say that it stands for the *inarticulate* [*anarthron*] nature of their chattering (as if it [its inarticulate nature] is what "has articulation").[192] The Bacchae wander in the mountains and love the wilderness because wine is produced not in cities but in the countryside. Dionysus was called 'Dithyrambos,' either because it draws attention to the *double door* [*dithuron*] of the mouth and makes people blurt out secrets or because *it makes* [*dia*] *the young go up to doors* [*thuras anabain(ontes)*] or *barge into* [*embain(ontes)*] them, that is, fall against them and dislodge the bolts. (People thought he was destructive of absolutely everything; also, that he was a warrior and first established the practice of the triumph for military victories. The 'triumph' [*thriambos*] got its name from the *shouting* [*thro(ein)*] and *lampooning* [*iamb(izein)*], which is why in military triumphs the crowds use anapests when they jeer.)[193] The jay is sacred to him as a chattering bird, and they call him 'Foxlike' [*bassareus*], from *to talk* [*bazein*], and Eiraphiotes, from *venting one's wrath* [*erin aphienai*]. He is crowned with ivy because of its resemblance to the vine and because its flowers are like clusters of grapes (also, it brings down trees, creeping up through them and twining around their lower parts with some strength). Theatrical performances are put on in the service of Dionysus because they are appropriate for celebrations—like song and the kithar: "For they are the offerings of the feast."[194] There is a myth that Dionysus was torn apart by the Titans and put back together

---

190. I.e., to suggest autumn; see 59,15–17 above.
191. Torres (2011, 50–53) argues that this is a creative allusion to the Roman institution of the Bacchanalia.
192. I cannot make sense of this parenthesis, and Lang might be right to delete it.
193. Some have seen allusion to Roman practice here: see Most 1989, 2030 n. 123.
194. Homer, *Od.* 1.52; 2.430.

τῆς Ῥέας, αἰνιττομένων τῶν παραδόντων τὸν μῦθον ὅτι οἱ γεωργοί, θρέμματα γῆς ὄντες, συνέχεαν τοὺς βότρυς καὶ τοῦ ἐν αὐτοῖς Διονύσου τὰ μέρη ἐχώρισαν ἀπ' ἀλλήλων, ἃ δὴ πάλιν ἡ εἰς ταὐτὸ [62,15] σύρρυσις τοῦ γλεύκους συνήγαγε καὶ ἓν σῶμα ἐξ αὐτῶν ἀπετέλεσε. καὶ ὁ παρὰ τῷ ποιητῇ δὲ μῦθος, ὡς φεύγων ποτὲ τὴν Λυκούργου ἐπιβουλὴν ὁ θεὸς ἔδυ κατὰ θαλάττης, εἶθ' ἡ Θέτις αὐτὸν διέσωσεν, ἐμφανῆ τὴν διάνοιαν ἔχει. τιθῆναι μὲν γάρ εἰσι τοῦ Διονύσου [62,20] αἱ ἄμπελοι· ταύτας δ' ὁ Λυκοῦργος τρυγητὴς ὢν ἐσκύλευσε καὶ ἀπεκόσμησεν, εἶθ' ὁ οἶνος θαλάττῃ μιγεὶς ἀσφαλῶς ἀπετέθη. καὶ περὶ μὲν Διονύσου τοσαῦτα.

(31) Ἡρακλῆς δ' ἐστὶν ὁ ἐν τοῖς ὅλοις λόγος [63,1] καθ' ὃν ἡ φύσις ἰσχυρὰ καὶ κραταιά ἐστιν καὶ ἀπερίγενητος οὖσα, μεταδοτικὸς ἰσχύος καὶ τοῖς κατὰ μέρος καὶ ἀλκῆς ὑπάρχων. ὠνόμασται δὲ τάχα ἀπὸ τοῦ διατείνειν εἰς τοὺς ἥρωας, ὡς αὐτοῦ ὄντος τοῦ κλεΐζεσθαι [63,5] τοὺς γενναίους ποιοῦντος· ἥρωας γὰρ ἐκάλουν οἱ παλαιοὶ τοὺς ἁδροὺς τοῖς σώμασι καὶ ταῖς ψυχαῖς καὶ κατὰ τοῦτο τοῦ θείου γένους μετέχειν δοκοῦντας. οὐ δεῖ δὲ ὑπὸ τῆς νεωτέρας ἱστορίας ἐπιταράττεσθαι· διὰ γὰρ ἀρετὴν ἠξιώθη τῆς αὐτῆς τῷ θεῷ προσηγορίας ὁ [63,10] Ἀλκμήνης καὶ Ἀμφιτρύωνος υἱός, ὥστε δυσδιάκριτα γεγονέναι τὰ τοῦ θεοῦ ἴδια ἀπὸ τῶν περὶ τοῦ ἥρωος ἱστορουμένων. τάχα δ' ἂν ἡ λεοντῆ καὶ τὸ ῥόπαλον ἐκ τῆς παλαιᾶς θεολογίας ἐπὶ τοῦτον μετενηνεγμένα εἴη. στρατηγὸν γὰρ αὐτὸν ἀγαθὸν γενόμενον καὶ [63,15] πολλὰ μέρη τῆς γῆς μετὰ δυνάμεως ἐπελθόντα οὐχ οἷόν τε γυμνὸν ἔδοξε περιεληλυθέναι, ξύλῳ μόνον ὡπλισμένον, ἀλλὰ τοῖς ἐπισήμοις τοῦ θεοῦ μετὰ τὸν ἀπαθανατισμὸν ὑπὲρ τῶν εὐεργετουμένων κεκοσμῆσθαι. σύμβολον δ' ἂν ἑκάτερον εἴη ῥώμης καὶ γενναιότητος· [63,20] ὁ μὲν γὰρ λέων τὸ ἀλκιμώτατον τῶν θηρίων ἐστί, τὸ δὲ ῥόπαλον τὸ καρτερώτατον τῶν ὅπλων. καὶ τοξότης δ' ἂν ὁ θεὸς παρεισάγοιτο κατά τε τὸ πανταχοῦ διικνεῖσθαι [64,1] καὶ κατὰ τὸ ἔντονόν τι ἔχειν καὶ τὴν τῶν βελῶν φοράν· στρατηλάτην δ' οὐκ ἄλογον τοιούτοις ὅπλοις πεποιθότα εἰς τὰς παρατάξεις ἀπαντᾶν. οἰκείως δὲ παρέδοσαν αὐτὸν Κῷοι τῇ Ἥβῃ συνοικοῦντα ὡς [64,5] ὁλοσχερέστερον αὐτὸν[195] τὴν διάνοιαν ὄντα, ὡς εἴρηται "νέων τι δρᾶν μὲν εὐτονώτεραι χέρες,

---

195. del. Lang (1881), Torres (2018).

again by 'Rhea.' The tradition through which this myth comes is hinting that farmers, who are sons of the soil, gathered in the grapes and separated out the different parts ["of Dionysus"] in them. They are all brought back together when the must *is poured* [*(sur)rusis*] back in, and a single body is made of them again. There is a clear meaning to the poet's story that the god, fleeing a plot of Lycurgus, once submerged himself in the sea where he was saved by 'Thetis': vines are the *nurses* [*tithēnai*] of Dionysus; these Lycurgus, being a vine gatherer, took as spoil and carried off; subsequently the wine was mixed with seawater and safely stored away.[196] So much for Dionysus.

(31) 'Heracles' is universal reason, thanks to which nature is strong and mighty, being indomitable as well, and it also gives strength and power to its various parts. The name comes, perhaps, from the fact that it extends to *heroes* [*hērōes*] and is what makes the noble *famous* [*kle(izesthai)*]. For the ancients called heroes those who were so strong in body and soul that they seemed to be part of a divine race. There is no need to be disturbed by the more recent story: the son of Alkmene and Amphitryon was deemed worthy of the same name as the god because of his virtue, so that it has become hard to distinguish what belongs to the god from the stories about the hero.[197] The lion skin and the club may have originated with ancient theology and been transferred to the latter—it cannot have seemed right that a good military leader who launched powerful attacks on many parts of the earth would have gone around naked, armed only with wood; rather, then, the hero was decorated with these badges of the god when his services had earned him apotheosis. Both the lion skin and the club can be a symbol of force and nobility; for the lion is the most powerful of the beasts, the club the mightiest of weapons. Traditionally, the god is an archer because he extends everywhere and because even the path of his missiles is somehow unwavering—and it is not an irrational commander who faces his enemies with his trust in weapons like this. The Coans have an apposite tradition according to which he lives with Hebe,[198] as one more perfect than her in intelligence—as it is said: "The hands of the young are fitter for action, but

---

196. Coan wine involved the admixture of seawater; see Cato, *Agr.* 112 (but also 24 for the use of seawater, and indeed must, in the production of Greek wine more generally).

197. Cf. Sextus Empiricus, *Adv. math.* 9.35–36. Hermes (see 25,21–22 above) gives another example of homonymy in the tradition.

198. The name means "youth."

ψυχαὶ δ' ἀμείνους τῶν γεραιτέρων πολύ." ὑπονοῶ δὲ καὶ τὴν παρ' Ὀμφάλῃ λατρείαν ἐκείνῳ πιθανωτέραν εἶναι προσήκειν, ἐμφαινόντων πάλιν διὰ [64,10] τούτου τῶν παλαιῶν ὅτι καὶ τοὺς ἰσχυροτάτους ὑποτάττειν δεῖ ἑαυτοὺς τῷ λόγῳ καὶ τὰ ὑπὸ τούτου προσταττόμενα ποιεῖν, εἰ καὶ θηλύτερόν τι κατὰ τὴν θεωρίαν καὶ τὴν λογικὴν σκέψιν προσπίπτει ἐκ τῆς ὀμφῆς,[199] ἣν οὐκ ἀτόπως ἂν δόξαιεν Ὀμφάλην προσηγορευκέναι. [64,15] τοὺς δὲ δώδεκα ἄθλους ἐνδέχεται μὲν ἀναγαγεῖν οὐκ ἀλλοτρίως ἐπὶ τὸν θεόν, ὡς καὶ Κλεάνθης ἐποίησεν· οὐ δεῖν δὲ δοκεῖ πανταχοῦ[200] εὑρεσίλογον πρεσβεύειν.

C.3.

(32) [65,1] Ἐχομένως τοίνυν, ὦ τέκνον, Ἀπόλλων ὁ ἥλιός ἐστιν, Ἄρτεμις δὲ ἡ σελήνη· διὰ τοῦτο γὰρ καὶ τοξότας αὐτοὺς ἀμφοτέρους παρήγαγον, τὴν ὡσανεὶ ἄφεσιν πόρρω τῶν ἀκτίνων αἰνιττόμενοι. καλοῦνται δὲ ὁ [65,5] μὲν ἥλιος ἕκατος διὰ τοῦτο,[201] ἡ δὲ ἑκάτη τῷ ἔκαθεν δεῦρο ἀφιέναι καὶ ἀποστέλλειν τὸ φῶς, ὥστε παρακειμένως καὶ ἑκατηβόλους αὐτοὺς προσηγορεύκασιν. ἔνιοι δὲ τὸν Ἕκατον καὶ τὴν Ἑκάτην ἄλλως ἐτυμολογοῦσιν, ὡς τῶν τεθειμένων αὐτοῖς τὰ ὀνόματα ταῦτα [65,10] ἑκὰς αὐτοὺς εἶναι εὐχομένων καὶ τὴν ἐξ αὐτῶν βλάβην μὴ προσπελάζειν αὐτοῖς· δοκοῦσι γὰρ καὶ φθείρειν ἔσθ' ὅτε τὸν ἀέρα καὶ τῶν λοιμικῶν καταστάσεων αἴτιοι γίνεσθαι· διὸ καὶ τοὺς ὀξεῖς θανάτους αὐτοῖς ἀνετίθεσαν οἱ πάλαι, καὶ ὁ ποιητὴς ὡς ἐμφανές τι ἐν [65,15] τῷ λοιμῷ παρεισάγει τὸν Ἀχιλλέα λέγοντα ὅτι ζητητέος μάντις, "ὅς κ' εἴποι ὅτι τόσσον ἐχώσατο Φοῖβος Ἀπόλλων." τούτου δ' ἕνεκεν οἴονται κατ' εὐφημισμὸν τὴν μὲν Ἄρτεμιν ἀπὸ τοῦ ἀρτεμεῖς ποιεῖν, ὅ ἐστιν ὑγιεῖς, ὠνομάσθαι, [65,20] τὸν δ' Ἀπόλλωνα ὡς ἀπολύονθ' ἡμᾶς τῶν νόσων ἢ ἀπελαύνοντα ἀφ' ἡμῶν αὐτὰς ἢ ἀπολλύντα[202] ταύτης [66,1] τετευχέναι τῆς προσηγορίας, καθ' ἣν ἔννοιαν καὶ παιήων ἐκλήθη καὶ ἰατρὸς ἔδοξεν εἶναι. τινὲς δὲ αὐτόθεν Ἀπόλλωνα αὐτὸν ἀπὸ τοῦ ἀπολλύναι φασὶν εἰρῆσθαι· καὶ γὰρ τὸν ἀπολλύντα ταύτην τὴν διακόσμησιν τοῦτον [66,5] εἶναι διὰ τοῦ διατμίζειν ἀδιαλείπτως πάντοθεν αὐτῆς τὸ ὑγρὸν καὶ τῷ αἰθέρι προσκατατάττειν· τάχα δ' ἂν καὶ ἀπὸ τοῦ ἁπλοῦν καὶ λύειν

---

199. Lang (1881), "Addenda et corrigenda"; τῇ ὀμφῇ Lang (1881), main text, Torres (2018).

200. Torres (2018); † πανταχοῦ Lang (1881) (obelisk added in "Addenda et corrigenda").

201. [ἥλιος] ἕκατος [διὰ τοῦτο] Lang (1881), Torres (2018).

202. del. Lang (1881); ἢ ἀπολούντα Torres (2018).

the souls of the older are better by far."[203] I suspect that it is more plausible that the service to 'Omphale' refers to him [the god]; through it, the ancients showed again that even the strongest ought to submit themselves to reason and to do what it enjoins, even if its *voice* [*omphē*] (which it would not be extraordinary to call 'Omphale') happens to call for the somewhat feminine activity of contemplation and rational inquiry. It is also possible to explain the Twelve Labors as referring to the god, as Cleanthes in fact did. But ingenuity should not always win the day.

C.3. Fire

(32) Next, then, my child: Apollo is the sun, and Artemis the moon. This is why they represent both of them as archers, hinting at how far their rays shoot, as it were. The one, the sun, is called 'Hecatos' while the other is called 'Hecate' for this reason: because they shoot light and send it here *from afar* [*hekathen*]. (They have likewise also come to be called 'Hecateboloi.')[204] Some give a different etymology for 'Hecatos' and 'Hecate,' as names given to them by people who were praying that they be *far away* [*hekas*] and that their harmful effects should not reach them. For sometimes they seem to corrupt the air and to be responsible for pestilential states—which is why the ancients attributed sudden deaths to them. And the Poet represents Achilles as saying during the plague, as if it was something obvious, that a soothsayer should be sought "who might say why Phoebus Apollo raged so much."[205] Because of this, they think that we are dealing with euphemisms: 'Artemis' being named from making things *stable* [*atremeis*], that is, healthy, and 'Apollo' being so addressed as *delivering* [*apoluōn*] us from diseases, or *driving them away* [*apelaunōn*] from us, or *destroying* [*apolluōn*] them. (This notion led to his being called Paieon ["Healer"] and considered a physician.) For the same reason, some say that it [the sun] was called 'Apollo' from *to destroy* [*apollunai*]; for this is what destroys the present world order by continually evaporating the moisture from everywhere in it and making it part of the aether.[206] So perhaps the name is also from his *reducing* [*haploun*] and disintegrating the composition of substance—

---

203. Euripides, from the lost *Bellerophontes*, TrGF 291.
204. *Bolē* is another word for shot, so *hekathen-boloi*, "shots from afar."
205. Homer, *Il.* 1.64.
206. See *SVF* 2.593.

τὸ συνεστὸς τῆς οὐσίας ἢ καὶ τὸ σκότος ὡσὰν ἁπλῶν εἰρημένος εἴη. οἰκείως δὲ καὶ ἀδελφοὺς αὐτοὺς παρεισήγαγον ἐμφερεῖς [66,10] ἀλλήλοις ὄντας καὶ ὁμοειδῆ κίνησιν κινουμένους καὶ δύναμιν παραπλησίαν ἐν τοῖς ὅλοις ἔχοντας καὶ τρέφοντας ὁμοίως τὰ ἐπὶ γῆς.

Εἶθ' ὁ μὲν Ἀπόλλων ἄρρην ἀνεπλάσθη, θερμότερον ὢν πῦρ καὶ δραστικώτερον, ἡ δ' Ἄρτεμις θήλεια, ἀμβλυτέραν καὶ ἀσθενῆ [66,15] τὴν δύναμιν ἔχουσα. βούπαιδος δ' ἡλικίαν ὁ Ἀπόλλων ἔχει, καθ' ἣν καὶ οἱ ἄνθρωποι εὐειδέστατοι ἑαυτῶν φαίνονται· κάλλιστος γὰρ ὀφθῆναι καὶ νεαρώτατός ἐστιν ὁ ἥλιος. μετὰ δὲ ταῦτα Φοῖβος μὲν λέγεται διὰ τὸ καθαρὸς εἶναι καὶ λαμπρός· ἐπιθέτοις ἄλλοις οἰκείως[207] εἰς [66,20] αὐτὸν χρῶνται, χρυσοκόμαν καὶ ἀκειρεκόμαν προσαγορεύοντες, [67,1] ἐπειδὴ χρυσωπός ἐστι καὶ ἔξω πένθους καθεστὼς διὰ τὴν ἁγνότητα· Δήλιον δὲ αὐτὸν ὠνόμασαν καὶ Φαναῖον ἀπὸ τοῦ δηλοῦσθαι δι' αὐτοῦ τὰ ὄντα καὶ φωτίζεσθαι τὸν κόσμον, ὡς καὶ Ἀναφαίου Ἀπόλλωνος [67,5] ἱερὸν ἱδρύσαντο, τοῦ ἀναφαίνοντος πάντα· τούτῳ δ' ἠκολούθησε καὶ τὸ τὴν Δῆλον καὶ Ἀνάφην ἱερὰς αὐτοῦ νομισθῆναι. διὰ δὲ τὸν εἰρημένον σαφηνισμὸν τῶν πραγμάτων καὶ τὴν μαντικὴν αὐτῷ προσῆψαν καὶ εὑρεθέντος τοῦ ἐν Δελφοῖς μαντείου τὸν Ἀπόλλωνα προσωνόμασαν [67,10] Πύθιον ἀπὸ τοῦ δεῦρο ἐρχομένους τοὺς ἀνθρώπους πυνθάνεσθαι τὰ καθ' ἑαυτούς· ἐλέχθη δὲ καὶ ὁ τόπος ὀμφαλὸς τῆς γῆς οὐχ ὡς μεσαίτατος ὢν αὐτῆς, ἀλλ' ἀπὸ τῆς ἀναδιδομένης ἐν αὐτῷ ὀμφῆς, ἥτις ἐστὶ θεία φωνή. λοξῶν δὲ καὶ περισκελῶν ὄντων τῶν χρησμῶν, [67,15] οὓς δίδωσι, λοξίας ὠνόμασται· ἢ ἀπὸ τῆς λοξότητος τῆς πορείας, ἣν ποιεῖται διὰ τοῦ ζῳδιακοῦ κύκλου. μουσικὸς δὲ καὶ κιθαριστὴς παρεισῆκται τῷ κρούειν ἐναρμονίως πᾶν μέρος τοῦ κόσμου καὶ συνῳδὸν αὐτὸ πᾶσι τοῖς ἄλλοις μέρεσι ποιεῖν, μηδεμιᾶς αὐτῶν[208] ἐκμελείας [67,20] ἐν τοῖς οὖσι θεωρουμένης, ἀλλὰ καὶ τὴν τῶν χρόνων πρὸς ἀλλήλους συμμετρίαν ἐπ' ἄκρον ὡς ἐν ῥυθμοῖς τηροῦντος αὐτοῦ καὶ τὰς τῶν ζῴων φωνάς, [68,1] ὡς αὖ τοὺς τῶν ἄλλων σωμάτων ψόφους, διὰ τὸ ξηραίνεσθαι χρησίμως ὑπ' <αὐτοῦ> τὸν ἀέρα ἀποδιδόντος καὶ δαιμονίως ἡρμόσθαι πρὸς τὰς ἀκοὰς ποιοῦντος.[209] ἀπὸ

---

207. Torres (2018); om. Lang (1881).
208. del. Lang (1881), Torres (2018).
209. Cf. von Arnim at *SVF* 1.503. Lang (1881) prints: καὶ τὰς τῶν ζῴων φωνὰς καὶ (καὶ τοὺς Torres [2018]) ὡσαύτως τοὺς τῶν ἄλλων σωμάτων ψόφους, οἳ διὰ τὸ ξηραίνεσθαι χρησίμως ὑπὸ τὸν ἀέρα ἀποδίδονται, δαιμονίως (καὶ δαιμονίως Torres [2018]) ἡρμόσθαι πρὸς τὰς ἀκοὰς ποιοῦντος. But for the essential connection of air with sound and hearing, see 74,9–10 below with note (see 22,3–4; *SVF* 2.859), and for one way in which air is formed is by evaporation, i.e., the process by which the sun dries out the earth, see 66,5–6.

or the darkness as well[210]—as if he were called 'Haplon' ["Simple"]. It is appropriate that they should be presented as brother and sister, since they are like each other and move in the same pattern and have a similar power in the universe and both alike nourish things on the earth.

Apollo was represented as male, since fire is warmer and more active, Artemis as female, being less active and her power being weak. Apollo has the age of a grown boy, when men appear at their most handsome; for the sun is the most beautiful and youthful thing to see. Beyond this, he is called Phoebus ["radiant"] because he is pure and bright. There are other appropriate epithets for him: they apply Golden Haired and Unshorn to him, since the sun looks golden and stands beyond grief because of its holiness.[211] They called him 'Delian' and 'Phanaian' because what exists is *revealed* [*dēlou(sthai)*] by it, and the cosmos lit up—so also they established a temple of 'Anaphaian' Apollo, who *brings to light* [*anaphainōn*] all things. It is as a consequence of this that Delos and Anaphe came to be considered his shrines. Because of the aforementioned elucidation of things, he was associated with prophecy, and when the oracle in Delphi was discovered, they gave Apollo the epithet 'Pythian,' since people come here to *learn* [cf. *puth(esthai)*] things that concern themselves. The place was called the 'navel' [*omphalos*] of the world not because it is right in the middle of it but because the oracular *voice* [*omphē*], which is the speech of god, was given out there. Because the oracles it gives are *oblique* [*loxoi*] and difficult, he was called 'Loxias'—or because of the oblique course [of the sun] through the zodiacal circle. He has been represented as a musician and kithar player because it strikes every part of the cosmos tunefully and makes it harmonious in all of its parts; none of them, of all that exists, can be considered out of tune. Rather, it preserves to the highest degree, as if rhythmically, a mutual balance in the timings of things[212]—as it does the voices of living creatures, and similarly the sounds made by all other bodies,[213] since it produces the necessary air through its drying action and makes it wonderfully adapted to hearing.

210. Presumably because the reduction of substance is to pure fire or light—a reminder that this destruction is not a death.

211. The hair was often shorn as an act of mourning (see Plato, *Phaed.* 89b), and bereavement was considered a source of ritual pollution (see Parker 1983, ch. 2).

212. The "times" (lit.) are generally taken to be the seasons, but the cosmic context might suggest a broader sense of the way in which the life cycle of each part complements those of all the others.

213. The phrasing of this clause seems to derive from the first line of the pseudo-Aristotelian *De audibilibus* (800a1–5), but it may also suggest Plato, *Leg.* 669c–d, which argues that the Muses would not wish to mix voices with other sounds.

ταύτης δὲ τῆς ἀρχῆς καὶ Μουσηγέτης ἐκλήθη καὶ ἐπίσκοπος [68,5] καὶ αὐτὸς παιδείας[214] μετὰ τῶν Μουσῶν ἐνομίσθη· "ἐκ γάρ τοι Μουσέων καὶ ἑκηβόλου Ἀπόλλωνος ἄνδρες ἀοιδοὶ ἔασιν ἐπὶ χθονὶ καὶ βασιλῆες"—φησὶν ὁ Ἡσίοδος. διὰ τοῦτο γὰρ καὶ ἱερὸς αὐτοῦ ὁ κύκνος τῷ μουσικώτατον καὶ λευκότατον ἅμα εἶναι τῶν [68,10] ὀρνέων, ὁ δὲ κόραξ ἀλλότριος διά τε τὸ μιαρὸς εἶναι καὶ διὰ τὴν χροιάν. ἡ δὲ δάφνη καίπερ δαφοινή τις οὖσα στέμμα αὐτοῦ ἐστιν, ἐπειδὴ εὐερνές τε καὶ ἀειθαλὲς φυτόν ἐστι· τυγχάνει δὲ καὶ εὐέκκαυστος οὖσα καὶ πρὸς τὰς καθάρσεις οἰκεῖόν τι ἔχουσα, ὥστε μὴ ἀλλοτρίως [68,15] ἀνακεῖσθαι τῷ καθαρωτάτῳ καὶ καυστικωτάτῳ θεῷ. τάχα δὲ καὶ τὸ ὄνομα αὐτῆς, προστρέχον πως τῷ διαφαίνειν, ἐπιτηδείαν αὐτὴν ἐποίησε πρὸς τὰς μαντείας [69,1] εἶναι δοκεῖν. ὁ δὲ τρίπους διὰ τελειότητα τοῦ τῶν τριῶν ἀριθμοῦ δέδοται αὐτῷ· δύναται δὲ καὶ ἀπὸ τῶν τριῶν παραλλήλων κύκλων, ὧν ἕνα μὲν τέμνει κινούμενος τὴν ἐνιαύσιον κίνησιν ὁ ἥλιος, δυοῖν δ' ἐφάπτεται. [69,5] ἐπεὶ δ' ἐν τοῖς λοιμοῖς ὡς ἐπίπαν δοκεῖ τὰ θρέμματα πημαίνεσθαι πρῶτον καὶ συνεχέστερον ἢ καθ' αὑτὰ φθείρεσθαι λοιμικῶς, κατὰ τοῦτο καὶ τὴν τῶν ποιμνίων ἐπιμέλειαν ἀνέθηκαν αὐτῷ, νόμιον καὶ λύκιον καὶ λυκοκτόνον προσαγορεύοντες. ἀγυιεὺς δ' [69,10] ἐκλήθη δεόντως ἱδρυθεὶς ἐν ταῖς ἀγυιαῖς· καταυγάζει γὰρ ταύτας καὶ πληροῖ φωτὸς ἀνατέλλων, ὡς ἐκ τῶν ἐναντίων εἴρηται τὸ "δύσετό τ' ἠέλιος σκιόωντό τε πᾶσαι ἀγυιαί." καὶ λεσχηνόριον δ' αὐτὸν προσηγόρευσαν διὰ τὸ τὰς [69,15] ἡμέρας ταῖς λέσχαις καὶ τῷ ὁμιλεῖν ἀλλήλοις συνέχεσθαι τοὺς ἀνθρώπους, τὰς δὲ νύκτας καθ' ἑαυτοὺς ἀναπαύεσθαι. παιᾶνα δ' αὐτὸν ἐκάλεσαν εἴτουν κατ' ἀντίφρασιν καὶ ἐξιλαστικῶς, ἵνα μὴ νόσους αὐτοῖς ἐπιπέμπῃ μηδὲ φθείρῃ τὸν ἀναπνεόμενον ὑπ' αὐτῶν [69,20] ἀέρα, εἴτε καὶ ὡς τῷ ὄντι τοῦ αὐτοῦ ὑγιείας τῷ σώματι [70,1] αἰτίου γινομένου διὰ τῆς τοῦ περιέχοντος εὐκρασίας. (33) κατ' ἀκόλουθον πάλιν τὸν Ἀσκληπιὸν υἱὸν αὐτοῦ ἔφασαν γενέσθαι, τὸν δοκοῦντα τοῖς ἀνθρώποις ὑποδεδειχέναι τὴν ἰατρικήν· ἐχρῆν γὰρ καὶ [70,5] τούτῳ τῷ τόπῳ θεῖόν τι ἐπιστῆσαι. ὠνομάσθη δὲ ὁ Ἀσκληπιὸς ἀπὸ τοῦ ἠπιοῦσθαι[215] καὶ ἀναβάλλεσθαι τὴν κατὰ τὸν θάνατον γινομένην ἀπόσκλησιν. διὰ τοῦτο

---

214. παίζειν Lang (1881).
215. Torres (2018); ἠπίως ἰᾶσθαι Lang (1881).

This is the origin of his being called Leader of the Muses, and along with the Muses the overseer of education: "For from the Muses and Far-Darting Apollo, men are singers on earth and kings," says Hesiod.[216] And this is the reason why the swan is sacred to him: it is at the same time the most musical and the whitest of birds, but the crow is alien to him because it is raucous and because of its color. The 'laurel' [*daphnē*] is his garland, since, although it is somewhat *tawny* [*daphoinē*] in color, it is a vigorous evergreen plant. It happens to be the most flammable as well and is somehow appropriate for purification rites, so its dedication to the purest and most fiery god is not inappropriate. And perhaps its name, which is a bit like *making clear* [*diaphainein*], made it seem that the plant should be associated with prophecy. The tripod is dedicated to Apollo because the number three is perfect. It might also be to do with the three concentric circles,[217] one of which is cut by the sun as it moves through its yearly course, while the other two are touched by it. Because it mostly seems to happen that the young are the first to get sick when there is a plague and are ill for longer, or perish by themselves of the plague, they dedicated the care of flocks to him, calling him God of the Pasture, Lycian ["Lupine"], and Wolf Killer. And he was called Aguieus ["Wayside"], of course, where his statue was set up in the 'streets' [*aguiai*]; for he *illuminates* [(*kat*)*aug*(*azei*)] them and fills them with light as he rises—as, conversely, it is said: "The sun sets, and all the streets were darkened."[218] They also called him 'Leschenorios' because men spend their days in *public buildings* [*leschai*],[219] mingling with each other, but the nights they spend resting by themselves. They called him Paian ["Healer"]—whether, indeed, by antithesis, to appease him, so that he should not send diseases to them or corrupt the air they breathed,[220] or whether it was because he is in fact himself the cause of bodily health by making the immediate environment well tempered. (33) Consequently, Asclepius was said to be his son. He was thought to have handed the art of medicine to mankind—for in this field, too, some knowledge of the divine was necessary. 'Asclepius' was named from the *stiffness* [*aposklē*(*sis*)] that comes about at death being *softened* [*ēpiōs*] and put off. This is why they

---

216. *Theog.* 94–95.
217. I.e., the circles extending out from the two tropics and the equator.
218. Homer, *Od.* 2.388.
219. The word for "men" here (*anthrōpoi*) could mean "people," but Cornutus evidently means it as a synonym for *anēres* (which can only mean "men"), giving as the full etymology *lesch-aner-*.
220. This was the explanation given above at 65,18–66,2.

γὰρ δράκοντα αὐτῷ παριστᾶσιν, ἐμφαίνοντες ὅτι ὅμοιόν τι τούτῳ πάσχουσιν οἱ χρώμενοι τῇ ἰατρικῇ [70,10] κατὰ τὸ οἱονεὶ ἀνανεάζειν ἐκ τῶν νόσων καὶ ἐκδύεσθαι τὸ γῆρας, ἅμα δ' ἐπεὶ προσοχῆς ὁ δράκων σημεῖον, ἧς πολλῆς δεῖ πρὸς τὰς θεραπείας. καὶ τὸ βάκτρον δὲ τοιούτου τινὸς ἔοικεν εἶναι σύμβολον· παρίσταται γὰρ δι' αὐτοῦ ὅτι, εἰ μὴ ταύταις ταῖς ἐπινοίαις ἐπεστηριζόμεθα [70,15] ὅσον ἐπὶ τὸ συνεχῶς εἰς ἀρρωστίαν ἐμπίπτειν, κἂν θᾶττον τοῦ δέοντος σφαλλόμενοι κατεπίπτομεν. λέγεται δὲ ὁ Χείρων τετροφέναι τὸν Ἀσκληπιὸν κἂν τοῖς τῆς ἰατρικῆς θεωρήμασιν ἠσκηκέναι, τὴν διὰ τῶν [71,1] χειρῶν ἐνέργειαν τῆς τέχνης ἐμφαίνειν αὐτῶν βουλομένων. παραδέδοται δὲ καὶ γυνὴ τοῦ Ἀσκληπιοῦ, Ἠπιόνη, τοῦ ὀνόματος οὐκ ἀργῶς εἰς τὸν μῦθον παρειλημμένου, δηλοῦντος δὲ τὸ πραϋντικὸν τῶν ὀχλήσεων [71,5] διὰ τῆς ἠπίου φαρμακείας.

(34) Ἡ δ' Ἄρτεμις φωσφόρος μὲν ἐπωνομάσθη διὰ τὸ καὶ αὐτὴ σέλας βάλλειν καὶ φωτίζειν ποσῶς τὸ περιέχον, ὁπόταν μάλιστα πανσέληνος ᾖ, δίκτυννα δ' ἀπὸ τοῦ βάλλειν δεῦρο[221] τὰς ἀκτῖνας—δίκειν γὰρ τὸ βάλλειν—ἢ ἀπὸ τοῦ [71,10] διικνεῖσθαι τὴν δύναμιν αὐτῆς εἰς πάντα τὰ ἐπὶ γῆς ὡς διικτύννης αὐτῆς οὔσης. κυνηγέτιν δ' αὐτὴν καὶ θηροκτόνον καὶ ἐλαφηβόλον καὶ ὀρεσίφοιτον παρεισήγαγον ἤτοι τρέπειν εἰς τὰ ἄγρια βουλόμενοι τὴν ἐξ αὐτῆς βλάβην ἢ ἐπειδὴ μάλιστα νυκτὸς καταφαίνεται, [71,15] πολλὴ δ' ἐν τῇ νυκτὶ ἡσυχία πανταχοῦ καθάπερ ἐν ταῖς ὕλαις καὶ ταῖς ἐρήμοις ἐστίν, ὥστε ἐν τοιούτοις τισὶ χωρίοις αὐτὴν πλάζεσθαι δοκεῖν, ἔξωθεν ἤδη τούτῳ προσπεπλασμένου τοῦ κυνηγετεῖν αὐτὴν τοξότιν οὖσαν. συνῳδὸν δὲ τούτῳ καὶ τὸ τοὺς κύνας [71,20] ἱεροὺς αὐτῆς νομισθῆναι πρός τε τὰς θήρας ἔχοντας [72,1] ἐπιτηδείως καὶ ἀγρυπνεῖν ἐν ταῖς νυξὶ καὶ ὑλακτεῖν πεφυκότας. κυνηγία δ' ἔοικε καὶ τὸ μὴ διαλείπειν αὐτὴν ὁτὲ μὲν διώκουσαν τὸν ἥλιον ὁτὲ δὲ φεύγουσαν, εἶτα ἐν τῷ ζῳδιακῷ μετερχομένην ζῴδια καὶ ταχέως [72,5] συνιοῦσαν· οἰκεῖον γὰρ κυνηγίᾳ καὶ τὸ τάχος· προσγειότατόν τε τῶν οὐρανίων οὖσαν αὐτὴν περὶ τὰς κορυφὰς τῶν ὀρῶν ἔφασαν ἀναστρέφεσθαι. οὐχ ἑτέρα δ' οὖσα αὐτῆς ἡ Ἑκάτη τρίμορφος εἰσῆκται διὰ τὸ τρία σχήματα γενικώτατα ἀποτελεῖν τὴν σελήνην, μηνοειδῆ [72,10] γινομένην καὶ πανσέληνον καὶ τρίτον

---

221. Torres (2018); om. Lang (1881).

dedicated the snake to him: it shows that those who benefit from medicine experience something like the snake in becoming, as it were, rejuvenated after their disease and putting off old age. At the same time, the snake is a symbol of careful attention, of which much is needed in medical treatment. The staff seems to be a symbol of something of the sort as well: the suggestion made by it is that we would fall into illness constantly if we did not rely on medical understanding, and, deprived of what we needed, would collapse more quickly. 'Chiron' is said to have nurtured Asclepius and to have trained him in the science of medicine, thanks to people who wanted to show that the exercise of an art is through the *hands* [*cheirōn*].[222] The wife of Asclepius, according to tradition, is 'Epione'—a name which was not incorporated into mythology idly: it points out how distresses are soothed through *gentle* [*ēpios*] medicine.

(34) Artemis acquired the epithet Phosphoros ["light-bringer"] because it [the moon], too, emits light and illuminates the surroundings to some extent, especially when it is a full moon. She is called 'Dictynna' from its shooting rays of light here—for to *cast* [*dikein*] is to shoot—or else from the fact that its power *reaches* [*diiknei*(*sthai*)] everything on earth, as if she were 'Diiktynes.' She was represented as Huntress and Beast Slayer and Deer Shooter and Mountain Wanderer either because people wanted to deflect the harm that comes from it onto wild beasts or because it shines during the night in particular and everywhere is very peaceful during the night—as peaceful as woods and deserts, which thus seem appropriate haunts for her. (To this was added the fiction that she uses her archery to hunt, and it is of a piece with this that dogs came to be thought sacred to her, since they are suitable for hunting—and they stay awake at night and bark. It is like a hunt with hounds, the way that it [the moon] never stops either pursuing or fleeing the sun; also, because it "chases" the animals in the zodiac and swiftly catches them up—speed being something associated with a hunt as well.) They said that she dwells in the mountaintops, since it is the nearest of the heavenly bodies to earth. Hecate, who is the same as Artemis, is represented as three in form because the moon makes three kinds of shape: it is in turns crescent shaped and full, and then they

---

222. This is not so banal a claim as it sounds: some philosophers valued *theoretical* attainment in the arts, even in medicine, over their practice—like the musical expert in Plutarch who is proud of not being able to play any instrument (*Quaest. conv.* 657d–e). Where to strike the balance was an especially controversial topic in contemporary Platonism; see Boys-Stones 2018, ch. 16.

τι ἄλλο σχῆμα πλάττουσιν ἀναλαμβάνουσαν, καθ' ὃ πεπλήρωται μὲν αὐτῆς ὁ μηνίσκος, οὐ πεπλήρωται δ' ὁ κύκλος. ἐντεῦθεν ἤδη καὶ τριοδῖτις ἐπεκλήθη καὶ τῶν τριόδων ἐπόπτης ἐνομίσθη διὰ τὸ τριχῶς μεταβάλλειν [72,15] ὁδεύουσα διὰ τῶν ζῴων. τοῦ δ' ἡλίου διὰ τῆς ἡμέρας μόνον φαινομένου, αὐτὴν καὶ νυκτὸς καὶ σκότους ὁρωμένην καὶ μεταβάλλουσαν νυχίαν τε καὶ νυκτιπόλον καὶ χθονίαν ἐκάλεσαν καὶ τοῖς καταχθονίοις θεοῖς ἤρξαντο συντιμᾶν, δεῖπνα ἐμφέροντες αὐτῇ. προσανεπλάσθη δὲ [72,20] τούτῳ καὶ τὸ μιαίνειν τὴν γῆν ταύτην καὶ μιαίνειν[223] [73,1] ὥσπερ τοὺς κατοιχομένους καὶ τὸ ταῖς φαρμακίσι συνεργεῖν καὶ ἐπάγεσθαι ταῖς οἰκίαις, εἶτα τελευταῖον τὸ πένθεσι καὶ φόνῳ χαίρειν, ἐξ οὗ τινες προήχθησαν ἐπὶ τὸ καὶ θυσίαις αὐτὴν ἀτόποις καὶ σφαγιασμοῖς ἀνθρώπων [73,5] ἱλάσκεσθαι θέλειν. καθιέρωσαν δὲ καὶ τὴν τρίγλαν αὐτῇ διὰ τοὔνομα. ἐνοδία δέ ἐστιν οὐ δι' ἄλλο τι ἢ διὸ καὶ Ἀπόλλων ἀγυιεύς. δοκεῖ δὲ τοῖς πλείστοις ἡ αὐτὴ εἶναι καὶ Εἰλείθυια, ἀπαύστως εἰλουμένη καὶ θέουσα περὶ τὴν γῆν, ἣν εὔχονται ἐλθεῖν αὐταῖς ἠπίαν καὶ λυσίζωνον [73,10] αἱ ὠδίνουσαι, λύουσαν τὸ ἐσφιγμένον τῶν κόλπων πρὸς τὸ ῥᾷον καὶ ἀπονώτερον ἐκπεσεῖν τὸ κυισκόμενον, λεγομένης αὐτῆς καὶ Ἐλευθοῦς. πλείους δ' Εἰλείθυιαι παραδέδονται καθ' ὃν λόγον πλείους Ἔρωτες· πολύτροποι γὰρ καὶ οἱ τοκετοὶ τῶν γυναικῶν ὡς [73,15] αἱ τῶν ἐρώντων ἐπιθυμίαι. φανερῶς δ' ἡ σελήνη τελεσφορεῖσθαι τὰ συλλαμβανόμενα ποιεῖ καὶ ταύτης ἐστὶ τό τε αὔξειν αὐτὰ καὶ τὸ ἀπολύειν τῶν φερουσῶν πεπανθέντα. οὐ θαυμαστὸν δ' εἰ κατ' ἄλλην μὲν ἔμφασιν παρθένον ὑπενόησαν τὴν Ἄρτεμιν ἄχραντον καὶ [73,20] ἁγνὴν οὖσαν ὁμοίως τῷ ἡλίῳ, κατ' ἄλλην δὲ ἐπίκουρον [74,1] τῶν τικτουσῶν, ἐπ' αὐτῇ κειμένου τοῦ εὐτοκεῖσθαι τὰ τικτόμενα, κατὰ τρίτην δὲ φρικῶδές τι καὶ χαλεπὸν ἔχουσαν, οἵαν ἔφαμεν περὶ τῆς Ἑκάτης ὑπόνοιαν εἶναι.

---

223. [καὶ μιαίνειν] Lang (1881), Torres (2018).

represent it, thirdly, taking on another shape, when the crescent is filled but it is not quite a circle. This is why she was called Goddess of the Forked Way and was thought to look over forks in the road:[224] it is because of the threefold change it undergoes as it journeys through the zodiac. And since the sun only shines during the day, but it [the moon] is also seen at night and in the dark and, what is more, is seen changing, they called her Goddess of the Night and Night Wanderer and Chthonian, and they started to worship her in company with the chthonian deities, introducing dinners in her honor. The fiction was added that it pollutes this earth, and pollutes it as the dead do; and that she helps witches and plots with them against households; and finally that she rejoices in grief and slaughter—which is what led some people to want to propitiate her with unusual sacrifices and human slaughter. The 'mullet' is sacred to her because of its name.[225] She is called Enodia ["Wayside"] for exactly the reason that Apollo is called Aguieus.[226] Most people think that Artemis is the same as 'Eileithuia,' who unceasingly *turns* [*eilou(menē)*] and *rushes* [*theousa*] around the earth. Those in labor pray that she should come to them as Gentle and Looser of the Girdle, as she loosens the constriction of the womb so that the child that has been conceived might fall out easily and without labor. So she is called 'Eleutho,' too.[227] Tradition has it that there is more than one Eileuthuia, for just the same reason that there is more than one Eros; for the births experienced by women are as varied as lovers' desires.[228] Obviously, the moon brings to term creatures that have been conceived, and it is due to her that they grow and are released from their carriers when ready. There is nothing extraordinary in the fact that people thought of Artemis in one sense as a virgin, pure and holy like the sun; in another as assistant to those giving birth, responsible for the safe delivery of children;[229] and in a third sense as somewhat terrifying and baleful, which is the notion we said was behind Hecate.

---

224. I.e., three-way intersections (something more transparent in the Greek).
225. *Trigla*, suggesting "three" again.
226. See 69,9–13 above.
227. I.e., suggesting "release" again (*eklu-*) or, just possibly, "arrival" (*eleusis*).
228. See 47,17–18 above.
229. See Plato, *Theaet.* 149b–c.

C.4.

(35) [74,5] Τελευταῖον δὲ τὸν δεχόμενον τὰς ψυχὰς ἀέρα Ἅιδην, ὡς ἔφην, διὰ τὸ ἀειδὲς προσηγόρευσαν. μὴ φαινομένων δ' ἡμῖν τῶν ὑπὸ γῆν, ἐκεῖσε χωρεῖν τοὺς διαλλάττοντας διεβόησαν. Κλύμενος ὁ Ἅιδης λέγεται τῷ αἴτιος εἶναι τοῦ [74,10] κλύειν· ἀὴρ γὰρ πεπληγμένος ἡ φωνή. εὔβουλον δὲ καὶ εὐβουλέα κατὰ ἀποδυσπέτησιν ὠνόμασαν αὐτὸν ὡς καλῶς περὶ τῶν ἀνθρώπων βουλευόμενον διὰ τοῦ παύειν αὐτοὺς ποτε τῶν πόνων καὶ τῶν φροντίδων. ἐπονομάζεται δὲ ἐπιθετικῶς καὶ πολυδέκτης καὶ [74,15] πολυδέγμων καὶ πολύαρχος πολλούς τε δεχόμενος καὶ τῶν λεγομένων πλειόνων ἢ πολλῶν ἄρχων. πυλάρτην δὲ αὐτὸν ὁ ποιητὴς προσηγόρευσεν ὡς ἀκριβῶς ἡρμοσμένας τὰς πύλας ἔχοντα καὶ μηδένα ἀνιέντα. ὁ δὲ Χάρων ἴσως μὲν κατ' ἀντίφρασιν ἐκ τῆς χαρᾶς ὠνομάσθη· [74,20] δύναται δὲ καὶ ἀπὸ τοῦ χωρεῖν ἢ τοῦ χανδάνω[230] τὸ ἔτυμον ἔχειν ἢ ἀπὸ τοῦ κεχηνέναι.[231] ὁ δὲ Ἀχέρων ἀπὸ τῶν γινομένων ἐπὶ τοῖς τετελευτηκόσιν ἀχῶν παρήχθη καὶ ἡ Ἀχερουσία λίμνη. φανερὸν δὲ πόθεν καὶ ὁ Κωκυτὸς καὶ ὁ Πυριφλεγέθων τὴν κλῆσιν [75,1] ἔσχον, πάλαι καιόντων τοὺς νεκροὺς καὶ κωκυτὸν ἐγειρόντων τῶν Ἑλλήνων, διὰ τοῦτο καὶ δαίμονας αὐτοὺς ἀπὸ τοῦ κεκαῦσθαι καλούντων. ἡ δ' ἄορνος λίμνη φυσικώτερον ἴσως ἀπὸ τοῦ ἀέρος προσηγορεύθη· [75,5] καίτοι καὶ τὸν σκότον ἔσθ' ὅτε καὶ τὴν ὁμίχλην ἀέρα οἱ παλαιοὶ ἐκάλουν, εἰ μὴ νὴ Δία οὕτως ἀπεχρήσαντο τῇ τοῦ ἀέρος γλαυκότητι ὡς καὶ τῶν λεγομένων φασγανίων οἷς στέφουσι τὸν Πλούτωνα. στέφουσι δὲ αὐτὸν καὶ ἀδιάντῳ πρὸς ὑπόμνησιν τοῦ αὐαίνεσθαι [75,10] τοὺς τελευτῶντας καὶ μηκέτι τὸ διερὸν ἴσχειν, στέρεσθαι δὲ τῆς παραιτίας τοῦ διαπνεῖσθαι καὶ θάλλειν ἰκμάδος. ἐντεῦθεν ὑπονοητέον καὶ τοὺς ἀλίβαντας μεμυθεῦσθαι· ἐν Ἅιδου εἰσὶ διὰ τὴν τῆς λιβάδος ἀμεθεξίαν τῶν νεκρῶν. οἰκείως δὲ τοῖς κατοιχομένοις [75,15] καὶ ὁ νάρκισσος ἔχειν ἔδοξε καὶ τῶν Ἐριννύων ἔφασαν αὐτὸν στεφάνωμα εἶναι, προσεδρεύσαντες τῇ παραθέσει τῆς νάρκης καὶ τῷ οἷον διαναρκᾶν τοὺς ἀποθνήσκοντας.

---

230. ἢ τοῦ χανδάνω del. Lang (1881), Torres (2018).
231. ἢ ἀπὸ τοῦ κεχηνέναι del. Lang (1881), Torres (2018).

C.4. Air

(35) Finally, the air which receives souls is 'Hades,' as I said, so called because it is *unseen* [*aeides*];[232] it is because things beneath the earth are not apparent to us that they put it about that the dead go there. Hades is said to be Famous [*klumenos*] because this air is the cause of *hearing* [*kluein*]: sound is air that has been struck.[233] Despair led them to call him 'Prudent' [*euboulos*] and the "Prudent One" [*eubouleus*]; the idea was that he *plans* [*bouleu(omenos)*] well [sc. *eu*-] for men by bringing an end at some time to their toils and cares. His epithets include: 'Much Receiving' and 'Receptive of Much' and 'Ruler over Many' because he *receives many* and *rules over* the so-called majority or the *many*. The Poet called him 'Gatekeeper,' as holding his gates tightly closed and letting none out.[234] 'Charon' was perhaps named by antithesis from *joy* [*chara*], but it might be that its etymology is *contain* [*chōr(ein)*] or *gape* [*cha(ndanō)*]—or *yawn* [(*ke*)*chēn(enai)*]. 'Acheron' and the 'Acherousian' lake came about because of the *sorrows* [*achē*] which come to the dead. It is clear where the names of 'Kokytus' and Pyriphlegethon ["blazing with fire"] come from: the Greeks of old used to burn their corpses and raise a *wail* [*kōkutos*]. Because of this they also called the dead 'daemons,' which comes from burning as well.[235] The 'Aornos' lake perhaps has its name with some regard to science from *air* [*aēr*], although sometimes the ancients called darkness and mist 'air' as well—unless, by Zeus, they were appealing to the gray of the air,[236] which it shares with the so-called gladioli with which they garland Pluto. They also garland him with 'maidenhair' [*adiantos*], as a reminder that the dead dry out and no longer [sc. *a*-] hold *moisture* [*dieron*] and are deprived of the water that is needed to breathe and flourish. This is why myths call them 'corpses' [*alibantes*]: the dead are in Hades because they lack [sc. *a*-] a share in the *wet* [*libas*]. The 'narcissus' was appropriately associated with the dead, and they said that it was the wreath of the Erinnyes, noting its similarity to *numbness* [*narkē*]—and because the dead grow, as it were, *numb* [(*dia*)*narkan*].

---

232. See 5,2–4 above.
233. E.g., Diogenes Laertius, *Vit. phil.* 7.55 (of which the most relevant part is included in *SVF* 1.74).
234. Homer, several times in the *Iliad* (e.g., 8.367) and once in the *Odyssey* (11.277).
235. Cornutus presumably has in mind the word *daiein*.
236. See n. 31 above.

D.

Οὕτω δ' ἂν ἤδη καὶ τἆλλα τῶν μυθικῶς παραδεδόσθαι [76,1] περὶ θεῶν δοκούντων ἀναγαγεῖν ἐπὶ τὰ παραδεδειγμένα στοιχεῖα, ὦ παῖ, δύναιο, πεισθεὶς ὅτι οὐχ οἱ τυχόντες ἐγένοντο οἱ παλαιοί, ἀλλὰ καὶ συνιέναι τὴν τοῦ κόσμου φύσιν ἱκανοὶ καὶ πρὸς τὸ διὰ συμβόλων [76,5] καὶ αἰνιγμάτων φιλοσοφῆσαι περὶ αὐτῆς εὐεπίφοροι. διὰ πλειόνων δὲ καὶ ἐξεργαστικώτερον εἴρηται τοῖς πρεσβυτέροις φιλοσόφοις, ἐμοῦ νῦν ἐπιτετμημένως αὐτὰ παραδοῦναί σοι βουληθέντος· χρησίμη γὰρ αὐτῶν καὶ ἡ ἐπὶ τοσοῦτον προχειρότης ἐστί. περὶ δὲ ἐκείνων καὶ [76,10] περὶ τῆς θεραπείας τῶν θεῶν καὶ τῶν οἰκείως εἰς τιμὴν αὐτῶν γινομένων καὶ τὰ πάτρια καὶ τὸν ἐντελῆ λήψῃ λόγον οὕτω μόνον ὡς εἰς τὸ εὐσεβεῖν ἀλλὰ μὴ εἰς τὸ δεισιδαιμονεῖν εἰσαγομένων τῶν νέων καὶ θύειν τε καὶ εὔχεσθαι καὶ προσκυνεῖν καὶ ὀμνύειν κατὰ τρόπον [76,15] καὶ ἐν τοῖς ἐμβάλλουσι καιροῖς καθ' ἣν ἁρμόττει συμμετρίαν διδασκομένων.

D. Epilogue

In the same way, my child, you will now also be able to refer the rest of what, in mythical form, the tradition has been pleased to pass down about the gods to the elements that have been set out, in the conviction that the ancients were far from mediocre but were capable of understanding the nature of the cosmos and ready to express their philosophical account of it in symbols and enigmas. It has all been said at greater length and in more detail by earlier philosophers, but I wanted now to pass it on to you in abbreviated form; an ability to handle these [symbols and enigmas] even to this extent is useful. But as to those [traditions], and the service of the gods, and what is appropriately done to their honor, you will thus grasp both your ancestral customs and also a perfect [philosophical] account when the young are led only to piety and not to superstition and are taught to sacrifice and pray and worship and swear in due form, as circumstances demand, and in proportionate manner.[237]

---

237. A similar thought is found in Epictetus, *Ench.* 31.4–5: "Whoever takes care to pursue and avoid what he ought is at the same time cultivating piety, but it is also appropriate to pour libations and to sacrifice and offer first fruits, in each case following ancestral tradition." See also Cicero, *Nat. d.* 2.71–72.

3
On Pronunciation or Orthography

3.1. Preface

3.1.1. Introduction

In the Greek grammatical tradition, orthography was a part of grammatical science narrowly concerned with identifying which letters were to be used in the representation of which sounds (see chs. 2, 4, 18, 20 in the following). However, as we can see in these extracts, the term came to be used by Roman grammarians to cover further questions about how words are, were, or ought to be pronounced (chs. 1, 2, 9, 13, 17) and about how, independently of their pronunciation, they ought to be written (chs. 3, 4, 7, 10, 11, 14, 15, 18).[1] (One question is whether spelling ought to follow pronunciation. Cornutus takes a flexible line; see *Orthography*, ch. 4 and note the contrasting approaches in chs. 5 and 14.) The more expansive acceptation of the word gradually encouraged the emergence of orthographical writing as a genre of its own, a genre of which Cornutus's *Pronunciation or Orthography* is an early example; in fact, we can only be sure of one that is earlier.[2]

Orthography in its most basic sense is obviously an important component of elementary grammatical education,[3] but Cornutus's work does not

---

1. It may be worth observing that Cassiodorus's introduction is the only thing that tells us that there we are dealing with a plurality of extracts (note *ista relata*)—or even that we have anything less than a full work. Length and lacunae (in chs. 4, 5, and 13) aside, it reads like any other work on orthography we know; its address to Aemilius gives it a plausible beginning, and the targets of cross-references (in chs. 11, 13, and 14) are all present and correct.

2. By Verrius Flaccus, who probably died around the time that Cornutus was born. Fragments in Funaioli 1907, 509–23; see esp. A11 = Suetonius, *Gramm.* 19.

3. See remarks by Quintilian, *Inst.* 1.4.6–17 and 1.7.33–34.

come across as a school text, or in any case not an elementary one. There is the technical level of some of the questions it addresses, its readiness to advise *innovation* on established conventions (chs. 2, 18), and, not least, the withering polemic against Varro (esp. ch. 16), which seems to speak to a well-informed readership interested in technical controversy. It is rather more likely that the work was connected with Cornutus's interest in the Latin poetical tradition, especially Virgil; the technical study of orthography was often motivated by questions about how earlier writers spoke and wrote the language (see chs. 4, 5, 9, 20).[4] But it is also natural to make the connection with Cornutus's interest in etymology (see introduction, §1.4.1.2); through its concern with understanding the choices of older writers, orthography has a lot to do with tracing the way words evolve and concerns itself with evidence that can be gleaned from the written language for the origins of words (e.g., chs. 3, 7, 12, 14, 15, and esp. 17).

3.1.2. Further Reading

Latin orthographical texts (up to Alcuin, in the ninth century) are collected in the same volume that contains the sixth-century work by Cassiodorus in which the extracts from Cornutus are preserved: Keil (1880). Quintilian did not devote a separate study to orthography, but, as a near contemporary of Cornutus, comparison might usefully be made with the relevant section of his *Institutes of Oratory* (1.7). For further discussion and context, see Gourinat (2008, esp. 80–82 for the link with etymology), De Paolis (2010), and especially now Zetzel (2018).

---

4. And Virgil was not only earlier but prone himself to archaism (see Quintilian, *Inst.* 1.7.18). The grammarian Nisus, another (presumed) younger contemporary of Cornutus, is someone else who was remembered both for work in orthography (he is mentioned several times in Velius Longus, *Orthography*, 76,7–80,2 [Keil 1880]) and for interest in Virgil (Donatus, *Vit. Verg.* 42). (Fragments in Mazzarino 1955, 332–39.)

3.2. Text and Translation

Annaei Cornuti de enuntiatione uel orthographia ista relata sunt:

1. Animaduerti quosdam, Aemili amice, eruditos etiam m litteram nec ubi oporteat dicentes nec [147,25] ubi oporteat supprimentes. hoc ne fiat hinc obseruari poterit, si simul subiciam, siquid ad rectam scripturam pertinet et ad diuisionem syllabarum. igitur si duo uerba coniungantur, quorum prius m consonantem nouissimam habeat, posterius a uocali incipiat, consonans perscribitur quidem, ceterum in enuntiando durum et barbarum sonat. at si posterius uerbum quamlibet consonantem habuerit uel uocalem loco positam consonantis, seruat m litterae sonum. par enim atque idem est uitium ita cum uocali sicut cum consonante m litteram exprimere.

2. [148,5] Est quaedam littera in ꜰ litterae speciem figurata, quae digamma nominatur, quia duos apices ex gamma littera habere uideatur. ad huius similitudinem soni nostri coniunctas uocales digammon appellare uoluerunt, ut est uotum uirgo. Itaque in prima syllaba digamma et uocalem oportuit poni, ꜰotum ꜰirgo, quod et Aeoles fecerunt et antiqui nostri, sicut scriptura in [148,10] quibusdam libellis declarat. hanc litteram

[Cassiodorus:] The following [extracts] are copied from Annaeus Cornutus, *On Pronunciation or Orthography*.

1. I have noticed, Aemilius my friend,[1] that some people, even educated people, fail to pronounce the letter m where they ought to and fail to suppress it where they should. It will be possible to see how to avoid this if I make a suggestion about orthography and the division of syllables at the same time. So, then: if two words are adjacent, and the first ends in the consonant m while the second begins with a vowel, the consonant is to be written, but it sounds labored and unidiomatic if it is pronounced.[2] But if the second word begins with any consonant at all, or with a vowel taking the place of a consonant,[3] the sound of the letter m is preserved. It is likewise a fault, and of equal severity, to pronounce the letter m the same way with a vowel and with a consonant.

2. There is a letter written as ϝ, called the *digamma*, because it looks like a gamma with two crossbars. In light of their similarity to its sound, our own people wanted to call conjoined vowels "digamma"—as in *uotum*, *uirgo*.[4] So in the first syllable one ought to put a digamma with the vowel—ϝ*otum*, ϝ*irgo*—as the Aeolians did, and our ancestors, too, as the writing in some books make clear. Terentius Varro, when he wanted to indicate this

---

1. It would be nice to think that this might be the Virgilian commentator Aemilius Asper (mentioned alongside Cornutus in F37). Asper is usually dated towards the end of the second century CE, but Cornutus himself forms the only secure *terminus post quem* for him (Asper responds to him in the continuation of F47), and there is no reason why they might not have been contemporaries. But equally, the Aemilii were an ancient consular family, and there is no shortage of (other) suitably prominent contemporaries to whom Cornutus may be dedicating his work.

2. This is borne out by metrical evidence: Latin verse writing assumes that a phrase such as *dictum est* will be pronounced as two syllables, not three.

3. I.e., the consonantal forms of the vowels u (pronounced "w" before another vowel) and i (pronounced "y" before another vowel). These are what, in para. 2 below, Cornutus calls "conjoined vowels."

4. The point of this paragraph is blunted by the distinction in English between the letters u and v (not to mention w), which is often observed even in writing Latin, but these were not distinguished by the Romans. By "conjoined vowel," Cornutus means consonantal u (pronounced w), as he goes on to explain.

Terentius Varro dum uult demonstrare, ita perscribit, VAV. qui ergo in hac syllaba sonus est, idem litterae erit. nos hodie u litteram in duarum litterarum potestatem coegimus: nam modo pro digamma scribitur, modo pro uocali. uocalis est, cum ipsa per se est: hoc enim cum ceteris quoque uocalibus patitur. si [148,15] cum alia uocali est, digamma est, quae est consonans. tres uocales quibusdam uidentur esse sub una syllaba uae. errant, si ita putant: nam nusquam apud Graecos neque apud Latinos ex tribus uocalibus syllaba constat. quare hic quoque digamma erit et duae uocales.

3. Similiter sed cadit in quaestionem, et aliis per t, aliis per d placet [148,20] scribi. apud antiquos enim scio pro sed sedum fuisse: unde nos duabus litteris nouissimis ablatis reliquas litteras salua d in usu habemus: quem ad modum si quaeras "sat qua littera scribi oportet?" dicemus per t, quia integrum eius sit satis.

4. [149,1] Q littera tunc recte ponitur, cum illi statim u littera et alia quaelibet una pluresue uocales coniunctae fuerint, ita ut una syllaba fiat: cetera per c scribuntur. hoc Lucilio quoque uidetur. non nulli putant auribus deseruiendum atque ita scribendum, ut auditur. est enim fere certamen [149,5] de recta scriptura in hoc, utrum quod audimus, an quod scribi oporteat, scribendum sit. ego non omnia auribus dederim. quotidie sunt qui per co cotidie scribant, quibus peccare licet desinere, si scient quotidie [inde] tractum esse a quot diebus, hoc est omnibus diebus. qui syllaba per qui scribitur; si diuiditur, ut sit cui ut huic, per c. hoc item in ceteris

3. On Pronunciation or Orthography 145

letter, wrote VAV:[5] the sound in this syllable ["waw"] is that of the letter. Today, we force the u to have the role of two letters: sometimes it is written instead of the digamma, sometimes instead of a vowel.[6] It is a vowel when it is on its own—as is the case with all vowels. But if it is with another vowel, it is a digamma, which is a consonant. Some people think that *uae* ("woe!") consists of three vowels in one syllable. They are wrong if they think that; three vowels never make one syllable, either in Greek or in Latin, so this would be a digamma and two vowels.

3. Similarly, the word *sed* ("but") falls under consideration. Some people see fit to write it with t, but others with d, because I know that for the ancients it was *sedum* rather than *sed*, and from them we get our word by removing the last two letters and keeping the rest, including d. In the same way, if you ask, "What letter should one use for *sat* ('enough')?" we will say t, because the full word is *satis*.

4. The letter q is placed correctly when the letter u and some other vowel or vowels are immediately joined to it so as to make one syllable. Otherwise, c is written. Lucilius thought that, too.[7] Some think that one should be led by the ears and write as one hears. This amounts to little short of a battle in the field of orthography—whether we are to write what we hear or what ought to be written. I would not concede everything to the ears. There are those who write *quotidie* ("daily") as *cotidie*, with *co*. They might desist from their error if they knew that *quotidie* is derived from *quot dies* ("as many days as there are"), that is, every day.[8] When *qui* is a syllable, it is written as *qui*; when it is divided, as in *cu-i* (compare *hu-ic*),[9] it is written with c. We shall note again in other cases that the letter c goes

---

5. Varro, frag. 270 (Funaioli 1907).

6. This sentence has been taken as evidence that the composition of the *Orthography* preceded the (short-lived) introduction of the digamma into the official alphabet by Claudius in 47 CE (referred to approvingly by Quintilian, *Inst.* 1.7.26); Rocca-Serra (2008) suggests that Claudius might even have been influenced by Cornutus.

7. Perhaps the second-century writer of satires (an inspiration to Persius: *Life of Persius* ad fin.).

8. Quintilian is dismissive of this view (*Inst.* 1.7.6).

9. A laudable recent innovation, according to Quintilian (*Inst.* 1.7.27). Note that *huic* is given by Cornutus here to provide a parallel example of a dative (of *hic*, "this") that, like the dative *cui* (of *qui*, "who"), is bisyllabic. (Its own possession of a -c is purely incidental.)

notabimus, [149,10] ut diuisionem c littera sequatur. si tamen secundum antiquam enuntiationem fuerit † quia genetiuus et ablatiuus non diuiditur.

5. Causa per unam s: nec quemquam moueat antiqua scriptura: nam et accussare per duo s scripserunt, sicut fuisse diuisisse esse et † causasse per duo s scriptum inuenio. in qua enuntiatione quo modo duarum consonantium [149,15] sonus exaudiatur, non inuenio.

6. Vostra olim ita per o, hodie per e, ut aduorsa aduersa, peruorsa peruersa, uotare uetare, uortex uertex, conuollere conuellere, amploctere amplectere.

7. Malo qui putant ab eo quod est graece μᾶλλον [comparativo modo] [149,20] descendisse et per duo l scribunt, peccant. non enim a graeco translatum est, sed ab antiquorum consuetudine, qui primo magis uolo dixerunt, postea a pluribus elisionibus hoc uerbum angustauerunt, ut mage uolo, [150,1] deinde mauolo, quod frequentissimum apud illos est: nouissimo in hoc substitit, ut malo esset. sed malle per duo l: magis uelle enim est. item nolo per unum l, nolle per duo l: nolo enim neuolo est, nolle ne uelle. denique ut se uerbum habet, ita ea quae ex illo componuntur.

8. [150,5] Alia sunt quae per duo u scribuntur, quibus numerus quoque syllabarum crescit. similis enim uocalis uocali adiuncta non solum non cohaeret, sed etiam syllabam auget, ut uacuus ingenuus occiduus exiguus. eadem diuisio uocalium in uerbis quoque est, ut metuunt statuunt tribuunt acuunt, ergo hic quoque c littera, non q apponenda est.

with division. However, if it were according to ancient pronunciation <...> because the genitive and ablative are not divided.[10]

5. *Causa* ("cause") is written with one s. Do not let anyone be swayed by ancient writing—for they also wrote *accussare* ('accuse') with double s; also *fuisse* ("to have been"), *diuisisse* ("to have divided"), *esse* ("to be"), and <...> I do find *caussae* written with a double s: I cannot find a way of pronouncing it by which the sound of a double consonant can be heard.[11]

6. *Vostra* was once written with o, nowadays with e; similarly, *aduorsa/aduersa*, *peruorsa/peruersa*, *uotare/uetare*, *uortex/uertex*, *conuollere/conuellere*, *amploctere/amplectere*.[12]

7. People who think that *malo* ("I prefer") comes from the Greek μᾶλλον ("rather"), so that it should be written with double l, are wrong. For it is not a borrowing from Greek but established by the usage of the ancients, who originally said *magis uolo* ("I have more wish for"), then shortened it to this word via a series of elisions: *mage uolo*, then *mauolo* (which is to be found *passim* in their writings); finally, it reached the point where it became *malo*. *Malle* ("to prefer"), however, has a double l because it is *magis uelle* ("to have more wish for"); similarly, *nolo* ("I do not want") with one l but *nolle* ("not to want") with two: for *nolo* is *neuolo*, *nolle* is *ne uelle*. And what goes for the verb goes for compounds made from it.

8. Some words are written with a double u, which increases the number of their syllables, too. For a vowel joined to a like vowel does not coalesce with it; in fact, it actually increases the number of syllables. For example: *uacuus, ingenuus, occiduus, exiguus*.[13] There is the same division of vowels in verbs: for example, *metuunt, statuunt, tribuunt, acuunt* (so that here, too, the letter c, not q, is to be used).[14]

---

10. Something is evidently missing, but the point might have concerned *cuius* and *quo*, the genitive and ablative forms of *cui*; perhaps Cornutus suggested writing *quius* for the genitive.

11. Of course one can *lengthen* the pronunciation of the -s-, and indeed, Latin poetical meter requires extra length to be given to double consonants. So Cornutus's point might tell us something about how everyday speech actually sounds (on qu-/c-, see n. 18 below), or he might simply be saying that there is no qualitative difference in this case (even if there is a quantitative one). Quintilian says that the writing of double s continued as late as Cicero and Virgil (*Inst.* 1.7.20).

12. "Opposite," "askew," "forbid," "whirlpool" (or "top"), "uproot," "embrace." *Vostra*, or, more familiarly, *uestra*, means "your."

13. "Empty," "freeborn," "setting," "small."

14. "They fear," "they establish," "they apportion," "they sharpen." For the point about c/q, see para. 4 above.

9. [150,10] Lacrumae an lacrimae, maxumus an maximus, et siqua similia sunt, quo modo scribi debeant, quaesitum est. Terentius Varro tradidit Caesarem per i eius modi uerba solitum esse enuntiare et scribere: inde propter auctoritatem tanti uiri consuetudinem factam. sed ego in antiquiorum multo libris, quam Gaius Caesar est, per u pleraque scripta inuenio, optumus [150,15] intumus pulcherrumus lubido dicundum faciundum maxume monumentum contumelia minume. melius tamen est et ad enuntiandum et ad scribendum i litteram pro u ponere, in quod iam consuetudo inclinauit.

10. Vineas per e quidam scribendas tradiderunt, si hae significarentur, quas in agris uidemus; at contra per i, uinias, illas sub quibus latere [150,20] miles solet, quod discrimen stultissimum est, nam neque aliunde uineae castrenses dictae sunt, quam quod uineis illis agrestibus similes sunt.

11. Extinguunt per duo u: qualem rationem supra reddidi de q littera, quam dixi oportere in omni declinatione duas uocales habere, talis hic [151,1] quoque intellegenda est. extinguo est enim, et ab hoc extinguunt, licet enuntiari non posit.

12. Interuallum duas l habet: uallum enim ipsum non aliter scribitur, a quo interuallum. Varro dicit interualla esse spatia quae sunt inter capita [151,5] uallorum, id est stipitum quibus uallum fit; unde cetera quoque spatia interualla dicuntur.

13. Obseruanda pusillo diligentius est praepositionum cum uerbis aut uocabulis compositio, ut consonantes nouissimas praepositionum sciamus non durare, sed mutari plerumque, itaque non numquam quae consonantes [151,10] uerborum aut uocabulorum primo loco sunt, easdem necesse est fieri et in praepositionibus, aut propter leuitatem aut quia omnino enuntiari saepe litterae praepositionum non possunt. quando autem fiant, quando non, sono internoscemus: accedo duo c, attuli duo

9. *Lacrumae* or *lacrimae* ("tears"), *maxumus* or *maximus* ("greatest"), and the like: we should ask how to spell them. Terentius Varro says that Caesar used to pronounce and spell them with i; the practice caught on, thanks to the influence of such a great man.[15] But I find the spelling with u in many books which predate Gaius Caesar: *optumus, intumus, pulcherrumus, lubido, dicundum, faciundum, maxume, monumentum, contumelia, minume*.[16] Nevertheless, it is better to pronounce and write i instead of u, which is the tendency now.

10. Some say that *uineas* is to be written with e when the word means the things we see in the fields ("vines") but with i, *uinias*, when it means the things beneath which soldiers hide[17]—which is a very stupid distinction, since the military *uineae* are so called for no other reason than that they look like the agricultural *uineae*.

11. *Extinguunt* ("they extinguish") is written with double u. The reason is similar to the one I gave above in my discussion of the letter q, when I said that it ought to have two vowels in every occurrence. For *extinguo* is the verb from which *extinguunt* comes—even though one cannot pronounce it.[18]

12. *Ineruallum* ("interval") has a double l; that is how *uallum* ("palisade") is written, and *interuallum* comes from it. Varro says that an *interuallum* is the space between the tops of the *ualli*, that is, of the stakes from which a *uallum* is made. From this, other spaces are called *interualla*, too.[19]

13. One ought to keep a fairly careful eye on the combination of prefixes with verbs or nouns; we need to be clear that the final consonants of the prefixes do not persist but usually change. Sometimes, then, the consonants at the beginning of the verbs or nouns have to be duplicated in the prefix—either because of weakening or because letters of the prefix cannot be enunciated at all. We know by the sound when letters are duplicated and when not: *ac-cedo* has double c, *at-tuli* double t, *as-siduus* double s,

---

15. Varro, frag. 269 (Funaioli 1907). Quintilian says that the practice originated with an inscription *to* Caesar (*Inst.* 1.7.21).

16. "Best," "innermost," "most beautiful," "lust," "to be said," "to be done," "especially," "monument," "insult," "least of all."

17. These were constructions to shield soldiers while doing siege work.

18. I.e., one does not pronounce the two vowels to make two syllables, so that *extinguunt* sounds like "extingunt" to just the extent that *quotidie* sounds like "cotidie" (para. 4 above). But at least in principle (perhaps not so much in practice), there ought to have been some difference in sound: qu- and gu- here are labiovelars, not velars with vowels.

19. Varro, frag. 276 (Funaioli 1907).

t, assiduus duo s, arrideo duo r, appareo duo p, annuo duo n, alligo duo l. in his non solum [151,15] propter leuitatem consonantes mutantur, sed et quia nullo modo sonare d littera potest. est ubi sonet et ubi scribatur, cum f consonanti adiungitur, ut adfluo adfui adfectus: at contra b non sonat, ut offui offero offendo. in aliis etiam consonantibus idem patitur, ut suggero <...> ostendi enim supra digamma consonantis uim habere. est ubi b, quod uix credibile est, in s [151,20] cogatur, ut suscipere sustinere suspendere suscitare, et quod antiqui dixerunt sustollere, nos praeterito sustuli. item ex praepositio ad f litteram formatur, ut effluo effodio effero efficio; nec minus in s formatur, ut [152,1] escendo. alicubi tamen sonat et ob hoc necessario scribitur, ut exsilio exsicco. itaque ubi sonuerit, ibi ponemus.

14. Tamtus et quamtus in medio m habere debent, quam enim et tam est, unde quamtitas quamtus tamtus, nec quosdam moueat, si n sonat: [152,5] iam enim supra docui n sonare debere, tametsi in scriptura m positum sit.

15. Exsilium cum s: ex solo enim ire est, quasi exsolium, quod Graeci ἐξορισμόν dicunt: antiqui exsoles dicebant.

16. H sicut in quaestione est, littera sit necne, sic numquam dubitatum est secundo loco a quacumque consonante poni debere, quod solus Varro [152,10] dubitat. uult enim auctoritate sua efficere ut h prius ponatur ea littera, cui adspirationem confert, et tanto magis hoc temptat persua-

ar-rideo double r, *ap-pareo* double p, *an-nuo* double n, *al-ligo* double l.[20] In these cases, the consonants are changed not just through being weakened but because the letter d cannot be made to be heard at all. Sometimes the consonant is both heard and written—when it is joined to the consonant f: for example, *ad-fluo, ad-fui, ad-fectus*.[21] But b, on the other hand, is not heard: *of-fui, of-fero, of-fendo*[22]—and the same thing happens with other consonants, as I show <…> for I pointed out above that the digamma has the force of a consonant.[23] There are times when b—although you would hardly believe it—is made to be an s: for example, *sus-cipere, sus-tinere, sus-pendere, sus-citare*; also *sus-tollere*, as the ancients said it, and we have the past tense *sus-tuli*.[24] Again, in the preposition *ex* there is a change to the letter f, as in *ef-fluo, ef-fodio, ef-fero, ef-ficio*, but it can also change to s, as in *escendo*.[25] However, sometimes it is heard and so must be written, as *ex-silio, ex-sicco*.[26] So, when it is heard, then we put it down.

14. *Tamtus* ("so much") and *quamtus* ("how much") ought to have m in the middle; they are from *quam* and *tam*, from which we get *quamtitas* ("quantity"), *quamtus, tamtus*. Nor should anyone be worried if n is heard; in fact, I made it clear above that one *ought* to pronounce n, even though m is written.

15. *Exsilium* ("exile") with s: it comes from *ex solo ire* ("go from the land") as if the word were *exsolium* (the Greeks say *exorismon*).[27] The ancients talked about *exsoles* ("exiles").

16. Whether h is a letter or not is in question, but it was never in doubt that it should be placed *after* its consonant. Only Varro doubts it: he wants to bring it about, by his authority, that h be placed *before* the letter on which it confers aspiration and strives the more to make the case because

---

20. "I approach," "I brought," "persistent," "I smile at," "I appear," "I assent to," "I bind." In each case the prefix is ad- ("to[wards]").

21. "I abound," "I was present," "emotion."

22. "I opposed," "I offer," "I meet." The prefix is *ob*- ("against").

23. Something reasonably substantial has been lost in the ellipsis marked, because ob- is not, as a matter of fact, assimilated to consonantal u as it is to f in the preceding examples (e.g., *ob-uius*, "in the way of").

24. "Hold up," "support," "suspend," "rouse"; and "raise"/"I raised." The prefix is sub- ("[from] under").

25. "I flow out," "I dig out," "I bear out," "I effect," "I ascend." *Ex*- of course means "out [from]."

26. "I leap out," "I drain off."

27. The Greek suggests "away from the border."

dere, quod uocalibus quoque dicit anteponi, ut heres hircus. sed Varronem praeterit consonantem ideo secundo loco h recipere, quod non possit ante se adspirationem nisi uocalis habere. itaque et ante et post h littera cuicumque [152,15] uocali adiungatur, [non] sonabit. haec enim natura uocalium est, ut ante se aut post se h litterae enuntiationem non impediant. praeterea [153,1] in libro qui est de grammatica Varro, cum de litteris dissereret, [ita] h inter litteras non esse disputauit, quod multo minus mirum, quam quod x quoque litteram esse negat. in quo quid uoluerit, nondum deprehendi, ipsius uerba subiciam: "e litterarum partim sunt et [153,5] dicuntur, ut a et b; partim dicitur neque sunt, ut h et x; quaedam neque sunt neque dicuutur, ut φ et ψ."

17. Vehemens et uemens apud antiques et apud Ciceronem lego, aeque prehendo et prendo, hercule et hercle, nihil et nil. haec obseruari eatenus poterunt, consuetudine potius quam ratione, in his praecipue uerbis quae [153,10] adspirationem habere debent.

18. Y littera antiqui non semper usi sunt, sed aliquando loco illius u ponebant: itaque in illorum quidem libris hanc scripturam obseruandam censeo, Suriam Suracusas sumbola sucophantas, at in nostris corrumpi non debet. illud etiam non uideo, quare huic litterae h adspirationis [153,15] gratia admoueam. ipsa enim per se adspiratiua est et quocumque uocabulo primum locum habuerit, adspiratur, Yacinthus Yllus Ymettus; et tanto magis adspiratio addenda non est, quanta apud Latinos uocabula non sunt hac littera notata.

(he says) it is also placed *before* vowels—as *heres* ("heir"), *hircus* ("goat").²⁸ But it has eluded Varro that a consonant takes the h after it because it is impossible for anything but a vowel to have aspiration before it. So the h will be heard whether it goes before or after the vowel. For this is the nature of vowels, that they do not impede the pronunciation of the letter h either before or after them. What is more, in his book *On Grammar*, when he is talking about letters, Varro takes the position that h is not a letter—something much less surprising than the fact that he also denies that x is a letter! What he means by this, I have not yet worked out, so I shall append his own words: "Some of the letters both *are* [real letters] and *are pronounced*, as a and b; others are *pronounced* but *are not*, as h and x. Some neither *are* nor *are pronounced*, as φ and ψ."²⁹

17. I read *uehemens* and *uemens* in the ancients, and in Cicero, equally, *prehendo* and *prendo*, *hercule* and *hercle*, *nihil* and *nil*.³⁰ These [contractions] may be adopted if one is following usage rather than reason—especially in the case of those words which ought to have aspiration.

18. The letter y was not always used by the ancients, but sometimes they would put u in its place. So I think this way of writing ought to be observed at least for their books, *Suriam, Suracusas, sumbola, sucophantas*,³¹ but our own writing ought not to be tampered with. And I do not see why I should add the letter h to aspirate it. It is aspirated in itself, and every word which it begins is aspirated: Yacinthus, Yllus, Ymettus.³² And there is all the more reason not to add aspiration because in Latin words are not written with this letter.³³

---

28. Varro, frag. 279 (Funaioli 1907).

29. Varro frag. 49 (Funaioli 1907). The argument against x being a real letter was that it represented a combination of phonemes (/k/ + /s/), each of which has its own letter already: so Marius Victorinus, *Ars gramm.* 3.8 (and see Quintilian, *Inst.* 1.4.9, noting its redundancy for this reason). The status of h comes into question because it has no semantic value in Latin (it never affects meaning): Quintilian calls it "more a breath than a letter" (*Inst.* 1.5.19). In denying that ψ and φ are pronounced, Varro may have meant simply that they are not part of the native phonetic repertoire of Latin—they certainly *are* pronounced in Greek, as, indeed, is ψ in words borrowed into Latin from Greek.

30. "Violent," "I grasp," "by Hercules!" "nothing."

31. "Syria," "Syracuse," "symbols," "sycophant." The letter y always represents the Greek upsilon, so it is only used in Greek borrowings (as these words are).

32. I.e., (the names) "Hyacinthus," "Hyllus," "Hymettus."

33. "This letter" being y. Cornutus's point seems to be that (1) y is only used for borrowings from Greek (see n. 31 above), but (2) there is no Greek word that begins

19. [154,1] Varroni etiam placet r litteram, si primo loco ponatur, non adspirari. lector enim ipse, inquit, intellegere debet Rodum, tametsi h non habet, Rhodum esse, retorem rhetorem. sed eadem obseruatio non necessaria est [r littera]. sunt enim uerba primo loco r litteram habentia non minus [154,5] latina quam graeca. itaque merito auferemus [aut amouebimus] adspirationem, Roma regina rapa rodus.

20. Z in antiquis libellis modo scriptum est, modo non, sed pro illo duo s ponebantur crotalizo crotalisso, malacizo malacisso et his similia. sed uiderint illi qui, cum uerbis integris Graecorum uti non erubuerunt, erubescendum [154,10] crediderunt litteras graecas intermiscere. nobis satius est alieno bene uti, quam nostro ineleganter.

19. Varro also wanted the letter r not to be aspirated when at the beginning of a word; the reader himself, he said, ought to understand that *Rodum*, although it does not have an h, is *Rhodum*, and *retor rhetor*.³⁴ But the same rule does not impose itself, because there are Latin words which begin with r as well as Greek ones, so we are quite right to remove the aspiration: *Roma, regina, rapa, rodus*.³⁵

20. In ancient books, the z is sometimes written—but sometimes not; instead, double s is used: *crotalizo/crotalisso* ("I clap"), *malacizo/malacisso* ("I soften"), and similar words.³⁶ But people who show no embarrassment in using entire Greek words, yet believe it embarrassing to put Greek letters into the mix, ought to think it over. For me, it is preferable to make good use of someone else's property than clumsy use of one's own.

---

with an unaspirated upsilon. (Rare exceptions listed in LSJ are late or dialectal, and see LSJ, s.v. Υ/υ.) Since (3) in the written Greek of the time it was not normal to mark aspiration (and when it is marked, it is with a diacritic, not a letter), Cornutus concludes: (4) Υ-/υ- is already pronounced "hy," so prefixing the letter h is both macaronic and redundant.

34. Varro, frag. 280a (Funaioli 1907).

35. "Rome," "queen," "turnip," "lump." Keil (1880) has Rodus ("R[h]odes") for the last, but Cornutus needs examples of native Latin words that are unaspirated—that being the point of the contrast with Greek borrowings, which are (always) aspirated. If not *rodus* (a form of *raudus* marked "dubious" by *OLD*, s.v.), then perhaps *rodo*, "eat away."

36. Once again, the issue is the treatment of a Greek letter (zeta), only used with Greek loanwords.

4
Fragments and Testimonia

4.1. Preface

With two exceptions, only material mentioning Cornutus by name is included.[1] There is room for more speculative identification of material that derives from Cornutus, especially in Servius's commentaries on Virgil (see the bibliography with the concordances), but there is no way of doing this with any useful objectivity or, since it generally relies on similarity with what we know already, in a way that promises any material improvement to our understanding of Cornutus.

The arrangement of the evidence in this section is purely thematic. It has not seemed useful to use different rubrics for testimonia (third-party reports from or about Cornutus) and fragments properly speaking (quotations from his work), nor to distinguish the more secure from the less certain evidence for the philosopher Cornutus; where there are reasons for doubt or caution, these are set out in the notes.

Details of editions used will be found in the index of sources; deviations are noted.

4.2. Texts and Translations

4.2.1. Life

F1. Diogenes Laertius, *Vit. phil.* index locupletior[2]

Ἐν τῷ ζ' Ζήνων, Κλεάνθης, Χρύσιππος, Ζήνων Ταρσεύς, Διογένης, Ἀπολλόδωρος, Βοηθός, Μνησαρχίδης, Μνησαγόρας, Νέστωρ, Βασιλείδης, Δάρδανος,

---

1. The exceptions are F51 and F54; see n. 92 below.
2. Dorandi 2013, 66,23–29.

Ἀντίπατρος, Ἡρακλείδης, Σωσιγένης, Παναίτιος, Ἑκάτων, Ποσειδώνιος, Ἀθηνόδωρος, Ἀθηνόδωρος ἄλλος, Ἀντίπατρος, Ἄριος, Κορνοῦτος.

Book 7 [of Diogenes Laertius, *Lives of the Eminent Philosophers*] covers: Zeno, Cleanthes, Chrysippus, Zeno of Tarsus, Diogenes, Apollodorus, Boethus, Mnesarchides, Mnesagoras, Nestor, Basilides, Dardanus, Antipater, Heraclides, Sosigenes, Panaetius, Hecato, Posidonius, Athenodorus, another Athenodorus, Antipater, Arius, Cornutus.[3]

F2. Suda κ.2098[4]

Κορνοῦτος· δύω συγγραφέε Ῥωμαίων ἤστην, Τῖτος Λίβιος, οὗ διαρρεῖ πολὺ καὶ κλεινὸν ὄνομα, καὶ Κορνοῦτος. πλούσιον μὲν οὖν ἀκούω καὶ ἄπαιδα τοῦτον, σπουδαῖον δὲ οὐδὲν ὄντα. τοσαύτη [158,30] δὲ ἦν ἡ διαφορότης ἐς τούσδε τοὺς ἄνδρας τῶν ἀκροωμένων, ὡς τοῦ [159,1] μὲν Κορνούτου παμπλείστους ἀκούειν, θεραπείᾳ τε καὶ κολακείᾳ τοῦ ἀνδρὸς συρρέοντας καὶ διὰ τὴν ἀπαιδίαν ἐλπίδι κληρονομίας· τοῦ γε μὴν Λιβίου ὀλίγους, ἀλλὰ ὧν τι ὄφελος ἦν καὶ ἐν κάλλει ψυχῆς καὶ ἐν εὐγλωττίᾳ. καὶ ταῦτα μὲν ἐπράττετο. ὁ χρόνος δὲ ὁ ἄπρατός τε καὶ [159,5] ἀδέκαστος καὶ ἡ τούτου φύλαξ καὶ ὀπαδὸς καὶ ἔφορος ἀλήθεια, μήτε χρημάτων δεόμενοι, μηδὲ μὴν ὀνειροπολοῦντες ἐκ κλήρου διαδοχήν, μήτ' ἄλλῳ τῳ αἰσχρῷ καὶ κιβδήλῳ τε καὶ καπήλῳ καὶ ἥκιστα ἐλευθέρῳ ἁλισκόμενοι, τὸν μὲν ἀνέφηναν καὶ ἐξεκάλυψαν, ὥσπερ κεκρυμμένον θησαυρὸν καὶ κεχανδότα πολλὰ καὶ ἐσθλά, τὸ τοῦ Ὁμήρου, [159,10] τοῦτον τὸν Λίβιον· τοῦ δὲ πλουσίου καὶ μέντοι καὶ περιρρεομένου τοῖς χρήμασι λήθην κατεχέαντο τοῦ Κορνούτου. καὶ ἴσασιν ἢ τις ἢ οὐδεὶς αὐτόν. οὗτος ὁ Κορνοῦτος Λεπτίτης φιλόσοφος· Λεπτὶς δὲ πόλις Λιβύης· γεγονὼς ἐν Ῥώμῃ ἐπὶ Νέρωνος καὶ πρὸς αὐτοῦ ἀναιρεθεὶς σὺν τῷ Μουσωνίῳ. ἔγραψε πολλὰ φιλόσοφά τε καὶ [159,15] ῥητορικά.

---

3. For the authenticity of this index, see Dorandi 1992. Diogenes Laertius, *Vit. phil.* 7 is devoted to Stoics, so we can derive from this (chronological) list not only confirmation of Cornutus's rough date (younger than Arius, who taught the emperor Augustus) but also his identification as a Stoic and one considered preeminent in his generation.

4. Adler 1928–1935, 158,27–159,15. The Suda here evidently confuses our Cornutus (the subject of the last lines, from "This Cornutus") with a historian of the same name: perhaps C. Caecilius Cornutus (see *FRH* 1:426–27 with *FRH* 54 T1; and further below at F63 with n. 115).

Cornutus: There were two Roman writers, Titus Livy, who left a great and glorious name, and Cornutus. I hear that the latter was rich and childless but not at all a good man. There was a great difference in the audiences these men drew. Very many went to hear Cornutus, streaming in to cultivate and flatter the man in the hope of inheriting something from him, since he was childless. Rather few went to hear Livy, but they got some benefit from him, both in the beauty of his soul and his eloquence. So this is what used to happen, but time, which cannot be bought or bribed, and truth, the guardian and companion and protector of time, neither of which need possessions or dream of a share in inheritance, neither of which is in thrall to any shameful, crooked, illiberal cheat, brought this man Livy to light and uncovered him, as if he were a hidden treasure store, "holding many wonderful things," as Homer put it.[5] But they poured oblivion over the wealthy Cornutus with his superabundance of possessions: hardly anyone has heard of him. This Cornutus was a Leptite philosopher (Leptis is a Libyan city). He was in Rome at the time of Nero and, along with Musonius,[6] was executed by him. He wrote many philosophical and rhetorical works.

F3. Eudocia, *Viol.* 590 (Περὶ Κορνούτου)[7]

Κορνοῦτος Λεπτίτης[8] (ἡ δὲ Λέπτις πόλις Λιβύης), φιλόσοφος, γεγονὼς ἐν Ῥώμῃ ἐπὶ τοῦ Νέρωνος καὶ πρὸς αὐτοῦ ἀναιρεθεὶς σὺν τῷ Μουσωνίῳ. ἔγραψε δὲ πολλὰ φιλόσοφα καὶ ῥητορικά.

Cornutus the Leptite (Leptis is a Libyan city) was a philosopher. He was in Rome at the time of Nero and, along with Musonius, was executed by him. He wrote many philosophical and rhetorical works.

---

5. *Od.* 4.96 (of the palace of Menelaus).

6. I.e., the Stoic philosopher Musonius Rufus (who, among other things, taught Epictetus).

7. Flach 1880, 448,7–11 = Hesychius, *Onom.* 361 (Flach 1882, 123,16–19).

8. Λεπτίνης manuscripts. But the close parallel with the last line of F2 shows that this is an error of transcription, helped no doubt by the fact that Leptines is a Greek personal name.

F4. Stephanus, *Ethnica*[9]

Τέργις, πόλις ἐν Λιβύῃ πρὸς τῇ Αἰθιοπίᾳ. τὸ ἐθνικὸν Τεργίτης, ὡς τῆς Λέπτις Λεπτίτης. οὕτως καὶ ὁ φιλόσοφος Κορνοῦτος ἐχρημάτιζε Λεπτίτης.

Tergis: a city in Libya, near Ethiopia. The ethnic is Tergite, as the ethnic of Leptis is Leptite. So the philosopher Cornutus was known as Leptite.

F5. Stephanus, *Ethnica*[10]

Θέστις, πόλις Ἀράβων. καὶ ἄλλη Λιβύης. ὁ πολίτης ἑκατέρας Θεστίτης. ἐκ δὲ τῆς Λιβυκῆς Κορνοῦτος φιλόσοφος Θεστίτης χρηματίζων.

Thestis: an Arabian city. There is another in Libya. A citizen of either is a Thestite; Cornutus the philosopher is called Thestite because of the Libyan one.[11]

F6. *IRT* 306 = *AE* (1926): 162[12]

> ... C]ornut[us ...
> ... templu]m Neptun[I ...

> <...> Cornutus <...> temple of Neptune <...>

F7. Cassius Dio, *Hist. Rom.* 62.29.1–4

[1] Ὁ δὲ Νέρων ἄλλα τε γελοῖα ἔπραττε, καί ποτε καὶ ἐπὶ τὴν τοῦ θεάτρου ὀρχήστραν ἐν πανδήμῳ τινὶ θέᾳ κατέβη καὶ ἀνέγνω Τρωϊκά τινα ἑαυτοῦ ποιήματα· καὶ ἐπ' αὐτοῖς θυσίαι πολλαί, ὥσπερ καὶ ἐπὶ τοῖς ἄλλοις ἅπασιν οἷς ἔπραττεν, ἐγένοντο. [2] παρεσκευάζετο δὲ ὡς καὶ τὰς τῶν Ῥωμαίων πράξεις ἁπάσας συγγράψων ἐν ἔπεσιν, καὶ περί γε τοῦ πλήθους τῶν βιβλίων, πρὶν

---

9. Meineke 1849, 616,23–617,2.
10. Meineke 1849, 312,10–12.
11. Presumably, this outlying testimony is the result of error or confusion.
12. This is what remains of an inscription on a sea-facing structure in Leptis from some time in the first century CE, apparently a shrine dedicated to Neptune by Cornutus. If this is the philosopher (see Romanelli 1925, 134; Brouquier-Reddé 1992, 94), it suggests that he maintained a close connection with the city after moving to Rome.

καὶ ὁτιοῦν αὐτῶν συνθεῖναι, ἐσκέψατο, παραλαβὼν ἄλλους τε καὶ Ἀνναῖον Κορνοῦτον εὐδοκιμοῦντα τότε ἐπὶ παιδείᾳ. [3] καὶ αὐτὸν ὀλίγου μὲν καὶ ἀπέκτεινεν, ἐς νῆσον δ' οὖν ἐνέβαλεν, ὅτι τινῶν τετρακόσια ἀξιούντων αὐτὸν βιβλία γράψαι, πολλά τε αὐτὰ εἶναι ἔφη καὶ μηδένα αὐτὰ ἀναγνώσεσθαι, καί τινος εἰπόντος "καὶ μὴν Χρύσιππος, ὃν ἐπαινεῖς καὶ ζηλοῖς, πολὺ πλείω συνέθηκεν" ἀπεκρίνατο ὅτι "ἀλλ' ἐκεῖνα χρήσιμα τῷ τῶν ἀνθρώπων βίῳ ἐστίν." [4] ὁ μὲν οὖν Κορνοῦτος φυγὴν ἐπὶ τούτῳ ὦφλεν, ὁ δὲ δὴ Λουκανὸς ἐκωλύθη ποιεῖν, ἐπειδὴ ἰσχυρῶς ἐπὶ τῇ ποιήσει ἐπῃνεῖτο.

Among the many ridiculous things Nero did, he once stood on the stage of a theater at a public performance and read poems of his own about Troy, and many sacrifices were made in their honor, just as for everything else he did. He planned a comprehensive history of the Romans in epic verse, and he made inquiries about how many books he would need before he composed any of them, taking advice from, among others, Annaeus Cornutus, who was at that time a respected cultural figure. He all but executed him, exiling him to an island, because when it was estimated that he [Nero] would be writing four hundred books, he [Cornutus] said that that was a lot and that no one would read them. Someone said: "But Chrysippus, whom you praise and imitate, composed many more."[13] He answered: "But they are useful for human life." Cornutus earned himself exile for this, while Lucan was forbidden from writing, since he had been wildly praised for his poetry.[14]

F8. Constantine VII Porphyrogenitus, *De sententiis*[15]

Ὅτι ἐπαγγελλομένου Νέρωνος ὡς τετρακόσια γράφειν βιβλία πολλὰ αὐτὰ εἶναι ἔφη Ἀννέας Κορνοῦτος καὶ μηδένα αὐτὰ δύνασθαι ἀναγινώσκειν. εἰπόντος δὲ Νέρωνος "καὶ Χρύσιππος, [251] ὃν ἐπαινεῖς καὶ ζηλοῖς, πολλῷ πλείονα ἔγραψεν," ἀπεκρίνατο ἐκεῖνος "ἀλλ' ἐκεῖνα χρήσιμα τῷ τῶν ἀνθρώπων βίῳ,"[16] καὶ διὰ τοῦτο ἐφυγαδεύθη.

---

13. See *Life of Persius* 38 with n. 7.
14. One might take this narrative to be *ben trovato*, but Furentes González (1994, 464) suggests that it is *vero* and testimony to the "uninhibited speech" (*parrhēsia*) characteristic of the philosopher.
15. Boissevain 1905, 250,32–251,3.
16. χρησιμωτάτων ἀνθρώπων βίος ἐστί manuscripts. But this makes no sense (lit.:

Nero said that he was going to write four hundred books, and Anneas [sic] Cornutus said that that was a lot and that no one would be able to read them. Nero said: "Chrysippus, whom you praise and imitate, wrote many more!" He answered: "But they are useful for human life." Because of this he was sent into exile.

F9. Cassius Dio, *Roman History* (excerpts)[17]

ἀλλ' ἦν μὲν καθάπαξ τοῖς ἀγαθοῖς τε καὶ πεπαιδευμένοις ἔγκοτος. τὸ δὲ πλεῖστον καὶ κράτιστον ἐπὶ παραλόγοις αἰτίαις ἀπανηλώκει τῆς βουλῆς μέρος, τοὺς μὲν ὅτι εὐγενεῖς, τοὺς δὲ ὅτι περιουσίας ἔχοντας, τοὺς δὲ ὅτι σώφρονες ἦσαν μισῶν τε καὶ κολάζων. Μουσώνιόν τε καὶ Κορνοῦτον μικροῦ μὲν ἐδέησεν ἀποκτεῖναι, τῆς δὲ Ῥώμης ἐξήλασεν, ἄλλο μὲν οὐδὲν ἐπικαλῶν, ὅτι δὲ σοφοὶ καὶ ἄριστοι βίον ἐγενέσθην.

He [Nero] had an unremitting grudge against anyone who was good and well educated. He annihilated the largest and most powerful part of his council on charges which made no sense: some of them he hated and punished because of their nobility, some because they were wealthy, some because they were reasonable. He just stopped short of executing Musonius and Cornutus, but he drove them from Rome because they were wise and excellent men—he made no other allegation.

F10. Eusebius, *Chron.* 2 (Canon)

(1) In the Latin version of Jerome, for the third year of the 211th Olympiad/the thirteenth year of Nero's rule/sixty-seven years *post Christum* (Helm 1956, 184,23–26): Nero cum caeteris uiris insignibus et Octauiam uxorem suam interfecit, Cornutumque philosophum, praeceptorem Persii, in exsilium fugat.

(1) (67 CE) Nero, along with other distinguished men, also killed his wife Octavia and sent Cornutus the philosopher, Persius's teacher, into exile.

"They are the life of the most useful men"), and it is easily seen as a corruption of the relevant line in F7 [3].

17. Boissevain 1895–1901, 3:755,34–40 = John of Antioch, frag. 90 (Mueller 1851, 575a) = Constantine VII Porphyrogenitus, *De uirtutibus et uitiis* (Boissevain 1905, 183,10–16).

(2) From the Armenian translation, for the first year of the 211th Olympiad/the tenth year of Nero's rule (Aucher and Awgarean 1818, 2:272):

Ներոն բնդ այլ արւ փառաւորւ և զհերքարիա զկին իւր սպան. նոյն և զկորնուտոս փիլիսոփոսն հալածեաց.

(2) (65 CE) Nero, with other illustrious men, killed his wife Octavia [Hok'tabia]. The same also expelled Cornutus [Kornutos] the philosopher.[18]

4.2.2. Exegesis of Greek Theology

F11. Porphyry 12T[19] quoted at Eusebius, *Hist. eccl.* 6.19.8

Συνῆν τε γὰρ ἀεὶ τῷ Πλάτωνι, τοῖς τε Νουμηνίου καὶ Κρονίου Ἀπολλοφάνους τε καὶ Λογγίνου καὶ Μοδεράτου, Νικομάχου τε καὶ τῶν ἐν τοῖς Πυθαγορείοις ἐλλογίμων ἀνδρῶν ὡμίλει συγγράμμασιν, ἐχρῆτο δὲ καὶ Χαιρήμονος τοῦ Στωϊκοῦ Κορνούτου τε ταῖς βίβλοις, παρ' ὧν τὸν μεταληπτικὸν τῶν παρ' Ἕλλησιν μυστηρίων γνοὺς τρόπον ταῖς Ἰουδαϊκαῖς προσῆψεν γραφαῖς.[20]

Origen was always in the company of Plato and the books of Numenius and Cronius, of Apollophanes and Longinus, of Moderatus, Nicomachus, and the more famous of the Pythagoreans, and he used the works of Chaeremon the Stoic and Cornutus, from which he learned the allegorical character of the Greek mysteries—something he went on to ascribe to the Jewish Scriptures.[21]

F12. Jerome, *Epist.* 70.4[22]

Hunc imitatus Origenes decem scripsit Stromateas Christianorum et philosophorum inter se sententias conparans et omnia nostrae religionis dogmata de Platone et Aristotele, Numenio Cornutoque confirmans.

---

18. Timothy Greenwood very kindly supplied this translation from the Armenian.
19. Smith 1993, 16.
20. This text is also recycled into the Suda entry for Origen: see ω.182 (Adler 1928–1935, 617.4–10).
21. Origen is the third-century Christian theologian. The other writers mentioned are second-century Platonists and Pythagoreans. For Chaeremon, see the introduction, p. 13.
22. Hilberg 1910, 705,18–20.

Origen imitated him [Clement of Alexandria] in writing the ten-book *Stromata*, comparing the views of Christians and philosophers with each other, finding support for all the tenets of our religion in Plato and Aristotle, Numenius and Cornutus.

F13. Tzetzes, *Ad Lyc.* 177 (ad Πελασγικόν)[23]

Σὺν γὰρ θεῷ φάναι, καὶ τοῦ πολυΐστορος Ἀλεξάνδρου καὶ Ἀπολλοδώρου καὶ Ῥηγίνου τοῦ πολυμνήμονος καὶ Ἀρτέμωνος τοῦ Περγαμηνοῦ [88.1] καὶ Κασσάνδρου τοῦ Σαλαμινίου καὶ τῶν λοιπῶν ἱστορικῶν ἱστορικώτεροι καθεστήκαμεν καὶ ἀλληγορεῖν ἐπιστάμεθα καὶ ὑπὲρ Κορνοῦτόν τε καὶ Παλαίφατον καὶ Δομνῖνον καὶ Κεφαλίωνα καὶ Ἡράκλειτον καὶ τοὺς ἄλλους, ὁπόσοι ἢ ἑτέρωθεν ἀρυσάμενοι ἢ ἀφ' ἑαυτῶν γράφοντες ἠλληγόρησαν.

With the help of God, I am determined to speak more historically than Alexander Polyhistor and Apollodorus and Rheginus the Memorious and Aremon of Pergamum and Cassander of Salamnia and the rest of the historians, and I know how to allegorize better than Cornutus and Palaephatus and Domninus and Cephalion and Heraclitus[24]—and whoever else allegorized, whether their writing drew on other sources or came from themselves.

F14. Tzetzes, *Exegesis of the Iliad*[25]

Ἕτεροι δὲ, τῆς ἀλληγορίας τῶν θεϊκῶν ὀνομάτων, ὥσπερ καὶ ὁ Κορνουτός,[26] κἄνπερ ἀλληγορῇ ἀσυμβίβαστα. αὐτὰ μὲν γὰρ καθ' ἑαυτὰ λεγόμενα, εἶναί τι δοκοῦσι· πρὸς δὲ τὴν τῆς Ἰλιάδος γραφὴν οὐ συνᾴδει συμβιβαζόμενα.

Others [dealt with] the allegorical meaning of divine names, as Cornutus, too—although these do not make for allegory in combination; the names

---

23. Scheer 1908, 2:87,32–88,6.

24. Palaephatus: date unknown, author of the rationalising *Incredibilia*. Domninus: perhaps the fifth-century Neoplatonist from Larissa. Cephalion: a second-century rhetor/historian. Heraclitus: author of the *Homeric Problems*; probably to be dated to the later first or early second century CE (cf. introduction, p. 48).

25. Hermann 1812, 3,17–21.

26. Κρουνοῦτος manuscripts. But it seems reasonable to emend this as an error of transmission, given the correct form of Cornutus's name elsewhere in Tzetzes.

are seen to be something or other spoken on their own, but they do not cohere in combination—unlike the *Iliad*.[27]

F15. Tzetzes, *All. Il.* 18.655–659

> Ὅτι δ' οὐδεὶς ἐτόλμησεν ἀλληγορῆσαι τάδε,
> ὁρᾶτε τὸν Ἡράκλειτον, καὶ τὴν μιμὼ σὺν τούτῳ,
> τὴν ἀλαζόνα σφίγγα δὲ μᾶλλον τὴν ἐπηρμένην,
> Κορνούτους, Παλαιφάτους τε πάντας ἀλληγοροῦντας,
> καὶ τά ἐμὰ βιβλίδια, τὸ εὐτλές τε τόδε.

No one before has dared to allegorize these things; you can see this if you look at Heraclitus and the ape with him, at that boastful (or, rather, arrogant) sphinx,[28] and at all the Cornutuses and Palaphatuses who wrote allegories—and then at my little booklets, including this worthless one here.

F16. Tzetzes, *All. Od.* proem 35–38

> Ἔχεις Δημοῦς τὸ σύγγραμμα καὶ τὸ τοῦ Ἡρακλείτου,
> Κορνοῦτον καὶ Παλαίφατον, καὶ τὸν Ψελλὸν σὺν τούτοις,
> καὶ εἴ τις ἄλλος λέγεται γράψας ἀλληγορίας
> ἀνερευνήσας εὔρισκε καὶ τὰ τοῦ Τζέτζου βλέπε.

You have Demo's book, and Heraclitus's, you have Cornutus and Palaephatus, and Psellus with them—and anyone else you can seek out and find who is said to have written allegories; then look at what Tzetzes wrote!

---

27. This observation is echoed in seminal works in twentieth-century studies of Cornutus's *Greek Theology* which emphasize that this work is more about etymology (the meanings behind individual names) than allegory (what the gods represent within extended narratives). See the introduction, §1.4.1.2.

28. The "ape" is Demo (see *All. Od.*, proem 32–34), date uncertain (perhaps fifth or sixth century); the sphinx is probably the Byzantine philosopher Michael Psellus, who read the sphinx as an image of the human being but also, implicitly, as an image of the allegorical interpreter—and so of himself; see his *Phil. min.* 1.44 with Miles (2014).

F17. Theodoretus, *Graec. affect. cur.* 2.94–95

Σαγχωνιάθων μὲν οὖν ὁ Βηρύτιος τὴν Φοινίκων θεολογίαν ξυνέγραψε· μετήνεγκε δὲ ταύτην εἰς τὴν Ἑλλάδα φωνὴν Φίλων, οὐχ ὁ Ἑβραῖος, ἀλλ' ὁ Βύβλιος, τὸν δὲ Σαγχωνιάθωνα λίαν τεθαύμακεν ὁ Πορφύριος· Μανεθὼς δὲ τὰ περὶ Ἴσιδος καὶ Ὀσίριδος καὶ Ἄπιδος καὶ Σαράπιδος καὶ τῶν ἄλλων θεῶν τῶν Αἰγυπτίων ἐμυθολόγησε· [2.95] Διόδωρος δὲ ὁ Σικελιώτης κοσμογονίαν ξυνέγραψε· τὴν δὲ τοῦ Ἀσκραίου ποιητοῦ Θεογονίαν οἶδε καὶ τὰ μειράκια· ὁ δέ γε Ὀδρύσης Ὀρφεὺς τὰς Αἰγυπτίων τελετὰς τοὺς Ἕλληνας ἐξεπαίδευσε. Κάδμος δὲ τὰς Φοινίκων· Κορνοῦτος δὲ ὁ φιλόσοφος τὴν Ἑλληνικὴν θεολογίαν ξυντέθεικε· Πλούταρχος δὲ καὶ Ἀέτιος τὰς τῶν φιλοσόφων ἐκπαιδεύουσι δόξας· τὸν αὐτὸν δὲ καὶ ὁ Πορφύριος ἀνεδέξατο πόνον, τὸν ἑκάστου βίον ταῖς δόξαις προστεθεικώς

Sanchuniathon of Beirut wrote out the Phoenician theology; Philo translated it into Greek (not Philo the Jew, but Philo of Byblos). Porphyry was an enthusiastic admirer of Sanchuniathon. Manetho wrote the mythologies of Isis and Osiris and Apis and Sarapis and all the other Egyptian gods. Diodorus of Sicily composed a cosmogony; even young children know the *Theogony* of the Ascraean poet.[29] Orpheus of Odrysa taught the Greeks the Egyptian mysteries, Cadmus those of the Phoenicians. Cornutus the philosopher put together a *Greek Theology*; Plutarch and Aetius instructed the Greeks in the opinions of the philosophers—and Porphyry expended the same energy adding a biography to the account of their doctrines in each case.

F18. *Etymologicum Magnum* 408,52–56

Ζεύς· Ὁ θεός. Κορνοῦτος ἐν τῷ περὶ Ἑλληνικῆς θεολογίας φησίν, ὅτι ψυχή ἐστι τοῦ παντὸς κόσμου, παρὰ τὸ ζωὴ καὶ αἰτία εἶναι τοῖς ζῶσι τοῦ ζῆν· καὶ διὰ τοῦτο βασιλεὺς λέγεται τῶν ὅλων, ὡς καὶ ἐν ἡμῖν ἡ ψυχή.

Zeus: the god. Cornutus, in *On Greek Theology*, says that he is the soul of the whole cosmos, so called from *life* and from its being "the cause to living things of their *being alive*. For this reason, too, he is said to be the king of the universe, as our soul is in us."[30]

---

29. I.e., Hesiod.
30. Cornutus, *Greek Theology*, 3,3–8.

4.2.3. On Aristotle's *Categories*

For general orientation on the early commentary tradition on Aristotle's *Categories*, see Griffin (2015; pp. 139–45 for Cornutus in particular). As with many of the early commentators, known to us only through selective and polemical reports from much later, the literature has struggled to identify adequate and serious motivation for Cornutus's interest; I set out my own suggestion above (introduction, §1.4.1.1).

We are usually not told from which of Cornutus's works citations derive, and we cannot assume that they all derive from the work (or works) dedicated to discussion of the *Categories*, the *Against Athenodorus and Aristotle* (see above, §1.6, T4); F20, for example, draws on a rhetorical work, and Simplicius tells us that Porphyry, our ultimate source for most if not all of the fragments in this section, cast his net wide in his treatment of Stoic views (see Simplicius, *On the Categories*, 2,8–9 [Kalbfleisch 1907]). For this reason, the following fragments are presented in the order in which the topics they treat arise in the *Categories* itself.

F19. Porphyry, *On the Categories*[31]

[Ἐρώτησις] Ἀλλ' εἰ ἐνθάδε εἰς δέκα γένη διεῖλεν τὰς σημαντικὰς φωνάς, πῶς ἐν τῷ Περὶ ἑρμηνείας εἰς δύο, εἰς ὄνομα καὶ ῥῆμα;

[Ἀπόκρισις] Ὅτι ἐνθάδε μὲν περὶ τῆς προηγουμένης θέσεως τῶν λέξεων τῆς κατὰ τῶν πραγμάτων ποιεῖται τὸν λόγον, ἐν δὲ τῷ Περὶ ἑρμηνείας περὶ τῆς δευτέρας, ἢ οὐκέτι ἐστὶ περὶ τῶν σημαντικῶν λέξεων τῶν πραγμάτων, καθό [58,35] εἰσι τούτων σημαντικαί, ἀλλὰ περὶ τῶν σημαντικῶν λέξεων τοῦ τύπου τῶν φωνῶν, καθὸ τύποι εἰσὶ τοιούτων· τύπος γὰρ τῆς φωνῆς τὸ εἶναι ἢ ὄνομα ἢ ῥῆμα. καὶ τὸ κυρίαν δὲ εἶναι τὴν λέξιν ἢ μεταφορικὴν ἢ ἄλλως [59,1] τροπικὴν τῆς δευτέρας ἐστὶ περὶ τῶν φωνῶν πραγματείας καὶ οὐ τῆς πρώτης.

[Ἐρώτησις] Ἆρα οὖν τὴν διαφορὰν ταύτην πάντες ἔγνωσαν οἱ περὶ τῶν κατηγοριῶν τι γράψαντες;

[59,5] [Ἀπόκρισις] Οὐδαμῶς· οὐ γὰρ ἂν οἱ μὲν περὶ τῶν γενῶν τῶν ὄντων προηγουμένως ᾤοντο ἐνταῦθα πραγματεύεσθαι, οἱ δὲ ἀντέλεγον ἀθετοῦντες αὐτῶν τὴν διαίρεσιν ὡς πολλὰ παριεῖσαν καὶ μὴ περιλαμβάνουσαν ἢ καὶ πάλιν πλεονάζουσαν.

[Ἐρώτησις] Τίνες εἰσὶν οὗτοι;

---

31. Busse 1887, 58,30–59,14.

[59,10] [Ἀπόκρισις] Οἱ περὶ Ἀθηνόδωρον καὶ Κορνοῦτον οἱ τὰ ζητούμενα περὶ τῶν λέξεων καθὸ λέξεις, οἷα τὰ κύρια καὶ τὰ τροπικὰ καὶ ὅσα τοιαῦτα, (διαφοραὶ γάρ ἐστι λέξεων καθὸ λέξεις εἰσί) τὰ τοιαῦτα οὖν προφέροντες καὶ ποίας ἐστὶ κατηγορίας ἀποροῦντες καὶ μὴ εὑρίσκοντες ἐλλιπῇ φασιν εἶναι τὴν διαίρεσιν, ὡς ἂν μὴ πάσης φωνῆς σημαντικῆς εἰς αὐτὴν περιλαμβανομένης.

[Question:] If he here[32] divides significant vocalizations into ten genera, why is it that in *On Interpretation* he divides them into two, namely, nouns and verbs?

[Answer:] Because here he is discussing the primary imposition of words on things, while in *On Interpretation* he is discussing their secondary imposition, which is no longer concerned with words that signify things insofar as they signify them, but rather with words as signifying a type of vocalization insofar as they are types of such things—and to be a noun or verb is to be a type of vocalization.[33] And whether a word is literal or metaphorical, or some other kind of [59.1] trope, has to do with this second treatment of vocalizations and not the first.

[Q:] So has everyone who has written on the *Categories* known the difference?

[A:] Not at all; otherwise there would not have been people who thought that the genera of what exists were primarily at issue there, or people who responded by rejecting the division for missing out many items and failing to encompass them—or, again, for including too much!

[Q:] Who are these people?

[A:] The followers of Athenodorus and Cornutus, who take the inquiry to be about words insofar as they are words—e.g., about what is literal, what is a trope, and so on (for these are differences between words insofar as they are words). Since this is what they think, they are confused about what sort of things the categories are, and because they fail to discover this, they say that the division is defective for not encompassing every significant vocalization.

---

32. I.e., Aristotle, in the *Categories*.

33. For example, the vocalization "dog" signifies an animal (primary imposition) but also a noun (i.e., the noun "dog": secondary imposition).

F20. Porphyry, *On the Categories*[34]

[Ἀπόκρισις] Διαίρεσις μὲν γάρ ἐστι τομὴ τοῦ γένους εἰς εἴδη, ἐνταῦθα δὲ οὐ γένος ἓν διαιρήσεται εἰς εἴδη δέκα, ἀλλὰ δέκα γένη ἐκθήσεται. καταρίθμησις οὖν ἐστιν, ἣν ποιήσεται τῶν πρώτων γενῶν καὶ τῶν κατὰ τὰ πρῶτα γένη δέκα κατηγοριῶν.

[Ἐρώτησις] Τί οὖν φησιν;

[86,15] [Ἀπόκρισις] "Τῶν κατὰ μηδεμίαν συμπλοκὴν λεγομένων ἕκαστον ἤτοι οὐσίαν σημαίνει ἢ ποσὸν ἢ ποιὸν ἢ πρός τι ἢ ποῦ ἢ ποτὲ ἢ κεῖσθαι ἢ ἔχειν ἢ ποιεῖν ἢ πάσχειν." καὶ λαμβάνει τούτων ἑκάστου δηλωτικὰ παραδείγματα, οἷον "οὐσίας μὲν ὡς τύπῳ εἰπεῖν ἄνθρωπος, ἵππος" καὶ τῶν ἄλλων τὸ πρόσφορον εἰς παράστασιν παράδειγμα.

[86,20] [Ἐρώτησις] Ἆρα οὖν πάντες συγχωροῦσι τὴν εἰς τὰ αὐτὰ γένη καταρίθμησιν τῶν σημαντικῶν λέξεων πρώτως καὶ προηγουμένως τῶν πραγμάτων;

[Ἀπόκρισις] Οὐδαμῶς· Ἀθηνόδωρος γὰρ ᾐτήσατο ὁ Στωϊκὸς βιβλία γράψας Πρὸς τὰς Ἀριστοτέλους κατηγορίας Κορνοῦτός τε ἐν ταῖς Ῥητορικαῖς τέχναις καὶ ἐν τῇ πρὸς Ἀθηνόδωρον ἀντιγραφῇ καὶ ἄλλοι πλεῖστοι.

[86,25] [Ἐρώτησις] Ἆρα οὖν ὀρθῶς ἀντιλέγουσιν;

[Ἀπόκρισις] Οὐδαμῶς.

[Ἐρώτησις] Πόθεν τοῦτο δῆλον;

[Ἀπόκρισις] Ὅτι πρὸς πάντα σχεδὸν ἀντεῖπεν αὐτοῖς ἀντιγράψας καὶ ἐπιδείξας, ὅπως σφάλλονται.

[86,30] [Ἐρώτησις] Τίς δὲ ὁ τρόπος τῆς ἀντιλογίας;

[Ἀπόκρισις] Τριττός· οἱ μὲν γὰρ ὅτι πλεονάζει ἡ καταρίθμησις, οἱ δὲ ὅτι ἐλλείπει, οἱ δὲ ὅτι τινὰ ἄλλα ἀντὶ ἄλλων παρείληφε γένη.

[A:] A division cuts a genus into species, but here there is not going to be one genus divided into ten species; rather, ten genera will be set out. So it is an enumeration which he will make of the primary genera and of the predications made according to the primary genera.

[Q:] Well, what does he say?

[A:] "If you say anything uncombined, it signifies either a substance, a quantity, a quality, a relative, a 'where,' a 'when,' a disposition, a condition, an action, or an affection."[35] And he takes examples to clarify each, for

---

34. Busse 1887, 86,10–32.
35. Aristotle, *Cat.* 1b25–27.

example, "Substances, to give a quick outline, include man, horse"—and an appropriate example to illustrate the others, too.

[Q:] So does everyone agree with his enumeration of these as the genera of words that primarily and principally signify things?

[A:] Not at all. The Stoic Athenodorus attacked it and wrote a work *Against Aristotle's Categories*; so did Cornutus, both in his *Rhetorical Handbook* and in the *Response to Athenodorus*, and so did many others.

[Q:] Are they right to object?

[A:] Certainly not.

[Q:] Why is that obvious?

[A:] Because what he wrote gives them their responses on just about every point and shows where they go wrong.

[Q:] What is the nature of the criticism?

[A:] It is of three kinds: some object that his enumeration contains too many items, some that it is deficient, and some that there are genera it includes instead of others.

F21. Simplicius, *On the Categories*[36]

Λοιπὸν δὲ τὸ περὶ τῆς εἰς τὰ κεφάλαια διαιρέσεως τοῦ βιβλίου λέγειν ὑπολείπεται, ἅ τινες μὴ ἐπιστήσαντες ὅπως τε κατ' ἄρθρα διῄρηνται καὶ ὅπως τήν τε πρὸς τὸν ὅλον σκοπὸν χρείαν ἀποπληροῦσι καλῶς καὶ τὴν [18,25] πρὸς ἄλληλα συνέχειαν διασῴζουσιν, στοιβηδὸν κεῖσθαι νομίζουσιν τὰ κεφάλαια κατὰ τὸν ὑπομνηματικὸν τρόπον. καὶ δὴ καὶ ἀντιλέγουσιν αὐτῷ τινες ἀθετοῦντες τὴν διαίρεσιν, οἱ μὲν ὡς πλεονάζουσαν μάτην, οἱ δὲ ὡς πολλὰ παρεῖσαν ὥσπερ Κορνοῦτος καὶ Ἀθηνόδωρος, οἵτινες περὶ λέξεων οἰόμενοι τὸν σκοπὸν εἶναι καθὸ λέξεις εἰσίν, πολλὰς λέξεις προβάλλοντες τὰς μὲν κυρίας, [18,30] τὰς δὲ τροπικάς, ἐλέγχειν οἴονται τὴν διαίρεσιν, ὡς οὐ πάσας τὰς λέξεις [19,1] περιλαβοῦσαν· οἳ καὶ διαίρεσιν τῶν ὀνομάτων οἴονται ποιεῖσθαι εἰς ὁμώνυμα καὶ συνώνυμα καὶ παρώνυμα καὶ εἶναι τὸ βιβλίον παντοδαπῶν θεωρημάτων σωρείαν ὑπολαμβάνουσιν λογικῶν τε καὶ φυσικῶν καὶ ἠθικῶν καὶ θεολογικῶν· εἶναι γὰρ τὰ μὲν περὶ ὁμωνύμων καὶ συνωνύμων καὶ παρωνύμων σκέμματα [19,5] λογικά, ἔτι δὲ καὶ τὸ περὶ τῶν ἀντικειμένων, τὰ δὲ περὶ κινήσεως φυσικά, ἠθικὰ δὲ τὰ περὶ ἀρετῆς καὶ κακίας, ὥσπερ θεολογικὰ τὰ περὶ τῶν δέκα γενῶν φιλοσοφήματα.

---

36. From the proem; Kalbfleisch 1907, 18,22–19,7.

Fragments and Testimonia   171

We are just left to talk about the division of the book into headings. Some people do not understand how it is divided into parts and how those parts contribute beautifully to the overall purpose of the work while maintaining continuity with each other—so they think that the headings are bundled together in the manner of a notebook.[37] What is more, there are people who criticize it and reject its division, some on the ground that it includes too much to no end, others because it misses out a lot—for example Cornutus and Athenodorus. They thought that the purpose of the work was words insofar as they are words, and alleged many words, both literal and metaphorical, and thought that they were refuting the division for not containing all words. [19.1] They also think that work makes a division of substantives into homonyms, synonyms, and paronyms[38] and that the book is a heap of various claims in logic, physics, ethics, and theology—with the reflections on homonyms, synonyms, and paronyms belonging to logic, along with those on the contraries, the reflections on change belonging to physics, those on virtue and vice to ethics, and with the issues raised by the ten genera belonging similarly to theology.[39]

---

37. An example adduced by these (unnamed) people is discussed later, at 44,3–4. There is no suggestion that Cornutus and Athenodorus are among them (although we learn later in the passage that they, too, think that the *Categories* lack structure), but this context is needed to show that it is unclear what "division" in the next lines (which do bear on Cornutus) refers to. It would be natural to suppose that it refers to the tenfold division of the categories (as in other fragments here), but these earlier lines create the expectation that it refers instead to the formal organization of Aristotle's book.

38. Simplicius's position is that this is not a formal "division," since it is not exhaustive (the full list of -onyms would include polyonyms and heteronyms; see *On the Categories*, 23,4–5 [Kalbfleisch 1907]; similarly Porphyry, *On the Categories*, 60,34–38 [Busse 1887]).

39. Since the "physics" and "ethics" is to be found *within* the discussion of the ten categories, this must mean the very fact of there being ten genera (i.e., categories). ("Theology" is metaphysics, as, for example, at 4,23–24: καὶ τῶν θεωρητικῶν τὰ μὲν θεολογικά, ὡς ἡ Μετὰ τὰ φυσικά; cf. Aristotle himself at *Metaph.* 1026a18–19.) The fact that the Stoics think that the tenfold division is *as such* an exercise in metaphysics supports the view that even the Stoics do after all believe that the ten categories are divided according to a view about reality rather than language; see the introduction, §1.4.1.1.

F22. Simplicius, *On the Categories*[40]

Ἄλλοι δὲ πολλοὶ πρὸς αὐτὴν ἀμφεσβήτησαν, αὐτόθεν κατηγοροῦντες [62,25] τῆς εἰς τοσοῦτον πλῆθος διαιρέσεως, ὥσπερ Ἀθηνόδωρος ἐν τῷ Πρὸς τὰς Ἀριστοτέλους μὲν Κατηγορίας ἐπιγεγραμμένῳ βιβλίῳ, μόνην δὲ τὴν εἰς τοσοῦτον πλῆθος διαίρεσιν ἐξετάζοντι. καὶ Κορνοῦτος δὲ ἐν οἷς Πρὸς Ἀθηνόδωρον καὶ Ἀριστοτέλην ἐπέγραψεν καὶ οἱ περὶ τὸν Λούκιον δὲ καὶ τὸν Νικόστρατον, ὥσπερ πρὸς τὰ ἄλλα πάντα σχεδόν, οὕτως καὶ πρὸς [62,30] τὴν διαίρεσιν ἀντειρήκασιν.

Many others have had doubts about it [the division of the ten categories], criticizing the division from the start for being into just this number—for example, Athenodorus, in his book entitled *Against Aristotle's Categories*, but which only examines the division into this number.[41] Both Cornutus, in the books he entitled *Against Athenodorus and Aristotle*,[42] and the followers of Lucius and Nicostratus also attacked the division this way—as they did pretty well everything else.

F23. Simplicius, *On the Categories*[43]

Πρὸς δὲ Κορνοῦτον καὶ Πορφύριον τὴν ῥοπὴν κατὰ βαρύτητα καὶ κουφότητα θεωρουμένην ποιότητα λέγοντάς φησιν τὴν ῥοπὴν μὴ εἶναι βαρύτητα καὶ κουφότητα, ἀλλὰ μέτρον βαρύτητος καὶ κουφότητος.

---

40. Kalbfleisch 1907, 62,24–30. On *Cat.* 1b25–2a10, where the categories are first introduced.

41. τοσοῦτον: Hijmans (1975, 108) takes this to mean that the number is criticized for being *too great*, and see what Simplicius has to say about Xenocrates and Andronicus a little later (*On the Categories* [Kalbfleisch 1907, 63,22–24]). But this creates a contradiction between this fragment and the testimony of F19 and F21, so the better guide to meaning might be the immediately preceding lines in which we are told that Herminus worried about whether "the genera are *this many*" (εἰ τοσαῦτά ἐστιν τὰ γένη) and that by this he meant precisely that they might be *too few* (Kalbfleisch 1907, 62,17–20). Moraux (1984, 588–89) is probably right, then, that Athenodorus's objection is to the number itself (ten), without implying that this is too many.

42. Or perhaps "*Against Athenodorus* and *Against Aristotle*"; see §1.6, T4.

43. Kalbfleisch 1907, 129,1–4. On *Cat.* 4b20 and the category of quantity.

Cornutus and Porphyry say that the downwards thrust which is observed according to whether a thing is heavy or light is a *quality*.[44] Against them, he [Iamblichus] says that the downward thrust is not what it is to be heavy or light but is a measure of how heavy or light something is.

F24. Simplicius, *On the Categories*[45]

Εἴτε οὖν ὡς Ἀθηνόδωρος οἴεται πρός τι εἶναι κατὰ Ἀριστοτέλη, ἐφ' οὗ ἡ προσηγορία ἐπιζητεῖ τὸ πρὸς ὃ [187,30] λέγεται (ὁ γὰρ δοῦλον ἀκούσας ἐπιζητεῖ τὸν οὗ ἐστι δοῦλος), εἴτε ὡς Κορνοῦτος πρός τι εἶναί φησιν οἷς συμπροσπίπτει πρὸς ἕτερον ἡ σχέσις, οὐ μέντοι ἡ συντακτική, ὡς ἐπὶ τῶν ἐχόντων καὶ ἐχομένων, ἀλλ' ἡ πρὸς ὑπόστασιν, ὅταν αὐτῷ τῷ ᾧ εἶναι τὴν πρὸς ἕτερον ἀπόνευσιν ἔχῃ, κατ' οὐδένα τρόπον τὸ πηδάλιον ἢ τὸ πτερὸν πρός τί ἐστιν. οὔτε γὰρ ἐπιζητεῖ τι πρὸς [187,35] ὃ λέγεται οὔτε κατὰ τὴν πρὸς ἕτερον ὑποστατικὴν σχέσιν λέγεται· οὐσία γὰρ τὸ πηδάλιον καὶ ἡ κεφαλὴ καὶ τὸ πτερόν.

Athenodorus thinks that, according to Aristotle, a relative is something the term for which also suggests what it is said in relation to: if you hear "slave," you wonder *whose* slave. Cornutus says that things are relative when the state of each thing is relative to the other—not as a matter of syntax (as "having" and "being had") but as a matter of reality, when one thing is oriented towards another by being the very thing it is. On neither of these accounts is "rudder" or "wing" a relative;[46] they do not also suggest something which they are said in relation to; and they are not mentioned only as things whose real state is relative to something else: a rudder is a substance, and so is a head and a wing.

---

44. This is one occasion on which Simplicius agrees with Cornutus—and on which Cornutus disagrees with Athenodorus, who (along with Iamblichus here, and also Archytas and Ptolemaeus) thinks that "weight or downward thrust" is to be classified alongside magnitude and number under the category of quantity (Simplicius, *On the Categories*, 128,5–8 [Kalbfleisch 1907]).

45. Kalbfleisch 1907, 187,28–36. On *Cat.* 6b36–7b14: relatives and correlatives.

46. These are Aristotle's examples in the passage under scrutiny. (Simplicius's own view is that they are relatives as *parts* of, i.e., relative to, some whole.)

F25. Simplicius, *On the Categories*[47]

Κορνοῦτος δὲ ἀπορεῖ, εἰ τὸ ποῦ τοῦ τόπου καὶ τὸ ποτὲ τοῦ χρόνου κατὰ τὸν χαρακτηρισμὸν τῶν λέξεων διενηνοχότα εἰς ἰδίας κατατέτακται κατηγορίας διὰ τὸ τὴν πρόθεσιν περὶ χαρακτήρων εἶναι λεκτικῶν, τί δήποτε οὐχὶ καὶ ταῦτα τῇ κατηγορίᾳ ταύτῃ προσέθηκεν, οἷον τὸ Διωνόθεν καὶ εἰς [359,5] Δίωνα καὶ τὰ τοιαῦτα πολλὰ ὄντα· ὅμοια γάρ ἐστιν τῷ Ἀθήνηθεν καὶ εἰς Ἀθήνας. πρὸς δὲ ταῦτα ἐξαρκεῖ λέγειν ὅτι οὐ περὶ χαρακτῆρος λέξεώς ἐστιν ἡ τῶν κατηγοριῶν διαίρεσις· καθόλου γὰρ τὰς μὲν λεκτικὰς διαφορὰς εἰς ὄνομα ἀνῆγον ἢ ῥῆμα ἤ τι τοιοῦτον, οὐ μέντοι εἰς κατηγορίαν τινά, ἐπὶ δὲ τούτων ἔχεσθαι μὲν δεῖ τῶν φωνῶν, οὐ μέντοι κατὰ τὸ πτωτικὸν [359,10] σχῆμα τῆς λέξεως, ἀλλὰ διαιρούμενον τὰς σημασίας κατὰ τὰς τῶν ὄντων διαφοράς, ὅθεν οὔτε ὁ τόπος, ἐπειδὴ τὸν αὐτὸν χαρακτῆρα ἔχει τῷ ἵππος, οὔτε ὁ χρόνος, ἐπειδὴ τὸ αὐτὸ σχῆμα τῆς λέξεως ἔχει τῷ λύκος, τῆς αὐτῆς εἰσι κατηγορίας, ἀλλὰ τὰ μὲν τοῦ ποσοῦ ἐστιν, τὰ δὲ τῆς οὐσίας.

[359,15] Πάλιν δὲ ὁ αὐτὸς ἀνὴρ τὸ πόρρω καὶ ἐγγὺς εἰς τὸ πρός τι ἀνάγειν ἀξιοῖ τοπικὸν ἔχοντα τὸ ὑποκείμενον, Ἀνδρόνικος δὲ εἰς τὸ ποῦ τίθησιν αὐτὰ ἀόριστα κατὰ τόπον ὄντα.

Cornutus raises a problem: if the *where* differs from *place* and the *when* from *time* by the way that the words are characterized and have been assigned to their own categories because the point of the exercise is to explore the characters that words have, why then did he not put the following in this category [i.e., where], too: things like, for example, "away from Dion" and "towards Dion," and the many other examples there are like this? After all, they are like "away from Athens" and "towards Athens." To this it is enough to say that the division of categories is not about characterizing words; in general, people explain differences between words by appealing to *noun*, *verb*, and so on, not to some category. One ought not, however, to treat these vocalizations according to schemes of word inflection but to interpret their meanings in line with the distinctions between actual things. So place, which has the same character as *horse*, and time, which has the same verbal form as *wolf*, are not in the same category: the former belongs to the category of quantity, the latter to that of substance.

---

47. Kalbfleisch 1907, 359,1–17. On the category *where*.

Again, the same person thinks that one should put *far* and *near* in the [category of] relative, the substrate being place, but Andronicus puts them into the category of where, since their place is indefinite.

F26. Simplicius, *On the Categories*[48]

Καὶ οἱ Στωικοὶ δὲ παραλαβόντες τὸν ὁρισμὸν λέγοντα "τὸ καθόλου διάστημα [351,20] τῆς τοῦ παντὸς φύσεως" παρέτρεψαν τὸν λόγον ἐπὶ τὸ διάστημα τῆς κινήσεως, καὶ πλημμελοῦσιν οὗτοι, διότι τῶν Πυθαγορείων τὸ διάστημα φυσικὸν καὶ ἐν φυσικοῖς λόγοις καὶ εἰ οὕτω τις βούλοιτο καλεῖν ἐν τοῖς σπερματικοῖς, ὥς ποτε καὶ Κορνοῦτος ὀψὲ τοῦτο ὑπώπτευσεν, ἢ ὡς ἀκριβέστερον ἄν τις εἴποι κατὰ προτέρους λόγους καὶ τῶν σπερματικῶν λόγων τοὺς τῆς [351,25] ὅλης κοσμικῆς φύσεως, ἐν ᾗ καὶ ἡ ψυχὴ περιλαμβάνεται, τὸ διάστημα ἀφοριζομένων, οὗτοι σαφῶς μὲν οὐκ ἔχουσι διελέσθαι, ὁποῖον λέγουσι διάστημα, ἐοίκασι μέντοι μᾶλλον τὸ τῶν σωματοειδῶν κινήσεων σωματοειδὲς διάστημα ὑπολαμβάνειν ἢ ὥσπερ γραμμοειδές τι τοῦτο ἀποφαίνεσθαι, ὃ πολλῆς ἀτοπίας μεστὸν ἰδίᾳ δείκνυται ἐν τοῖς περὶ χρόνου λόγοις.

The Stoics inherited [from the Pythagoreans] a definition which calls [time] "the generic interval belonging to the nature of the universe" and changed it to "interval of movement."[49] This is a mistake. The Pythagoreans define the *interval* as the natural interval found *within* both natural principles and seminal principles (if you want to use this language—something Cornutus, too, once suggested later on),[50] or, to be more accurate, *in accor-*

---

48. Kalbfleisch 1907, 351,19–29. On the categories *when* and *where*.

49. At *On the Categories*, 360,15–16 (Kalbfleisch 1907) (= SVF 2.510), Simplicius specifies that Zeno defined time as "the interval of movement," and Chrysippus as "the interval of the movement of the cosmos."

50. The claim here seems to be that the (older) Stoics abandoned a definition of time in terms of the *principle* of movement, which Simplicius takes to be the (incorporeal) soul, and referred it instead to the actual movement of bodies; later on, Cornutus makes an adjustment back in the direction of the Pythagorean definition insofar as he linked time to the *principles* of corporeal movement—albeit these, for him, are features of the corporeal world (namely the seminal principles). ("Later on," then, more likely refers to a later period in Stoicism rather than a later period in Cornutus's own career.) A text that Simplicius might have had in mind for his view of the Pythagoreans is "Archytas," Περὶ τῶν καθόλου λόγων, 24,15–16 (Thesleff 1965) ("time is the moving number of something, or also, in general terms, the interval of universal nature"). See Moraux 1984, 594–97.

dance with the former principles and those of the seminal principles which are principles of cosmic nature as a whole (including soul). But the Stoics are not able to distinguish clearly what they mean by interval, although they seem rather to assume the bodily interval of bodily movements or like something of the nature of a line—which leads to much absurdity in their account of time.

4.2.4. Physics and Metaphysics

F27. Iamblichus, *On the Soul*, quoted at Stobaeus, *Ecl.* 1.49.43[51]

Ἆρά γε πνιγμῷ τῶν ἀρτηρίων ἀποκλειομένων τοῦ δέχεσθαι τὸ ἐκτὸς πνεῦμα, ἢ ἐκλυομένου τοῦ τόνου καὶ παριεμένου, ἢ τοῦ θερμοῦ ἐναποσβεννυμένου πως εἰς τὰ εἴσω τὰ ζῶντα πρότερον εἰσαῦθις ἀποθνῄσκει; ἀλλ᾽ εἰ οὕτως γίγνεται ὁ θάνατος, προαναιρεῖται ἢ συναναιρεῖται ἡ ψυχὴ τῷ σώματι, καθάπερ Κουρνοῦτος οἴεται.

Does what was formerly alive die when the arteries are choked and closed off from receiving breath from outside? Or when its tension is released and slackened? Or when the internal heat is somehow extinguished? If death comes about like this, then the soul is destroyed before, or at the same time as, the body—as Cornutus thinks.[52]

---

51. Wachsmuth and Hense 1884–1912, 1:383,24–384,2. On whether the soul dies with, before, or after the body.

52. The earlier Stoics had defined death as the separation of the soul from the body, and their view was that souls survived this separation for some time (although how long was a matter of debate; see *SVF* 2.809–22). So Festugière (1953), 230–32, n. 2 ad fin. suggests that a Stoic could not think that the soul perished *before* the body, and Zeller thinks it a "considerable deviation" even to suppose that it perished *with* it (1880, 693). But since the soul is a distinct corporeal entity on all Stoic accounts, it is not obvious why such views, however eccentric, would be in tension with the physical system at large. (It is hardly an objection that the definition of death would need to be refined, i.e., if it involved the soul perishing in the body *rather than* being separated from it.) In the *Greek Theology*, Cornutus talks of the souls of the dead being received by the "air" (5,5–6; 74,5–6), but this may mean that their matter is dispersed into the air when they perish, rather than that they *survive* to live there for some period.

F28. P.Oxy. 3649 = *CPF* 1.1*, 35 1T

Κορνούτου Περὶ ἑκτῶν β'

Cornutus, *On Haveables* (two books)[53]

F29. Syrianus, *On the Metaphysics*[54]

Παραφέρεται δὲ καὶ Βοηθὸς ὁ περιπατητικὸς ἐκ τῶν παρὰ τῷ Ἀριστοτέλει κατηχήσεων εἰς ταὐτὸν ἄγων τοῖς γενικοῖς τὰς ἰδέας· ᾧ καὶ τὸν Κορνοῦτον συντάττειν εὔλογον, οὐ πόρρω καὶ αὐτὸν ταύτης ὑπενεχθέντα τῆς δόξης· εἴτε γὰρ πρότερα τὰ γενικὰ τῶν καθ' ἕκαστα, οὐχ οὕτω πρότερα ὡς ἐξῃρημένα τῆς πρὸς αὐτὰ σχέσεως [106,10] οὐδ' ὡς τῆς οὐσίας αὐτῶν αἴτια, ἅπερ ὑπάρχει ταῖς ἰδέαις.

Boethus the Peripatetic misses what Aristotle is trying to say and identifies forms with genera. One might reasonably rank Cornutus along with him because his opinion is not very different from this. But if genera are prior to individuals, they are not prior in such a way that they no longer possess a state which is relative to them or become the causes of their substance—which is the case with forms.[55]

---

53. See Turner 1975. Sedley (2005, 118–20) argues for the likely metaphysical orientation of this work; he suggests that it concerned properties (things that can be "had"), explaining them in materialist terms opposed to the Platonic theory of forms.

54. Kroll 1902, 106,5–10.

55. Martini (1825, 93) and Moraux (1984, 601) place this fragment with Cornutus's interest in the *Categories*, although for different reasons. Martini thinks that the discussion of the *Categories* was essentially rhetorical in character (and the word *idea* is indeed used for rhetorical *style* as well as Platonic *form*). Moraux, on the other hand, takes *idea* to be "form," and supposes that the "genera" at issue here must be the categories. But to align Plato's forms with the sort of genera represented by the categories would take considerable ingenuity. More likely, Cornutus was making just the kind of metaphysical claim that Syrianus understands: his move would have been to suggest that Plato's *forms* were hypostasizations of *genera*, i.e., *natural kinds*; see something similar in Seneca, *Ep.* 58.19 and 65.7. Sedley (2005, 120–21) connects this fragment with F28.

4.2.5. Rhetoric

F30. Anonymous, *Commentary on Hermogenes's* Περὶ ἰδεῶν[56]

Δοκεῖ δὲ ὁ Κορνοῦτος σαφέστερον περὶ αὐτῶν εἰπεῖν· τὴν γὰρ Βασιλικοῦ παρίημι δόξαν· φησὶν οὖν ὁ Κορνοῦτος, κῶλόν ἐστι μόριον λόγου συγκείμενον ἐξ ὀνομάτων δύο ἢ καὶ πλειόνων, τελειοῦν ἐπὶ μέρος διάνοιαν, [931,5] εἶτα παρακατιὼν σαφέστερον τὸν λόγον ἐποίησεν, ἐπιμνησθεὶς αὐτοῦ· κῶλον γάρ ἐστι διανοίας μέρος ἀπαρτίζον πρὸς ἕτερον κῶλον παρακείμενον· τὸ γὰρ, εἰ τὸν χορευτὴν οὐδὲ ὁ προσκαλέσας ἀζήμιος ἔσται, κῶλον μέν ἐστι σαφῶς, οὐκ ἂν δὲ εἰλικρινῶς, οὐδὲ τὴν ἐπὶ μέρος παρέστησεν ἡμῖν [931,10] διάνοιαν μὴ προσλαβοῦσι· τὸν δὲ χορηγὸν αὐτὸν οὐδὲ ὁ συγκόψας οὐ δώσει δίκην. διαλαμβάνει δὲ καὶ περὶ τοῦ κόμματος ὁ Κορνοῦτος, σαφῶς οὑτωσί πως λέγων· κόμμα ἐστὶ λόγος διάνοιαν δηλῶν δύο ἢ τρισὶ λέξεσιν· οἷόν ἐστι τό· μηδὲν ἄγαν, καὶ τό· γνῶθι σαυτόν· ἔτι δὲ σαφέστερον [931,15] τὰ περὶ τοῦ κόμματος Ἀψίνου δόξειεν ἂν ἔχειν.

Cornutus seems to have spoken more clearly about these things (I shall leave Basilicus's views to one side). So Cornutus says: "A *colon* is a part of discourse composed of two or more words, partially completing a thought." Then further down he refers back to this and gives a clearer account: "A *colon* is part of a thought which completes it when associated with another *colon*." Take: "If not even the man who challenges the dancer to a fight is immune from penalty …." This is clearly a colon, but not in the pure sense, because it does not partially complete a thought for us unless we add: "… then the man who beats up the chorus leader will certainly not avoid punishment."[57] Cornutus also gets to grips with the *comma*. He gives

---

56. Walz 1834, 931,1–15. Graeven (1891, xxvii–xxviii) takes this passage to be part of a survey of rhetorical writers arranged in chronological order. This would mean that we are dealing with a different, later Cornutus: older than Apsines (i.e., presumably Apsines of Gadara, who must have been born almost a century after Annaeus Cornutus died) but younger than his teacher, Basilicus. Graeven (and after him, Reppe [1906, 60–61]) likewise assigned F33, F34, F35, and F36 to this putative rhetorician. Heath (2003, 152) succinctly shows that the argument does not stand up. (Nor does Graeven's inference from their shared definition of the colon that the Cornutus of this passage is the author of an anonymous rhetorical treatise known as Anonymus Seguerianus; see Graeven 1891, p. xxx; cf. Graeven 1895, 306–7 with Christ, Schmid, and Stählin 1924, 928.)

57. The example is from Demosthenes, *Mid.* 57.1.

this clear account: "A *comma* is a phrase which exhibits a thought in two or three words, as, e.g., 'Nothing in excess' or 'Know yourself.'" Apsines's definition of a comma would seem to be even clearer.

F31. [Julius Rufinianus], *Schem. dian.* 1[58]

Tertius usus est harum figurarum, quum gratia uenustatis adhibentur, [60,10] qui tamen ironiae est proximus. sed eius modi figurae, quae iuuenibus in schola lasciuiunt, ut Cornutus ait, minime maturae sunt et parum causis foroque conueniunt.

A third use of these figures is when sexual pleasures come into it—a use which is, however, close to irony. But figures like this, which titillate schoolboys, as Cornutus says, are very immature, and quite unsuitable for the law court or forum.

F32. Nicolaus Sophistes, *Progymnasmata*[59]

Ὁ ἀνὴρ γὰρ ἐκεῖνος αἰδέσιμος ὢν τέταρτον παρὰ τὰ τρία τὰ προλεχθέντα τὸ ἱστορικὸν ἐκάλεσε, μικτὸν ἀπὸ τῶν τριῶν εἶναι εἰπών. εἰ δὲ δοίη τις εἶναι τέταρτον, ὥσπερ οὖν καὶ δεῖ δοῦναι, οὐδὲν κωλύει καὶ τοῖς ἄλλοις ἕπεσθαι τοῖς μέχρι καὶ τριάκοντα εἰδῶν οἶμαι προελθοῦσιν· ἴσως δ' ἂν εὑρεθείη καὶ πλείονα· σχεδὸν γὰρ ὅσα ἐν ἀνθρώποις πράγματα, τοσοῦτοι καὶ λόγοι. ἀλλὰ λήσεταί τις οὕτω σύγχυσιν ἐργαζόμενος· διὸ ὑπ' ἐκεῖνα τὰ παρὰ τῷ Κουρνούτῳ ὀνομαζόμενα καὶ Πορφυρίῳ ἅπαντα χρὴ πειρᾶσθαι ἀνάγειν τὰ πράγματα, εἰδοποιοῦντας αὐτῶν τὰς ὑποθέσεις.

This venerable man [Aristotle] called a fourth type, alongside the three I have mentioned, *narrative*, saying that it was a mixture of those three. But

---

58. Halm 1863, 60,9–12. It is naturally tempting to suppose that this is a fragment of Cornutus's *On Figures of Thought* mentioned in F53. Context: figures of thought are used (1) when it is not safe to speak openly and (2) when it is not proper to speak bluntly.

59. Felten 1913, 55,10–21. Context: there are three types of speech, corresponding to three different types of audience: advisory, forensic, and panegyric. To allow more types than this is to risk confusion. Cornutus's view is standard among the Stoics; see Diogenes Laertius, *Vit. phil.* 7.42: "They say that rhetoric is itself tripartite: part of it is advisory, part forensic, part encomiastic."

if one allows that this is a fourth type, which one would have to, I do not think anything stops as many as another thirty coming in its train—perhaps you can find even more: there are pretty much as many speeches as human affairs. But someone who did this would create confusion. So we ought [20] to try to bring all affairs under the types named by Cornutus and Porphyry and use them to classify our propositions.

F33. Anonymous, *Prolegomena to Hermogenes's* Περὶ στάσεων[60]

Τί ἐστι τῆς ῥητορικῆς ἡ στάσις; καὶ λέγομεν, ὅτι συμβέβηκε τῷ λόγῳ τῷ ῥητορικῷ ἡ στάσις καὶ δύναμιν ἔχει συμβεβηκότος· ταύτης δὲ τῆς δόξης καὶ Λολλιανός ἐστι καὶ Κορνοῦτος.

What is a rhetorical "issue" (*stasis*)? We say that an issue is an accident of rhetorical speech and has the force of an accident. That is also the view of Lollianus and Cornutus.

F34. Syrianus, *On Hermogenes's* Περὶ στάσεων[61]

Κορνοῦτος δὲ τὴν ἀμφιβολίαν λέγων δύο εἶναι ἐν ταῖς στάσεσιν ἀμφιβολίας, τὴν μὲν περὶ ῥητὰ τὴν νομικὴν ἀμφιβολίαν, τὴν δὲ περὶ πράγματα τὴν στοχαστικήν, πρότερα δὲ εἶναι τὰ ῥητὰ τῶν πραγμάτων, προτέραν ἄρα καὶ τὴν νομικὴν ἀμφιβολίαν τακτέον.

Cornutus [thinks] ambiguity. He says that there are two types of ambiguity among issues: *legal* ambiguity, which has to do with the wording [of the law], and *conjectural* ambiguity, which has to do with the facts.[62] But the wording is prior to the facts,[64] so legal ambiguity should take priority, too.

---

60. Rabe 1931, 330,6–9. For doubts (probably ill motivated) over the identity of this Cornutus, see note to F30.

61. Rabe 1931, 60,19–23. Context: different people think different rhetorical issues should be addressed first. For the identity of Cornutus here and in F35, see note to F30.

62. There was controversy in antiquity both over whether ambiguity was a rhetorical *issue* (in the technical sense: *stasis*) and, if it was, how many species of it there were. The views of Cornutus here are close to those of at least some earlier Stoics known to have been interested in *stasis* theory; both Archedemus (*SVF* 3, Archedemus, frag. 11 = Quintilian, *Inst.* 3.6.31) and Posidonius (EK F189 = Quintilian, *Inst.* 3.6.37) treated ambiguity as an issue, and both thought there were two species—deal-

F35. Syrianus, *On Hermogenes's* Περὶ στάσεων⁶⁴

Τὴν ἀμφιβολίαν Κορνοῦτος πρώτην τῶν ἄλλων ἀξιοῖ τάττεσθαι στάσεων, δι' ἣν κατ' ἀρχὰς ἔφαμεν αἰτίαν· δύο γὰρ εἶναί φησιν ἐν ταῖς στάσεσιν ἀμφιβολίας, τὴν μὲν ἐν πράγμασι τὸν στοχασμὸν λέγων, τὴν δὲ ἐν ῥητοῖς τὴν ἀμφιβολίαν, πρότερα δὲ τὰ ῥητὰ τῶν πραγμάτων, προτέρα ἄρα καὶ ἡ περὶ τὰ ῥητὰ ἀμφιβολία μελετηθήσεται.

Cornutus thinks that ambiguity should be addressed before all other issues, for the reason we gave at the beginning: he says that there are two kinds of ambiguity among the issues, calling that relating to the facts *conjectural* and the ambiguity relating to wording *legal*, but the wording is prior to the facts, so ambiguity in phrasing is to be given priority in treatment as well.

F36. Suda λ.165⁶⁵

Λαχάρης, Λαχάρους, Ἀθηναῖος, σοφιστής· μαθητὴς Ἡρακλέωνος Ἀθηναίου, διδάσκαλος δὲ πλείστων, ἐνδόξων δὲ Εὐστεφίου καὶ Νικολάου καὶ Ἀστερίου· ἀκμάσας ἐπί τε Μαρκιανοῦ καὶ Λέοντος τῶν βασιλέων. ἔγραψε Περὶ κώλου καὶ κόμματος καὶ περιόδου, Διαλέξεις, Ἱστορίαν τὴν κατὰ Κορνοῦτον, Ἐκλογὰς ῥητορικὰς κατὰ στοιχεῖον.

Lachares: son of Lachares, an Athenian, a sophist, pupil of Heracleon of Athens, teacher of many, including the famous Eustephius, Nicolaus, and Asterius. His *floruit* was during the principate of Marcianus and Leo.⁶⁶ He wrote *On the Colon and Comma and Period*, *Dialects*, *Investigation* (the

---

ing respectively with words (*voces*) and facts (*res*) according to Posidonius; divided between "conjecture" and "definition" according to Archedemus. See Atherton 1993, esp. ch. 8.2. Atherton's study shows how interested the Stoics were in the topic of ambiguity more generally; Le Boulluec (1975, 317–18) and Long (1997, 210) make the connection with the exegetical challenge facing the Stoics in their exegesis of mythology.

63. That is, *qua* rhetorical *issues*: establishing the phrasing and intention of the law is a prior concern in court to establishing what happened.

64. Rabe 1931, 201,8–14. See note to F30.

65. This fragment, too, has been assigned to a hypothetical rhetorician instead of the philosopher; see note to F30 above. But there is also the further possibility that we might be dealing with the historian; see note to F2.

66. Emperors in 450–457 and 457–474 CE, respectively.

one written against Cornutus),[67] *Rhetorical Selections* (arranged alphabetically).

4.2.6. Fame as a Critic

F37. Augustine, *Util. cred.* 17[68]

"At absurda ibi dici uidebantur." quibus adserentibus? nempe inimicis, qualibet causa, qualibet ratione—non enim hoc nunc quaeritur—tamen inimicis. "cum legerem, per me ipse cognoui." ita ne est? nulla inbutus poetica disciplina Terentianum Maurum sine magistro adtingere non auderes, Asper, Cornutus, Donatus et alii innumerabiles requiruntur, ut quilibet poeta possit intellegi, cuius carmina et theatri plausus uidentur captare.

"What they [Christians] claim there is obviously absurd!" Who says? Their enemies! Enemies for whatever pretext or reason, that is not now the question, but their enemies nonetheless. "When I read them, I could see it for myself." Really? If you did not have an education in poetry, you would not dare to approach Terentianus Maurus without expert help;[69] Asper, Cornutus, Donatus, and any number of others are needed to be able to understand any poet, albeit their verses are seen to win applause at the theater.

4.2.7. On Virgil

Before Cornutus, only one person, C. Iulius Hyginus (a freedman of Augustus: Suetonius, *Gramm.* 20) is known to have published commentary on Virgil. (A certain Celsus, mentioned in the augmented version of Servius's commentary, is sometimes identified with an author of the first century CE, but he might well have lived a century or two later.)

---

67. Or possibly: *A History according to Cornutus*—who might in this case be the "other" Cornutus of F2 (above with note). However, the other books listed here make a discussion of linguistic or rhetorical issues more likely.

68. Zycha 1891, 21. An imagined opponent on Christian teachers and Augustine's response.

69. Terentianus was a second-century grammarian. Perhaps Augustine's point is that one cannot even understand the commentators without help or training, let alone the poetry itself—and so, mutatis mutandis, with scripture.

For the context and significance of Cornutus's work, see Zetzel (1981, ch. 3, esp. 38–41; and 2018, ch. 4.2); also Geymonat (1984) and Timpanaro (1986, ch. 3). Two prominent issues of controversy in the scholarship concern (1) whether Cornutus wrote a ten-work study of Virgil distinct from his commentary (see §1.6 above, T7 and T8) and (2) how far Cornutus's comments were inspired by a spirit of criticism (see my remarks on this in the introduction, §1.4.1.2). In view of this latter question—complicated further by the fact that at least one of the fragments, F53, derives from a rhetorical work—it is more often than not impossible to be sure about the source of a particular fragment on Virgil. For this reason, the fragments follow the sequence of Virgilian verses to which they pertain—starting with the *Eclogues*, moving on to the *Georgics* with F42, and finally the *Aeneid* from F45.

F38. Scholia Veronensia, *Ad Ecl.* 3.40[70]

Cornutus sic aestimat dictum esse, ut: "In medio mihi Caesar erit" pro "eminebit."

Cornutus judges that it means just what it does in the line "I will have Caesar in the middle"[71]—that is, "he will stand out."

F39. Junius Philargyrius, *Exp. Buc.* [*versio* I] ad 3.104–105[72]

Dicit Cornutus ab ipso Virgilio audisse se, quod Caelium Mantuanum quendam tetigit, qui consumptis omnibus facultatibus nihil sibi reliquit, nisi locum trium ulnarum spatium ad sepulturam.

---

70. Thilo and Hagen 1881–1902, 3.2:395,4–5. *Ecl.* 3.40: *in medio* (on two figures "in the middle" of a cup).
71. Virgil, *Georg.* 3.16.
72. Thilo and Hagen 1881–1902, 3.2:69,13–19. *Ecl.* 3.104–105: "dic quibus in terris, et eris mihi magnus Apollo, tris pateat caeli spatium non amplius ulnas" ("Tell me, and you will be my great Apollo: in what lands is the extent of the heavens no more than three *ulnae*?").

Cornutus says that he heard from Virgil himself about a man from Mantua called Caelius, who lost all of his resources and had nothing left but the space of three *ulnae* for a grave.[73]

F40. Scholia Veronensia, *Ad Ecl.* 6.9[74]

Cornutus putat hoc ad Musas pertinere.

Cornutus thinks this refers to the Muses.[75]

F41. Aulus Gellius, *Noct. att.* 2.6.1–2[76]

Nonnulli grammatici aetatis superioris, in quibus est Cornutus Annaeus, haut sane indocti neque ignobiles, qui commentaria in Vergilium composuerunt, reprehendunt quasi incuriose et abiecte uerbum positum in his uersibus: "candida succinctam latrantibus inguina monstris | Dulichias uexasse rates et gurgite in alto | a! timidos nautas canibus lacerasse marinis." [2] uexasse enim putant uerbum esse leue et tenuis ac parui incommodi nec tantae atrocitati congruere, cum homines repente a belua immanissima rapti laniatique sint. [3] item aliud huiuscemodi reprehendunt: "quis aut Eurysthea durum | aut inlaudati nescit Busiridis aras?" inlaudati parum idoneum uerbum esse dicunt, neque id satis esse ad faciendam scelerati hominis detestationem, qui, quod hospites omnium gentium immolare solitus fuit, non laude indignus, sed detestatione execrationeque totius generis humani dignus esset. [4] item aliud uerbum culpauerunt: "per tunicam squalentem auro latus haurit apertum," tamquam si non

---

73. An *ulna* as a measure of length is "the span of the outstretched arms" (LSJ, s.v.). The fact that Cornutus could not possibly have heard this (or anything else) from Virgil naturally suggests caution, but it does not rule it out that the story ultimately derives from Virgil.

74. Thilo and Hagen 1881–1902, 3.2:398,8–9. *Ecl.* 6.9: *non inussa cano* ("I do not sing what has not been asked for").

75. I.e., it is the Muses who ask Virgil to sing what he sings. The question was debated; Servius, ad loc. (Thilo and Hagen 1881–1902, 2:66,6–8) lists Apollo, Augustus, and Maecenas (but not the Muses) as possibilities.

76. On *Ecl.* 6.75–77; *Georg.* 3.4–5; *Aen.* 10.314. See Macrobius, *Sat.* 6.7, which repeats the whole of *Noct. att.* 2.6 (including responses to the specific criticisms outlined in this extract) with only a little rewording—but no mention of Cornutus.

conuenerit dicere "auro squalentem," quoniam nitoribus splendoribusque auri squaloris inluuies sit contraria.

[1] Some grammarians of a former age who wrote commentaries on Virgil, among them Cornutus Annaeus,[77] men not lacking in erudition or breeding, criticize what they allege is the careless and undignified choice of verb in the following verses: "Fair loins girt with barking monsters | annoyed the Dulichian boats, and deep in the whirlpool—| alas!—tore at the timid sailors with dogs of the sea."[78] [2] For they think that "annoyed" is a slight and thin word, a word for a minor inconvenience, not one that suits such an enormity, in which men are being unceremoniously snatched up by a savage beast and butchered. [3] They criticize another line the same way: "Who does not know harsh Eurystheus | Or the altars of the unpraised Busiris?" "Unpraised" they say is an unsuitable word, inadequate to rouse abomination for this wicked man: he used to sacrifice guests from whatever nation and is not [just] unworthy of praise, but worthy of the hatred and execration of the whole human race. [4] Again, they find fault with another word: "Through a tunic caked with gold, [the sword] drank from his gaping side."[79] The allegation was that it does not work to say "caked" with gold, because being caked with dirt is the very opposite of the gleaming and shining of gold.

F42. Servius [Dan.], *Ad Georg.* 1.277[80]

Probus Orchus legit, Cornutus uetat aspirationem addendam.

Probus reads "Orchus"; Cornutus forbids addition of the aspiration.[81]

---

77. Most (1989, 2030, n. 118) notes that Cornutus is here called a *grammaticus* because of his publications on grammatical issues but countenances the possibility that it refers to his role as a teacher (sc. of younger children). However, Gellius is evidently using the word in his own voice to generalize over these authors, not reporting their professional title (and see the introduction, pp. 5–6).
78. The description is of Odysseus's ships caught in the whirlpool of Scylla.
79. This is Aeneas slaying Theron.
80. Thilo and Hagen 1881–1902, 3.1:195,19–20. On *Georg.* 1.277: *pallidus Orcus* (pale Orcus, i.e., Death).
81. Cornutus concerns himself with marking and pronouncing aspiration at *Orthography*, paras. 16–19, but none of the considerations there explain the issue in

F43. Pseudo-Placidus, *Gloss.* I23[82]

Cornutus uentrem, Plinius edacitatem.

Cornutus: "belly"; Pliny: "voracious appetite."

F44. Servius [Dan.], *Ad Aen.* 1.45[83]

Cornutus ait inflixit uerius, quod sit uehementius.

Cornutus said that "dash against" is truer, since it is more energetic.[84]

F45. Servius [Dan.], *Ad Aen.* 1.150[85]

Multi non uolant, sed uolunt inuenisse se dicunt. sed Cornutus "uerendum," ait, "ne praeposterum sit faces uelle, et sic saxa, cum alibi maturius et ex ordine dictum sit 'arma uelit poscatque simul rapiatque inuentus.'"

Many people say they have found not "fly" but "they wish for." But Cornutus said: "One would have to worry that this is not the moment to 'wish for torches' or, likewise, rocks. It is more timely and follows the right sequence when, elsewhere, he says: 'Let the men wish for arms, demand them at once, and seize them!'"[86]

---

this case. As Zetzel notes (1981, 40–41), Cornutus may simply have been explaining a reading ("Orcus") he found in copies of the text known to him.

82. Pirie and Lindsay 1930, 65. On *Georg.* 3.431 and the meaning of the word *ingluvies* (*ingluuiem*).

83. Thilo and Hagen 1881–1902, 1:32,3–4. *Aen.* 1.45: *infixit* ("impaled").

84. "Truer" might mean "truer to life" (cf. *vere* in F56), but Cornutus might conceivably be arguing for an alternative reading, one "truer" to what Virgil wrote.

85. Thilo and Hagen 1881–1902, 1:64,9–13. *Aen.* 1.1.50: *iamque faces et saxa uolant* ("now fly torches and rocks").

86. *Aen.* 7.340. The argument concerns which manuscript reading to adopt ("found" means found in some manuscripts). For those Cornutus is opposing here, see Zetzel 1981, 39; Geymonat 1984, 898.

F46. Servius, *Ad Aen.* 1.488[87]

Cornutus tamen dicit uersu isto "uadimus inmixti Danais" hoc esse soluendum.

Cornutus says that this is explained by the line, "We proceed, mingling with the Greeks."

F47. Scholia Veronensia, *Ad Aen.* 3.691[88]

Cornutus: num indecore hoc dicitur, qum sit Ulixes hostis Aeneae?

Cornutus: Surely it is jarring to say this, since Ulysses is Aeneas's enemy?

F48. Placidus, *Glossary*[89]

Magmentem: alii pinguissimum exterum, alii secunda prosecta. Cornutus quid mactatur, quidquid dis datur.[90]

Magmentem: some say that this is the fattiest outer part, others that it refers to the propitious cuts [of sacrificed meat]. Cornutus: "what is sacrificed, whatever is given to the gods."

---

87. Thilo and Hagen 1881–1902, 1:154,25–26. *Aen.* 1.488: *se quoque principibus permixtum agnouit Achiuis* ("He recognized himself mixed up with the Argive leaders"). Aeneas is looking at the paintings of the Trojan War in the sanctuary of Dido's new temple to Juno; the question for commentators is what part of the narrative appears in this particular scene. Cornutus quotes from Aeneas's own description of his escape from Troy in *Aen.* 2.396.

88. Thilo and Hagen 1881–1902, 3.2:429,22–34. *Aen.* 3.691: *comes infelici Ulixi* ("the companion of unfortunate Ulysses").

89. Goetz 1894, 116,5 = Pseudo-Placidus, *Gloss.* M7 (Pirie and Lindsay 1930, 67). Perhaps deriving from a comment on *Aen.* 4.57: ("They sacrifice"). As Jahn (1843, xix) noted, the word *magmentum* is similarly connected with the *mactare*, to sacrifice, in Servius's commentary on *Aen.* 4.57, and it is conceivable that this was the original context for Cornutus's note as well.

90. *datur* Bücheler 1879, 348, after Jahn 1843, xix n. 1; *distraitur* manuscripts.

F49. Scholia Veronensia, *Ad Aen.* 4.178[91]

Cornutus: <...> (quid) <...>e posset.

Cornutus: <...> what <...> is able.

F50. Macrobius, *Sat.* 5.19.1-4[92]

In libro quarto in describenda Elissae morte ait quod ei crinis abscisus esset his uersibus: "nondum illi flauum Proserpina uertice crinem | abstulerat Stygioque caput damnauerat Orco." deinde Iris a Iunone missa abscidit ei crinem et ad Orcum refert. [2] hanc Vergilius non de nihilo fabulam fingit, sicut uir alias doctissimus Cornutus existimat, qui adnotationem eius modi adposuit his uersibus: unde haec historia ut crinis auferendus sit morientibus, ignoratur: sed adsueuit poetico more aliqua fingere ut de aureo ramo. haec Cornutus. [3] sed me pudet quod tantus uir, Graecarum etiam doctissimus litterarum, ignorauit Euripidis nobilissimam fabulam Alcestim. [4] in hac enim fabula in scaenam Orcus inducitur gladium gestans quo crinem abscidat Alcestidis et sic loquitur: | ἡ δ' οὖν γυνὴ κάτεισιν εἰς Ἅιδου δόμους. | στείχω δ' ἐπ' αὐτήν, ὡς κατάρξωμαι ξίφει, | ἱερὸς γὰρ οὗτος τῷ κατὰ χθονὸς θεῷ, | ὅτῳ τόδ' ἔγχος κρατὸς ἁγνίσῃ τρίχα.

[1] In book 4, describing the death of Elissa, he says that a lock of her hair would be cut. These are the lines: "Not yet had Proserpina taken a golden lock from her head and consigned her to Stygian Orcus" (then Iris, sent by Juno, cuts the lock and turns her over to Orcus). [2] Virgil does not conjure up this tale out of nothing, as Cornutus supposes—an extremely erudite man in other respects. He annotated the verses like this: "The origin of this

---

91. Thilo and Hagen 1881-1902, 3.2:431,15-16. *Aen.* 4.178: *illam terra parens ira inritata* ("Her, mother Earth provoked to anger").

92. On *Aen.* 4.698-699: "Not yet had Proserpina"; and 6.136-141, the golden bough. The former passage marks the culmination of the suicide of Dido (also known as Elissa). See discussion (and a defense of Cornutus) in Rauk 1995. On the basis of this fragment, Cornutus has been identified as the source behind critical responses to Virgil noted elsewhere in the scholia; see esp. Cugusi 2003 (and overview in Setaioli 2003-2004, 360 with n. 177). This collection includes only the two passages that have the most obvious overlap with this one: F51 and F54. It is worth noting that nothing in the present fragment explicitly indicates disapproval on Cornutus's part; see the introduction, pp. 27-28.

story, that a lock of hair has to be taken from the dying, is unknown. But he (Virgil) had the poet's habit of invention—as in the case of the golden bough." So Cornutus. [3] But I am embarrassed that a man of his stature, extremely erudite in Greek literature, too, should be unaware of Euripides's well-known play, the *Alcestis*. [4] In this play, Orcus is brought onto the stage carrying a sword with which to cut off a lock of Alcestis's hair and says: "The woman will go down into the halls of Hades! I am coming at her with sword for sacrifice; for when this weapon consecrates the hair of someone's head to one of the infernal gods, he is sacred to that god" (*Alc.* 73–76).

F51. Servius, *Ad Aen.* 3.46[93]

Vituperabile enim est, poetam aliquid fingere, quod penitus a ueritate discedat. denique obicitur Vergilio de mutatione nauium in nymphas; et quod dicit per aureum ramum ad inferos esse descensum; tertium, cur Iris Didoni comam secuerit. sed hoc purgatur Euripidis exemplo, qui de Alcesti hoc dixit, cum subiret fatum mariti.

It is a matter of criticism if a poet invents something which gets too far from the truth. So people criticize Virgil for the ships that change into nymphs (*Aen.* 9.120–122), for saying that a golden bough gives a means of descent to the underworld (*Aen.* 6.136–141), and, thirdly, because Iris cut off Dido's hair (*Aen.* 4.698–699)—although the latter is cleared up by the precedent given by Euripides, who says this about Alcestis when she went to take on her husband's fate.

F52. Scholia Veronensia, *Ad Aen.* 5.488[94]

Adnotat Cornutus, quod indecenter sacram matri suae auem sagittis figendam constituerit. sed uidelicet Homerum secutus est; sed et eodem modo

---

93. Thilo and Hagen 1881–1902, 1:344,23–28. On *Aen.* 4.698–699; 6.136–141; and 9.120–122. This comes, however, in the context of commentary on *Aen.* 3.46. For its possible relevance to Cornutus, see note to F50, but note that there is no independent check for Cornutus's interest in the changing of ships into nymphs.

94. Thilo and Hagen 1881–1902, 3.2:435,3–7. On *Aen.* 5.488–489: "He hung from a high pole a winged dove tied with a cord, as a target for their iron."

quamcunque aliam auem expositam queri potuit, quia singula genera alitum Diis quibuscunque sacrata sunt.

Cornutus has a note saying that it was unseemly for him [Aeneas] to decide on setting up for their arrows a bird which was sacred to his mother. But I suppose he (Virgil) was following Homer, and it would be possible to make the same complaint about any other bird which was hung up because every species of bird is sacred to some god.[95]

F53. Aulus Gellius, *Noct. att.* 9.10[96]

Quod Annaeus Cornutus uersus Vergilii, quibus Veneris et Vulcani concubitum pudice operteque dixit, reprehensione spurca et odiosa inquinauit.

[1] Annianus poeta, et plerique cum eo eiusdem Musae uiri, summis adsiduisque laudibus hos Vergilii uersus ferebat, quibus Vulcanum et Venerem iunctos mixtosque iure coniugii, rem lege naturae operiendam, uerecunda quadam translatione uerborum, cum ostenderet demonstraretque, protexit. [2] sic enim scripsit: "ea uerba locutus Optatos dedit amplexus placidumque petiuit Coniugis infusus gremio per membra soporem." [3] minus autem difficile esse arbitrabantur, in istiusmodi re dicenda, uerbis uti uno atque altero breui tenuique eam signo demonstrantibus, sicut Homerus dixerit: παρθενίην ζώνην et λέκτροιο θεσμόν et ἔργα φιλοτήσια, [4] tot uero et tam euidentibus ac tamen non praetextatis, sed puris honestisque uerbis uenerandum. [5] sed Annaeus Cornutus, homo sane pleraque alia non indoctus neque inprudens, in secundo tamen librorum, quos *De figuris sententiarum* conposuit, egregiam totius istius uerecundiae laudem insulsa nimis et odiosa scrutatione uiolauit. nam cum genus hoc figurae probasset et satis circumspecte factos esse uersus dixisset: "membra tamen inquit "paulo incautius nominauit."

---

95. For Homer, see *Il.* 23.850–855. Note that the first response may imply the assumption that Cornutus's remark was a question about Virgil's choices, not those of his character.

96. On *Aen.* 8.404–806. Cugusi (2003, 230) notes parallels in the grammatical tradition on periphrasis; Setaioli (2003–2004, 363–64) conversely argues that Cornutus's real concern here was not ethical but cosmological: he is concerned that Virgil's association of Vulcan with *erotic* heat obscures his real connection with *cosmic* fire. Whatever the case, it is important to note that Aulus is guilty of considerable hyperbole here; Cornutus's "criticism," when it comes, is far more restrained and limited than he leads us to expect.

[Title:] *That Annaeus Cornutus tainted those verses of Virgil in which he spoke chastely and frankly about Venus and Vulcan sharing a bed, with disgusting and odious criticism.*

[1] The poet Annianus,[97] and many who shared the same Muse, used continually to heap the highest praise on those verses in Virgil where he gives an explicit description of Vulcan and Venus joined in conjugal embrace—something which nature requires us to conceal—yet modestly veiled through the use of metaphor. [2] This is what he writes: "Having spoken these words, he (Vulcan) gave the embrace she desired and, melting into his wife's bosom, sought peaceful sleep throughout his limbs." [3] The easier thing, they thought, in this sort of description is to use one or two words and gesture at the matter with a brief allusion—as when Homer talks about the "maiden's girdle" or "bed rites" or "acts of love." [4] No one else had used so many and such explicit words to describe the private and respectable matter of two people chastely sharing a bed—yet words which were pure and decent and avoided all obscenity. [5] But Annaeus Cornutus—neither an ignorant nor a foolish man, for the most part, in fact—in book 2 of his work *On Figures of Thought* overstepped the mark when he trampled on their extraordinary praise for all this reverence, violating it with his odious probing. Although he approved of this kind of figure and said that the verses had been crafted with circumspection enough, he nevertheless said that "he [Virgil] was little thoughtless in using the word 'limbs.'"

F54. Servius, *Ad Aen.* 9.81[98]

Figmentum hoc licet poeticum sit, tamen quia exemplo caret, notatur a criticis: unde longo prooemio excusatur.

This [transformation] is, of course, poetic invention; however, it lacks precedent, as the critics note, and that is why it is explained by a long preface.

---

97. Probably the second-century friend of Aulus Gellius, so Cornutus obviously could not have had him in mind, but there is no reason why some of the "many who shared the same Muse" might not have predated Cornutus's comments.

98. Thilo and Hagen 1881–1902, 2:316,22–24. On the long lead-up from *Aen.* 9.81 to the transformation of the Trojans' ships into nymphs at 120–122. The circumstantial thread connecting Cornutus with this remark runs through F51 to F50.

F55. Servius [Dan.], *Ad Aen.* 9.348⁹⁹

Cornutus nocte legit et adnotauit "utrum nocte pro morte, an cum multa nox esset?"

Cornutus reads "night" and commented: "Either 'night' stands for 'death,' or the point is that the night was deep."

F56. Servius, *Ad Aen.* 9.672¹⁰⁰

Apparet quia hunc locum male intellexit Donatus, dicens, commissam portam, id est creditam, Pandaro et Bitiae: qui duces non erant. Cornutus uere et melius sensit, dicens, "portam quae ducis imperio commissa" fuerat, hoc est clausa, eam aperuerunt.

It appears that Donatus understood this passage badly, because he says that the gate was "committed" to, that is, "put in the charge of," Pandarus and Bitias—who were not commanders. Cornutus made a suggestion which is better and truer [to life] when he says: "'The gate which, on the order of the general, was committed,' i.e., 'closed'—this they opened."

F57. Charisius, *Art of Grammar*¹⁰¹

Annaeus Cornutus ad Italicum de Vergilio libro X, "iamque exemplo tuo etiam principes ciuitatium, o poeta, incipient similia fingere."

[On the usage *civitatium*:] Annaeus Cornutus to Italicus on Virgil book 10: "Poet! Now by your example even the leaders of states (*civitatium*) will begin to invent like things."¹⁰²

---

99. Thilo and Hagen 1881–1902, 2:340,23–25;. On *Aen.* 9.348: after Asius kills Rhoetus, his sword comes out with, literally, "much death" (*et multa morte recepit*), at least in our text but apparently not in Cornutus's.

100. Thilo and Hagen 1881–1902, 2:370,19–23; with immediate reference to 9.675: *portam, quae ducis imperio commissa, recludunt* (Pandarus and Bitias open one of the gates of Troy).

101. Barwick and Kühnert 1964, 159,27–29. On *Aen.* 10? Alternatively, the reference is to book 10 of a work by Cornutus *On Virgil*. See §1.6, T7.

102. Rocca-Sera (1988) reads this as a dedication to the poet Italicus in the light of his composition of the *Punica* (begun in the 80s); Fuentes González (1994, 465)

F58. Charisius, *Art of Grammar*[103]

Aetius Philologus librum suum sic edidit inscriptum, "An amauerit Didun Aeneas," ut refert Plinius, consuetudinem dicens facere hanc Callisto, hanc Calypso, hanc Io, hanc Allecto. itaque et L. Annaeus Cornutus in Maronis commentariis Aeneidos X Didus ait, "hospitio Didus exceptum esse Aenean."

[On the usage *Didun*:] Aetius the literary scholar published his book with this title: *Did Aeneas Love Dido (Didun)?* That is what Pliny relates, saying that he employed the same custom for "Callisto," the same for "Calypso," the same for "Io," the same for "Allecto." So Lucius[104] Annaeus Cornutus as well, in his commentary on Maro, *Aen.* 10, says *Didus* ("Dido's"): "Aeneas was received into Dido's hospitality."[105]

F59. Servius (italics = [Dan.]), *Ad Aen.* 10.547[106]

Prouerbialiter dictum est, ac si diceret, non mirum sic occisum esse eum qui sibi plurimum adrogabat. *Cornutus*[107] *ut sordidum inprobat.*

This is a proverbial saying, and, if he said it, it is no wonder that he was killed: he was claiming far too much for himself. Cornutus disapproves of him as someone lacking honor.[108]

---

notes that there is nothing to rule out the poet being Virgil himself, "Italicus" being the "leader of a state," Ti. Catius Asconius Silius Italicus, consul for 68.
  103. Barwick and Kühnert 1964, 162,6–11.
  104. This is the sole attestation to Cornutus's Roman *praenomen*, Lucius. (But see also F64 below.)
  105. Aetius and Cornutus followed the Greek declension of these names (nom. -ō, acc. -(o)un, gen. -(o)us). The alternative would have been to treat them as if they were Latin nouns in -o, which would have given *Didonem* in Aetius's title and *Didonis* in the quotation from Cornutus. It is a curious, and perhaps relevant, fact about the *Aeneid* that the name Dido always appears in the nominative.
  106. Thilo and Hagen 1881–1902, 2:448,5. On *Aen.* 10.547: *dixerat ille aliquid magnum* (Anxur "had made a grand claim"). Note that the ascription to Cornutus relies on an emendation of the manuscripts.
  107. *Corintus* [Dan].
  108. Kragelund (2016, 145, n. 5): "Cornutus condemns it" (i.e., Virigil's "prosaic" style here) "as base." Kragelund (2016) is also among those who think that F52 con-

194   L. Annaeus Cornutus: *Greek Theology*, Fragments, and Testimonia

4.2.8. On Lucan[109]

F60. Bern scholia to Lucan, *Bel. civ.* 1.214[110]

Porfurion puniceum interpretatus est quasi phoeniceum (propter rubras aquas), quem ad modum ἐρυθρὰν θάλασσαν dicimus rubrum mare. Cornutus uero sic: quasi puniceum lapidem habens aut ripas.

Porphyry understood *puniceus* as if it were *phoeniceus*, used here on account of the red waters—just as we say ἐρυθρὰ θάλασσα, "red sea." But Cornutus thus: "as if having red stones or banks."

F61. Bern scholia to Lucan, *Bel. civ.* 3.375[111]

In Cornuto: Caesar cum Massiliam iter deuerteret, Quintum Fabium in Hispaniam praemisit. Massilian autem aduersus Caesarem defensauit praetor Apollonides, urbi qui praefuit, classi autem Parmeno.

In Cornutus: Caesar, when he had made a diversion to Massilia, sent Quintus Fabius into Spain. But the praetor Apollonides, who was in charge of the city (while Parmeno was in charge of the fleet), defended Massilia against Caesar.

---

cerns a criticism of the author rather than a comment about his character (q.v. above with note).

109. Cichorius (1922, 261–69) argued that the Cornutus mentioned in the Bern scholia in connection with Lucan was the author of a historical work on the second civil war—and probably the very Cornutus confused with the philosopher in F2. He is followed by Nock (1931, 1004); Furentes González (1994, 471); *FRH* 1:426–27. On the other hand, Euzennat, Salviat, and Veyne (1968–1970, 23–24) judge this less likely than an identification with the philosopher—an identification we could make, as they note, without ascribing to him a full-blown commentary on Lucan.

110. Usener 1869, 25,10–13 = *FRH* 54 F1. On *Bel. civ.*1.214, where the Rubicon is described as "red" (*puniceus*).

111. Usener 1869, 109,28–32 = *FRH* 54 F2. On *Bel. civ.* 3.375: Caesar is laying siege to Massilia (modern Marseille) (*aut procul amuro tumulus surgentis inaltum telluris*).

F62. Bern scholia to Lucan, *Bel. civ.* 3.381[112]

In Cornuto sic: aggeres illic .LX. pedes altos aterum fecit ad portum, quem locum portus † pedeon uocant, alterum ad locum in occidentem adsurgentem † urbisplicia dixerunt.[113]

Thus in Cornutus: There he made mounds 60 feet high at the gate, one at the port, the one they call the <...> Port, and another rising in the west <...>

4.2.9. Miscellaneous

F63. Charisius, *Art of Grammar*[114]

In mundo pro palam et in expedito ac cito: Plautus in *Pseudolo* "quia sciebam," inquit, "pistrinum in mundo fore." Caecilius quoque, ut Annaeus Cornutus,[115] libro Tabularum Castarum Patris Sui,[116] profecto qui nobis: "in mundo futurum lectum"

---

112. Usener 1869, 110,6–9 = FRH 54 F3. On *Bel. civ.* 3.381: Caesar conceives a plan to build a rampart joining the hill on which he is encamped with the citadel of Massilia (*tunc res inmenso placuit s[tatura] l[abore]*).

113. *Pedeon* and *urbisplicia* have defied compelling explanation, but see Euzennat, Salviat, and Veyne 1968–1970 for possible corrections that square the text with the topography of Masillia.

114. Barwick and Kühnert 1964, 261,17–24. On the meaning of the phrase *in mundo*. The following translation is offered *exempli gratia*, the line parsed in order to allow mention of Annaeus Cornutus without his presence having a determinative bearing on the reconstruction of the mysterious title or the identification of Caecilius (whom Cornutus is merely quoting).

115. *ut T. Annaeus Cornutus*, Stroux (1930), suggesting that Titus was the son of the philosopher, who collected and published some of his father's notes (the "wax tablets"; see next note). *Caecilius [ut Annaeus] Cornutus*, Cichorius (1922, 267–68): this Caecilius Cornutus might then be a candidate for the historian confused with the philosopher in F2.

116. *libro tabernariarum* † *patris sui* † Jahn (1843), xxi (i.e., a comedy of the type called *tabernariae*, with a title having something to do with a father); *Hypobolimaeus Rastraria*, Reppe (1906, 72) (see SRPF 2:50–51); *libro tabularum cast[a]rensium*, Bücheler (1879, 347) (military memoirs of Cornutus's father); *tabulae catasterismorum*, Cichorius (1922, 268) (*Tables of the Constellations*), *libro tabularum ceratarum patris sui*, Stroux (1930, 361) ("a book from his father's wax tablets").

In mundo is used to mean "openly" and "without hindrance" and "quickly." Plautus in the *Pseudolus* says, "because I knew the mill would *immediately* be ...."[117] Also Caecilius[118] in his *Records of His Father's Camps* (as Annaeus Cornutus notes), who certainly [gives] us: "It will be chosen *openly*."[119]

F64. Fulgentius, *Exp. serm. antiq.* 20[120]

Tittiuilicium dici uoluerunt fila putrida quae de telis cadunt; ut Plautus in Cassina ait: "Non ego hoc uerbum empsim tittiuilicio," id est re admodum uilissima. Nam et Marcus Cornutus in satyra sic ait: "Tittiuiles Flacce do tibi."

By *tittivilicium* they mean the dirty threads that hang down from the loom—as Plautus says in the *Casina*: "I would not pay a *tittivilicium* for that claim," i.e., not even the very cheapest thing.[121] And Marcus Cornutus, too, in his *Satires* says this: "Flaccus, I give you *tittiviles*."

---

117. The line (*Pseud.* 499), given here a little inaccurately and abbreviated, is actually: *pistrinum in mundo scibam, si dixem, mihi* ("I knew the mill would be mine immediately, if I said").

118. Since this follows a quotation from Plautus, some people have assumed the comic writer, Caecilius Statius: Jahn (1843, p. xxi, n. 1), Reppe (1906, 71–72), Stroux (1930, 360); others have seen a historian: Nock (1931, 1004) (and see n. 115 above).

119. Or the quotation may start with "who certainly" (see Stroux 1930, 358–59).

120. Helm 1898, 117,13–17. *Quid sit tittiuilicium* (What a *tittiuilicium* is). This is probably the correct form for Fulgentius (although manuscripts also give *titiuilicium* and *textiuilicium*). But Paul the Deacon, in his epitome of Festus's *De significatione uerborum* (s.v.) has *tittibilicium*, which is a plausible contender for what was originally in Plautus; the tradition for the *Casina* itself has various corruptions at this point. For reasons to doubt an ascription to Annaeus Cornutus, see §1.6, T10.

121. Plautus, *Cas.* 347.

5
Cornutus and Persius

Text and Translation

Aules Persius Flaccus natus est pridie Non. Dec. Fabio Persico L. Vitellio coss., decessit VIII Kal. Dec. P. Mario Afinio Gallo coss. natus in Etruria Volaterris, eques Romanus, sanguine et [5] affinitate primi ordinis uiris coniunctus. decessit ad VIII miliarium uia Appia in praediis suis.

Pater eum Flaccus pupillum reliquit moriens annorum fere VI. Fuluia Sisennia nupsit postea Fusio equiti Romano et eum quoque extulit intra paucos annos. [10] studuit Flaccus usque ad annum XII aetatis suae Volaterris, inde Romae apud grammaticum Remmium Palaemonem et apud rhetorem Verginium Flauum. cum esset annorum XVI, amicitia coepit uti Annaei Cornuti, ita ut nusquam ab eo discederet; inductus aliquatenus in philosophiam est. [15] amicos habuit a prima adulescentia Caesium Bassum poetam et Calpurnium Staturam, qui uiuo eo iuuenis decessit. coluit ut patrem Seruilium Nonianum. cognouit per Cornutum etiam Annaeum Lucanum, aeque tum auditorem Cornuti. nam Cornutus illo tempore criticus fuit sectae [20] Porticus,[1] qui libros philosophiae reliquit. sed Lucanus mirabatur adeo scripta Flacci, ut uix se retineret recitantem a clamore: quae illius essent uera esse poemata se ludos facere. sero cognouit et Senecam, sed non ut caperetur eius ingenio. usus est apud Cornutum duorum conuictu doctissimorum [25] et sanctissimorum uirorum acriter tunc philosophantium, Claudi Agathini[2] medici Lacedaemonii et Petroni Aristocratis Magnetis, quos unice miratus est et aemulatus, cum aequales essent Cornuti, minor ipse. idem decem fere annis summe dilectus a Paeto

---

1. Most 1989, 2046; *tragicus fuit sectae poetae* manuscripts. Most's reading has won general assent—although, e.g., Kragelund (2016, 103, 145) accepts this text as (our only) evidence that Cornutus was a tragedian.

2. Clausen (1959), following Osann (1844); Agatur(r)ini manuscripts. The correction is based on an identification with the pneumaticist mentioned by Galen at *De differentia pulsuum* (Kühn 1821–1833, 8:674,8–11) and with Agathinus the Spartan, who founded an eclectic form of medical theory (Pseudo-Galen, *Def. med.* 14 [Kühn 1821–1833, 19:353,5–8, with Hatzimiachali 2011, 20–24]).

5.1. *Life of Persius*

Aules Persius Flaccus was born on December 4 in the consulship of Fabius Persicus and Lucius Vitellius (= 34 CE). He died on November 24 in the consulship of Publius Marius and Afinius Gallus (= 62 CE). He was born in the Etrurian town of Volaterra, as a Roman knight with connections by blood and marriage with men of the highest rank. He died on his estate some eight miles along the Appian Way.

His father died when he was about six, and left him as a ward. (Fulvia Sisennia[3] subsequently married Fusius, a Roman knight—but buried him, too, not many years later.) Flaccus studied at Volaterra up to the age of twelve, then at Rome with the grammarian Remmius Palaemo and the rhetorician Verginius Flavus. When he was sixteen, he formed such a friendship with Annaeus Cornutus that he was never separated from him. He was introduced to philosophy to some extent by him.[4] From early adolescence, he was friends with Caesius Bassus, the poet, and with Calpurnius Statura, who died young during his lifetime. He treated Servilius Nonianus as a father. Through Cornutus, he met his contemporary Annaeus Lucan, who was also taught by Cornutus (for Cornutus was at that time a critic, of the Stoic school, who left books of philosophy). Lucan so admired Flaccus's writings that when he recited them he could hardly stop himself from shouting out that they were *real* poems, while his own were bagatelles. Later on, he met Seneca, too, but was not taken with his character. At Cornutus's place, he associated with two extremely learned and good men, who were then keenly engaged in philosophy: Claudius Agathinus, a physician from Sparta, and Petronius Aristocrates, from Magnesia.[5] He admired them enormously and emulated them—they being of Cornutus's age, and he younger. Again, for about ten years he was a great favorite of

---

3. Persius's mother, according to a scholion to *Sat.* 6.6.
4. For Cornutus as teacher of Persius, see F10 and the introduction, p. 6.
5. For Agathinus, see note to the text ad loc. Aristocrates might be the grammarian mentioned at Galen, *De compositione medicamentorum* (Kühn 1821–1833, 12:879,4; cf. 878,16).

Thrasea est, ita ut peregrinaretur [30] quoque cum eo aliquando, cognatam eius Arriam uxorem habente.

Fuit morum lenissimorum, uerecundiae uirginalis, famae pulchrae, pietatis erga matrem et sororem et amitam exemplo sufficientis. fuit frugi, pudicus.

[35] Reliquit circa HS uicies matri et sorori. scriptis tantum ad matrem codicillis Cornuto rogauit ut daret HS $\overline{XX}$, aut ut quidam, $\overline{C}$; ut alii uolunt, et argenti facti pondo uiginti et libros circa septingentos Chrysippi siue bibliothecam suam omnem. uerum Cornutus sublatis libris pecuniam sororibus, [40] quas heredes frater fecerat, reliquit.

Scriptitauit et raro et tarde; hunc ipsum librum inperfectum reliquit. uersus aliqui dempti sunt ultimo libro, ut quasi finitus esset. leuiter contraxit Cornutus et Caesio Basso, petenti ut ipse ederet, tradidit edendum.

Scripserat [45] in pueritia Flaccus etiam praetextam †uescio et opericon† librum unum et paucos sororum Thraseae[6] in Arriam matrem uersus, quae se ante uirum occiderat. omnia ea auctor fuit Cornutus matri eius ut aboleret. editum librum continuo mirari homines et diripere coeperunt.

[50] Decessit autem uitio stomachi anno aetatis XXX.

---

6. Manuscripts; [*sororum Thraseae*] Clausen (1959), but excising these words does not obviously help, at least so long as we assume that Perstius's mother was Fulvia Sisennia (see translation, n. 3).

Paetus Thrasea, to the extent that he sometimes travelled abroad with him. (He was related to his wife, Arria.)

He had the most gentle manners and a chaste modesty, had a fine reputation, and showed exemplary piety towards his mother, sister, and aunt. He was upright and blameless.

He left about two million sesterces to his mother and sister. In codicils written only for his mother, he asked her to give Cornutus 20,000 sesterces (or, as some say, 100,000), and, as others insist, twenty pounds of silver and around seven hundred books by Chrysippus (that is, his whole library) as well.[7] (In fact, Cornutus took the books but left the money to the sisters whom their brother had made his heirs.)

He wrote infrequently and slowly. He left this very book unfinished;[8] some verses were removed from the last book to make it seem finished. Cornutus lightly emended it and, when Caesius Bassus asked if he might publish it, gave it to him to publish.

As a child, Flaccus had also written a historical play, <...> one book, and a few verses of Thrasea's sisters on their mother Arria,[9] who had killed herself in front of her husband. Cornutus saw to it that his mother destroyed all these. People immediately began to admire the published volume and hunt it out.

He died of a stomach ailment at the age of thirty.

---

7. It is wildly implausible that Persius *only* had books by Chrysippus in his library, as this line clearly implies. (The author of the *Life of Persius* may have wanted to make a statement about his philosophical commitment by mentioning them at all, but to do so with such hyperbole would sit uneasily with the claim at line 14 that Persius was engaged with philosophy only "to some extent," *aliquatenus*.) One possibility is that we are meant to understand a qualification of the claim from the context: that the books constitute Persius's entire collection *of Stoic*, or maybe even *of Chrysippean*, books. Another is that the text ought to emended to say that what Persius had was the whole "library" of *Chrysippus*'s books, i.e., everything that Chrysippus published (*bibliothecam* [*suam*] <*eius*> *omnem*). That would be more of a stretch (apart from the need for emendation, it does not give a natural sense to *bibliotheca*), but, as it happens, seven hundred would be about right for Chrysippus's oeuvre: we can extrapolate the number from the surviving fragment of the catalogue of Chrysippus's books at Diogenes Laertius, *Vit. phil.* 7.189–202, and we know that the total number was greater than four hundred: see F7, F8, and Diogenes Laertius, *Vit. phil.* 10.26–27.

8. This line shows that the *Life of Persius* was written to preface an edition of the *Satires*.

9. No version of the transmitted text makes much sense here, and we do not have the parameters needed to suggest a plausible emendation.

Sed mox ut a schola magistrisque deuertit, lecto Lucili libro decimo uehementer saturas componere instituit. cuius libri principium imitatus est, sibi primo, mox omnibus detrectaturus cum tanta recentium poetarum et oratorum [55] insectatione, ut etiam Neronem illius temporis principem inculpauerit. cuius uersus in Neronem cum ita se haberet: "auriculas asini Mida rex habet," in eum modum a Cornuto, ipse tantummodo, est emendatus: "auriculas asini quis non habet?" ne hoc in se Nero dictum arbitraretur.

5.2. Persius, *Sat.* 5

Part 1

[1] Vatibus hic mos est, centum sibi poscere uoces,
centum ora et linguas optare in carmina centum,
fabula seu maesto ponatur hianda tragoedo,
uolnera seu Parthi ducentis ab inguine ferrum.
[5] "quorsum haec? aut quantas robusti carminis offas
ingeris, ut par sit centeno gutture niti?
grande locuturi nebulas Helicone legunto,
si quibus aut Procnes aut si quibus olla Thyestae
feruebit saepe insulso cenanda Glyconi.
[10] tu neque anhelanti, coquitur dum massa camino,
folle premis uentos nec clauso murmure raucus
nescio quid tecum graue cornicaris inepte
nec scloppo tumidas intendis rumpere buccas.
uerba togae sequeris iunctura callidus acri,
[15] ore teres modico, pallentis radere mores
doctus et ingenuo culpam defigere ludo.
hinc trahe quae dicis mensasque relinque Mycenis
cum capite et pedibus plebeiaque prandia noris."
non equidem hoc studeo, pullatis ut mihi nugis
[20] pagina turgescat dare pondus idonea fumo.

Part 2

Secrete loquimur. tibi nunc hortante Camena
excutienda damus praecordia, quantaque nostrae

Soon after leaving school and his teachers, he read the tenth book of Lucilius's work and devoted himself with passion to composing satires. He imitated the beginning of his book to make fun of himself, first of all, but then of everyone—with such intense criticism of contemporary poets and orators that he even hit out at Nero, who was emperor then. He had a verse against Nero that went: "King Midas has the ears of a donkey"; Cornutus himself emended it thus: "Who doesn't have the ears of a donkey?" [*Sat.* 1.121] so that Nero would not think that it was said against him.

5.2. Persius, *Sat.* 5
Translated by Simon MacPherson

Part 1

For poets, it's tradition to ask for a hundred voices,
to wish for a hundred mouths and tongues for poetry, one hundred.
The tale on offer could be tragic, a gloomy actor gaping out his play,
or else a Parthian's wounded groin, and (drawn-out long) the blade.
[5] "What's it all for? How many gobbets of full-strength verse
are you piling in—to need a hundred gullets' worth of labors?
Speakers in the grand manner can get their clouds from Helicon,
But is anyone up for boiling Procne's or Thyestes's pan,
time and again, for Glycon to make a meal of, tastelessly?
[10] Forcing winds in a wheeze of bellows is not for you.
It's for lumpen metal, furnace cooked. Crass pomposity's not your style,
with a harsh crows-caw delivery or a strangled whisper.
No risk that you'll burst swollen cheeks with a deflating pop!
In language you dress Roman; your skill is harsh disjointedness of words;
[15] your style is rounded moderation. Your learning scrapes away at
sick behavior and with pointed Roman banter skewers vice.
So source your subjects local. Let Mycenae keep her feasts
(both head and feet). Get familiar with the food of ordinary folk."
Well I've no desire to bulk my page with dark-robed trifles,
[20] their only use to give a spurious weight to smoke.

Part 2

This is our private conversation. To you, at the Muse's bidding,
I give my heart for tough interrogation. How much, Cornutus,

pars tua sit, Cornute, animae, tibi, dulcis amice,
ostendisse iuuat. pulsa, dinoscere cautus
[25] quid solidum crepet et pictae tectoria linguae.
hic ego centenas ausim deposcere fauces,
ut quantum mihi te sinuoso in pectore fixi
uoce traham pura, totumque hoc uerba resignent
quod latet arcana non enarrabile fibra.

Part 3

[30] Cum primum pauido custos mihi purpura cessit
bullaque subcinctis Laribus donata pependit,
cum blandi comites totaque inpune Subura
permisit sparsisse oculos iam candidus umbo,
cumque iter ambiguum est et uitae nescius error
[35] diducit trepidas ramosa in compita mentes,
me tibi supposui. teneros tu suscipis annos
Socratico, Cornute, sinu. tum fallere sollers
adposita intortos extendit regula mores
et premitur ratione animus uincique laborat
[40] artificemque tuo ducit sub pollice uoltum.

Part 4

Tecum etenim longos memini consumere soles
et tecum primas epulis decerpere noctes.
unum opus et requiem pariter disponimus ambo
atque uerecunda laxamus seria mensa.
[45] non equidem hoc dubites, amborum foedere certo
consentire dies et ab uno sidere duci.
nostra uel aequali suspendit tempora Libra
Parca tenax ueri, seu nata fidelibus hora
diuidit in Geminos concordia fata duorum
[50] Saturnumque grauem nostro Ioue frangimus una,
nescio quod certe est quod me tibi temperat astrum.

of the inner me belongs to you, dear friend, it is a joy
to put on record. Take my soul and strike it, making careful note
[25] of what sounds firm and what's linguistic cover of painted plaster.
Now I'd dare demand one hundred throats to show,
with voice untainted, how much you're fixed in my heart's complexity.
So, my words may reveal the whole of what is hidden,
deep within my being, impossible to express in full.

Part 3

[30] I was anxious. My purple toga and its protective power had given way.
Boyhood's amulet hung, offered in the house to its girded gods.
The new brightness of my outfit, the coaxing of my peers,
licensed my eyes, broadcast over all Subura offered.
At the splitting of the road, lack of lived experience makes for a wrong turn
[35] and disturbed ideas veer off into thicketed byways.
I gave myself to you for adoption. Socratic in your embrace,
Cornutus, you lifted up my vulnerable years. Deceptive in your subtlety,
you applied your measure's edge, straightened behavior's twists and turns.
Reason was brought to bear. My mind struggled to be mastered,
[40] took on the shape of its design, molded by your thumb.

Part 4

I remember eating up the length of daytime hours with you
and subtle dinners plucked with you in earliest hours of night.
Our work and rest were side by side, arranged so they were one.
We relaxed from serious study with a meal of some restraint.
[45] Have no doubt our contract is mutual and secure.
It comes from a single star sign, the agreement of our days.
It was, perhaps, by Fate (and its grasp on truth secure)
that our times were allotted and poised on Libra's scale.
Or perhaps the hour of birth belonging to the loyal pair
split, in Gemini, the destiny of a heartbeat shared.
[50] We're breaking Saturn's grimness, then, as part of Jupiter's team.
There is some star I'm certain that's aligning me with you.

Part 5

Mille hominum species et rerum discolor usus;
uelle suum cuique est nec uoto uiuitur uno.
mercibus hic Italis mutat sub sole recenti
[55] rugosum piper et pallentis grana cumini,
hic satur inriguo mauult turgescere somno,
hic campo indulget, hunc alea decoquit, ille
in uenerem putris; sed cum lapidosa cheragra
fregerit articulos ueteris ramalia fagi,
[60] tunc crassos transisse dies lucemque palustrem
et sibi iam seri uitam ingemuere relictam.

Part 6

At te nocturnis iuuat inpallescere chartis;
cultor enim iuuenum purgatas inseris aures
fruge Cleanthea. petite hinc, puerique senesque,
[65] finem animo certum miserisque uiatica canis.
"cras hoc fiet." idem cras fiat. "quid? quasi magnum
nempe diem donas!" sed cum lux altera uenit,
iam cras hesternum consumpsimus; ecce aliud cras
egerit hos annos et semper paulum erit ultra.
[70] nam quamuis prope te, quamuis temone sub uno
uertentem sese frustra sectabere canthum,
cum rota posterior curras et in axe secundo.

Part 7

Libertate opus est. non hac, ut quisque Velina
Publius emeruit, scabiosum tesserula far
[75] possidet. heu steriles ueri, quibus una Quiritem
uertigo facit! hic Dama est non tresis agaso,
uappa lippus et in tenui farragine mendax.
uerterit hunc dominus, momento turbinis exit
Marcus Dama. papae! Marco spondente recusas
[80] credere tu nummos? Marco sub iudice palles?
Marcus dixit, ita est. adsigna, Marce, tabellas.
haec mera libertas, hoc nobis pillea donant.

Part 5

Humans come in a thousand types, the color of their ways diverse:
each with individual wants, their lives express no single prayer.
Under a fresh-risen sun, one may trade for Italian goods
[55] a shriveled pepper or seed of cumin blanching white.
One opts for swollen fullness and drink-soaked slumbers.
One gives way to sport's addiction, one is rendered down by dice throw,
another is rotten from desire. But once the stoniness of gout
has fractured their joints like beech tree boughs,
[60] disgust comes for marshy half-lit days they've crossed.
They moan (too late) for the life they've left behind.

Part 6

Your paleness comes from passion for nighttime study.
You may cultivate young men: but Cleanthes's harvest is what you sow
in their scoured-out ears. Here boys and old men both should seek
[65] the safety of an end in mind, resources for their gray-haired pain.
"It'll get done tomorrow." But it does need to get done tomorrow.
"Surely it's no problem, giving me an extra day?" The next day comes,
so yesterday's tomorrow's eaten up. And soon the next tomorrow
is thief of all our years, just a little beyond our reach, always.
[70] That wheel rim spins close by, under the self-same structure,
but you won't succeed in catching up. You are only a rear wheel
after all. You are speeding and spinning on a different axle.

Part 7

We do need freedom, but not the sort where any Roman, newly enrolled,
has title by ticket to adulterated grain. Truth and you are strangers
[75] if citizenship for you is just the act of twirling round.
Take Dama the stable lad, without a bean, befuddled by wine
and bleary eyed: he'd tell you a lie for a pinch of animal feed.
Master gives him a turn and from that spinning motion.
Out comes Marcus Dama. Hey presto! You won't refuse a loan;
[80] if Marcus underwrites it, grow pale with fear with Marcus on the jury.
Marcus has pronounced, it must be so. Marcus, sign here please!
Freedom taken neat, that's what wearing the cap of liberty means.

"an quisquam est alius liber, nisi ducere uitam
cui licet ut libuit? licet ut uolo uiuere, non sum
[85] liberior Bruto?" "mendose colligis" inquit
Stoicus hic aurem mordaci lotus aceto,
"hoc relicum accipio, 'licet' illud et 'ut uolo' tolle."

Part 8

"Vindicta postquam meus a praetore recessi,
cur mihi non liceat, iussit quodcumque uoluntas,
[90] excepto siquid Masuri rubrica uetabit?"
disce, sed ira cadat naso rugosaque sanna,
dum ueteres auias tibi de pulmone reuello.
non praetoris erat stultis dare tenuia rerum
officia atque usum rapidae permittere uitae;
[95] sambucam citius caloni aptaueris alto.
stat contra ratio et secretam garrit in aurem,
ne liceat facere id quod quis uitiabit agendo.
publica lex hominum naturaque continet hoc fas,
ut teneat uetitos inscitia debilis actus.

Part 9

[100] Diluis elleborum, certo conpescere puncto
nescius examen? uetat hoc natura medendi.
nauem si poscat sibi peronatus arator
luciferi rudis, exclamet Melicerta perisse
frontem de rebus. tibi recto uiuere talo
[105] ars dedit et ueris speciem dinoscere calles,
ne qua subaerato mendosum tinniat auro?
quaeque sequenda forent quaeque euitanda uicissim,
illa prius creta, mox haec carbone notasti?
es modicus uoti, presso lare, dulcis amicis?
[110] iam nunc adstringas, iam nunc granaria laxes,
inque luto fixum possis transcendere nummum
nec gluttu sorbere saliuam Mercurialem?
"haec mea sunt, teneo" cum uere dixeris, esto
liberque ac sapiens praetoribus ac Ioue dextro.

"A free man is (what else?) someone who can live his life
as he wants. I can live as I want. So I am more free
[85] than Brutus am I not?" "A fallacy of conflation," is what
the Stoic here says, for vinegar's bite has given his ears a wash.
"The rest is fine, but get rid of 'can' and 'as I want'"

Part 8

"I've left the praetor. I'm my own man now. His rod of office has made me so.
So why can't I follow where my inclination commands me?
[90] Not those red-letter don'ts of course, the ones in Masurius's law."
Listen and learn. Drop your anger, your turned-up nose, your curling sneer.
Your ancient grandmothers' sayings? I'll root them up and out your lungs.
It is not in the praetor's remit to give a detailed brief to fools
on what duty means, how to micromanage a life that's swiftly gone.
[95] Easier to get a barrack corporal playing the harp!
Reason opposes it, is chatting away (for your ear only):
"No one should do what he'll corrupt by doing it."
This truth is there in human as well as nature's law.
Crippling ignorance makes it impossible to get things done.

Part 9

[100] You're mixing a dose of hellebore but lack all skill
in balance calibration? So what healing means—that is what's saying no!
A plowboy in boots wants to be captain but doesn't know his Morning Star.
Even a minor sea god would bewail the death of standards!
And are you poised, ready to react, your ankle placed just so?
[105] Is defining the characteristics of truth in your skill set
(no telltale sound of copper-layered falsity in gold)?
Is your to-do list to hand? And the one of what to avoid?
The first labeled white, the second black?
Your needs are modest, your expenditure curbed? You're hospitable with
    friends?
[110] You can stop your grain outflows, then let them flow free?
A penny is stuck in the mud: can you walk past it
without Mercurial salivation and the greediness of spittle?
"This is mine. It is what I possess." Only when you can say and mean it
will you count with Jupiter as wise and free, not just officialdom.

Part 10

[115] Sin tu, cum fueris nostrae paulo ante farinae.
pelliculam ueterem retines et fronte politus
astutam uapido seruas in pectore uolpem,
quae dederam supra relego funemque reduco.
nil tibi concessit ratio; digitum exere, peccas,
[120] et quid tam paruum est? sed nullo ture litabis,
haereat in stultis breuis ut semuncia recti.
haec miscere nefas nec, cum sis cetera fossor,
tris tantum ad numeros Satyrum moueare Bathylli.
"liber ego." unde datum hoc sumis, tot subdite rebus?
[125] an dominum ignoras nisi quem uindicta relaxat?
"i, puer, et strigiles Crispini ad balnea defer"
si increpuit, "cessas nugator?" seruitium acre
te nihil inpellit nec quicquam extrinsecus intrat
quod neruos agitet; sed si intus et in iecore aegro
[130] nascuntur domini, qui tu inpunitior exis
atque hic quem ad strigilis scutica et metus egit erilis?

Part 11

Mane piger stertis. "surge" inquit Auaritia, "eia
surge." negas. instat. "surge" inquit. "non queo." "surge."
"et quid agam?" "rogat! en saperdas aduehe Ponto,
castoreum, stuppas, hebenum, tus, lubrica Coa.
tolle recens primus piper et sitiente camelo.
uerte aliquid; iura." "sed Iuppiter audiet." "eheu,
baro, regustatum digito terebrare salinum
contentus perages, si uiuere cum Ioue tendis."
[140] iam pueris pellem succinctus et oenophorum aptas.

Part 10

[115] You used to be the same grade flour as the rest of us. So, chances are,
you won't have changed your spots. Your brow may be smooth and shiny,
but you still retain the filthy deceit of a fox-like heart.
I revoke any slack I've given you, taking a pull on the rope.
Reason makes no concessions: a finger out of line and you're at fault.
[120] It doesn't get smaller than that. Tons of incense won't answer your prayer
for a tiny speck of wisdom to stick fast in an idiot.
Mixing the two is against the rules. If you're crass in other ways,
three steps of Bathyllus's Satyr is all you'll ever dance.
"But I'm free." Why take this as read? You're at the mercy of events.
[125] Aren't there any masters but the one you were freed from by the praetor's rod?
"Get on boy. Take Crispinus's strigils to the baths," someone bawls.
"Stop dreaming, you slacker." But slavery and its harshness
does not act on you, does it? Nothing enters you from outside
and sets your muscles into motion. It is on the inside that masters are born
[130] in that less-than-healthy liver of yours. Are you any less hauled in or disciplined
than any slave forced to get scrapers by fear of his master's strap?

Part 11

It's morning. You're snoring lazily. "Get up," says Greed. "Come on,
get up!" You say no. She insists. "Get up," she says. I can't. "Get up."
Why should I? "You have to ask? To bring sprats from Pontus,
[135] castor oil, tows of flax, ebony, fragrance, and glinting fabrics from Cos.
Be first to grab the freshest pepper—don't wait and water the camel.
Borrow money, swear you'll repay it." But Jupiter will hear. "Oh dear.
If you're happy still to use that finger, scrape that salt cellar,
then carry on! You can taste, often, and live on Jupiter's terms."
[140] All geared up then, you load your slaves with baggage and wine.

Part 12

Ocius ad nauem! nihil obstat quin trabe uasta
Aegaeum rapias, ni sollers Luxuria ante
seductum moneat: "quo deinde, insane, ruis, quo?
quid tibi uis? calido sub pectore mascula bilis
[145] intumuit quam non extinxerit urna cicutae?
tu mare transilias? tibi torta cannabe fulto
cena sit in transtro Veiientanumque rubellum
exhalet uapida laesum pice sessilis obba?
quid petis? ut nummi, quos hic quincunce modesto
[150] nutrieras, pergant auidos sudare deunces?
indulge genio, carpamus dulcia, nostrum est
quod uiuis, cinis et manes et fabula fies,
uiue memor leti, fugit hora, hoc quod loquor inde est."

Part 13

En quid agis? duplici in diuersum scinderis hamo.
[155] huncine an hunc sequeris? subeas alternus oportet
ancipiti obsequio dominos, alternus oberres.
nec tu, cum obstiteris semel instantique negaris
parere imperio, "rupi iam uincula" dicas;
nam et luctata canis nodum abripit, et tamen illi,
[160] cum fugit, a collo trahitur pars longa catenae.

Part 14

"Daue, cito, hoc credas iubeo, finire dolores
praeteritos meditor" (crudum Chaerestratus unguem
adrodens ait haec.) "an siccis dedecus obstem
cognatis? an rem patriam rumore sinistro
[165] limen ad obscenum frangam, dum Chrysidis udas
ebrius ante fores extincta cum face canto?"
"euge, puer, sapias, dis depellentibus agnam

Part 12

Get a move on, onto the ship. Nothing to stop you subjecting the Aegean
to the massiveness of your speedy craft. Unless Luxury beguiles you, takes
      you off first
for a spot of advice. "Where oh where are you rushing to next, you fool?
What do you really want? That red-hot bile, the virility of your heart,
[145] is so puffed up—not even a jug of hemlock could snuff it out.
Leaping across the sea? Using a coil of hemp rope on the rowers' bench
as your dinner couch? Is some Veiian red in a squat container
breathing out fumes, polluted by deadening pitch?
Just what is your goal? Sweating at a greedy 11 percent,
[150] those coins fattened up at a modest five? Give in to what's natural,
let's seize our pleasures: life's for living and it belongs to us.
Ashes are what you will become, and shades and a closed book.
Live with death in mind. Time flies, and what I am saying is subtracted
      from it."

Part 13

What to do? Pulled by hooks in different directions, you don't know
[155] which one to go with. You must submit
to each of your masters in turn, in turn abandon your task.
And not even when you have put up a resistance, refused to accept
those persistent commands, can you say, "I have now broken my bonds."
A bitch may struggle at her bonds, may even break the lock, but still,
[160] as she runs off, a long part of the chain's still trailing from her neck.

Part 14

"Listen to me, Davus, I've got a plan! To put my troubles behind me,
bring them to an end." As Chaerestratus says this, he bites his raw and
      bleeding nails.
"My relations are dry as dust. But am I to disgrace them,
destroy my inheritance by scandal? Outside a house of ill repute?
Chrysis's doors are soaking wet. And here I am in front of them,
[165] singing, drunk, that torch of mine already long snuffed out."
Good news, my boy! If you've any sense, you'll offer the gods a slaughtered
      lamb.

percute." "sed censen plorabit, Daue, relicta?"
nugaris. solea, puer, obiurgabere rubra,
[170] ne trepidare uelis atque artos rodere casses.
nunc ferus et uiolens; at, si uocet, haut mora dicas
"quidnam igitur faciam? nec nunc, cum arcessat et ultro
supplicet, accedam?" si totus et integer illinc
exieras, nec nunc.

Part 15

                    Hic hic quod quaerimus, hic est,
[175] non in festuca, lictor quam iactat ineptus.
ius habet ille sui, palpo quem ducit hiantem
cretata Ambitio? "uigila et cicer ingere large
rixanti populo, nostra ut Floralia possint
aprici meminisse senes. quid pulchrius?" at cum
[180] Herodis uenere dies unctaque fenestra
dispositae pinguem nebulam uomuere lucernae
portantes uiolas rubrumque amplexa catinum
cauda natat thynni, tumet alba fidelia uino,
labra moues tacitus recutitaque sabbata palles.
[185] tum nigri lemures ouoque pericula rupto,
tum grandes galli et cum sistro lusca sacerdos
incussere deos inflantis corpora, si non
praedictum ter mane caput gustaueris ali.
 dixeris haec inter uaricosos centuriones,
[190] continuo crassum ridet Pulfenius ingens
et centum Graecos curto centusse licetur.

Celebrate your escape! "But, Davus, do you think she'll cry if I leave her?"
Don't be an idiot boy. You'll come under attack from that red slipper
[170] to stop your desperate gnawing at the nets of her captivity.
For now, your ferocity's untamed, but if she calls, you'll say a moment later,
 "What am I to do? It's genuine. She's calling me, pleading with me.
I should go to her now. Shouldn't I?" Look: you're in one piece.
So, not now. That's what I say!

Part 15

Over here! Here's what we are searching for,
[175] here it is! And it's not in symbols, wielded in empty ceremonial.
Is the wheedler in control, paraded, gaping in Ambition's whited toga?
"Get up early, get in those chickpeas—the crowd will be spoiling for a fight!
All so sunning old men can recall our Floral Festival. Nothing finer!"
But when the festive days of Herod come around,
[180] the lamps are placed just so at the oil-smeared window,
and, violet-adorned, they sick up their thick and fatty cloud.
The fish tail's engulfed in the red dish it swims in;
the jug's swelling with the whiteness of wine, as you move your lips in silence,
pale with fear at the Sabbath of the circumcised.
[185] What of the dark spirits, too, and the dangers of an egg once broken,
the bulked up Galli, the rattle of the one-eyed priestess?
Into you they've forged the gods that swell your bodies
if you don't taste your morning garlic three times as prescribed.
But say this in front of centurions with heavy veins
[190] and instantly some massive Pulfenius, with a rough laugh,
will offer a hundred cents for a hundred Greeks in clipped coin.

6
Index of Sources for the Fragments

Anonymous
    Commentary on Hermogenes's Περὶ ἰδεῶν (Walz 1834)
        931,1–15 = F30
    Prolegomena to Hermogenes's Περὶ στάσεων (Rabe 1931)
        330,6–9 = F33
Augustine
    De utilitate credendi (Zycha 1891)
        17 = F37
Aulus Gellius
    Attic Nights (Marshall 1968)
        2.6.1–4 = F41
        9.10 = F53
Cassius Dio
    Roman History (Boissevain 1895–1901)
        62.29.1–4 = F7
    Roman History (excerpts from John of Antioch) (Boissevain 1895–1901)
        3:755,34–40 = F9
Charisius
    Art of Grammar (Barwick and Kühnert 1964)
        159,27–29 = F57
        162,6–11 = F58
        261,17–24 = F63
Constantine VII Porphyrogenitus
    De sententiis (Boissevain 1905)
        250,32–251,3 = F8
    De virtutibus et vitiis (Boissevain and Büttner-Wobst 1906)
        183,10–16 = F9

Diogenes Laertius
    Lives of Eminent Philosophers (Dorandi 2013)
        index locupletior, 66 = F1
Etymologicum Magnum (Gaisford 1848)
        408,52–56 = F18
Eudocia
    Violarium (Flach 1880)
        no. 590, 448,7–11 = F3
Eusebius
    Chronicle (Armenian version) (Aucher and Awgarean 1818)
        2:274 = F10b
    Chronicle (Latin version of Jerome) (Helm 1956)
        184,23–26 = F10a
    History of the Church (Bardy 1952–1958)
        6.19.8 = F11
Fulgentius
    Expositio sermonum antiquorum (Helm 1898)
        20, 117,13–17 = F64
Hesychius
    Onomatologi (Flach 1882)
        123,16–19 = F3
Inscriptions
        AE (1926), no. 162 = F6
        IRT 306 = F6
Jerome
    Letters (Hilberg 1910)
        Ep. 70.4, 705,15–20 = F12
John of Antioch
    Fragments (Müller 1851)
        575, frag. 90 = F9
[Julius Rufinianus]
    De schematis dianoeas (Halm 1863)
        1, 60,9–12 = F31
Junius Philargyrius
    Explanatio in Bucolica Vergilii [*versio* I] (Thilo and Hagen 1881–1902)
        3.2:69,13–19 = F39
Macrobius
    Saturnalia (Willis 1970)
        5.19.1–3 = F50

6.7, see F41 (note)
Nicolaus Sophistes
    Progymnasmata (Felten 1913)
        55,10–21 = F32
Papyri
        P.Oxy. 52.3649 (Turner 1984) = F28
Placidus
    Glossary (Codex Parisinus Bibl. Nat. lat. nov. acquis. 1298) (Goetz 1894)
        116,5 = F48
Placidus, Pseudo-
    Glossary (Pirie and Lindsay 1930)
        I23, 65 = F43
        M7, 67 = F48
Porphyry
    On the Categories (Busse 1887)
        58,30–59,14 = F19
        86,210–32 = F20
    Fragments (Smith 1993)
        12T = F11
Scholia
    Bern scholia (on Lucan) (Usener 1869)
        25,10–13 = F60
        109,28–32 = F61
        110,6–9 = F62
    Scholia Veronensia (on Virgil) (Thilo and Hagen 1902)
    on the *Aeneid*
        429,22–23 (ad 3.691) = F47
        431,15–16 (ad 4.178) = F49
        435,3–7 (ad 5.488) = F52
    on the *Eclogues*
        395,4–5 (ad 3.40) = F38
        398,8–9 (ad 6.9) = F40
Servius
    On the Aeneid (Thilo and Hagen 1881–1902)
        1:32,3–4 [Dan.] (ad 1.45) = F44
        1:64,9–13 [Dan.] (ad 1.150) = F45
        1:154,25–26 (ad 1.488) = F46
        1:344,23–28 (ad 3.46) = F51
        2:316,22–24 (ad 9.81) = F54

2:340,23-25 [Dan.] (ad 9.346) = F55
2:370,19-23 (ad 9.672) = F56
2:448,3-5 (ad 10.547) = F59
   On the Georgics (Thilo and Hagen 1881-1902)
3.1:195,19-20 (ad 1.277) = F42
Simplicius
   On the Categories (Kalbfleisch 1907)
18,22-19,7 = F21
62,24-30 = F22
129,1-4 = F23
187,28-36 = F24
351,19-29 = F26
359,1-17 = F25
Stephanus
   Ethnica (Meineke 1849)
312,10-12 = F5
616,23-617,2 = F4
Stobaeus
   Anthology (Wachsmuth and Hense 1884-1912)
1.49.43 (1:383,24-384,2) = F27
Suda (Adler 1928-1938)
κ.2098 (Κορνοῦτος) = F2
λ.165 (Λαχάρης) = F36
ω.182 (Ὠριγένης) = F11
Syrianus
   On Hermogenes's περὶ στάσεων (Rabe 1893)
60,19-23 = F34
201,8-14 = F35
   On the Metaphysics (Kroll 1902)
106,5-10 = F29
Theodoretus
   Graecarum affectionum curatio (Canivet 1958)
2.94-95 = F17
Tzetzes
   Allegories of the Iliad (Matranga 1850)
18,655-59 = F15
   Allegories of the Odyssey (Hunger 1956)
35-38 (proem) = F16
   Commentary on Lycophron (Scheer 1908)

87,30–88,6 = F13
Exegesis of the Iliad (Hermann 1812)
   3,17–21 = F14

7
Concordances

Mazzarino 1955	This edition
A (*Testimonia*)	
1	F58
2	F2, F4
3	F2
4	*Pers.* 4
5	F2, F7, F9, F10
6	*Pers.* 5
7	*Pers.* 8, 10
8	*Pers.* 8
9	F53
10	F50
11	F2
11a	F17, F18
11b	F22
11c	F11 (Suda)
11d	F20
12	F64
13	—[1]
14	see F53
B (*Fragmenta*) (grammatical works only)	
1–16	*Orthography*, paras. 1–16

---

1. The *Scholia on Persius*, spuriously ascribed to Cornutus; see §1.6.4, T13.

16a	*Orthography*, para. 17
17	*Orthography*, para. 18
18	*Orthography*, para. 19
19	*Orthography*, para. 20
20	F38
21	F40
22	F41
23	F42
24	F44
25	F45
26	F46
27	F47
28	F49
29	F51
30	F52
31	F55
32	F56
33	F58
34	F59
35	F57
36	F53
37	F63
38	F43
39	F48
40 (*falsum*)	F39
41 (*falsum*)	—[2]

---

2. Servius, *Ad. Georg.* 3.135. See also Cugusi 2003, 233. But this relies on a hypothesis of Georges (1902, 298), who corrected the name *Lucretius* found in the manuscripts to *Cornutus* on the grounds (1) that no critic named Lucretius is known and (2) that there is thematic similarity with Cornutus F53 (Mazzarino 1955, 30). But (2) is illusory: the emended text claims that Cornutus treated sexual union more openly than Virgil, which is true enough if one has the *Greek Theology* in mind but contradicts the critical point in F53. As to (1): there is no reason to doubt that Servius had the *poet* Lucretius in mind; see, e.g., Thomas (1988, 64, on *Georg.* 3.135–137), comparing *Rer. Nat.* 4.1106–1107.

7. Concordances

Hays 1983	This edition

Appendix 1 (Life)

1	*Life of Persius*
2	Persius, *Sat.*5
3	F2
4	F7
5	F5
6	F4
7	F3
8	F10
9	F10
10	F9
11	F11
12	F12, F1

Appendix 2 (Fragments)

1	F19
2	F20
3	F21
4	F22
5	F23
6	F24
7	F26
8	F25
9	F57
10	F38
11	F40
12	F41
13	F42
14	F41
15a	F43
15b	—[3]

---

3. Placidus, *Gloss.*, s.v. *ingluuies*, on the basis of similarity with F43 (Hays 1893, frag. 15a), but all the overlap is with what is attributed to Pliny in the latter, not Cornutus.

16	F44
17	F45
18	F46
19	F51
20	F47
21	F58
22	F48
23	F49
24	F50
25	F52
26	F54
27	F55
28	F56
29	F41
30	F59
31	F53
32	F31
33	F20
34	F32
35	*Orthography*
36	F18
37	F17
38	F36
39	F14
40	F13
41	F27
42	F29
43	F34
44	F35
45	F30
46	F63

Other collections or lists of testimonia and fragments: Reppe 1906, 4–5 and 76–83; Nock 1931; on Virgil in particular: Suringar 1834, 116–24; Cugusi 2003, 239–40.

For material not included in this volume that might be traced back to Cornutus, although it does not name him, see (on Virgil) the many parallels listed with the evidence in Mazzarino 1955, 167–209; also Cugusi 2003, whose final list (at 239–40) adds Servius, *Ad Georg.* 3.135 (see n. 2

above); Servius [Dan.], *Ad Aen.* 11.554; Quintilian, *Inst.* 8.6.8; Macrobius, *Sat.* 5.18.18–21.

On the *Categories*, Griffin (2015, 153–65) suggests that we see Cornutus behind Dexippus, *On the Categories*, 11,1–12,31 (Busse 1887) (translated in full in the introduction, §1.4.1.1 above); Simplicius, *On the Categories*, 64,20–65,12 (Kalbfleisch 1907) (he suggests a transmission error that led to material from Cornutus being ascribed to "followers of Lucius"); and Plotinus, *Enn.* 6.1.5.14.

Bibliography

Adler, Ada, ed. 1928–1938. *Suidae lexicon*. 4 vols. Leipzig: Teubner.
Atherton, Catherine. 1993. *The Stoics on Ambiguity*. Cambridge: Cambridge University Press.
Aucher, Joannes Baptista, and Y. Awgarean, eds. 1818. *Eusebii Pamphili Caesariensis episcope, Chronicum bipartitum*. 2 vols. Venice: Lazarus.
Baltzly, Dirk. 2014. "Plato's Authority and the Formation of Textual Communities." *CQ* 64:793–807.
Bardy, Gustave, ed. 1952–1958. *Eusèbe de Césaré, Histoire ecclésiastique*. SC 31, 55, 73. 3 vols. Paris: Cerf.
Barnes, Jonathan. 1997a. *Logic and the Imperial Stoa*. PhA 75. Leiden: Brill.
———. 1997b. "Roman Aristotle." Pages 1–69 in *Philosophia Togata II: Plato and Aristotle at Rome*. Edited by Jonathan Barnes and Miriam Griffin. Oxford: Oxford University Press.
Barwick, Karl, and F. Kühnert, eds. 1964. *Flavii Sosipatri Charisii Artis grammaticae libri V*. BSGRT. Leipzig: Teubner.
Bellandi, F. 2003. "Anneo Cornuto nelle *Saturae* e nella *Vita Persi*." Pages 185–210 in *Gli Annaei: Una Famiglia nella Storia e nella Cultura di Roma Imperiale; Atti del Convegno internazionale di Milano-Pavia 2–6 maggio 2000*. Edited by Isabella Gualandri and Giancarlo Mazzoli. Como: New Press.
Berdozzo, F. 2009. "Text, Übersetzung und Anmerkungen." Pages 29–138 in *Cornutus: Die griechischen Götter; Ein Überblick über Namen, Bilder und Deutungen*. Edited by Heinz-Günter Nesselrath. SAPERE 14. Tübingen: Mohr Siebeck.
Betegh, Gábor. 2004. *The Derveni Papyrus: Cosmology, Theology, and Interpretation*. Cambridge: Cambridge University Press.
Boissevain, Ursul Philipp, ed. 1895–1901. *Cassii Dionis Cocceiani historiarum Romanorum quae supersunt*. Vols. 1–3. Berlin: Weidmann.
———, ed. 1905. *Excerpta de sententiis*. Vol. 4 of *Excerpta historica iussu imp. Constantini Porphyrogeniti confecta*. Berlin: Weidmann.
Boissevain, Ursul Philipp, and Theodor Büttner-Wobst, eds. 1906. *Excerpa de virtutibus et vitiis*. Vol. 2.1 of *Excerpta historica iussu imp. Constantini Porphyrogeniti confecta*. Berlin: Weidmann.
Bouhier, Jacques. 1729. "Remarques de M. le President Bouhier sur la dissertation critique." Pages 1133–46 in Joannes Jacobus Breitinger, "Exercitatio Critica in Vitam A. Persii Fl." Pages 1103–46 in *Amoenitates literariae, quibus variae observationes,*

scripta item quaedam anecdota et rariora opuscula exhibentur. Vol. 10. Edited by Johann Georg Schelhorn. Frankfurt: Bartholomaeus.

Bowen, Alan C., and Todd, Robert B. 2004. *Cleomedes' Lectures on Astronomy: A Translation of The Heavens*. Berkeley: University of California Press.

Boys-Stones, George R. 2001. *Post-Hellenistic Philosophy: A Study in Its Development from the Stoics to Origen*. HCS 42. Oxford: Oxford University Press.

———, ed. 2003a. *Metaphor, Allegory, and the Classical Tradition*. Oxford: Oxford University Press.

———. 2003b. "The Stoics' Two Types of Allegory." Pages 189–216 in *Metaphor, Allegory, and the Classical Tradition*. Oxford: Oxford University Press.

———. 2007. "Fallere Sollers: The Ethical Pedagogy of the Stoic Cornutus." Pages 77–88 in *Greek and Roman Philosophy 100 BC–200 AD*. Edited by R. W. Sharples and Richard Sorabji. BICSSup 94. London: Institute of Classical Studies.

———. 2009. "Cornutus und sein philosophisches Umfeld: Der Antiplatonismus der *Epidrome*." Pages 141–61 in *Cornutus: Die griechischen Götter; Ein Überblick über Namen, Bilder und Deutungen*. Edited by Heinz-Günter Nesselrath. SAPERE 14. Tübingen: Mohr Siebeck.

———. 2013. "Seneca Against Plato: *Letters* 58 and 65." Pages 128–46 in *Plato and the Stoics*. Edited by A. G. Long. Cambridge: Cambridge University Press.

———. 2016. "Philosophy as Religion and the Meaning of 'Providence' in Middle Platonism." Pages 317–38 in *Theologies of Ancient Greek Religion*. Edited by Esther Eidenow, Julia Kindt, and Robin Osborne. CCS. Cambridge: Cambridge University Press.

———. 2018. *Platonist Philosophy 80 BC to AD 250: An Introduction and Collection of Sources in Translation*. Cambridge: Cambridge University Press.

Brouquier-Reddé, Véronique. *Temples et cultes de Tripolitaine*. EAA. Paris: Éditions du CNRS, 1992.

Bücheler, Franz. 1879. "Coniectanea." *RM* 34:341–56.

Busch, Peter, and Jürgen K. Zangenberg, eds. and trans. 2010. *Lucius Annaeus Cornutus: Einführung in die griechische Götterlehre*. TF 95. Darmstadt: Wissenschaftliche Buchgesellschaft.

Busse, Adolf, ed. 1887. *Porphyrii isagoge et in Aristotelis categorias commentarium*. CAG 4.1. Berlin: Reimer.

Canivet, Pierre, ed. 1958. *Théodoret de Cyr: Thérapeutique des maladies hélleniques*. 2 vols. SC 57. Paris: Cerf.

Christ, Wilhelm von, Wilhelm Schmid, and Otto Stählin. 1924. *Geschichte des griechischen Litteratur*. Vol. 2.2. Munich: Beck.

Ciaffi, V. 1937. "Intorno all'autore dell'Octavia." *RFIC* 15:246–65.

Cichorius, Conrad. 1922. *Römische Studien. Historisches, Epigraphisches, Literargeschichtliches aus vier Jahrhunderten Roms*. Leipzig: Teubner.

Cizek, Eugen. 1972. *L'Époque de Néron et ses controverses idéologiques*. RA 4. Leiden: Brill.

Clarke, M. L. 1971. *Higher Education in the Ancient World*. London: Routledge & Kegan Paul.

Clausen, Wendell Vernon, ed. 1959. *A. Persi Flacci et D. Iuni Iuvenalis Saturae.* OCT. Oxford: Clarendon.
Clausen, Wendell Vernon, and James E. G. Zetzel, eds. 2004. *Commentum Cornuti in Persium.* BSGRT. Munich: Saur.
Cugusi, P. 2003. "Lucio Anneo Cornuto esegeta di Virgilio." Pages 211–44 in *Gli Annaei: Una Famiglia nella Storia e nella Cultura di Roma Imperiale; Atti del Convegno internazionale di Milano-Pavia 2–6 maggio 2000.* Edited by Isabella Gualandri and Giancarlo Mazzoli. Como: New Press.
Dawson, David. 1992. *Allegorical Readers and Cultural Revision in Ancient Alexandria.* Berkeley: University of California Press.
De Paolis, Paolo. 2010. "L'insegnamento dell'ortografia latina fra Tardoantica e alto Medioevo: Teorie e manuali." Pages 229–91 in *Libri di scuola e pratiche didattiche: Dall'Antichità al Rinascimento; Atti del Convegno Internazionale di Studi, Cassino, 7–10 maggio 2008.* Vol. 1. Edited by Lucio Del Corso and Oronzo Pecere. Cassino: Università di Cassino.
Dorandi, Tiziano. 1992. "Considerazioni sull'index locupletior di Diogene Laerzio." *Prometheus* 18:121–26.
———, ed. 2013. *Diogenes Laertius: Lives of Eminent Philosophers.* CCTC 50. Cambridge: Cambridge University Press.
Duhot, Jean-Joël. 1991. "Y a-t-il des catégories stoïciennes?" *RIP* 45:220–44.
Duret, Luc. 1986. "Dans l'ombre des plus grands: II. Poètes et prosateurs mal connus de la latinité d'argent." *ANRW* 32.5:3152–346.
Euzennat, Maurice, François Salviat, and Paul Veyne. 1968–1970. "Les scholies bernoises de Lucain, César et Marseille antique." *Études Classiques* 3:13–24.
Evans, James, and J. Lennart Berggren, trans. 2006. *Geminos's Introduction to the Phenomena: A Translation and Study of a Hellenistic Survey of Astronomy.* Princeton: Princeton University Press.
Fabricius, Johann Albert. 1793. *Bibliotheca Graeca.* 4th ed. Vol. 3. Hamburg: Bohn.
Felten, Joseph, ed. 1913. *Nicolai Progymnasmata.* Vol. 11 of *Rhetores Graeci.* BSGRT. Leipzig: Teubner.
Festugière, André-Jean. 1953. *Les doctrines de l'âme.* Vol. 3 of *La révélation d'Hermès Trismégiste.* Paris: Gabalda.
Finamore, John F., and John M. Dillon. 2002. *Iamblichus: De anima; Text, Translation, and Commentary.* PhA 92. Leiden: Brill.
Fitzgerald, John T., and L. Michael White. 1983. *The Tabula of Cebes.* SBLTT 24. Chico, CA: Scholars Press.
Flach, Johann Louis Moritz, ed. 1880. *Eudociae Augustae Violarium.* BSGRT. Leipzig: Teubner.
———, ed. 1882. *Hesychii Milesii onomatologi quae supersunt.* Leipzig: Teubner.
Fuentes González, Pedro Pablo. 1994. "Cornutus [C190]." Pages 460–73 in *Dictionnaire des Philosophes Antiques.* Vol. 2. Edited by Richard Goulet. París: CNRS.
Funaioli, Gino, ed. 1907. *Grammaticae Romanae Fragmenta.* Vol. 1. BSGRT 290. Leipzig: Teubner.
Gaisford, Thomas, ed. 1848. *Etymologicum Magnum.* Oxford: Oxford University Press.

Gale, Thomas. 1688. *Opuscula mythologica, physica et ethica: Græce et Latine*. Amsterdam: Wetstein.
Georges, Heinrich. 1902. *Die antike Vergilkritik in den Bukolika und Georgika*. PhilSup 9. Leipzig: Dieterich'sche Verlagsbuchhandlung.
Geymonat, M. 1984. "Cornuto." Pages 897–98 in *Enciclopedia Virgiliana*. Vol. 1. Edited by F. Della Corte. Rome: Istituto della Enciclopedia italiana.
Gill, Christopher, trans. 2013. *Marcus Aurelius: Meditations, Books 1–6*. Oxford: Oxford University Press.
Goetz, Georg, ed. 1894. *Placidus liber glossarum: Glossaria reliqua*. Vol. 5 of *Corpus glossariorum Latinorum*. Leipzig: Teubner
Goulet, Richard, ed. 1994–2018. *Dictionnaire des Philosophes Antiques*. 7 vols. Paris: CNRS.

———. 2013. "Ancient Philosophers: A First Statistical Survey." Pages 10–39 in *Philosophy as a Way of Life: Ancients and Moderns; Essays in Honor of Pierre Hadot*. Edited by Michael Chase, Stephen R. L. Clark, and Michael McGhee. Oxford: Wiley Blackwell.
Gourinat Jean-Baptiste. 2005. "Explicatio fabularum: La place de l'allégorie dans l'interprétation stoïcienne de la mythologie." Pages 934 in *Allégorie des poètes, allégorie des philosophes: Études sur l'herméneutique de l'allégorie de l'Antiquité à la Réforme*. Edited by Gilbert Dahan and Richard Goulet. Paris: Vrin.

———. 2008. "Cornutus: Grammairien, rhéteur et philosophe stoïcien." Pages 53–92 in *Grammairiens et philosophes dans l'Antiquité gréco-romaine*. Edited by Brigitte Pérez and Michel Griffe. Montpellier: Presses Universitaires de la Méditerranée.
Graeven, Hans, ed. 1891. *Cornuti artis rhetoricae epitome*. Berlin: Weidmann.

———. 1895. "Ein Fragment des Lachares." *Hermes* 30:289–313.
Griffin, Michael J. 2015. *Aristotle's Categories in the Early Roman Empire*. OCM. Oxford: Oxford University Press.
Hadot, Iseltraut. 2005. *Arts libéraux et philosophie dans la pensée antique: Contribution à l'histoire de l'éducation et de la culture dans l'antiquité*. Paris: Vrin.
Hahm, David E. 1977. *The Origins of Stoic Cosmology*. Columbus: Ohio State University Press.
Halm, Carl, ed. 1863. *Rhetores Latini minors*. Leipzig: Teubner.
Hatzimichali, Myrto. 2011. *Potamo of Alexandria and the Emergence of Eclecticism in Late Hellenistic Philosophy*. Cambridge: Cambridge University Press.
Hays, Robert Stephen. 1983. "Lucius Annaeus Cornutus' Epidrome (Introduction to the Traditions of Greek Theology): Introduction, Translation and Notes." Diss., University of Texas at Austin.
Heath, Malcolm. 2003. "Porphyry's Rhetoric." *CQ* 53:141–66.
Helm, Rudolf, ed. 1898. *Fabii Planciadis Fulgentii V.C. opera*. Leipzig: Teubner.

———, ed. 1956. *Die Chronik des Hieronymus*. Vol. 7 of *Eusebius Werke*. GCS 47. Berlin: Akademie Verlag.
Hermann, Gottfried, ed. 1812. *Draconis Stratonicensis liber de metris poeticis; Ioannis Tzetzes exegesis in Homeri Iliadem*. Leipzig: Weigel.
Herrmann Leon. 1980. "L. Annaeus Cornutus et sa rhétorique à Herennius Senecio." *Latomus* 39:144–60.

Hijmans, B. L. 1975. "Athenodorus on the Categories and a Pun on Athenodorus." Pages 105–14 in *Kephalaion: Studies in Greek Philosophy and Its Continuation Offered to C. J. de Vogel*. Edited by Jaap Mansfeld and Lambertus Marie de Rijk. PhTS 23. Assen: Van Gorcum.

Hilberg, Isidor, ed. 1910. *Sancti Eusebii Hieronymi Epistulae*. Vol. 1. CSEL 54. Vienna: Tempsky.

Hiller, Eduard. 1878. *Theonis Smyrnaei philosophi platonici: Expositio rerum mathematicarum ad legendum Platonem utilium*. Leipzig: Teubner.

Höhler, Wilhelm, ed. 1867. *Die Cornutus-Scholien zum ersten Buche der Satiren des Juvenals*. JCPSup 23. Leipzig: Teubner.

Horst, Pieter Willem van der. 1981. "Cornutus and the New Testament: A Contribution to the Corpus Hellenisticum." *NT* 23:165–72.

———, ed. and trans. 1984 *Chaeremon: Egyptian Priest and Stoic Philosopher; The Fragments Collected and Translated with Explanatory Notes*. EPRO 101. Leiden: Brill.

Hunger, Herbert, ed. 1956. "Johannes Tzetzes, Allegorien zur Odyssee Buch 1–12: Kommentierte Textausgabe." *BZ* 49:249–310.

Jahn, Otto, ed. 1843. *Auli Persii Flacci Satirarum liber: Cum scholii antiquis*. Leipzig: Breitkopf & Haertel.

Kalbfleisch, Karl. 1907. *Simplicii in Aristotelis Categorias commentarium*. CAG 8. Berlin: Reimer.

Keil, Heinrich. 1880. *Scriptores de orthographia*. Vol. 7 of *Grammatici Latini*. Leipzig: Teubner.

Krafft, Peter. 1975. *Die handschriftliche Überlieferung von Cornutus' Theologia Graeca*. BKA 2.57. Heidelberg: Carl Winter Universitätsverlag.

Kragelund, Patrick. 2016. *Roman Historical Drama: The Octavia in Antiquity and Beyond*. Oxford: Oxford University Press.

Kroll, Wilhelm, ed. 1902. *Syriani in Metaphysica commentaria*. CAG 6.1. Berlin: Reimer.

Kühn, Carl Gottlob. 1821–1833. *Claudii Galeni opera omnia*. 20 vols. Leipzig: Cnobloch.

Lang, Karl Heinrich von, ed. 1881. *Cornuti Theologiae Graecae Compendium*. Leipzig: Teubner.

Le Boulluec, Alain. 1975. "L'allégorie chez les Stoïciens." *Poétique* 23:301–21.

Leo, Friedrich. 1904."Didymos περὶ Δημοσθένους." *Nachrichten der Göttinger Gesellschaft der Wissenschaften* (Philologisch-historische Klasse): 254–61.

Lévy, C. 2004. "Sur l'allégorèse dan l'ancien Portique." Pages 221–33 in *L'Allégorie de l'Antiquité à la Renaissance*. Edited by Brigitte Pérez-Jean and Patricia Eichek-Lojkine. Paris: Champion.

Liebl, Hans. 1888. *Die Disticha Cornuti, auch Cornutus oder Distigium des Jo. v. Garlandia genannt, und der Scholiast Cornutus: Mit dem Text des Cornutus antiquus und novus; Programm der kgl. Studien-Anstalt Straubing*. Straubing: Lechner'schen.

Lobel, Edgar, and Denys Page, eds. 1955. *Poetarum Lesbiorum fragmenta*. Oxford: Clarendon.

Long, A. A. 1992. "Stoic Readings of Homer." Pages 41–66 in *Homer's Ancient Readers: The Hermeneutics of Greek Epic's Earliest Exegesis*. Edited by Robert Lamberton and John J. Keaney. Princeton: Princeton University Press.

———. 1997. "Allegory in Philo and Etymology in Stoicism." Pages 198–210 in *Wisdom and Logos: Studies in Jewish Thought in Honor of David Winston*. Edited by David T. Runia, David Winston, and Gregory E. Sterling. SPhiloA 9. BJS 312. Atlanta: Scholars Press.

———. 2003. "Roman Philosophy." Pages 184–210 in *The Cambridge Companion to Greek and Roman Philosophy*. Edited by D. N. Sedley. Cambridge: Cambridge University Press.

Marshall, Peter K., ed. 1968. *Aulus Gellius: Noctes Atticae*. 2 vols. OCT. Oxford: Clarendon.

Martini, Gerardus Joannes de. 1825. "De L. Annaeo Cornuto philosopho stoico." Diss., Leiden.

Marx, F. 1894. "Annaeus" (9). *RW* 1:2, cols. 2227–35.

Matranga, Pietro, ed. 1850. *Anecdota Graeca e mss. bibliothecis Vaticana, Angelica, Barberiniana, Vallicelliana, Medicea, Vindobensii*. Vol. 1. Rome: Bertinelli.

Mazzarino, Antonius. 1955. *Grammaticae Romanae Fragmenta Aetatis Caesareae*. Vol. 1. Torino: Loescher.

Meineke, August, ed. 1849. *Stephan von Byzanz: Ethnika*. Berlin: Reimer

Miles, Graeme. 2014. "Living as a Sphinx: Composite Being and Monstrous Interpreter in the 'Middle Life' of Michael Psellos." Pages 11–24 in *Conjunctions of Mind, Soul and Body from Plato to the Enlightenment*. Edited by Danijela Kambaskovic. Dordrecht: Springer.

Moraux, Paul. 1984. *Der Aristotelismus im I. und II. Jh. n. Chr.* Vol. 2 of *Die Aristotelismus bei den Griechen von Andronikos bis Alexander von Aphrodisias*. Peripatoi 6. Berlin: de Gruyter.

Morford, Mark. 2002. *The Roman Philosophers: From the Time of Cato the Censor to the Death of Marcus Aurelius*. London: Routledge.

Morison, Benjamin. 2005. "Les catégoires d'Aristote comme introduction à la logique." Pages 103–19 in *Les Catégories et leur histoire*. Edited by Otto Bruun and Lorenzo Corti. Paris: Vrin.

Most, Glenn W. 1989. "Cornutus and Stoic Allegoresis: A Preliminary Report." *ANRW* 36.3:2014–65.

———. 1993. "Die früheste erhaltene griechische Dichterallegorese." *Rheinisches Museum* 136:209–12.

———. 2016. "Allegoresis and Etymology." Pages 52–74 in *Canonical Texts and Scholarly Practices: A Global Comparative Approach*. Edited by Anthony Grafton and Glenn W. Most. Cambridge: Cambridge University Press.

Mueller, Ian. 1969. "Stoic and Peripatetic Logic." *AGP* 51:173–87.

Müller, Carl, ed. 1851. *Fragmenta historicorum Graecorum*. Vol. 4. Paris: Didot.

Nesselrath, Heinz-Günter, ed. 2009. *Cornutus: Die griechischen Götter; Ein Überblick über Namen, Bilder und Deutungen*. SAPERE 14. Tübingen: Mohr Siebeck.

Niehoff, M. R. 2007. "Did the *Timaeus* Create a Textual Community?" *GRBS* 47:167–91.

Nock, Arthur Darby. 1931. "Kornutos." *RW* Supplement 5, cols. 995–1005.
Osann, Friedrich, ed. 1844. *L. Annaeus Cornutus De natura deorum*. Göttingen: Libraria Dieterichiana.
Parker, Robert. 1983. *Miasma: Pollution and Purification in Early Greek Religion*. Oxford: Clarendon.
Pépin, Jean. 1958. *Mythe et Allégorie: Les origines grecques et les contestations Judaeo-Chrétiennes*. Paris: Aubier.
Pià Comella, Jordi. 2011. "De La nature des dieux de Cicéron à l'Abrégé de Cornutus: Une nouvelle répresentation des élites dans la réflexion théologique?" *Camenae* 10:1–27.

———. 2014. *Une piété de la raison: Philosophie et religion dans le stoïcisme impérial des Lettres à Lucilius de Sénèque aux Pensées de Marc Aurèle*. Turhout: Brepols.
Pirie, J. W., and Wallace Martin Lindsay, eds. 1930. *Placidi glossae*. Vol. 4 of *Glossaria Latina*. Paris: Les Belles Lettres.
Rabe, Hugo, ed. 1893. *Syriani in Hermogenem commentaria*. Vol. 2. BSGRT. Leipzig: Teubner.

———, ed. 1931. *Prolegomenon sylloge*. Vol. 14 of *Rhetores Graeci*. Leipzig: Teubner.
Ramelli, Ilaria, ed. 2003. *Anneo Cornuto: Compendio di Teologia Greca*. Milan: Bompiani.

———, ed. 2007. *Allegoristi dell'età classica: Opere e frammenti*. Milan: Bompiani.

———, ed. 2008. *Stoici romani minori*. Milan: Bompiani.
Rauk, John. 1995. "Macrobius, Cornutus, and the Cutting of Dido's Lock." *CP* 90:345–54.
Reppe Rudolf. 1906. "De L. Annaeo Cornuto." Diss., Leipzig.
Ribbeck, Otto. 1866. *Prolegomena Critica ad P. Vergili Maronis opera maiora*. Leipzig: Teubner.
Rocca-Serra, Guillaume. 1963. "Pour une édition de Cornutus." *BAGB* 1:348–50.

———. 1982. "Exégèse allégorique et idéologie impériale: L'*Abrégé* de Cornutus." Pages 61–72 in *Neronia 1977: Actes du 2e colloque de la Société internationale d'études néroniennes (Clermont-Ferrand, 27–28 mai 1977)*. Edited by Jean-Michel Croisille and Pierre-Maurice Fauchere. Clermont-Ferrand: ADOSA.

———. 1988. "Cornutus: Abrégé des traditions relatives à la théologie grecque; Introduction, traduction et commentaire." PhD thesis, Paris.

———. 2008. "Du bon usage du digamma." Pages 281–87 in *Ars pictoris, ars scriptoris: Mélanges de peinture, histoire et littérature offerts à Jean-Michel Croisille*. Edited by Fabrice Galtier and Yves Perrin. Clermont-Ferrand: Presses universitaires Blaise Pascal.
Romanelli, Pietro. 1925. *Leptis Magna*. Rome: Società editrice d'arte illustrata.
Russell, D. A., and David Konstan, eds. and trans. 2005. *Heraclitus: Homeric problems*. WRGW 14. Atlanta: Society of Biblical Literature.
Salles, Ricardo. 2015. "Two Early Stoic Theories of Cosmogony." Pages 11–30 in *Causation and Creation in Late Antiquity*. Edited by Anna Marmodoro and Brian D. Prince. Cambridge: Cambridge University Press.
Scheer, Eduard, ed. 1908. *Lycophronis Alexandra*. Vol. 2. Berlin: Weidmann.
Schmidt, Bruno. 1912. "De Cornuti theologiae graecae compendio." Diss., Leipzig.

Sedley, David N. 2002. "The Origins of Stoic God." Pages 41–89 in *Traditions of Theology: Studies in Hellenistic Theology, Its Background and Aftermath*. Edited by Dorothea Frede and André Laks. PhA 89. Leiden: Brill.

———. 2003. *Plato's Cratylus*. Cambridge: Cambridge University Press.

———. 2005. "Stoic Metaphysics at Rome." Pages 117–42 in *Metaphysics, Soul, and Ethics in Ancient Thought: Themes from the Work of Richard Sorabji*. Edited by Ricardo Salles. Oxford: Oxford University Press.

Setaioli, Aldo. 2003–2004. "Interpretazioni stoiche ed epicuree in Servio e la tradizione dell'esegesi filosofica del mito e dei poeti a Roma (Cornuto, Seneca, Filodemo), I." *IJCT* 10:335–76.

Smith, Andrew, ed. 1993. *Porphyrii philosophi fragmenta*. BSGRT. Stuttgart: Teubner.

Steinmetz, Peter. 1986. "Allegorische Deutung und allegorische Dichtung in der alten Stoa." *RM* 129:18–30.

Stern, Jacob, trans. 1996. *Palaephatus: On Unbelievable Tales*. Wauconda: Bolchazy-Carducci.

Stroux, Johannes. 1930. "Vier Zeugnisse zur römischen Literaturgeschichte der Kaiserzeit." *Phil* 86:338–68.

Struck, Peter T. 2004. *Birth of the Symbol: Ancient Readers at the Limits of Their Texts*. Princeton: Princeton University Press.

Sullivan, John Patrick. 1985. *Literature and Politics in the Age of Nero*. Ithaca: Cornell University Press.

Suringar, Willem H. D. 1834. *Historia critica scholiastarum latinorum*. Vol. 2. Leiden: Luchtmann & Cyfveer.

Theiler, Willy. 1982. *Poseidonios: Die Fragmente*. 2 vols. TK 10. Berlin: de Gruyter.

Thesleff, Holger. 1965. *The Pythagorean Texts of the Hellenistic Period*. Åbo: Åbo akademi.

Thilo, Georg, and Hermann Hagen, eds. 1881–1902. *Servii grammatici qui feruntur in Vergilii carmina commentarii*. 3 vols. Leipzig: Teubner.

Thomas, Richard F., ed. 1988. *Virgil: Georgics*. Vol. 1. Cambridge: Cambridge University Press.

Thorsteinsson, Runar M. 2010. *Roman Christianity and Roman Stoicism: A Comparative Study of Ancient Morality*. Oxford: Oxford University Press.

Timpanaro, Sebastiano. 1986. *Per la storia della filologia virgiliana antica*. Rome: Salerno.

Torre, Chiara. 2003. "Cornuto, Seneca, i poeti e gli dei." Pages 167–84 in *Gli Annaei: Una Famiglia nella Storia e nella Cultura di Roma Imperiale; Atti del Convegno internazionale di Milano-Pavia 2–6 maggio 2000*. Edited by Isabella Gualandri and Giancarlo Mazzoli. Como: New Press.

Torres, José Bernardino, trans. 2009a. "Δεύς in Cornutus." *Mnemosyne* 62:628–34.

———. 2009b. *Mitógrafos griegos: Paléfato, Heráclito, Anónimo Vaticano, Eratósthenes, Cornuto*. BCG 376. Madrid: Gredos.

———. 2010. "Mitos didácticos: El significativo caso de Anneo Cornuto." Pages 95–101 in *Artes ad Humanitatem: Actes del XVI Simposi de la Secció Catalana de la SEEC*. Vol. 1. Edited by Esperança Borrell Vidal and Pilar Gómez Cardó. Barcelona, SEEC.

———. 2011. "Roman Elements in Cornutus's Ἐπιδρομή." Pages 41–54 in *Vtroque sermone nostro: Bilingüismo social y literario en el imperio de Roma / Social and Literary Bilingualism in the Roman Empire.* Pamplona: EUNSA.
———. 2016. "The *Homeric Hymns*, Cornutus, and the Mythographical Stream." Pages 187–202 in *The Reception of the Homeric Hymns.* Edited by Andrew Faulkner, Athanassios Vergados, and Andreas Schwab. Oxford: Oxford University Press.
———, ed. 2018. *Cornuti Theologiae Graecae compendium.* Leipzig: Teubner.
Trapp, Michael. 2007. *Philosophy in the Roman Empire: Ethics, Politics and Society.* Aldershot: Ashgate.
Turner, E. G., ed. 1984. "3649. Cornutus, περὶ ἑκτῶν β." Pages 12–13 in vol. 52 of *The Oxyrhynchus Papyri.* Edited by Helen M. Cockle. London: Egypt Exploration Society.
Usener, Hermann, ed. 1869. *M. Annaei Lucani: Commenta Bernensia.* Leipzig: Teubner.
Vian, F. 1952. "La guerre des Géants devant les penseurs de l'Antiquité." *REG* 65:1–39.
Wachsmuth, Curt. 1897. *Ioannis Laurentii Lydi Liber de ostentis et calendaria Graeca omnia.* Leipzig: Teubner.
Wachsmuth, Curt, and Otto Hense, eds. 1884–1912. *Ioannis Stobaei Anthologium.* 5 vols. Berlin: Weidmann.
Walz, Christianus, ed. 1834. *Rhetores Graeci.* Vol. 7. 2 parts. Stuttgart: Cotta.
Welare, J., trans. 1549. "Phornuti Speculatio de deorum natura." Pages 151–70 in *C. Iulii Hygini: Augusti liberti fabularum liber.* Basel: Heruagium.
Wickert, L. 1897. "L. Annaeus Cornutus [A609]." *PIR* 1:100.
Willis, James A., ed. 1970. *Ambrosii Theodosii Macrobii, Saturnalia.* 2nd ed. BSGRT. Leipzig: Teubner.
Wojciechowski, Michał, trans. 2016. *Pseudo-Cornutus, Przegląd greckich poglądów na bogów (Epidrome).* Starożytne Teksty Religijne. Olsztyn: Wydział Teologii Uniwersytetu Warmińsko-Mazurskiego.
Zeller, Eduard. 1919–1923. *Die Philosophie der Griechen in ihrer geschichtlichen Entwicklung.* 6th ed. 3 vols. Leipzig: Reisland.
Zetzel, James E. G. 1981. *Latin Textual Criticism in Antiquity.* New York: Arno.
———. 2018. *Critics, Compilers, and Commentators: An Introduction to Roman Philology, 200 BCE–800 CE.* Oxford: Oxford University Press.
Zycha, Joseph, ed. 1891. *Sancti Aureli Augustini: De utilitate credendi, De duabus animabus, Contra Fortunatum, Contra Adimantum, Contra epistulamfundamenti, Contra Faustum.* CSEL 25. Vienna: Tempsky.

General Index

Acheron (river), 135
addressee
   of the *Greek Theology*, 5, 6 n. 17, 42
   of the *Orthography*, 143 n. 1
Adonis, 113, 115
Adrasteia, 67
Aeficianus (Stoic), 9 n. 23, 13
Aegean. *See* Briareos
aegis, 63, 95
Aelian, Claudius (Stoic), 12
Aemilius Asper (commentator on Virgil), 143
Agathinus, Claudius, of Sparta (medic), 6, 13, 198 n. 2, 199
Agathodaemon. *See* Good Daemon
Aglaia (Grace), 75
Aigle, 75
Akmon, 55
Alekto (Erinnys), 65
Alexander of Aphrodisias (Aristotelian), 13
allegory, 25–28, 47–49, 163–65
   de facto, 26, 47–48
ambiguity. *See stasis*-theory
Amphitrite, 101
Andronicus (Aristotelian), 10, 15, 175
Aornos (lake), 135
Aphrodite, 91, 103, 105, 107, 115, 121
Apollo, 71, 125, 127, 129, 133
Apollodorus of Athens (writer on the gods), 49
Apsines of Gadara (grammarian), 178 n. 56, 179
Archedemus (Stoic), 57 n. 7, 180 n. 62

Ares, 91, 99
Aristocrates, Petronius, of Magnesia (grammarian), 6, 13, 199
Aristotelianism, 9, 10, 11, 16–24, 30, 34
Aristotle, 48, 93 n. 116, 164
   Categories, 11–12, 13, 14, 15–24, 35, 167–76
Arius Didymus (Stoic), 158
Arrian (Stoic), 12–13, 113 n. 169
Artemis, 125, 127, 131, 133
Asclepius, 129, 131
Astraios, 107
Atargatis, 59
Athena, 83, 91, 93, 95, 97, 99
Athenodorus (Stoic), 13, 15–24, 35, 158, 168, 170, 171, 172, 173
Atlas, 107
Atropos (Lot), 67
Baal (Phoenician deity), 5
Bacchae, 121
Bacchanalia, 121 n. 191
Basilicus (grammarian), 178
Boethus (Aristotelian), 17 n. 41, 22 n. 48, 177
Briareos, 83
Caesar, C. Iulius, 149
Celsus (commentator on Virgil), 182
Cephalion (rhetor, historian), 164
Chaeremon of Alexandria (Stoic), 9 n. 23, 13, 163
Chaos, 85
Charon, 135
Chiron, 131
Christianity, 8

-239-

Chrysippus (Stoic), 10, 11, 27 n. 55, 31, 32 n. 66, 35, 57 n. 7, 107 n. 151, 158, 161–62, 175 n. 49, 201
Cicero, M. Tullius, 7, 38, 48, 147 n. 11, 153
Claudius (emperor), 145 n. 6
Cleanthes (Stoic), 10, 11 n. 27, 32 n. 66, 35, 57 n. 7, 125, 158, 207
Cleomedes (Stoic), 13
Clitomachus (Academic), 5 n. 10
colon, 178
comma, 178–79
Cornutus, C. Caecilius (historian), 158 n. 4, 181 n. 65, 194 n. 109, 195 n. 115, 196 n. 118
cosmogony, 29–31
cosmopolis, 34, 59
Day (goddess), 85
death, 32, 38, 176
Demeter, 111, 113, 115, 117
Demo (grammarian), 165
Derveni papyrus, 49
Dexippus (Platonist), 19–21
Dido, 188–89, 193
digamma, 2 143, 145, 151
Dike. *See* Justice
Dione, 103
Dionysus, 97, 117–23, 128
Domninus (grammarian), 164
Earth (goddess), 46, 61, 73, 85
Eileithuia, 133
Eirene. *See* Peace
Eleusis, 113
Enyo, 99
epanorthōsis, 27 n. 55
Epictetus (Stoic), 3 n. 6, 8 n. 20, 9 n. 23, 12, 159 n. 6
Epicureanism, 9 n. 25, 10
Epimetheus, 89, 91
Epione, 131
Erato (Muse), 71
Erebos, 85
Erinnyes, 65, 135
Eros, 85, 105, 107, 133
ethics, 30–31, 32–34

etymology, 25–26
 gestural, 107, 113
Euanthe, 75
Eunomia (Season), 117
Euphrosyne (Grace), 75
Eurydome, 73
Eurymedousa, 73
Eurynome, 73
Euterpe (Muse), 71
fate, 31, 67, 205
Fortune (goddess), 67
Gaia. *See* Earth
Galen of Pergamum (medic), 9 n. 23, 13
Ge. *See* Earth,
Geminus (Stoic), 13
Good Daemon, 109
Gorgon, 95
Graces, 63, 73, 75, 91, 103
grammaticus, Cornutus as?, 5–6, 14–15, 185
Hades, 57, 65, 113, 135, 189
Harmony (goddess), 99
Hasdrubal. *See* Clitomachus
Heaven. *See* Ouranos.
Hebe, 123
Hecate, 125, 131, 133
Hephaestus, 29, 75, 91, 93
Hera, 26, 27 n. 55, 46, 57, 73, 83, 91
Heracles, 81, 123
Heraclitus (writer on Homer), 48, 164, 165
Hermes, 75–81, 103
Hesiod, 44, 46, 85–89, 166
Hestia, 111
Horai. *See* Seasons
Hyginus, C. Iulius (commentator on Virgil), 182
Hyperion (Titan), 87
Iapetos (Titan), 87
Ignatius Celer, P., of Beirut (Stoic), 8 n. 23
Iris, 77, 188–89
Isis, 113, 166
Juno, 188
Jupiter, 205, 209, 211
Justice (Season), 63, 117

General Index

Kalliope (Muse), 71
Kleio (Muse), 69
Klotho (Lot), 67
Koios (Titan), 87
Kokytus (river), 135
Kore, 111
Krios (Titan), 87
Kronos (Titan), 46, 57, 59, 61, 89
Lachares (sophist), 181–82
Lachesis (Lot), 67
Leptis Magna, 2, 4–5, 35, 159–60
Leukothea, 103
Litai. *See* Prayers
Livy (historian), 159
logic, debate over, 19–24
Lollianus (grammarian), 180
Lucan, M. Annaeus (poet), 3 n. 5, 6, 7 n. 18, 161, 194–95, 199
Lucilius, C. (poet), 145, 203
Lucius (Platonist), 16, 172
Maenads, 119
Maia, 79
Manilius (Stoic), 12
Marcus Aurelius (emperor), 8, 9 n. 25, 12
Megaira (Erinnys), 65
Mela, L. Annaeus, 3 n. 6
Melpomene (Muse), 71
Metis, 93
Mnemosyne (Titan), 69, 73, 87
Muses, 69, 129, 184
Musonius Rufus, C. (Stoic), 159, 162
Nemesis, 67
Neptune, 160
Nereus, 103
Nero (emperor), 2, 7, 13 n. 32, 159, 161–63, 203
Nicostratus (Platonist), 16, 172
Night (goddess), 85
Nike. *See* Victory
Nisus (grammarian), 140 n. 4
Nymphs, 103, 107, 119, 189
Octavia (the tragedy), 37–38
Okeanos (Titan), 46, 61, 87
Omphale, 125
Opis, 67

Origen (the Christian), 163–64
Osiris, 113, 166
Ourania (Muse), 71
Ouranos (Heaven), 46, 53, 59, 61, 73, 85
Palaephatus, 49, 164, 165
Pan, 107
Peace (Season), 117
Pegasus, 103
Peripatetics. *See* Aristotelianism
Persephone, 115
Persius (poet), 2, 5, 6, 10, 162, 197–215
Phoebe (Titan), 87
Plato
    Cratylus, 48
    Timaeus, 12, 35, 41, 44–47
Platonism, 10, 11, 15, 16–17, 30–31, 34 nn. 71–72, 35, 77 n. 72, 93 n. 119, 97 n. 131, 132 n. 222
Plautus, L. Sergius (Stoic), 13 n. 33
Plautus, T. Maccius (playwright), 196
Pleiades, 107
Plutarch (Platonist), 4, 6, 31 n. 65, 33 n. 67, 166
Pluto, 59, 135
Polymnia (Muse), 71
Porphyry (Platonist), 4 n. 9, 17–24, 166, 167, 173, 180, 194
Poseidon, 5 n. 11, 57, 83, 101, 103
Posidonius (Stoic), 26 n. 54, 33, 34 n. 70, 35, 47 n. 8, 57 n. 7, 158, 180 n. 62
Prayers (goddesses), 65
Priapus, 109
Prometheus, 89, 91
Proserpina, 188
Pyriphlegethon (river), 135
Pythagoreanism, 9, 15, 175
Rhea (Titan), 26, 46, 57, 59, 87, 123
Rhetoric to Herennius, 38
Roman philosophy, 1, 7–8, 9, 12
Saturn, 205
Satyrs, 119
Seasons (goddesses), 63, 117
Seneca, L. Annaeus (Stoic), 3 n. 5, 7, 12, 32, 199
Servius, 27 n. 57, 157

Silenoi, 119
Silius Italicus (poet), 2, 192
Simplicius (Platonist), 17, 18, 23, 167
Skirtoi, 119
stasis-theory, 28, 180–81
Stoicism, 7–13
superstition, 33
Tartarus, 61, 85
Terpsichore (Muse), 71
Tethys (Titan), 46 61, 87
Thaleia (Grace), 75
Thaleia (Muse), 71
Thaumas, 107
Theagenes of Rhegium, 47
Theia (Titan), 87
Themis (Titan), 89, 117
Thetis, 83, 123
time, 175–76
Tisiphone (Erinnys), 65
Titans, 87, 121
Triptolemos, 113
Triton, 101
triumph, 121
Varro (grammarian, Academic), 140, 143, 149–55
Velius Longus (grammarian), 140 n. 4
Venus, 190–91
Verrius Flaccus, M. (grammarian), 139 n. 2
Vestal Virgins, 111 n. 163
Victory (goddess), 63, 97
Virgil, 1, 2, 5, 25, 27–28, 140, 182–93
Vulcan, 190–91
war, 117
Zeno (Stoic), 10, 158, 175 n. 49
Zeus, 26, 27 n. 55, 46, 55–69, 73, 79, 83, 89, 91–95, 99, 109, 117, 166

www.ingramcontent.com/pod-product-compliance
Lightning Source LLC
Chambersburg PA
CBHW032109220426
43664CB00008B/1190